# A Novel Approach to Criminal Courts

# A Novel Approach to Criminal Courts

**David R. Lynch**
PROFESSOR OF CRIMINAL JUSTICE
WEBER STATE UNIVERSITY

CAROLINA ACADEMIC PRESS
Durham, North Carolina

Names: Lynch, David R. (David Richard), author.
Title: A novel approach to criminal courts / by David R. Lynch.
Description: Durham, North Carolina : Carolina Academic Press, LLC, 2019. |
    Includes bibliographical references and index.
Identifiers: LCCN 2019010381 | ISBN 9781531014551 (alk. paper)
Subjects: LCSH: Criminal procedure—United States. | Criminal justice,
    Administration of—United States. | LCGFT: Textbooks.
Classification: LCC KF9619.85 .L96 2019 | DDC 345.73/05—dc23
LC record available at https://lccn.loc.gov/2019010381

eISBN: 978-1-5310-1456-8


Carolina Academic Press
700 Kent Street
Durham, North Carolina 27701
Telephone (919) 489-7486
Fax (919) 493-5668
www.cap-press.com

Printed in the United States of America

*To my wife, Kathleen, who made my academic career possible.*

# Contents

## UNIT 5: THE PROSECUTOR AND PRE-TRIAL MATTERS

## UNIT 6: ATTEMPTING TO SETTLE

## UNIT 7: HEADING TOWARD TRIAL

## UNIT 8: JUDGE, LAWYER, JUROR

## UNIT 9: THE TRIAL GETS UNDERWAY

## UNIT 10: THE STATE LANDS ITS BLOWS

# Preface

This "teaching novel" is meant for use in courses on the American criminal courts, criminal court process, and related subjects. Some might find a "textbook novel" such as this to be a somewhat unorthodox pedagogical tool, so a few words of explanation regarding the approach may be in order.

The book takes the reader on a journey through the American criminal courts by telling the fictional story of a burned-out former public defender turned high school math teacher, who very reluctantly agrees to represent one of his students charged with double vehicular homicide. The case starts in juvenile court but quickly winds up waived to adult court for ultimate jury trial there. The reader then vicariously travels through the entire adult criminal court process, beginning with a preliminary hearing, and continuing on through such steps as pretrial motions, plea bargaining, jury selection, the trial itself, sentencing, and appeal. As the tale unfolds, the reader learns the "ins and outs" of criminal court process: how these various steps are done in real life. Perhaps even more important, the reader experiences the inner society or the "behind the scenes" world of a courthouse. Hence, the heart and soul of defense attorneys, prosecutors, court schedulers, judges, witnesses, jurors, presentence investigators, and others are portrayed in the book's pages.

The book consists of 45 (not too lengthy) chapters. Since most semesters in American universities consist of 15 weeks, these 45 chapters are combined in such a way as to form 15 units, composed of two to four related chapters apiece.

To further help with the pedagogy, all 45 chapters contain bolded key terms, representing real world concepts of importance embedded within the fictional story. Furthermore, each of the 45 chapters ends with a dozen or so questions for classroom discussion.

I have attempted to "teach" students about the courthouse in a way that I wished I had been taught prior to accepting my first job after law school as a public defender. It is my hope that the book will be both educational and stylistically pleasing.

David R. Lynch
January 14, 2019

# Unit 1
# Setting the Stage

**Chapter 1: Law Is a Jealous Mistress**

**Chapter 2: "Attorney" Jack Day**

This unit sets the stage for the entire book. The unit's chapters introduce the reader to the protagonist, a former public defender turned high school math teacher, who is recruited by his principal to help a student charged with two counts of vehicular homicide. Chapter 1 sets the scene in the high school, while Chapter 2 provides some character development by providing a flashback to the protagonist's law school days and ultimate finding of a job as a public defender.

# 1

# Law Is a Jealous Mistress

Very few, if any, of Mr. Day's current high school math students knew that he had worked six years or so ago as a gifted, local public defender. Jack Day had reinvented himself successfully and completely within the very first couple of years at the school. However, Jack's boss, Father Joseph Skelly, principal of the Catholic high school where Jack had sought asylum from the law, remembered. He considered Jack to be something of a saint given his devotion to his students and lack of complaints regarding his pay, all of which struck Father Skelly as kind of funny since he had heard that saintly Jack's nickname among his adversaries in the district attorney's office had been "the prince of darkness."

Jack was a young person playing a **young person's game** when he had quit the practice of criminal law, a couple of years shy of his 30th birthday. Public defending, a profession filled with unrelenting stress, is typically a job that leads to rapid **burnout.** Yet, Jack, a maverick in his office, had burned out a little sooner than anyone had expected. Father Skelly had thought it strange that Jack, a lawyer with a degree from a top law school, specifically an **Ivy League law school** (Penn), would ever have even wanted to serve as a poorly paid public defender to begin with. Yet, though it is uncommon, it is far from being rare. Top law schools consider public defending to be an acceptable and noble calling for their graduates to undertake, at least for a little while. Heaven forbid that any of them should choose prosecution, however. Liberal Ivy League and

other top law school professors (stupidly) consider prosecutors to be the
**legal profession's untouchables**.

Even stranger to Father Skelly was Jack's application years ago to join
his faculty. At the time, Skelly was not even sure that Jack was qualified
to teach. Jack may have minored in math as an undergraduate, but he
did not have an education degree of any kind. Skelly knew that without
an education degree, the public schools would never hire him. Skelly
also knew that teaching is a profession, requiring specialized training
and skills. He resented other professionals who sometimes assumed that
teaching can be a type of default career that any other professional could
do well. Still, given the low pay that he could offer at his underfunded,
private school, Principal Skelly had to consider that Jack was one of the
only people with a math background of any kind to have applied for the
job. Furthermore, Jack had impressed Skelly by convincing him that he
was genuinely passionate about teaching. Jack also seemed to possess
strong people skills. Ultimately, Skelly decided to take a chance on him.
Jack did not disappoint. He worked hard to learn the teaching craft and
eventually turned out to be a very good fit for St. Francis.

St. Francis High School was founded in 1937 in suburban Philadelphia to help educate the children and grandchildren of the large masses
of Irish and Italian immigrants who had helped settle the area. The quar-
ter-mile long, red brick school was located in Brunswick, a town of about
35,000 people centered in a county of about 300,000. Brunswick was 11
miles down the road from the town of Center Square, the county seat
where Jack had worked as a young lawyer fresh out of school.

Oh, how Jack had loved public defending! He loved it in no small part
because he was so good at it. After three long years of law school, he had
become sick of reading books and writing papers. He liked dealing with
the **soft skills** (emotional control, strong communication skills, ability
to read people well) that the practice of criminal law required. Sure, his
law schoolmates were all making three times his salary by now. However,
they worked twice as many hours as he did, doing boring **corporate law**
(representing the interests of major companies). Jack's best friend used
his big brain all day proofreading and double-checking thick corporate
contracts written by someone else. Jack was not going to waste whatever
spark of creativity that lurked within him doing work like that.

Jack also liked being a public defender because he could be one of "liberty's last champions," the logo on his office softball team's t-shirts, which opponents took as a joke but which all of the defenders took quite seriously. Jack also liked the chance he had to "stick his finger in the eye of **the man**," who he considered to be anyone associated with the criminal justice system (including police, prosecutors, judges, and correctional officials). Jack always figured that since America locked up a higher percentage of its people than any other country, including even a higher percentage than all past generations of Americans ever did, his being a disruptive **cog in the machine** from time to time was not such a bad thing after all.

Yeah, Jack had drunk the Kool-Aid, for sure. However, for a long time it had never made him sick. Yet, that eventually changed.

About three years into his budding legal career, something happened that caused Jack to start spiraling down into mental instability. Jack had beaten a DUI rap for a client on a technicality. The client celebrated by immediately getting drunk and slamming his huge pickup truck into a car filled with a young family. The mother survived (though in a wheelchair for life), but the father, young daughter, and grandpa all perished. The drunk, behind the wheel of a much heavier vehicle, got out of it with a mere broken nose and arm.

Upon first hearing of these deaths, Jack developed a panic attack, something he had never experienced before. He had a colleague drive him to the ER, thinking he was having a cardiac event. However, all of the tests came back clear. It was the psychiatrist who the hospital emergency department called in for a consult, who first told Jack what really must have occurred.

Jack took a few days off from work to clear his soul but was soon back at the job. Nevertheless, the panic attacks returned, each one coming sooner than the previous one, and all of them occurring during work. Once, during a bail reduction hearing (in a DUI case of all things), Jack actually vomited in the hallway right after the judge agreed to release Jack's client on his own recognizance.

Jack tried to hang in there for a few more weeks, but his boss wound up ordering him to temporarily go on county disability pay. That is when Jack started looking for a job outside of the law. That is how he wound up at St. Francis.

Jack never again had a panic attack after becoming an educator. Sure, high school kids can try the patience and nerves of anyone, but Jack was able to cope. He was used to working in the high stakes, **verbal combat zone** of criminal law. As a lawyer, fighting and dealing with conflict was a key part of his job. True, the classroom can be a real jungle but so could the tumultuous world of the criminal courts.

Jack was surviving his jungle one day when one of the school office secretaries paged him over his classroom intercom voice box. The school day was nearly over, and the secretary asked Mr. Day to come see the principal before he went home. Jack's students teased him about being in "big trouble with the old man."

When class was over, Jack quickly finished some record keeping and then walked the hundred yards to the head office suite located in the dead center of the long school building. Upon entering the suite, he chatted briefly with the receptionists and then reported to the good Father's office.

"Thanks for coming by, Jack," began Father Skelly.

"Sure, what's up, Father?" Jack was curious but completely at ease with this kindly old man. Years ago, Father Skelly invited Jack to start calling him "Joe" when students were not around, but Jack simply could not bring himself to be so casual with an ordained priest. A concern that was perhaps a little bit odd, since Jack was not even a Catholic.

"Jack, I think you know a senior in this school by the name of Richard Mahan. I think he goes by 'Rich.'"

"Rick, actually, with a 'K.' Rick Mahan. Yes, I know him very well. He was in my precalculus course last semester. Good kid. A nearly straight-A student. Very polite. Kind of quiet but a good kid."

Father Skelly smiled nervously and continued. "Have you heard any rumors about him circulating about?"

"No, nothing. Why, what's the matter?" Jack could not imagine how Rick Mahan could possibly be in trouble.

"Not many people know about this yet," began the old Jesuit. "But Rick was arrested two days ago on some very serious charges and is in juvenile lockup. Thank heaven he is still just 17 and a minor."

A look of sincere concern swept over Jack's face. "Is it sex stuff?"

"No, they are accusing him of," a nervous Father Skelly looked down at his notes, "Homicide by vehicle while DUI, two counts. I guess that means two people got killed."

Jack without hesitation replied, "That's exactly what it means." Father Skelly noticed that Jack looked a little pale. An awkward moment of silence developed while Father Skelly carefully considered his next words.

Jack instead broke the silence by asking, "Is there something I could do to help?"

"You mean you possibly could give the family a bit of legal advice?" the surprised old man responded in a hopeful tone of voice.

"Oh, no, no. Nothing legal. Is there something I could do as a teacher to help the kid?"

"Well, school work is the least of Rick's worries in life right now. Maybe you could just tell me what kind of time he is facing if convicted of two counts of vehicular homicide."

Jack relaxed a bit and replied, "Well, it is a really, really good thing that he is still a juvenile. That means he will go to juvenile court where the emphasis is entirely on rehabilitation and not on punishment. Juvenile court judges bend over backward to avoid incarcerating kids, even when they have done something major. However, with two dead victims, Rick will probably have to do some time. The worst they could give him though, it being a juvenile matter, is to lock him up until he turns 21."

"I thought that juvenile courts lose their jurisdiction at age 18," responded the priest.

"Yeah, **juvenile court jurisdiction** ends at 18, but **juvenile correctional jurisdiction** extends until age 21. Since Rick is almost 18, the most he would have to do is three years. But he might even do less than that."

"Even with not one but two dead victims?"

"Yeah, even so."

"Well, you seem to know your stuff still, Jack. I want to ask you a big favor. Would you consider attending his juvenile trial or whatever it is called? Just to observe things and make sure all goes well. I know you stopped being a lawyer over cases like this, especially DUI homicide stuff. But it would really help me out if I could tell Rick's parents that you'd be observing the proceedings."

"Well, I don't see the point," replied Jack. "Anyway, juvenile adjudication hearings are closed to the public. I could not attend if I wanted to. Keeping proceedings confidential are all part of the **rehabilitation focus** of this type of court."

"What if the parents invite you to sit with them?"

Jack reluctantly admitted, "Yeah, maybe that would work. Do you think they want this?"

"I know for a fact that they do. They are concerned that their kid pulled one of the bad apples in the local public defenders' office. I mean, this bum will not even return their phone calls. I suggested that maybe you could go as an observer, and they really latched on to that idea. I know it would help them just having you sit with them as a sort of a comfort companion."

"I am not a support dog, Father," Jack countered. "Look, I don't know about all of this. I am sure Rick's lawyer is fine. In fact, **public defender effectiveness** is as good as or better than the effectiveness of average privately retained lawyers. I hear from my old law pals that 9 out of the 10 public defenders in our county these days are sharp. Rick would do just fine with any one of those nine. I would bet that Rick's lawyer is simply super busy and not just blowing them all off. After all, the case is just a few days old."

"Who is the 10th lawyer? The one that is not sharp?" demanded Skelly.

"Some in-law of the head public defender, a lazy, dumb butt named 'Pete Snarr.' I hear that Snarr's nickname among his office mates is the '**cop out king**' because he will sell out his client in a second just to dispose of a case. Snarr actually took four attempts to pass the Pennsylvania bar exam, known to be one of the easier state bar exams in the country. All of the other PD's though are super smart and super hard working."

"Yeah, but what if Rick's lawyer is Snarr? Will you agree to go and sit with the Mahan's in court?"

"Sure, Father. Let me know if you hear he got Snarr."

Father Skelly looked down again at his notes. As Jack saw the look of frustration sweep across Skelly's face, Jack knew who Rick Mahan's lawyer would be. Jack sighed. "Rick actually pulled Pete Snarr, didn't he?"

"Yes," groaned the normally proper and polite Father Skelly. "That lazy dumb butt of a cop out king will be his guy."

~

## Key Terms Found in This Chapter

Young person's game

Burnout

Ivy League law school

Legal profession's untouchables

Juvenile correctional jurisdiction

Corporate law

The man

Cog in the machine

Verbal combat zone

Juvenile court jurisdiction

Soft skills

Rehabilitation focus

Public defender effectiveness

Cop out king (or queen)

## Questions for Class Discussion

1. Why is public defending sometimes considered to be a "young person's game"?
2. Could you defend people accused of a crime for a living?
3. What are some of the specific types of things that might lead public defenders to "burnout"?
4. Should public defenders be paid as much as prosecutors? More?
5. What sort of jobs would you expect graduates of Ivy League and similar law schools to get?
6. Why do some elite law school professors consider public defending to be more acceptable than prosecuting?
7. What sort of "soft skills" do effective public defenders need to possess?
8. Do graduates of elite law schools tend to possess "soft skills" in greater abundance than graduates of average law schools?
9. Would you rather work in corporate law or criminal law? What are some of the pros and cons of each?
10. What are some of the things that public defenders can do to become "cogs in the state's machine"?
11. Who are some of the people who public defenders must fight that turns criminal court into a "verbal combat zone"?
12. Why was Attorney Jack Day happy to hear that the defendant was only 17? What is the major difference in focus between juvenile court and adult criminal court?
13. How could it even be possible that public defenders tend to be just as effective on average as privately retained criminal defense attorneys?

14. What advantage is there to being a "cop out king" (or "cop out queen")? Would you be tempted to become such a person if you were a public defender? What do you think of such attorneys?

# 2

# "Attorney" Jack Day

Jack Day never planned to become a lawyer. He was an English major with a math minor in college. All of his literary friends thought his love of math was weird, and all of his math friends thought the same in reverse. Jack was not sure what he was going to do when he graduated until his (then) fiancée rather made up his mind for him.

"Jack," she announced one day, "Let's both go to law school together. My dad says he is sure you would like it. I know that I will." Jack's future father-in-law was a wealthy partner in a big law firm. Even so, Jack resisted the idea…at first.

Eventually, Jack found himself leaning toward law school. Majoring in English had posed no problem. There is no **preferred pre-law major**. Unlike medical school, law school does not even have a set of **required pre-law courses** or even a single course that one needs to take for admission.

Jack really had no idea what else to do with his life. It was not as if employers were beating down English majors' doors with offers of lucrative employment. Jack figured that between his fiancée, her well-connected father, Jack's 90th percentile score on the **LSAT** (the "Law School Admission Test" that his fiancée insisted he take), and his 3.8 GPA, maybe law school was not such a bad idea.

With a mixture of apathy and hesitation, Jack finally applied to just two schools: the University of Pennsylvania (a stretch school for anybody) and the Delaware Law School (for him, a **safety school**). Both schools accepted him. Getting into Penn was lucky because Jack had not applied to any schools between the extremes of stellar and mediocre, a reckless course of action. He chose the University of Pennsylvania's School of Law over Delaware because it was Ivy League. Jack's future father-in-law was very proud of his newfound protégé. He was also quite pleased with his daughter, even though Penn had rejected her, and she wound up having to matriculate at Delaware. Jack's fiancée (Jennifer) was happy because at least she and Jack were within an hour's drive of one another. "It's still very romantic," she assured Jack.

That simple hour's drive wound up being quite a burden for the couple, both crushed by the demands of being first year law students. Jennifer and Jack saw one another two or three times each week for the first month. However, their reunions dwindled down to once per week before too long.

Jack studied hard and was determined to excel. His goal was to be selected to join the coveted **law review**, a student-produced repository of scholarly articles written by law professors, which would require a top 10% performance in his first year grades.

Jennifer, on the other hand, worked hard for the first month but soon decided that all of the endless, difficult reading that law school required was very "boring." She stopped attending by early November. On the day she dropped out of school, she telephoned Jack to tell him that news along with the revelation that she had a new boyfriend, an oral surgeon whom she was already now living with in an upscale neighborhood just north of Wilmington. "Sorry, Jacky," Jennifer said in a tone quite lacking in actual sorrow, "Have a nice life."

Jack responded at first by throwing himself even harder into his studies, finishing the semester just shy of the top 10%. It was not until Christmas break at his parents' home that the thought of "What the hell am I doing in law school?" suddenly occurred to Jack. He felt like a fool who let others, especially that "betrayer Jennifer," talk him into entering a program that he never would have chosen but for her influence.

Returning to classes post-break only intensified Jack's pain. He came to realize that he really had no interest in ever being a lawyer. "Jennifer was right. This material is boring," Jack lamented. The thought of working hard at something he no longer had any passion for seemed daunting. Yet, if he were to drop out of school, what could he do? He

2 · "ATTORNEY" JACK DAY

had no idea. He decided to finish out the first year and then make a final decision.

The second semester was every bit as grinding as had been the first, even more so now. Jack's patience with the **case method** (where students inefficiently "discover" the law by reading endless appellate case after case) grew thin. He also began to internally rebel at the **Socratic method** of instruction used in law schools (in which professors aggressively grill students by asking them constant in-your-face questions without ever providing answers).

Jack's grades began to tumble along with his enthusiasm. Because of his stellar performance the first semester, he still managed to finish out the first year in the top half of his class. Not bad for an Ivy League school.

Jack spent summer break working in a gas station. Unlike most of his classmates, he had not bothered applying for summer legal internships. "What would be the point?" he wondered, since dropping out of law school was now his presumed course of action.

Summer ended and classes resumed. Jack could not believe he found himself back there yet again reading cases and being hazed by instructors. He pictured himself to be almost as a twig being pushed relentlessly along in a powerful river current.

He hated every class he took except criminal law and constitutional law. "At least those two subjects have some kick to them," he considered. Jack saved his utter contempt for the endless stream of business-related law courses. His schedule always seemed to be full with those, however, since that was mostly what the professors offered. Apparently, business law was where all the money was. For the most part, his fellow students seemed fascinated with the idea of making a lot of money.

After three long years, Jack had finally completed the dismal, torturous marathon. He had quite nearly dropped out of school yet again at the end of his second year. However, realizing that he was then two thirds through, he did not have the heart to negate all of the sacrifices he had made up to that point. "I've sunk too much pain into all of this to just chuck it away now," he reasoned.

On Jack's last day in the law school building, he stopped by the registrar's office to request that they mail him his diploma.

"Aren't you coming to graduation? You can get it there," explained the secretary.

"No, I have other plans," explained Jack.

The secretary looked at him as if he were crazy to skip graduation. She disapprovingly wrote down his request nevertheless. "Did it ever occur to you that maybe your parents would have enjoyed attending graduation?" she snidely remarked after Jack had thanked her for her assistance.

Upon leaving the school for the last time, Jack literally gave the building "the finger" as he exited the door. Driving home to his parents' house, he tried to weigh his future options. "Should I even take the bar exam?" he wondered. "That is a lot of studying for someone who might never practice law." Jack was right about the studying part. It was arduous. The better the law school the less it prepares one to pass the local bar exam. Lesser law schools, which cater entirely to locals, tend to have higher bar passage rates than the elite, national law schools that recruit students from all over the country. The lesser schools can afford to become essentially a **3-year bar review** course. However, the national schools have no state bar exam for which to specifically prepare their diverse students. Besides, the elite schools think it beneath them to engage in such a vocational mission. "Our main purpose is not to train you but to educate you so that you can learn to **think like a lawyer**," they told students like Jack repeatedly. It took Jack forever to figure out what they meant by all of that. He finally realized they wanted their graduates to be able to think critically, analytically, and creatively.

At his father's insistence, Jack wound up studying for and passing the Pennsylvania bar exam. His dad even paid for the extensive course that Jack took online. The **bar exam** extended over two days: a multiple choice test on the first day and essay questions on the second. Jack studied enough to know that he had passed the test even before receiving the fat, thick envelope announcing the results. (A thin envelope meant that you had failed.)

Jack was now Pennsylvania attorney #19-1885. He had a state-issued attorney identification card to prove it. Now, if he only had a job.

Jack finished the summer after graduation working at the same gas station where he had worked during summer while in school. He thought often about applying for one of the corporate law positions worthy of an Ivy law graduate but just could not bring himself to do it.

It was his mother who suggested that he apply for a job at the local public defender's office. "Weren't there any classes you liked in law school?" his mother asked him one day.

"Well, criminal law was interesting," admitted Jack. "That and constitutional law."

"Then why don't you try for a job as a constitutional lawyer, Jack?"

"Because Mom, those are some of the highest sought after jobs in the country. Everyone loves constitutional law. I would have to have finished at the very top of my Ivy League law school class even to have a shot. As you know, I did not exactly finish at the top of my class."

"What about criminal law, then? Maybe you could get a job as a prosecutor or some such thing."

Jack had never considered working in criminal law. Nobody who graduates from Penn goes into criminal law. It is the **lowest paying legal specialty**. Yet, Jack had to admit that it paid more than pumping gas. "You might be on to something, Mom," Jack acknowledged. "I'll look into it."

Jack did more than just look into it. His parents happily watched as Jack applied to every district attorney's office in the metropolitan area. Jack also applied to every public defender's office in the area while he was at it. This approach of would-be criminal lawyers applying simultaneously to both prosecutor and defender offices is actually quite common. Rather than preferring one or the other, many applicants simply apply to both and go to work for whoever is the first to make them an offer.

Two weeks passed when Jack received a phone call from the chief public defender of the county next door. "I love it when I get resumes from strong schools like Penn," Jack was told on the phone. "I only try to hire attorneys from the best schools. They don't make any better public defenders than graduates of ordinary law schools, but image is kind of important to me."

"Geeze," Jack thought. "There really is a **lawyer glut** out there."

Jack arranged with the public defender to be interviewed the following Monday morning. Jack quickly ran out and bought a new suit and tie. "They won't believe that I can think like a lawyer if I don't look like one," Jack figured.

Monday morning came and Jack reported on time to the receptionist in the courthouse basement offices of the county public defender's office. Jack thought it unfair when he saw that the district attorney's office was located on the rather opulent main floor, while the public defender's of-fice had to endure the indignity of a dingy basement. Oddly, Jack rather liked the setup that way. "These public defenders might just be my kind of folks," he considered.

Jack had barely sat down in the waiting room when "Big Mike" Fin-negan emerged to greet him. "You must be Jack Day. I am Michael Fin-negan, the public defender. You can call me 'Big Mike' or just plain 'Mike.' I get called 'Big Mike' a lot since I am about the shortest person that anyone has ever met who was not born BCE. Come on back to my office."

Jack followed Mike and both took their seats in Mike's office. Jack listened to Mike as he asked, "So, why does an Ivy Leaguer like you want to work for $70,000 per year defending a bunch of guilty people?"

Jack was not sure how to respond to that. He decided to be brutally honest. "I am one of those guys who went to law school by mistake. I hated it. I know everyone hates law school, but at least they could look forward to becoming a corporate lawyer someday. I was not even sure I wanted to be a lawyer, of any kind. Since graduating, I have been pump-ing gas at Ronnie's Super Shell for just over minimum wage. I only took the bar exam this summer because my dad made me. Then my mom, who I must have been worrying sick, suggested I look for a job in crimi-nal law. She only suggested that because I mentioned to her that criminal law was just about the only course I found very interesting in school. Before my mother brought it up, going into criminal law had never oc-curred to me. Yet, as soon as she suggested it, the very idea immediately made me excited. Being here today, in your offices, in this courthouse, I feel an energy and an excitement that I have not felt in years. If you hire me, I promise you that I will work hard to help our clients. I will work smart and hard. As for the $70,000 salary, it sure beats what I am making pumping gas."

Big Mike swiveled in his chair for a few moments. "So far, you sound crazy enough to fit in with the rest of us. How do you feel about the death penalty?"

"I oppose it."

"No, really, tell me the truth. My hiring decision won't be affected by your position. In fact, I myself support the death penalty, as a private citizen."

"I truthfully oppose it," Jack insisted.

"OK, Jack, here is the deal. I am going to bring in my **first assistant public defender**. She helps me run the office. She hates the death penalty with a burning passion. She has devoted her professional life to defending people charged with capital murder. She handles all of those cases for us as well as helping me to supervise all of the other assistant public defenders. She says she will quit if I ever let anyone else handle our occasional death penalty case. She hates the death penalty that bad. I think she believes she is on some kind of mission from God or something, but I have always been too afraid to ask."

"OK, Mike. I'd be happy to meet her."

"Oh, you will be doing more than just meeting her. I want you to make the strongest, most compelling argument that you can to her in favor of the death penalty. That way, I can judge if you have what it takes to be a public defender."

"But I am against the death penalty, Mike," Jack protested.

"I know that. If we wind up hiring you, you will have to argue passionately for clients you hate, for motions you would not grant if you were the judge, and for verdicts you would never vote for if you were on the jury. That is the job. In addition, you will have to think on your feet. They shove us into court hearings all the time with no chance to prepare. Therefore, I want you to argue in favor of the death penalty, a position you do not personally support. I want you to do this right now with no chance to prepare. I want you to make this argument before the most hostile audience imaginable, my obsessed first assistant. If she is impressed, you got the job, Ivy man."

Jack sat there astonished while Big Mike left to round up his first assistant. Jack stood as Mike reentered the room with an intense-looking woman in tow. "Jack, this is Kathy Bell. Kathy, this is Jack Day." Jack shook her hand and nodded, smiling. Kathy nodded back, no smile.

"Mr. Jack Day is applying for the opening we have for a new **APD**," Mike the PD noted. "He wants to tell you why you should change your mind and start favoring the death penalty in this country, Kathy."

"Oh, he does, does he? I would really like to hear what he has to say!"

Big Mike nodded at Jack, "Counselor, you may begin your argument. You have seven minutes. I suggest you take all of that time."

Jack straightened his tie and cleared his throat as he rose to his feet. Mike and Kathy sat down and settled in to watch the spectacle. If ever

Jack had to be creative, now was the time. A thought suddenly jumped into Jack's head that gave him courage. "I have done this sort of thing before," he assured himself. "I have done this each time one of those aggressive law professors grilled me in class over homework cases we read. I can do this."

In truth, Jack did do it. He systematically hit on point after point on why the death penalty was appropriate for our society to maintain. He spoke about the law. He spoke about morality. He spoke about philosophy. He spoke about justice. He spoke about proper constitutional interpretation. He spoke about ancient tradition. He spoke about evolving standards of right and wrong (and lack thereof). He even brought up and knocked down all of the arguments on the other side. He easily filled up the entire seven minutes. Then Jack sat down.

"What do you think, Kathy," asked Big Mike. "He was pretty good wasn't he?"

"Good?" exclaimed Kathy. "I was good when you put me through this type of test years ago on my interview day. I would have to say that this candidate is not just good but damn good! Hell, he is the freaking prince of darkness himself. He almost convinced me to go over to the dark side on the death penalty."

"I guess that means you are hired, Jack," Mike announced. "Could you start tomorrow? As you might imagine, we are kind of swamped around here."

## Key Terms Found in This Chapter

Preferred pre-law major

Required pre-law courses

LSAT

Safety school

Law review

Case method

Socratic method

Three-year bar review

Think like a lawyer

Bar exam

Lowest paying legal specialty

Lawyer glut

First assistant public defender

APD

# Questions for Class Discussion

1. Even though there is no preferred pre-law major, do you person-ally think that some majors would better prepare students for law school than others? If so, which ones?

2. Why do you suppose that unlike medical schools, law schools do not even require a certain set of pre-law courses to be taken while yet an undergraduate? Is that a responsible policy for them to have?

3. In your opinion, is it fair for law school admission committees to put a lot of weight on the LSAT? Should high GPA's count much more?

4. Can you name any probable "safety schools" in your state that aspiring law school students could apply to just to be careful?

5. Why do you suppose it matters for students of elite schools to "make law review" if they already are on course to graduate from a top law school anyway?

6. If the "case method" of instruction is indeed an inefficient way to learn the law, then why do law professors insist on subjecting students to it?

7. In your opinion, does the Socratic method of instruction unfairly tend to favor some types of students over others?

8. After reading the chapter, what would you think of a law school that brags about having a higher bar passage rate than other more elite law schools in the area?

9. Given the sometime unpopular image of lawyers, is helping law students to "think like a lawyer" a bad thing?

10. How would you feel if you spent three years in law school only to repeatedly fail the bar exam? Do you think this ever happens to students? What would you do if that happened to you?

11. Why do you suppose that criminal law is the lowest paying legal specialty? Would that fact deter you from practicing criminal law if you were a law school graduate?

12. Whose fault is it that there is a generation-long "lawyer glut" in this country?

13. How much should new, full-time assistant public defenders make in your opinion? Should they be paid less, more, or the same as full-time assistant district attorneys?

# Unit 2
# Juvenile Court and Beyond

**Chapter 3: Hello, Kiddie Court**

**Chapter 4: Goodbye, Kiddie Court**

**Chapter 5: The Preliminary Non-hearing, Hearing**

This unit portrays what juvenile court is like and what it is like to experience it both as an attorney and as a client. The concept of "waiver" to adult court is illustrated, and the purposes behind the first step of the process in adult court—the preliminary hearing—are illustrated.

# 3

# Hello, Kiddie Court

Nearly a decade had now passed since Jack Day had first joined the office of the public defender. During those 10 years, Jack had delivered the three wonderful years of service as a public defender, had his breakdown over the DUI deaths, started a new career in the high school, and enjoyed six years of success as a popular teacher.

Given his past psychological trauma, Jack really did not want to get involved all these years later in anything legal, especially a case involving DUI and people dying. Could there possibly be a more perfect storm to trigger Jack's old demons? Yet a 3-part, virtuous cocktail consisting of Jack's loyalty to Father Skelly, Jack's protective impulses regarding one of his accused students, mixed with Jack's disgust regarding ineffective defenders like Pete Snarr induced the former courthouse maverick to at least provide some emotional support by attending the juvenile court proceedings as a guest of young Rick Mahan's parents.

Jack asked Father Skelly to set up a lunchtime meeting the next day at school with Rick's parents in Skelly's office. The boy would not be present since he was still in juvenile lockup awaiting court proceedings. Unlike adult court, juvenile court never sets bail. After a brief **detention hearing**, a juvenile is simply either detained or else released with no money exchanging hands. Apparently, the court had chosen to detain Rick. At least Rick could count on a prompt process going forward. What takes months to happen in criminal court often only takes days or weeks to occur in juvenile court. The complete absence of juries in juvenile court is a big reason for the faster pace, along with the focus on what is in the **best interests of the child**, the governing philosophy of juvenile courts. Slow justice is not in the best interests of a child.

This whole concept of "best interest" started in Illinois in the late 1800s when a group of highly concerned women known as **child savers** got involved in pushing for reform in the courts. Thanks to them, juvenile courts emerged as something quite different from just trickle- down versions of adult court with its obsession on punishment. Instead, juvenile courts adopted a legal principle known as ***parens patriae***, in which the state (i.e., the juvenile judge) was to assume a parental role in trying to provide rehabilitative services to the young offender. The idea was that **juvenile intake workers**, working for the juvenile court, would screen incoming files and **divert** most cases away from a judge by arranging counseling for a young offender, negotiating community service, imposing curfews on the child, etc., in lieu of formal court proceedings. However, some cases, of course, are much too serious for such informal dispositions. In such matters, the intake worker will file a **petition** (similar to an indictment in adult court) asking a judge to find the child to be **delinquent** (i.e., responsible for an act that would be considered a crime if one were an adult). Once a judge finds a child to be delinquent, the judge would order a **social investigation** (akin to a presentence investigation in adult court) to be done by the juvenile probation office, after which the judge would schedule a **disposition hearing** (similar to a sentencing hearing in adult court) to decide the child's fate. Since few parents would lock up their own child for any misconduct less than horrific, so too are juvenile judges reluctant to incarcerate juveniles found to be delinquent. Most frequently, delinquent children are put on formal probation and assigned a juvenile probation officer who works intensely with the child to help set his or her course straight. Sometimes, however, a juvenile judge sees no option other than to incarcerate (**to place**) the child in a **secure facility** (essentially a youth jail).

Being a former public defender, Jack knew all of the above and took great comfort in these concepts. He knew that young Rick was a dozen times better off going through the juvenile justice system than he would if he were tried as an adult. Not only would the court's focus be on helping, rather than punishing Rick, but a finding of delinquency would generate no criminal record whatsoever, giving him a fresh start for his soon-to-be adult life. A finding of delinquency is a **civil finding**, not a criminal one, and it is not considered to constitute a conviction of any kind. Not only that, but as a juvenile, Rick's court records would be **sealed** and forever kept secret from the public. Plus, as noted earlier, the worst possible outcome imaginable for Rick would be to get locked up in a juvenile facility for three years, since juvenile correctional jurisdiction ends at age 21, and Rick was just a couple of months from turning 18.

When Rick's parents showed up the next day to meet with Jack in Father Skelly's office, Jack painstakingly educated them on the above concepts. He knew that this would be a help to them and was a type of "legal service" that in no way would risk summoning back Jack's anxieties. The parents listened intently and thanked Jack for the lesson. It did make them feel more knowledgeable and empowered.

Father Skelly also found the session useful since Rick was not the school's first, and no doubt would not be its last, student to get into trouble with the law. When Jack appeared to be taking a breather, Father Skelly asked the Mahans if they had heard anything yet about when Rick's next juvenile court appearance would take place.

"Yes," replied Mrs. Mahan, pulling out a very official-looking legal notice from her purse. "This sheet says that Rick, his attorney Peter Snarr, and Assistant District Attorney Sara Carter are ordered to appear in Courtroom #3, next Tuesday at 9:30 a.m., before Judge Leonard Watson so that arguments can be heard on the commonwealth's petition for waiver."

Everyone in the room looked at Jack. Jack remained poker-faced and quiet. Finally, Mr. Mahan chose to break the silence by remarking, "Apparently, this 'waiver' thing is something being requested by the prosecutor Sara Carter. Waiver sounds like it might be something good. Is this a good thing? Does it mean that the state wants to go a little easy on Rick? Mr. Day, Please tell us that this is something good."

Jack looked straight into the familiar eyes of Father Skelly to buy a few seconds and gather up some courage. Skelly realized instantly that some bad shoe was about to drop. Jack then shifted his gaze to the faces of the waiting parents and tried to remain professionally calm while breaking some very bad news.

"Waiver is not something the state wants in order to help Rick out," Jack stated resolutely. "I am afraid it is very, very much the opposite."

"Why, what exactly is waiver, Jack?" queried Father Skelly.

Jack now spoke directly to the parents, even though Skelly had asked the question. "When a juvenile court orders **waiver**, the juvenile judge is essentially relinquishing all of the benefits and protections associated with juvenile court and ordering the case be transferred to adult court for processing there. In essence, the prosecutor is asking the juvenile court judge to order that Rick be tried as an adult and, if convicted, punished as an adult. My guess is that since she is going to all this trouble, the prosecutor probably wants Rick to do a bunch more time than three years for these alleged two homicides. I think the prosecutor wants Rick to do some long, hard time in adult prison."

Both Mr. and Mrs. Mahan gasped simultaneously as if on cue. Father Skelly sprang from his seat and approached the terrified couple, placing each of his pastoral hands on one each of their respective shoulders. "Jack, the boy is not yet even 18 years old. He has not even graduated from high school. How can he be tried as an adult?" Skelly hotly demanded.

Jack went back into lecture mode but tried to explain things without coming across as too detached. "Every state sets a **presumptive age** for adult court jurisdiction. Most states, like our state, have chosen this age to be 18. Some states have chosen 17 and a half dozen or so have chosen 16. Nevertheless, whatever age is chosen by a state, this age is just presumptive. What that means is that sometimes, in the 'interests of justice,' some people below the cutoff age should be processed in adult court."

"Who gets to decide this waiver thing, the prosecutor?" inquired Father Skelly. Skelly was now speaking for the parents who were too emotional to talk.

"No, the judge decides using his or her discretion. The prosecutor can petition the court for waiver, which apparently this Sara Carter is doing. A juvenile judge can also waive a case *sua sponte*, which is a Latin phrase meaning…"

"Latin for 'on one's own accord,'" interjected the priest of Rome. "What did you mean when you said a judge will use 'his or her discretion' in deciding waiver? What factors typically sway a judge to not follow the normal rule that someone under 18 is still a kid and should be treated as a kid?"

"There are **three main waiver factors** that juvenile judges mostly consider in deciding whether or not to waive a case to adult court," Jack explained. "First, the age of the child. The closer the child is to being 18, the more likely waiver could happen. Second, the gravity of the current offense. The more serious the charge, the more likely waiver will be ordered. Finally, the youth's prior juvenile record. The more extensive a delinquent past, the more likely waiver will be ordered since the court begins to lose its patience in trying to rehabilitate someone who keeps coming back. Thus, for example a 12 year old who shoplifts a candy bar and has never been in trouble before has about a 0% risk of being waived to adult court. On the other hand, a 17 year old who robs someone at knife point and who had been processed as a juvenile before for a prior, so-called delinquent act of armed robbery stands a pretty high chance of being waived."

"But our son has never, ever been to juvenile court before," Mrs. Day defensively noted. "This is his first time. He never so much as received a school detention, like, in his whole life."

"Yes, so he has a shot at staying in juvenile court," confirmed Jack. "However, a judge does not have to have all three factors present to waive a case. In your son's case, the charges are very serious—two counts of vehicular homicide while drunk driving—and Rick is very nearly 18. Let's hope that this judge has some compassion since it is Rick's first time in trouble and rejects the prosecutor's petition. I would if I were the judge."

At this point, the meeting spiraled down before Jack even had the chance to ask the parents what the actual, alleged, specific facts of the case against their son were. He was sure that the parents (and young Rick and Rick's lawyer) all had been given a paper on that. What proof did the police have that Rick had been driving while intoxicated? How did the accident happen? Did Rick make any incriminating statements? Were there any breath or blood tests done on Rick? Who exactly died? Jack wanted to know but could not ask given the invectives that the parents were now bouncing around the room regarding that "evil bitch," Assistant District Attorney Sara Carter. Jack would just have to wait until the hearing to learn of the particulars.

The meeting ended with Father Skelly assuring Mr. and Mrs. Mahan that Jack would attend the waiver hearing as a guest of the family. As to that promise, Jack quickly uttered, "No problem, I'll be there." However,

Jack wished that Father Skelly had had the decency to consult him more thoroughly first. "I really, really don't want to get sucked into this," Jack thought. "I am not their defense attorney. That would be Public Pretender, Peter Snarr," he silently despaired.

∿

## Key Terms Found in This Chapter

| | |
|---|---|
| Detention hearing | Disposition hearing |
| Best interests of the child | To place |
| Child savers | Secure facility |
| Parens patriae | Civil finding |
| Juvenile intake workers | Sealed |
| Divert | Waiver |
| Petition | Presumptive age |
| Delinquent | Sua sponte |
| Social investigation | Three main waiver factors |

## Question for Class Discussion

1. Why do you suppose that bail involving an exchange of money is not used in the juvenile court system?
2. Is it fair to the victims of juvenile bad actors that juvenile judges are supposed to focus primarily on the "best interests" of the juvenile offender?
3. Do you have any ideas of what might have motivated the women in the late 1800s known as the "child savers" to get involved in a juvenile justice movement?
4. Are you okay with the notion that the government must step in as the ultimate parent when the real parents are unable or unwilling to help their own children?
5. Should first-time adult offenders of nonviolent crimes generally be diverted away from formal criminal court proceedings the same way that most first-time juvenile offenders are diverted from formal juvenile court proceedings?

6. Why do you suppose that juvenile court has adopted its own vocabulary (e.g., petitions, social investigations, placement, secure facilities, etc.) when there are perfectly good words used in the adult system that already describe those same sort of concepts?

7. What is a huge benefit of juvenile court matters being considered to be "civil" rather than "criminal" proceedings"?

8. Do you agree that juvenile court findings of delinquency should be "sealed" and kept hidden from potential employers, neighbors, and other members of the public? What, if any, exceptions to this policy should exist?

9. If you were a juvenile court judge, do you think that you would be stingy with "waiver" to adult court or more open than most other judges to the possibility?

10. What is the "presumptive age" for adult court jurisdiction in your state? Is that age old enough? Too old? At what point does the human brain become fully mature?

11. Why do you suppose that judges can waive juvenile matters to adult court *sua sponte* without so much as a request from a prosecutor? Do you agree that they should have this right?

12. The three main waiver factors include offender age, current offense gravity, and past record. Which of these three strike you as generally being the most important? Is there any age that is too young for waiver, no matter how bad the current offense is?

# 4

## Goodbye, Kiddie Court

Jack threw himself into teaching and the grading of homework while waiting for waiver hearing day to arrive. It did arrive, soon enough.

Father Skelly wanted to attend the proceedings for the sake of the parents but also for the sake of poor Jack. However, he was unable to find a substitute teacher to cover Jack's morning classes and therefore was forced to cover them himself. This meant that the unhappy Jack would be on his own to attend the proceedings with two very distraught parents. "Just swell, this is all just terrific," Jack silently ruminated as he took a seat right next to the fretting Mahans in Courtroom #3. "Skelly dragged me into this, and he is not even here. I have a bad feeling that this is not going to be a typical day in kiddie court."

Courtroom #3 was known among criminal lawyers and other **courthouse regulars** (the small "bar within a bar" who specialize in litigation) as **kiddie court**, a term that simultaneously showed most lawyers' contempt for and total ignorance of what takes place in the juvenile arena. Juvenile court proceedings involve children. Lawyers often foolishly equate matters that involve children as lacking in gravitas, a benighted attitude that is difficult to rectify given the lack of transparency that characterizes these secretive venues.

Young Rick, having taken his seat in Courtroom #3, was looking completely bewildered as he sat three feet in front of his parents at a large oak table. He shared this table with his attorney, Public Defender Peter Snarr.

At the other table, a few feet to the right, sat a 30-something, stick-thin woman who Jack correctly surmised to be Assistant District Attorney Sara Carter, or as Rick's parents unceasingly now called her, "the bitch." Next to the alleged "bitch" sat a cop in full police uniform. None of these officials knew who Jack was since both the public defender and prosecutor, and even the cop, had been hired after Jack had hung up his legal gloves.

Jack was silencing his mobile phone when Judge Leonard Watson, permanently assigned by the presiding judge of the county to handle all juvenile matters, abruptly entered the courtroom. A startled Jack instinctively rose to his feet despite no bailiff summoning "all rise." Jack sat back down when the judge waived him to do so. Jack had forgotten that juvenile judges typically do not like **overly formalizing** juvenile procedures since that distracts from the therapeutic environment of the proceedings.

Now that Jack had caught Judge Watson's attention, the judge asked why there were three adult spectators in the room. "These proceedings are **closed to the public** except for the two parents," the judge instructed. "Parents can stay as interested adults," the judge stated, "but any non-parent must explain his presence." The judge was looking directly at Jack at this point.

The judge knew what he was doing. The law does indeed require that juveniles be provided both a lawyer and at least one **interested adult**— typically a parent—to help advise them during court. Since juvenile court is confidential, the public is excluded. Secrecy is all part of the therapy. After the parents explained that Jack was a member of the bar, as well as their special guest, Jack was told he could stay. Knowing that Jack was a lawyer, though, caused the judge to consider that Jack looked familiar somehow.

"Do I know you?" Judge Watson asked Jack.

"Yes, Sir. I am Jack Day. I used to be a public defender here a few years back. But I worked solely in adult court."

"Oh, right," acknowledged the judge. "Good to see you again. Hope you are still lawyering somewhere but maybe getting paid more decently for it."

"Thank you, Your Honor," replied Jack. Jack did not bother updating the busy judge on the details of his alternative career.

The judge now focused his attention on young Rick Mahan. "Mr.

Mahan," began the judge, "I suppose that these are your parents sitting behind you?" (Juvenile judges often refer to defendants as "Mr." or "Ms." despite their youthful age.)

"Ah, yes, that's right," muttered Rick.

"I want you to know, young man, that you may consult with your parents, as well as with your attorney, whenever you feel the need. Understood?"

"Yes sir."

Judge Watson now turned his attention to Attorney Peter Snarr. "Mr. Snarr, have you had the chance to discuss this case with your client?"

"Yes," assured Snarr, who in reality had spent just 10 minutes discussing the case with Rick and his parents outside the courtroom. Two deputy sheriffs (used for transportation of prisoners and for courthouse security in many states, including Pennsylvania) had stood by to deter any thought of Rick's running.

"Very well," continued Judge Watson. Watson shifted his gaze to the prosecutor's table. "Ms. Carter, I understand that you have filed a motion for waiver to adult court. I would like to hear arguments on both sides about this. However, first, I call upon you to make an **offer of proof** so that I may know what the underlying facts of this case are all about. I have read the police reports in my file, but I would like to hear what you believe the commonwealth could prove were this to have been a full-blown adjudicatory hearing this day."

"What's going on?" Rick's father whispered toward Jack.

"The judge wants the prosecutor to tell him what facts she believes she would be able to prove if the case were to go to juvenile trial. Basically, the judge wants to know how horrible the incident was to help him better decide whether Rick should be tried as an adult. Seriousness of the current charges is a huge factor judges consider in waving juvenile court jurisdiction."

Sara Carter began to speak. Jack and Rick's father stopped their communications and sat back straight again in their chairs.

"Thank you, Your Honor," began Sara Carter, after she stole a peep at the recent whisperers. Now looking down at her yellow legal pad and then up again at the judge (a pattern she was about to repeat for the next couple of minutes), Carter announced, "The commonwealth is confident that it would prove the following facts beyond a reasonable doubt:

"First, that Rick Mahan, a teen just a few months shy of his 18th birthday, had been attending a party at the house of a schoolmate on the evening of April 5, along with about two dozen other partyers. The parents of the teen host were out of town on a business trip together. Beer was being served at this party, and young Mr. Mahan consumed beer. We know this because he admitted this to the police after they smelled alcohol on his breath at the 2-vehicle accident scene.

"Second, that in addition to drinking some beer, Mr. Mahan also consumed two tablets of the cold medicine and antihistamine known as Benadryl, which a girl at the party offered to him when he complained about a bad cold. We could prove this if necessary using the testimony of the girl. The girl would also testify that she told Rick that the medicine, which the state admits is both legal and sold without a prescription, would help him with his runny nose and coughs. She would further testify that she saw Rick take the time to read the print on the back of the box. This very box, which the state can produce, warns that Benadryl often has the side effect of causing drowsiness and that people taking it should not drive or operate machinery of any kind. There is also a warning that people should not take Benadryl along with alcohol since such a combination amplifies drowsiness. Rick admitted to the police that he had read the box yet took the medicine after already having consumed beer.

"Third, the Commonwealth would prove that around 10 p.m., Mr. Rick Mahan had tired of the party and decided to drive home. At this point, it had been about 30 minutes since Mr. Mahan had taken the cold medicine. The police will testify that Rick told them that he was not worried about falling asleep at the wheel because he felt completely sober and alert when he left. However, 15 minutes into his drive home, he struggled to stay awake and began to look for a safe place to pull his parents' jeep over for a brief nap. The next thing he remembered was waking up in his car to the promptings of a police officer at the scene. The officer told him there had been a wreck and asked if he was ok. Mr. Mahan said, "Yes," though his left shoulder later was found to have been dislocated by the force associated with the seatbelt.

"Fourth, the county coroner will testify that two people died at the scene of this accident: the 52-year-old driver of a Ford Focus and his 49-year-old wife. Neither had been wearing seatbelts, and tragically, both were ejected from this small vehicle on impact.

"Lastly, the commonwealth can produce a biochemist who works for the Pennsylvania State Crime Lab, who is a trained state expert on intoxication. She would testify that in her expert opinion, young Rick Mahan almost certainly fell asleep due to the interaction of alcohol with Benadryl."

Ms. Carter stopped talking and could sense that the judge "got it." Every lawyer knows to quit when she is ahead. "This completes the commonwealth's offer of proof," Carter concluded.

"Thank you for your summation of the commonwealth's anticipated case, Ms. Carter," responded Judge Watson. "Mr. Snarr, as defense counsel, do you have any issues with Ms. Carter's assertions?"

"Well, Your Honor, an offer of proof is hardly the same thing as actual proof. We have not heard from an actual witness today."

"We all realize that, Mr. Snarr," retorted the judge. "Is it not the situation here, however, that if the commonwealth could actually prove those facts as offered, we would not only be dealing with a set of serious charges but charges of the utmost seriousness? There are two dead bodies, and that is not contestable. Is there any reason you can think of that would suggest that Ms. Carter's offer of proof is something other than one made sincerely, that is, in good faith?"

Watching from the audience, Jack could tell that Snarr was a little unsure how exactly to respond. Pete Snarr thought for a few seconds, seemed to gain a little confidence, and finally said, "Your Honor, why would I doubt Ms. Carter's sincerity? She, like every member of the bar, is an **officer of the court** and as such is under a strict ethical obligation never to utter a lie in court. However, I would remind the court that even sincere people do not always convey what is objectively correct. This case is something for you to hear, from the actual witnesses to the events, so that a decision can be correctly made as to what really happened on that tragic night in question. These charges are very serious and need to be fully considered by a neutral judge like you, Sir, and not by Assistant District Attorney Carter."

Judge Watson subtly sighed before suggesting, "Well, Mr. Snarr, that gets us to the point of this whole waiver hearing doesn't it? If this case is at least hypothetically very serious, as I sense that even you seem to agree that it is, perhaps it is then potentially serious enough a matter for adult court to handle."

Judge Watson then suddenly fell silent. He stared down at his lap in deep reflection for ten or so seconds. He then continued, "Mr. Snarr, I frankly must tell you that the seriousness of the allegations seem to favor the state's application for waiver. Nevertheless, despite the gravity of the alleged facts, maybe there are reasons still to keep it before me. Mr. Snarr, let me hear what other reasons you might have as to why this juvenile court should not waive this matter to adult court for trial there."

Observing from the audience, Jack Day could see that this judge wanted to give young Rick a fair and balanced hearing before deciding to send him off to the fiery furnace of adult court. It seemed to Jack that the judge had nearly made up his mind but wanted Snarr to present whatever he could first.

"Very well, Your Honor," began Snarr. "I am not going to sit here and try to portray this alleged incident as some kind of normal teenage in-discretion. I know that there are two dead people involved. However, this was an accident. Nobody killed anyone on purpose. My client allegedly only had a small amount of beer. True, he supposedly took some cold medicine but just two capsules…"

"Mr. Snarr, I am sorry to interrupt. Perhaps, it would be better if you talked about your client's prior juvenile history. I do not think you are going to convince me that this is not a horrific set of alleged facts."

"Get it together, Pete," Jack was thinking to himself. "Follow the judge's lead here."

"Your Honor, if I may just suggest that this is a manslaughter case at most, not murder. That is all I was driving at."

"I get that, Mr. Snarr. Please move on," the irritated judge suggested.

"Well, I would add that my client is nearly 18 and has never been before this court or any court before. Even if Ms. Carter is right about her facts, and that is a big 'even if,' I would argue that my client's clean record calls for this case being retained in juvenile court. That is where it belongs. Thank you."

Jack reflected, "Well at least you got that important point in, Pete. It would have been nice, though, if you had **humanized** Rick a little more—brought in some sympathetic points like what a model student and obedient son he is. Juvenile judges are not used to dealing with model students and obedient sons."

"Ms. Carter, would you care to respond to Mr. Snarr's arguments?" asked the judge.

"Thank you, Your Honor." Before speaking further, Ms. Carter looked straight at Peter for a moment. She would show him how lawyering is supposed to be done.

"Your Honor, this case should be waived for two big reasons. First, of all, this so-called child is about as close to being at the cutoff age of 18 as one can get. He will be 18 in just two short months. If Mr. Mahan were 12 years old or 14 or even 16, okay, maybe he would be too young for you to waive, even in a horrendous double-homicide case. However, he is not any of those ages. He is 17 years and a whole bunch of months old.

"Second, you must consider the gravity of the facts of this case. If the commonwealth can prove its case as we believe we can, then Mr. Mahan is guilty of not just one but two counts of homicide by vehicle while DUI. You could not place him in a juvenile lockup for more than three years if you retain juvenile court jurisdiction. That would be just one-and-one-half years per dead victim. How would the surviving family members feel about that? What kind of message would we be sending to the community? I believe in compassion toward young people but not when it obliterates justice.

"Finally, Mr. Snarr talks about how this is Mr. Mahan's first time in trouble. Okay, but he allegedly killed two people. How is that for a 'first time in trouble?' Given his advanced age, coupled with the super seriousness of the charges, the commonwealth asks that this court waive its jurisdiction and transfer the matter to adult court for a proper trial. Thank you."

This young prosecutor's arguments really impressed Jack. For a second, she almost had him convinced. Yet, then he remembered what a great kid Rick really was. Jack thought, "The prosecutor did not know Rick. Neither did the judge. They both just saw a generic killer. Oh, why couldn't Snarr have prepared some organized talking points ahead of time as this prosecutor obviously has done? This is just another example of how attorney self-preparation wins cases."

Judge Watson's voice interrupted Jack's thoughts. "Thank you, Ms. Carter. Thank you too, Mr. Snarr. Give me a moment," he stated.

At this point, Judge Watson swung his chair sideways and stared at a mural on the wall. It was a mural of the scales of justice, with Lady Justice wearing her famous blindfold. After a minute or two, the judge swung his chair back into its forward position.

"It is the order of this court that the matter of Richard Mahan, involving two counts of alleged homicide by vehicle while DUI, be transferred to the adult Court of Common Pleas for a trial by jury. The juvenile court waives all jurisdiction in the matter. The district attorney's office is instructed forthwith to charge Richard Mahan as an adult and to cause a preliminary hearing on the charges to be scheduled promptly. My understanding is that 'promptly' means within the next 14 days, as required by the Pennsylvania Supreme Court. However, you can verify that by consulting the timelines written down in the Pennsylvania Rules of Court. Is there a motion for bail?"

"Your Honor, I ask that bail be set at $100,000," Ms. Carter responded.

"Your Honor, I ask that bail be set at no more than $5,000 or $10,000, if that. My client has nowhere to run. He is not a flight risk. One hundred thousand dollars is just plain ridiculous." Pete finally seemed upset.

"Bail is set at $100,000," the judge announced but only after first hesitating. "Unless and until bond is posted, I instruct that the defendant be remanded back to the juvenile detention center despite his now facing trial in adult court. I do not want this 17 year old locked up in our adult jail. Do you understand, deputy?"

"Yes, Your Honor," acknowledged the sheriff's deputy. "I will transport him back to juvenile lockup just where we found him."

"Very well, is there anything else?" asked the judge of the attorneys.

With nothing else said, the judge announced that the court was dismissed. On rising from the bench, the judge looked at young Rick who was gently crying. He then looked at Rick's mother who was also gently crying. He noticed that Rick's father was on the verge of crying. "So, I guess all of this sadness means that now I'm the bad guy," thought Judge Leonard Watson as he self-consciously walked toward the side door that led back to the welcome solitude of his chambers.

## Key Terms Found in This Chapter

Courthouse regulars                                    Interested adult
Kiddie court                                             Offer of proof
Overly formalizing                                   Officer of the court
Closed to the public                                        Humanized

## Questions for Class Discussion

1.  Would you rather be a "courthouse regular" or the type of lawyer
    who rarely goes to court? Which type of lawyers rarely appear in
    courthouses?
2.  In what ways could you argue that "kiddie court" is actually more
    important than adult criminal court?
3.  Besides making everyone "all rise," what are some other ways a
    juvenile court judge could avoid "overly formalizing" court pro-
    ceedings so as to enhance the therapeutic environment of juvenile
    court?
4.  Why should juvenile courts be closed to the public? What, if any,
    disadvantages to society are there in keeping juvenile court matters
    secret?
5.  If juveniles are provided with an attorney, why do they still need
    some other "interested adult" to advise them during court?
6.  Why did the juvenile judge want the prosecutor to make an "offer
    of proof" before deciding the waiver issue?
7.  Did it surprise you that lawyers, as officers of the court, are forbid-
    den ever to tell a lie in court? Do you agree with the additional rule
    that they are forbidden to call people to the stand who they know
    are planning to lie?
8.  Why is it so important for lawyers to try to humanize their clients
    to judges in juvenile court? How would you have tried to humanize
    young Rick if you were his attorney?
9.  After this case was waived to adult court, was setting bail at
    $100,000 "ridiculous" like Attorney Pete Snarr maintained? What
    differing amount, if any, do you think would have been fair?
10. Why was the judge so careful to make sure that young Rick would
    go back to juvenile hall rather than to adult jail to wait for trial?
    What sort of perils would a youthful Rick face in adult jail?

# 5

# The Preliminary Non-hearing, Hearing

Ten days had gone by since young Rick's waiver to adult court. Shortly after the waiver decision, Jack had told Father Skelly all about the disappointing result. Skelly had thanked Jack for his support and told Jack that the matter was no longer his problem. Jack was glad to hear that Father Skelly expected nothing further from him. Jack just wanted to go back to teaching. There was more than enough weird students and minor conflicts in his classroom to satisfy any desire he might have for some drama in his life.

Having just finished teaching his last class for the day, Jack was sitting at his desk doing paperwork when he sensed the presence of someone standing silently next to him. It was Father Joseph Skelly, flashing a tense smile.

"Geeze, Father. You kind of scared me. I did not hear you come in."

"Sorry, Jack. Did not mean to creep you out. How are your classes going?"

"Since when do you come to a teacher's classroom to ask that sort of question? What's really up, Father?"

"Well, if you really must know…"

"Wait a minute, Father," interrupted Jack. "Is this something about Rick Mahan's case? We agreed that I am done with that."

"Oh, why, yes, I just wanted to fill you in on the latest. No harm in my just doing that. I did not come here to ask you to get involved. I figured you should know what is going on since you still care about Rick, right?"

"OK, what's going on with his case?" a wary Jack inquired.

"I thought you would never ask," responded Father Skelly. "Rick was scheduled for a preliminary hearing this morning before a **justice of the peace**. Is that what they are still called?"

"In some states, yes. However, the generic name for those lower court judges is technically **magistrate**. They go by different names depending on the state. In our state, they call them 'district justices.' So, what happened at the prelim? Were you able to go?"

Father Skelly nodded affirmatively. "I was free, so I decided to attend to show my support to Rick and his parents. Court was scheduled at 9:00 a.m., but Rick's hearing was not called until an hour later. I had to sit through some traffic cases and even some small claims civil court stuff. After sitting there for a full hour, the judge announced it was time for Rick's preliminary hearing. If you ask me, I think they were stalling that first hour for some reason. I did not see any witnesses hanging about."

"Ok, Father. So, what happened?"

"Absolutely nothing happened. The public defender told the court that he was waiving the preliminary hearing. The judge said, 'Okay, since the hearing has been waived, I hereby **bind the case over** to the Court of Common Pleas for a jury trial.' What does all that mean, Jack?"

With surprise in his voice, Jack demanded, "Who on earth was the public defender who opted to waive this preliminary hearing?"

"Peter Snarr," replied Skelly. "Who else?"

"Oh, no, you mean Rick is still stuck with Peter Snarr? I was hoping his case would get reassigned to some other lawyer once juvenile court was out of the picture."

"Well, Snarr told me that his boss wants him to take the case through to the very end. Snarr knows the case well, and apparently they don't want to reassign the case to some new, fresh lawyer at this point."

"The public defender's office must be going with **vertical representation**," opined Jack. "I think I heard they were using that model these days. Back in my day, the office used **horizontal representation** in which a different defender got the case at each different stage of the process. Therefore, the lawyer who did the prelim passed the case on to the lawyer who would try to get a plea bargain, who would pass the case on to the lawyer who did the trial, who would pass the case on to the lawyer who did the appeal. However, now it looks like they are going with vertical representation, where the same attorney takes the case from beginning to end."

"Is vertical representation a good thing?" asked Skelly.

"Not when your vertical lawyer is Pete Snarr," replied Jack.

"What is the purpose behind a preliminary hearing, Jack?" asked Skelly. "Snarr told Rick and his parents it was just a waste of everyone's time. Is that true?"

"No," Jack answered. "Well, yes… Sort of yes… But actually no."

"I see that law school really helped you speak clearly," joked Skelly.

Jack began, "It is true that this case would have been bound over for trial whether there was a preliminary hearing or not. But Snarr should never have waived it just because of that."

"Please do explain," requested the school principal.

"OK, I will try," asserted Jack. "A **preliminary hearing's official purpose** is for a judge or magistrate to determine if there is enough evidence to even have a trial. The prosecutor has to establish what is known as a *prima facie* **case**. If the prosecutor fails to establish that, then the charges will be dismissed."

"And what is a *prima facie* case?" Father Skelly inquired.

"I was getting to that," Jack noted. "A *prima facie* case means that there is enough proof to show that the defendant probably committed the crime—that there is probable cause, in other words. Later, during the jury trial, the state would have to prove that the defendant committed the crime beyond a reasonable doubt, not just that he probably did it. However, at the preliminary hearing stage, all a judge needs in order to bind over a case for trial is a finding of simple, 51% probability. This is a very low standard since it is doubtful the police would arrest somebody in the first place who did not at least probably commit a crime. So, since judges almost always find probable cause, a foolish lawyer might think that he might as well waive the hearing in the first place. I will say that only about 2% of cases are not bound over for trial pursuant to a preliminary hearing. And with what I know about the evidence so far in Rick's case, I am quite certain it would not be part of that 2% that gets dismissed."

"Then, why do you think that Snarr messed up by waiving the preliminary hearing? It sounds to me that it was no big deal either way," asserted Father Skelly.

Jack explained, "Because this is a very serious set of charges, and every responsible lawyer would insist on a preliminary hearing in order to use it as an **unofficial discovery tool**. You see, Father, in order to establish its *prima facie* case, the state would have to put on enough witnesses to prove each element of the charged offenses, at least to the level of probable cause like we discussed. While they are presenting these witnesses, the defense lawyer gets to listen and hear about their case. Even better, the defense lawyer can cross-examine each witness and use the cross-examination to explore the case against his client. That way, the defense can prod, probe, and start preparing for the eventual trial. Remember, there is no jury present, so this 'show and tell' can only benefit the defense. The state knows this, so the prosecutor's preliminary hearing strategy is to put on as little evidence as possible to prove the *prima facie* case—nothing more. The prosecutor knows that it does not take much for a preliminary hearing judge to 'pass the buck' and bind a case over for trial. Therefore, the prosecutor tends only to put on a **skeleton case**; in other words, he or she uses as few witnesses as possible to get the job done. At this level, a few key witnesses are all that is usually required to prove probable cause."

"Wow, that makes sense, Jack," admitted Skelly. "You really know your stuff still, don't you Jack?"

"Well, yeah, it's not like I am 80 years old—no offense Father. Oh, and one more sweet benefit of not waiving the preliminary hearing: you get to have a court stenographer present taking down every word each prosecution witness utters. Then, during the eventual trial, you can discredit the witness, or **impeach the witness** as lawyers call it, if he or she deviates in any way at trial from what was said at the preliminary hearing. Impeaching a witness is one way to create some reasonable doubt in the minds of the jurors."

Father Skelly looked puzzled. "Well, given all these unofficial benefits of the preliminary hearing, why would Peter Snarr have waived it?"

"Because he is a lazy piece of crap, Father," Jack explained matter-of-factly.

"Maybe you are being too hard on Snarr," speculated Father Skelly. "Doesn't the defense put on a case at a preliminary hearing after the state does? If the defense can use a preliminary hearing to discover the state's case, why couldn't the state use the preliminary hearing to discover the defense strategy? The defense does get to call witnesses and put on a defense at this stage, does it not?"

"Yes, they can if they want to," replied Jack. "At least that's the case in states like ours that use preliminary hearings instead of traditional grand juries. You see, Father, some state constitutions require the use of **grand juries** of ordinary citizens instead of one-judge, preliminary hearings to decide if enough probable cause exists for a trial. In those states, if a grand jury finds enough evidence to constitute probable cause, it will return an **indictment**, also known as a **true bill**. You may have heard of these words before. They just mean that the case will now go to trial. Preliminary hearing judges, on the other hand, who find probable cause issue what is called an **information**, which is essentially the same thing as their client being indicted. Here is where it gets tricky.

"In the grand jury states, only the prosecution gets to call witnesses and present a case. The defense just shuts up, sits there, and watches until it is over. They do not get to cross-examine the other side's witnesses or call their own witnesses in response. It really is one-sided, a real kangaroo court. However, most states use preliminary hearings instead of grand juries because their state constitution allows for it, and you do not have to drag in a bunch of jurors. In a preliminary hearing, defense attorneys can indeed try to 'beat the rap' at that very stage of the process through heavy cross-examination and by calling witnesses for the defense to testify. However, as useful as cross-examination of enemy witnesses is for the defense, presenting a defense case by calling defense witnesses is very rare at preliminary hearings. This is so because nearly always the judge is going to bind the case over for trial no matter what the defense witnesses say. So, why let the prosecutor discover your trial strategy by hearing what your defense witnesses have to say and by cross-examining them in advance of trial?"

"Oh, I get it," acknowledged Skelly. "Preliminary hearings can generate a lot more pre-trial discovery of the other side's case than grand jury proceedings. However, preliminary hearings really only should benefit the defense in terms of it being a discovery tool and a possible impeachment tool at trial. But the defense attorney needs to resist the urge of putting on any defense via witnesses at this stage. That just tips the prosecutor off in a matter that is probably going to be bound over for trial no matter what anyway."

"Father, you would have made a great lawyer," quipped Jack. "I think you followed the wrong calling."

Skelly smiled and said, "Why didn't Snarr just force the state to put on witnesses, sit back and learn, and then decline to put on any defense? That is what you are telling me a sensible lawyer would have done instead of simply waiving the hearing."

"Again, Father, it is because poor Rick has Pete Snarr who seems to lack sense. Or maybe he just does not care."

Father Skelly decided he had nothing to lose when he straightforwardly now asked, "Jack, would you be willing to take over the defense of our own Rick Mahan? He really needs a competent lawyer. Please, Jack."

Jack went dead silent for 30 straight seconds. With a tear in his eye and a frog in his throat, he quietly stated, "Yeah, Father. I'm all in."

∾

## Key Terms Found in This Chapter

| | |
|---|---:|
| Justice of the peace | Unofficial discovery tool |
| Magistrate | Skelton case |
| Bind the case over | Impeach the witness |
| Vertical representation | Grand juries |
| Horizontal representation | Indictment |
| Preliminary hearing's official purpose | True bill |
| Prima facie case | Information |

## Questions for Class Discussion

1. Some preliminary hearing states use magistrates (not all of whom are law school graduates) to decide if a case has enough evidence to go to trial, while others use full-blown, law-trained judges. Do you think magistrates are capable of deciding the existence (or not) of probable cause in a case?

2. Some states use grand juries instead of preliminary hearings to decide if cases have enough evidence to be bound over for trial. Would it surprise you that grand juries bind over an even higher percentage

of cases for trial than do preliminary hearing judges? Why do you think that this might be so?

3. Knowing what you now know about preliminary hearings and grand juries, which would you rather have in deciding whether your case should go to trial?

4. Does your state make use of preliminary hearing judges or grand juries in deciding if cases should be bound over for trials?

5. Does your state call its magistrates "justices of the peace," which is the traditional term for such officials, or does it give them a more modern title?

6. Why do you suppose that not all states require their magistrates to be graduates of law schools?

7. Would you be happier to learn that your public defender's office believed in using vertical representation or horizontal representation if you were using their services? If you were a public defender, which would you prefer as a worker?

8. If police can only arrest someone if there is probable cause that he or she committed a crime, then why do we need a court to also find the presence of probable cause in a pre-trial case?

9. If almost all preliminary hearing judges return an information, why should defense lawyers in preliminary hearing states refuse generally to waive a client's preliminary hearing?

10. How can a defense lawyer go about "discovering" the other side's case during a preliminary hearing? How can they prevent the prosecutor from doing the same to them?

11. Why cannot defense lawyers use grand jury proceedings to "discover" the other side's cases to the same degree that they can during preliminary hearings?

12. How can a defense lawyer sometimes make use of the preliminary hearing transcript to impeach a prosecution witness months later during a jury trial?

13. Why was Jack so upset at Public Defender Peter Snarr's performance on the day scheduled for young Rick's preliminary hearing?

# Unit 3
# Lawyer and Client

**Chapter 6: Jack Enters the Stage**

**Chapter 7: The Unlikely Villain**

This unit illustrates various challenges facing a lawyer and a client. It describes how Jack Day, the former public defender turned teacher, returns to his old lawyering ways by personally taking over the defense of Rick Mahan, a student. The unit discusses issues of competency of private lawyers versus public defenders and the role that criminal defenders are expected to play. It then turns its attention to the client and the hardships of pre-trial detention for a fish out of water such as young Rick Mahan.

# 6

## Jack Enters the Stage

Young Rick Mahan's parents were delighted when Father Skelly called them with the news that Jack Day was willing to take over their son's defense as a service to the family and school. They could tell that something was not quite right with the quality of representation that Public Defender Peter Snarr was giving their son. Their instincts told them that something was sorely lacking.

Mr. and Mrs. Mahan wasted no time in calling Jack on the phone to discuss next steps. Setting their phone to speaker function, they both thanked Jack profusely for coming to their son's aid.

"Thank you, thank you, Mr. Day, for getting our son away from those incompetent public defenders. We are so glad that he has a real lawyer now and not just some government, public defender hack."

Jack cringed a little inside when he heard the Mahans refer to privately retained lawyers as "real lawyers" as though public defenders were not. When Jack had worked as a public defender, he had heard this supposed **real lawyer** versus public defender distinction hundreds of times. He knew that nothing could be further from the truth.

"Well, you are welcome," responded Jack. "But please do not judge all public defenders by Peter Snarr. Every office has one bad apple. The truth is that, generally speaking, public defenders around the county do as **good a job or better** than privately retained criminal defense lawyers."

"How is that even possible?" asked Mrs. Mahan. Her tone of voice telegraphed total incredulity.

"Well, it is true," Jack assured. "My experience in the courts has been that whether you look at plea bargains negotiated, acquittals won at trial, or successful appeals, public defenders tend to get quite good results. It only makes sense. They see so much action that they inevitably wind up acquiring a strong set of skills. They also are part of a super-tight, daily **courtroom workgroup** with judges and prosecutors. Private criminal lawyers also get to become part of these ongoing workgroups but never to the extent of the public defenders. Public defenders really know what works, when it works, and with whom it works. Remember, I myself was one of those hack public defenders before I became a teacher. I was a graduate of an elite law school, as were most of my colleagues in the office. Our credentials far exceeded most of the local private criminal defense lawyers. That is often the case around the county, especially in large metro areas. It is hard to get a job as a public defender. Anyone can hang out a shingle and declare himself to be a private defense lawyer."

"Ok, fair enough," replied Mrs. Mahan. She knew better than to argue some point with which her son's new protector obviously had some lingering issues. "My husband and I are just glad we have you now. After the waiver hearing, we asked the head public defender to give us a different lawyer. She told us that things do not work that way. It was Snarr or nobody. We think you will be an upgrade from Snarr. Our son is on board with this too. When can you meet with him?"

"Right away," said Jack. "I plan to drive over to the juvenile detention center in the late afternoon after my classes. Is there anything you should tell me about Rick before I meet with him one-on-one?"

Rick's father now chose to speak up. "Just remember that despite the system now treating him like some kind of a fully grown adult, Rick really is just a scared kid who needs help. I mean, he drank one lousy beer and took a couple of over-the-counter cold tablets. I know there was a terrible accident, but destroying Rick is not going to fix things. Two wrongs do not make a right."

Rick felt better listening to what Mr. Mahan had just said. He had been feeling guilty and anxious defending someone who probably committed homicides while driving under the influence. In fact, that was the very type of crime that triggered his flight from the public defender's office years ago. Yet, "Destroying a mere boy like Rick maybe would be two wrongs trying to make a right," he silently considered.

Jack realized that even if Rick had fallen asleep at the wheel by engaging in reckless conduct, he did not deserve the many harsh years in prison that the state was obviously intent on pursuing. Most criminal defenders feel this way. In most cases, they do not see their role as getting their factually guilty client off "scot-free" but to help **mitigate the punishment** that they perceive as being draconian by western world standards — even by world standards.

Jack realized that he almost certainly would wind up trying to plea bargain Rick's case. Jack figured that simply arranging a deal should not necessarily trigger any of his old mental health demons. Helping Rick in this way was the right thing to do. If he could negotiate a sentence of months in the local county jail, rather than a sentence of years or decades in the horrors of state prison, everyone would win. "Long years in state prison would destroy Rick. That's for sure," Jack silently contemplated. "Even when Rick got out, he would be seriously messed up for life. Then there is the suffering of his parents to consider. It would just ruin their lives to see what prison life had in store for a super conventional kid like Rick who is utterly lacking in prison survival skills. Rick's only chance would to become some hardened wolf's personal punk or else just go crazy enough that people would leave him alone."

Jack ended his phone call with the Mahans while keeping his dark concerns for Rick to himself. At the end of school's sixth period, Jack Day the teacher donned the costume of Jack Day, **Esquire,** by changing into a suit and a tie. He then drove the eight miles to the juvenile facility where they had locked youthful Rick up, pre-trial.

At first, the detention center authorities refused to admit Jack since he no longer carried his old attorney identification card in his wallet. He got lucky, though, when one of the supervisors recognized him as a former public defender and thus a lawyer. Having gained entry, Jack was next escorted by a guard to a bland-looking conference room. "I'll go and fetch Richard Mahan for you and will be back shortly," said the guard.

Jack waited about five minutes until the guard returned to the room with Rick in tow. "I have to lock you both in this room while you chat in private," apologized the guard. "Just knock when you are done, and I will let you both out."

After the guard left, Jack looked to make sure that the door was shut. Jack then turned to a tired-looking young Rick and asked, "How are you holding up in here, Rick?"

"Not too well," sighed Rick. "This is not exactly St. Francis High School around here."

"I can only imagine," Jack sympathized. "Hang in there. Tomorrow morning I will be filing a motion to reduce your bail." Jack knew that this was one type of **critical early legal action** that thoughtful lawyers like to take in order to gain a client's confidence early in their representation. Gaining a client's confidence is an important first step that any lawyer should do in a case. It helps later when you need a client to take your advice. Getting bail reduced in a criminal case—or even just trying to—is one of just several ways to build that trust. Besides, Jack knew that Rick's bail had been set much too high.

"How long will it take to get my bail reduced to something my parents could afford? They told my parents they wanted $100,000 dollars. Who has that kind of money?" asked Rick.

Jack knew that many people unable to make bail have a **getting out obsession**. This obsession can be particularly pronounced among people locked up for the very first time in their lives. They feel like someone who has a splitting, intense headache. They can deal with other matters later, but first they want relief from the excruciating, immediate pain.

"Motion court is usually held late in the week, on Thursdays or Fridays. If I can file our motion to reduce bail tomorrow morning, we should get before the motions court judge late this week."

"Can't you get me out any sooner?" pleaded Rick.

"No, but I will work things as fast as is humanly possible," responded Jack.

"OK, thanks, Mr. Day. I am glad you are my lawyer. You were one of my favorite teachers too. It is kind of weird but good weird."

Jack stared at Rick with a concerned gaze. "Why don't you fill me in on what happened that horrible night when you got in the wreck?" he suggested.

"It's pretty much like the cops said," Rick began. "I did drink a beer at a party, just one. I did have this horrible cold. I probably should not have even gone out that night, but all of my friends were going to the party. I do not like to drink, but I thought I needed to have at least one beer so that I would fit in. Then I took a couple of cold pills that some girl offered to me after I kept coughing while talking to her."

"Did you read the box like the cops claim?"

"Yeah, I read the stupid box."

"Tell me about the accident," Jack prompted.

"All right. Well, halfway home I started having trouble staying awake. This had happened to me once before, and it really scared me. At that time, I had sworn to myself that if I ever got sleepy behind the wheel again, I would just pull over. However, when it happened again after the party, I was unable to find a place to quickly pull over, when boom; I was waking up after the crash with the cops all over the place. I do not remember crashing the car or anything. But I am sure I must have fallen asleep at the wheel. I am so, so, sorry for that man and woman who died! I am so, so sorry!" Rick broke into tears.

Jack let Rick cry it out a little. Then, Jack said, "Rick, you mentioned that falling asleep had happened to you once before. When was that?"

"Two or three months ago."

"Had you been drinking or taking any medicine then?" asked Jack.

"No, it just happened."

Jack filed this information away in his lawyer's mind for now. It could come in handy later.

"Rick, is it true you admitted to drinking a beer to the cops?"

"Yeah, I did. I told them just one beer though. And that was the truth. Just one."

Jack nodded to show his understanding. He then asked, "Rick, is it also correct that you told them you had read the writing on the box?"

"Yeah, I did admit that. Why? Is that a problem?" (Rick had read the information on the box about all of the many symptoms the medicine helped alleviate and the proper dosages. Jack had assumed that Rick was also admitting to having read all of the stern warnings about driving, etc., which actually Rick had not read.)

"Well, don't beat yourself up over the box." Jack suggested. "Do you remember when the cops read you your **Miranda warnings**?"

"What are those?" Rick inquired.

Jack explained, "You know, like 'you have the right to remain silent. You have the right to a lawyer present before talking to the cops.' Stuff like that."

"They told me my rights before even asking me anything. It sounded like a TV show. It was really weird."

Jack was a little disappointed that the cops had been so careful to read Rick his rights so early on in the encounter. He was hoping for a suppression issue in there somewhere. The cops must have been being extra careful that night to not even wait to read Rick his rights until making a formal arrest.

Rick interrupted Jack's thoughts by saying, "Next time I will know to shut up until I get a lawyer. The kids in here have taught me that. They call it 'lawyering up.' They say, 'always **lawyer up**, and the cops will stop asking you questions!'"

"That is good advice, Rick," confirmed Jack. "However, I doubt you will ever get in trouble again. You are not that kind of person."

"Tell that to the family of the dead people," lamented Rick.

Jack was about to move on but had a strange hunch. "Rick just to be clear, you did actually agree to talk to the cops after they read you your rights, correct?"

Rick nodded his head in the affirmative but then said, "I remember at first saying that 'maybe I need a lawyer' when the cop first asked me a question. The cop said, 'Well, is that what you want?' I then said, 'No, not really,' and then I just started answering his questions."

"Oh, that could be something potentially very useful," Jack declared. He mentally filed this information away as well for now. Jack remembered that the cops had never mentioned anything about "maybe I need a lawyer" in any of their police reports.

Jack spoke to Rick for a few more minutes, but nothing else that was particularly useful came from it. Finally, Jack figured it was time to leave so he knocked on the door. While waiting for the guard, Jack turned to Rick and said, "See you in a few days at the hearing on our petition to reduce bail."

"You mean I get to go to that hearing too and not just you?" asked Rick.

"Yes, they will transport you there in case the judge wants some information from you in making his decision. I will invite your parents too. See you then."

As the guard opened the door, Jack gave Rick a wave goodbye. Jack saw the look of exhaustion return to Rick's face. "If the kid thinks this place is rough, heaven forbid he gets shipped off to adult prison," fretted Jack to himself.

$\sim$

## Key Terms Found in This Chapter

Real lawyer

Good a job or better

Courtroom workgroup

Mitigate the punishment

Esquire

Critical early legal action

"Getting out" obsession

Miranda warnings

Lawyer up

## Questions for Class Discussion

1. Why was Attorney Jack Day so sensitive when Mrs. Mahan suggested that public defenders were not real lawyers?

2. Why do people assume that public defenders are inferior to privately retained counsel?

3. How is it possible that public defenders, on average, do as good a job as private attorneys who have so much more time on their hands to prepare their cases?

4. Why would public defenders tend to be even more entrenched in a system of courtroom workgroups than are privately hired attorneys?

5. What is meant by the idea that most defense lawyers see their role in most cases to be one of "mitigating the punishment"?

6. Would you feel comfortable helping criminals to have their punishment mitigated? Would you feel comfortable helping them to get off "scot-free"?

7. Have you ever heard of the title given to lawyers of "esquire" before?

8. Getting a client's bail reduced can be a "critical early legal action" a lawyer can do in order to gain a new client's confidence. What other early actions can you think of that can also establish confidence?

9. Why are people incarcerated for the first time so obsessed with making bail? Would you be obsessed? Why?

10. If "lawyering up" is a smart thing to do, why do so many people fail to do it? Is there ever a situation when an arrested person should not "lawyer up"?

11. What do you think of Jack for agreeing to take over this case? Do you think that is something you would do if you suffered from the same "demons" as did Jack?

12. As a people, how indebted should we feel to the thousands of people who serve as criminal defense attorneys? Should they warrant the same gratitude that many people feel toward prosecutors? Less gratitude? More gratitude?

13. Should we try to attract strong talent to public defending or offer the lowest possible salaries that will still attract some applicants to the job?

14. How could public defenders combat the image among the public and those charged with crimes that they are "lesser" lawyers? Should they try to combat this image?

# 7

# The Unlikely Villain

Rick Mahan was the oddest of ducks in juvenile lockup. For one thing, he was an adult court, pre-trial detainee. Though the juvenile judge had ordered Rick to be tried as an adult, he did not want the 17 year old thrown into jail with the adult wolves (yet).

The other way that Rick was an oddity in **juvie hall** was that he in no way fit the typical profiles of adult criminals or even those of the hard-core delinquents inhabiting his current location.

Breaking the law while a teenager is a very common thing to do. Luckily for most of us, we are never caught. Whether we are lucky or not, breaking minor laws once or twice without any violence is truly just youthful indiscretion and not any evidence of chronic antisocial personality. Our brief propensity for mischief will not continue into adulthood. However, there are youth who classify as exceptions. Their repeated, escalating delinquent acts (or their first-time spectacularly dangerous, single act) cause enough concern to a juvenile judge that these exceptional youths are eventually placed in a secure juvenile lockup instead of given the **standard disposition of juvenile court**: probation with conditions.

The juvenile court judge did not decide to lock up Rick due to a long history of repeated and escalating misdeeds. Nor did the judge feel compelled to protect society from a violent predator. Rather, Juvenile Court Judge Watson had placed Rick in juvenile hall simply because there was no place else for the boy to wait for his adult court trial. The inconve-

nient reality was that Rick had allegedly killed two people under circumstances that the state had alleged were not exactly accidental. Because of
the serious nature of the case, the juvenile judge had ordered Rick to be
tried as an adult and, while waiting for his jury trial, to be thrown into
juvenile detention alongside the varied assortment of chronic, incorrigible, and even sometimes violent, predators.

Rick did not feel like he was **incorrigible** (hardened, unchangeable
offender) nor a violent person by nature. Nobody else in the detention
center saw him in those ways either. Everyone there — the inmates, the
guards, and even Rick himself — saw Rick as being a clueless **fish** (a naïve
square who is brand new to detention).

St. Francis was the place where Rick fit in, even thrived. He was dili-
gent and smart enough to maintain nearly a 4.0 GPA, even late into his
current senior year. Rick had no problems with authority: he had never
come close to ever meriting a suspension or any other school disciplinary
action. Neither was Rick antisocial. In fact, he was very prosocial: his
classmates had elected him to be one of their student body officers for his
last year at St. Francis. In short, Rick's profile could be most succinctly
summarized by mentioning the pithy description given to him by those
compiling the soon-to-be-published, St. Francis High School yearbook:
"Rick Mahan, amiable genius who we vote as most likely to succeed."

Rick's successful life up to this point was mostly due to a combination
of good parents and good peers, along with some innate talents. Most
of the others locked up alongside Rick came from broken homes and/or
gang-filled neighborhoods. Unlike Rick, they mostly grew up in poverty,
which unfortunately is highly correlated with bad parenting and deviant
peers. Those few of Rick's new associates, who came from functional
families and stable neighborhoods, were often unlucky when it came to
idiosyncratic, mental disorders of various kinds.

Rick had not been saddled with an internal mental disorder of any
kind. He possessed empathy and therefore clearly was not a **psychopath.**
He had no trouble following rules and so did not suffer from **oppositional defiance disorder.** He tried to get along with others and hence was
not plagued with **antisocial personality disorder.** Indeed, unlike many
of his youthful, fellow inmates, he was not burdened with a behavioral
disorder of any kind.

Nor did Rick possess any of the typical **delinquency risk factors.** His
parents were neither neglectful, indulgent, nor authoritarian. His sib-

lings too were solid people. Outside the home, his peer group mostly consisted of the other law-abiding kids at his private, college-prep school—hardly a likely breeding ground for future felons of America.

As far as other various individual risk factors were concerned, Rick was neither particularly bad tempered, impulsive, nor anxious. Instead, he was slow to anger, thoughtful, and calm. Rick was a master at delaying gratification. He was successful at and consistently rewarded for following all of the rules of conventional society. In the parlance of the others in the lockup, conventional Rick was a **square**.

In fact, Rick found himself to be the biggest square in the place. Yet, this time, he was unwilling or unable to do what it would take to assimilate.

Back at school, Rick strived to assimilate. It was important to him always to fit in. In fact, Rick probably cared a bit too much about what others thought of him. This was the main reason that he had drunk beer at the party. Rick hated the taste of beer and was not infatuated with the idea of getting drunk. He only drank to be one with the group.

In juvenile lockup, Rick could not figure out how to become one with the group, or even if he should try. The few squares like him were all deeply mentally ill. Most of the rest were either bullies or creepy sheep. The **bullies** loved to fight and to intimidate others. They used violence and threats to get their way. The **sheep** sucked up to the bullies and tried constantly to curry their favor. The crazies were left to their own by nearly everybody, as were the very rare **stoics**—strong, silent types who just wanted to be left alone to do their time. Even though this secure juvenile facility included a small "high school" of sorts, complete with salaried teachers and even a principal, very few of the "students" tried to improve themselves by getting an education while there. Rick's instincts told him that he too should not put too much effort into schoolwork. This was not St. Francis.

Rick was not sure how to succeed in this place. He knew he did not have the personality to be a bully. He refused to be a creepy sheep. He was not crazy enough or stoic enough for others to leave him alone. He decided to pursue the only option he thought was left open to him: retreat from his newfound society as best he could.

While not in class, Rick spent most of his days just sitting in his cell. Since this was not adult jail, there were plenty of books in the library for him to checkout and read in his "room." Rick did have to come out for meals in the cafeteria, but he generally either sat alone (his preferred option) or at the table of crazies (his default). Frequently (meaning several times each day), one of the bullies would verbally abuse him while the sheep would jeer and laugh. Sometimes a bully would punch him, spit on him, or threaten his life. Rick knew that it was against the **inmate code** (informal set of peer rules) for him to seek help from a staff member. **Snitching** was considered to violate the code more than any other single thing since all the captives considered it to be an act of treason. Even if Rick were ever tempted to betray his new tribe, he sensed it was unlikely that any of the staff would even know what to do to help him.

Rick was on his own. Sometimes Rick was forced to fight back physically. He had to do this to avoid being labeled a weakling, a **punk**. Rick always lost such fights because even when he occasionally would get the upper hand over a bully, several of the sheep would jump in to make sure their hero won. Still, Rick would fight when he felt there was no other option.

From time to time, Rick worried about the ultimate outcome of his future trial. Did he have any chance of an acquittal? On the other hand, would being locked up somewhere, perhaps in a place even worse than this, become the type of life to which he must eventually grow accustomed? Despite such worries, Rick mostly was too concerned about immediate, daily survival to think deeply about his long-term future.

Rick's life was so hard that he did not even dare tell his parents during their weekly visits about the true depth of his suffering. He did constantly urge them, however, to remind his lawyer about the importance to him of having his bail amount reduced to a point his parents could afford. The frequency of their boy's requests constituted dark hints of the level of pain their son must be enduring. "If only Jack Day could get our son's bail reduced, we'll get him out of this horrible place," Rick's parents would assure one another.

"Please God, help my lawyer and my parents to get me out on bail," was Rick's own nightly prayer. Rick's second-most favorite activity of each day was this nightly prayer. He wished that this were so because of his deep piety. Yet, he knew it was mostly so because the ritual made him feel like he had some control left in his life. Besides, it was the last thing he would do before engaging in his most favorite daily activity of all: sleep.

## Key Terms Found in This Chapter

| | |
|---|---|
| Juvie hall | Square |
| Standard disposition of juvenile court | Bullies |
| Incorrigible | Sheep |
| Fish | Stoics |
| Psychopath | Inmate code |
| Oppositional defiance disorder | Snitching |
| Antisocial personality disorder | Punk |
| Delinquency risk factors | |

## Questions for Class Discussion

1. How would you personally feel if you were sent to a juvenile detention facility to wait for your day in court? Do you have the skills to succeed in such a place?

2. Should adult criminal sentencing courts try to take a cue from juvenile courts in bending over backward to impose probation instead of incarceration as a standard sentence, even in serious matters?

3. What sort of typical conditions should be imposed upon juveniles who are given probation instead of incarceration? Should different offenses result in different conditions?

4. Why do you suppose new, naïve inmates in juvenile lockup are referred to as "fish"?

5. Are most juvenile delinquents "psychopaths"?

6. Did you know anyone from your youth who seemed to suffer from "oppositional defiance disorder"? What was this person like? How did this person cause problems?

7. Why do you suppose some children become antisocial to the point of being pathological? What environments help children to grow up to be prosocial?

8. What are some of the major risk factors that help lead to delinquent life styles?

9. What, if anything, could the government do to better support the creation and maintenance of strong, healthy families?

10. Are you a "square"? If so, how did this happen?

11. If you were locked up, would you more likely become a bully, sheep, or stoic?

12. Other than the rule against snitching, what other rules do you imagine might constitute part of a juvenile detention facility's inmate code?

# Unit 4
# Bail and Arraignment

### Chapter 8: Freedom Held Hostage

### Chapter 9: Homeward Bound

### Chapter 10: Arraignment

This unit describes various pre-trial matters, with special focus on the purposes and process of bail, as well as the purposes and process of arraignment. The reader learns all about the setting and posting of bail and the nuances of arraignment as attorney Jack Day takes us—and his client—through the paces.

# 8

# Freedom Held Hostage

Bail is an ancient concept dating back many centuries. It is a primitive concept involving money kept as hostage. At one time, bail actually involved a human hostage rather than money. A relative or close friend of the accused would post himself as **bond** in order to secure the pre-trial release. If the accused chose to **abscond**, the person who posted himself as the bond would be punished as a substitute. This punishment could even include execution, if the crime called for that (which nearly every felony did back then).

Today, bail takes the form of money held hostage rather than use of actual human hostages. Yet, it is still quite a primitive and sketchy affair. Nevertheless, bail is as needed as much today as ever. There is arguably no such thing as the right to a speedy trial in the United States. It is a promise left largely unfulfilled, at least by any objective, rational measure.

True, the language of the Sixth Amendment to the Constitution guarantees not just the right to a jury trial in a criminal case but a "speedy" trial at that. However, courts facing thousands of cases per year with relatively few personnel simply have proven to be unable to deliver speed as promised.

Courts will never openly admit that they are slow in delivering due process. To do so would invite catastrophe. After dodging the issue for decades, the U.S. Supreme Court finally ruled in 1973 (in a case called

*Struck v. United States*) that failure to provide a speedy trial requires complete and permanent dismissal of the charges. No other weaker remedy, e.g., reduction of sentence, would suffice.

Still, speed is not provided. What the Supreme Court giveth, it taketh away. In the case of ***Barker v. Wingo***, another case from the same time period, the High Court provided an easy escape hatch for courts across America to continue their sluggish business as usual. It ruled that speed could not be defined using days, weeks, months, or (gasp) even years. Rather, it must be decided on a case-by-case basis, that is, to say subjectively, using squishy factors like "reasons for the delay" and "harm to the defendant."

In practice, the squishy factors provide cover for busy courts who simply cannot or will not be swift. In fact, in the *Barker* decision itself, the Supreme Court used its newfound squishy factors to ultimately rule that the lower court did not deny alleged murderer Barker speed, even though it took over five years for the state to give him his day in court.

Yes, the Sixth Amendment's right to speedy justice can often seem more like a mere form of words than it does an actual, enforceable right. It this sense, it has a lot in common with the Fourth Amendment. For a long time, the Fourth Amendment's guarantee of no "unreasonable searches and seizures" was simply words on paper with no teeth. It was not until 1961 that the Supreme Court, in the case of ***Mapp v. Ohio***, finally got around to ruling that there would be consequences attached to the police violating someone's Fourth Amendment rights. Specifically, the Court ruled that evidence obtained illegally would be suppressed. Yet, it took nearly 200 years from the drafting of the Bill of Rights to the 1960s for the promise of the Fourth Amendment to go into effect in state courts. Has the **Sixth Amendment** promise of speedy trials been achieved yet in the states? Jack did not think so. "Would waiting at a so-called fast food restaurant for two hours for your burger and fries seriously be considered 'fast food'?" Jack thought the analogy was a fair one.

Jack knew that judges in his county deeply resented any petition to dismiss a case due to lack of speed until at least one year had passed since the arrest. "Don't even bother," was the signal they had sent. Yet, Jack knew that sitting locked up for months or longer caused some serious **incarceration-related pre-trial harms** to individuals charged with crimes. People in lockup have their futures put completely on hold. They are handicapped in mounting a defense. They often worry themselves sick about what will ultimately happen to them. They feel the stigma of knowing that friends, work colleagues, and acquaintances must think that they are too dangerous or too much of a flight risk to be allowed out in polite society. They cannot hold a job and support their family. They cannot have physical intimacy with their spouse. They cannot escape boredom and bullies. The list goes on.

Jack did not want Rick rotting in lockup for month after month until the local courts finally got around to granting him his "speedy" trial. Jack had heard that locally, most cases were currently taking about six months to be scheduled for trial. Amazingly, it was the prosecutor's office who got to decide when a case would be scheduled for trial. They were the ones who would list it on the trial roster. True, some counties in the United States use neutral court administrators to schedule cases for court. Some counties let the judge assigned to the case decide the trial day. However, in Jack's county, it was a former adult probation officer now working in the district attorney's office who had this responsibility. "How is this even constitutional?" Jack often wondered. "The prosecutor not only gets to decide when a case comes to trial but even who the judge will be. Isn't that like the opposing team's coach getting to pick the time, place, and referee in a sporting match?"

Jack knew that the district attorney's office would not be in any rush to schedule Rick's case fast. Maybe if he had been charged with a minor misdemeanor and was willing to plead guilty in exchange for time served, Rick could get a prosecutor to schedule the guilty plea right now for court. However, Rick was not facing "time served" kind of charges. Additionally, he was not willing (at least not yet) to plead guilty. No, Rick was going to sit in lockup along with all of the other people charged with serious crimes (and even a few "unreasonable" folks charged with minor crimes who were not yet willing to plead guilty for a time served deal).

So, this is where bail comes in. Being out on bail does not get you a speedier trial, but at least you do not have to suffer the pains of jail while you wait. (Instead, you get to suffer out of jail—there are still harms waiting for trial even out of jail, just not as many nor as intense.)

Jack got to work early the day after his visit to Rick in lockup. He wanted to use his classroom computer's printer to print out a "motion to reduce bail" so that he could run over to the courthouse and file it during his lunch hour. Jack mostly remembered the mechanics of how to draft such a motion but made use of the internet to fill in the few fuzzy gaps.

In his motion, Jack stated that Rick's bail set at $100,000 was "excessive" and therefore violated the **Eighth Amendment** requirement that "excessive bail shall not be required." Jack knew that a **state of excessive bail** exists whenever it exceeds the amount reasonably calculated to ensure appearance for court. Therefore, Jack asserted several reasons why Rick posed no serious **flight risk**. He spoke of how Rick had no financial resources to go anywhere. He spoke of how Rick had no history of nonappearance. He mentioned that Rick had numerous and strong **community ties**: loving parents, warm home, close-knit school, plenty of local friends, long-time neighbors, etc., and that he had lived in the area all of his life. Finally, Jack noted that $100,000 was a king's ransom to working families like Rick's; far less parental money on the line would be more than enough to motivate Rick to not even consider failing to appear for court.

Lunch break soon came, and with motion in hand, Jack drove over to the courthouse. He parked a few blocks down the street from the stately columned, domed building made entirely of brick and stone. Upon entering the courthouse, Jack found his way to the clerk of court's office and asked, "Which judge has been assigned **motions court** this week?" A clerk told Jack that it was Judge Wood's week to handle all motions (bail reductions, motions for suppression, motions to postpone trials, motions to compel discovery, etc.) according to a schedule issued earlier in the year by the president judge of the county. "Is Judge Wood still assigned to Courtroom 2?" asked Jack, remembering the old days. "No, he is now in Courtroom 4, up on the third floor," the clerk replied.

Jack thanked the clerk and walked up a wide flight of marbled stairs to floor 3. On the way up, he crossed paths with an old bailiff who recognized Jack and looked surprised to see him once again in the old haunts.

Jack wandered down the hallway on floor 3 until he saw the old familiar, large wooden doors framing the opening to Courtroom #4. "I had a lot of adventures in there, didn't I?" thought Jack. Walking past the courtroom doors, Jack traveled another 15 feet until he reached the chambers of Judge Wood. (Judges typically have their office, or **chambers**, right next to the courtroom assigned to them—an interior office door provides a private short cut for the judge to enter the side of his or her courtroom without having to go out into the hall.)

Judge Wood's "chambers" actually consisted of two rooms: a reception room where his secretary/receptionist sat and his private office located behind that. Jack knew that he would not have to see the judge himself this day. He just needed the secretary to fill in a date and time for the bail hearing he was requesting. He had left those items blank on his motion paper.

"Hello, Agnes," Jack said with a broad smile. "Remember me?"

"Well, if it isn't the old Prince of Darkness himself, Jack Day!" responded the judge's secretary. "How the heck are you Jack? What brings you hear? I thought you moved to hell and were never coming back."

Jack forgot how edgy, even acerbic, Agnes's snarky wit could be. He knew she was just trying to be friendly. "Actually, I hang out with St. Francis and his holy people these days," Jack replied. "You may have heard that I have taken up shop at the Catholic high school."

"Yeah, I know. I thought it was funny your working there. You always seemed too irreverent to be religious."

"I am not particularly religious," confirmed Jack. "Neither am I even Catholic. I just teach math. Not a bad gig, really."

"Well, does your being here today mean that you are coming back to spend some lawyer time with us? Have you taken a case? We could use some of your special kind of shenanigans around here again, Jack."

"Yes, in fact I have taken a case," Jack acknowledged. "It is a case involving an alleged DUI where a guy and his wife got killed by a kid. The kid is my client. They are trying him as an adult."

"Oh, yeah, that case is getting some buzz around here. I hear the two victims were relatives of one of the judges but nobody related to Judge Wood," confided Agnes. "Man, when you come back, you don't mess around with some boring case, do you Jack?"

"Well, I am not sure that I am 'back.' I am just taking this case as a favor to my boss at the school. Plus, I kind of feel sorry for the kid and his parents. I am not even being paid."

"Once a lawyer for the poor, always a lawyer for the poor, Jack," lamented the secretary while gently shaking her head in sympathy. "I guess St. Francis at least is proud of you. Of course, that is, assuming you chose the morally correct side on this matter. I see a motion in your hand. I suppose you want me to write in a day and time?"

"Yes," Jack confirmed. "It is a motion to reduce bail, and the clerk

downstairs told me that Judge Wood pulled motions court this week."
Jack handed the paper to Agnes.

"Would this Thursday at 1:00 p.m. work for you, Jack?"

"I teach school. Anything after 3:00 available?"

"I'll put you down for 3:30, the last case of the day. You are lucky I
like you, Jack, even though you did leave us by going missing in action."

After the secretary marked the day and time on Jack's motion, she wrote
the same information down in the computer so that the judge would know.
Jack made some more small talk with her and then bid her "goodbye."

In the hallway, Jack filled in the day and time of the hearing on blank
spaces he had left on each of the two duplicate motions he had photo-
copied earlier from the original. He then walked downstairs to the clerk
of court's office and handed the original and both duplicates to one of
the clerks. The clerk stamped the original and its two copies with a stamp
indicating the day and time of the filing. The clerk then took the original
for official filing and handed the two stamped duplicates back to Jack.
Jack next walked down the hall to the office of the district attorney and
handed the receptionist one of the duplicates (Jack would be keeping the
second duplicate for his own records). "This is a bail reduction hearing
scheduled for this Thursday at 3:30 before Judge Wood," Jack instructed.
The receptionist nodded with understanding and said, "One of our prosecutors will see you then."

As Jack walked away, he reflexively took a deep breath to calm himself
down. Until then, he had not even realized he had been at all anxious.
Hopefully, come Thursday, his mental health would hold.

~

## Key Terms Found in This Chapter

| | |
|---|---|
| Bond | Eighth Amendment |
| Abscond | State of excessive bail |
| Struck v. United States | Flight risk |
| Barker v. Wingo | Community ties |
| Mapp v. Ohio | Motions court |
| Sixth Amendment | Chambers |
| Incarceration-related pre-trial harms | |

# Questions for Class Discussion

1. In what way is requiring money to post bond still a rather primitive concept?
2. Is it fair that extremely poor people sit in jail for trial while people of means usually get out?
3. Why do you suppose the remedy for failure to provide speed in setting trial dates is complete and permanent dismissal of the charges? Is that a good idea?
4. How do "squishy factors" provide cover to courts providing slow justice?
5. How long do you think most cases should drag on before speedy justice is deemed to have been denied? How long do you suppose the drafters of the Sixth Amendment would have tolerated court delay?
6. Do you agree that the promise of "speed" in our courts is a promise left unfulfilled? How did the *Mapp* case finally get around to fixing another problem that was a promise left unfulfilled?
7. In what ways is "justice delayed, justice denied"? What are some of the specific, pre-trial incarceration-related harms that people experience who are unable to make bail?
8. How would you feel if you waited many months in jail only to have the case against you rejected by a jury? Would you be happy? Bitter? Ambivalent?
9. What causes a "state of excessive bail" to exist?
10. What are some things that would make you a high flight risk?
11. What are some things that would make you a low flight risk?
12. Do you have enough community ties that you would be considered a low flight risk?
13. What sort of matters are taken care of in "motions court"?
14. How could the way that judicial chambers typically are situated in courthouses help lead to feelings of isolation and loneliness among judges?

# 9

# Homeward Bound

Thursday came and Jack made sure that he arrived in Judge Wood's courtroom 15 minutes early. Rick's parents were already there, and Jack sat next to them while waiting for Rick to be brought up from the courthouse's temporary lockup. In the meantime, Judge Wood was hearing and ruling on various motions that other lawyers were arguing that day in "motions court."

Even before Jack had arrived, Judge Wood had already heard and ruled upon a **motion to quash** the probable cause findings of a preliminary hearing judge, a motion to change the **trial venue** of a case due to pretrial publicity, a motion to compel discovery, and a motion for a **continuance** in order to postpone a trial. While waiting for Rick's case, Jack and the Mahans got to hear the arguments on a **motion *in limine***, in which a defense attorney was requesting that the prosecutor be ordered before trial to not even attempt to introduce certain evidence at trial that would unduly prejudice the jury. The judge wound up denying the request. "Not a good sign for us," thought Jack.

Finally, it was time for Jack's motion to reduce bail. Judge Wood decided to escape through a side door back into his chambers knowing that it would take the deputy sheriffs a few minutes to go and fetch Rick from the lockup in the basement. Once Rick was seated at the courtroom table (still in leg irons and handcuffs), Jack left his perch in the benches and took a seat next to him. A young assistant district attorney that Jack did not know took a seat at the table a few feet to the left. Both of these tables (defense and prosecution) were **beyond the bar**, that is, beyond the fence and gate that separated the lawyer's arena in a courtroom from the audience section. Jack felt some pride that despite his professional inactivity of the past few years, he was still **admitted to the bar**.

All waited quietly for a few more minutes for Judge Wood to return. When Judge Wood emerged through his chamber's door, a bailiff announced, "All rise." Judge Wood took his seat on the stand and motioned for everyone to have a seat.

The judge glanced at Jack and nodded, apparently inviting him to introduce his motion. Jack stood up and said, "Your Honor, as you may remember, my name is Jack Day. I am here today representing Rick Mahan in the case of Commonwealth v. Richard Mahan. We are here pursuant to a defense motion for reconsideration of bail that had been previously set by Judge Watson at $100,000. It is our contention that this bail is excessive and therefore in violation of the Eighth Amendment of the U.S. Constitution, as applicable to the states via the Fourteenth Amendment. It is our contention that this excessively high bail also violates the guarantees against excessive bail set forth in Pennsylvania's state constitution."

"Very well, Mr. Day," began Judge Wood. "By the way, Jack, welcome back to the practice of law! It has been far too long. Now, let's hear why you think the bail is excessive."

"Thank you, your honor," Jack said with a nod. "As you know, the sole purpose of bail is to ensure appearance at trial. Bail's purpose is not to punish someone in advance, nor has it any other lawful purpose. Earlier, my client's bail was set at the astronomical amount of $100,000. Even many upper middle class families would have a hard time coming up with that kind of money, let alone a working family like that of my young client, who, by the way, is only 17 years old and completely without his own assets."

Jack took a pause to collect his breath. He was breathing rather heavily at this point and worried he might start to sound nervous. Jack was mindful that his old history of panic attacks in court could strike him down at any moment. Jack awkwardly shuffled some papers for a few seconds to regain his full composure.

Feeling a little better, Jack continued, "Bail in this high amount might be appropriate were my client someone who had been arrested before and who failed to appear later for court. However, this is my client's very first arrest, and, consequently, he has no history of failing to appear as some defendants have."

Jack smiled at his client while subtly taking two more deep breaths between his teeth before continuing. "High bail could also be justified if my client had no community ties to anchor him here, for example, if all of his relatives lived far across the country and he was just here attending college or something. However, Rick is a 17-year-old young man who lives with his parents, who are sitting right behind him. He was born and raised in this local area. He has never lived anywhere but here. He has no money to fund any getaway. All of his friends live here. He attends high school here—yes, he is still in high school. Everybody he knows lives here. His community ties are about as strong as could be. The state says he is a man, but he really is just a boy with no resources to go anywhere but home."

Jack glanced over at the prosecutor, who simply stared back at him, expressing no emotion. "Your Honor," Jack continued, "One hundred thousand dollars might be a justifiable bond if my client or his family were wealthy enough that losing that sum would be no big deal to any of them. However, my client's parents combined make only $50,000 per year and live in an old rancher with a mortgage. You could require much less than $100,000 from them to inspire Richard Mahan to stick around and face his day in court. I would add that Rick is a straight-A student in school, and this is a strong indication that he lives and plays by the rules and that he is a highly responsible person." Jack paused to consider whether he had left out any good points. Not being able to think of any, he simply ended by saying, "Thank you, Your Honor." Jack took his seat and visibly exhaled loud enough for Judge Wood and Ms. Miller to both look mildly disturbed.

"Thank you, Mr. Day," replied Judge Wood. Glancing over at the prosecution table, Wood nodded at its occupant and said, "Ms. Miller, what have you to say in support of the bail amount 'as is?' Is it too high like Mr. Day suggests or is it right just where it is?"

Edith Miller, assistant district attorney, now rose to her feet. Though short, her intelligent and confident countenance made her appear rather formidable. "Your Honor, it is our contention that even bail in the amount of $100,000 is not going to cut it. I move that the bail amount be actually increased."

"How is that, Ms. Miller?" asked the judge. "At what amount do you argue it should be set?"

"I argue that Richard Mahan be denied bail in any amount," replied Miller. "He is alleged to have killed not just one but two people."

"Your Honor," Jack interjected. "This may be a homicide case, but it is not a capital case; the Eighth Amendment speaks of bail in **all but capital cases.**"

"That is no longer exactly true," replied Miller. "The Supreme Court ruled 30 years ago that bail could be denied entirely—even in noncapital cases—when a court determines that a defendant poses an immediate and substantial danger to society if allowed to remain free. **Future dangerousness** is a legitimate reason for a court now to deny bail in any amount. The Supreme Court has said that the language of the Eighth Amendment means that bail should not be excessive if bail is appropriate. However, bail is not appropriate when setting it poses a hazard to society's safety. It is the state's contention that a drunk driver who killed two people poses a huge, ongoing danger and should be denied bail in any amount."

Judge Wood looked at Jack for his response. Jack knew that Miller was correct as to the nuances of the law of bail. Yet, he wondered if Miller arguing for a complete denial of bail was sincere or merely a strategy to get the judge to "compromise" by keeping the bail amount unchanged. Judge Wood was wondering the same thing as Jack. (In fact, Miller was being sincere.)

Jack rose to his feet, looked at Ms. Miller, looked at his client Rick, looked at the judge and said, "Your Honor, releasing my client on bail would not pose a significant safety hazard to society. He did not intentionally hurt anybody. He is not psychotic. He is not sociopathic. He is not an alcoholic who drives unceasingly around the county. He is accused of drinking one beer, taking two cold tablets, and falling asleep at the wheel. He is not some crazed, evil killer. I would not object, as a condition of reduced bail, that Rick surrender his driver's license and agree to not drive until his case is disposed of."

"Would you be willing to do that as a condition of bail, young man?" asked Wood of Rick.

"Yes, Your Honor," confirmed Rick. "I promise."

"Ms. Miller I am not inclined to agree with your suggestion that bail be denied in any amount. What reasons can you now give me to keep bail where it is?"

"Well, Your Honor. These charges are serious, very serious indeed. If convicted, Richard Mahan could face many years in state prison. That could tempt anyone to fail to appear."

"Would you agree that his community ties are strong, Ms. Miller?" asked Judge Wood.

"Well, Your Honor," replied the prosecutor, "I would not disagree, but I would point out that even people with strong community ties some-times run to avoid long prison sentences. Bail set at $100,000 was deemed to be appropriate by Judge Watson who, as you know, is not just some justice of the peace. I would argue that Judge Watson was correct, and his decision on the matter should be given wide deference by this court."

"Not bad," thought Jack. "She is reminding Judge Wood that this bail amount was set by a peer colleague and not by some lowly magistrate as is usually the case."

Judge Wood's eyes narrowed as he stared back at Ms. Miller as if to communicate his resentment at Miller trying to pressure his decision by pitting him against a colleague. Turning his attention now to Jack, Wood asked, "Mr. Day, how much money could your client or his parents come up with if I were to consider reducing bail?"

Jack glanced back at the Mahans. The couple spoke back and forth for a few seconds, and Mrs. Mahan announced to Jack, in a voice heard by everyone in the room, "We only have about $2,000 in the bank, but we do have $40,000 in equity in our house; could we use that somehow?"

The aggressive prosecutor was itching to say something when Judge Wood waived her off. "It is the order of the court that bail be reset in this matter at $40,000 to be paid by cash or by the posting of property. Mr. Day, will you draft an order reflecting my decision for me to sign?"

"Yes, Your Honor, I will see that it gets to your chambers by tomorrow morning. In the meantime, I will help the Mahans to hire a **certified appraiser** to value their property and confirm their equity. I'll get that report to the clerk of court's office in the next few days."

"Very well, Mr. Day. Once you can confirm to the clerk of court's of-fice that the Mahans have at least $40,000 equity in their home, the clerk of court can put a **lien** on their property. Once the lien is in place, I will sign an order granting Richard Mahan's release on bail. Ms. Miller, have I missed anything?"

"Just that Richard Mahan must surrender his driver's license to the clerk of court and cannot drive his car as a strict condition of his continued release on bail, Your Honor," added Miller.

"Quite right, Ms. Miller," agreed Judge Wood. "Mr. Day, be sure to include such language in the bail reduction order you will be drafting for my signature."

"I will do so, Sir," Jack acknowledged.

Judge Wood rose and left through his side door. Jack looked at Rick, who seemed extremely relieved, almost tearfully so. Rick's parents actually were in tears—happy ones.

ADA Edith Miller nodded at Jack as she left the room. She completely ignored Rick and his parents.

Jack felt good. However, he knew that he really had only won one skirmish in a high-stakes, ongoing war. The road to ultimate victory would be a bumpy, slippery, hazardous, adventurous minefield.

~

## Key Terms Found in This Chapter

| | |
|---|---:|
| Motion to quash | Beyond the bar |
| Certified appraiser | Trial venue |
| Admitted to the bar | Lien |
| Continuance | All but capital cases |
| Motion in limine | Future dangerousness |

## Questions for Class Discussion

1. What do you suppose an attorney would have to convince a law-trained judge in order to have the results of a preliminary hearing before a lower court judge (e.g., a justice of the peace) quashed?

2. Why would a "motion *in limine*" be necessary if a judge could simply instruct a jury to "disregard" improper evidence introduced by one side during a trial?

3. What are some reasons a lawyer might request a "continuance"? If you were a judge, would you probably be stingy or liberal in granting such requests?

4. When should a judge grant a motion to change venue? Why would a judge be rather reluctant to grant such a request?

5. What structure in the courtroom makes it possible for lawyers "admitted to the bar" to actually physically pass "beyond the bar"?

6. If a lawyer becomes inactive, should his or her bar membership expire entirely at some point? If not, what would you require (if anything) for an inactive lawyer to be allowed to resume the practice of law?

7. The Eighth Amendment speaks of capital cases as not being appropriate for bail. In the 1700s when the amendment was written, what sort of cases constituted capital ones?

8. Is "future dangerousness" something that courts can accurately predict to a degree that would make it fair to deny someone bail in any amount? Could you make an argument that such predictions are voodoo science at best?

9. How does one go about posting real estate as bond? Is it necessary to sell said real estate first?

10. How would you guess that one could post a bag of pretty objects purporting to be actual jewels as bond? Under what circumstances should the court accept this bag of objects?

11. Did it surprise you that judges expect the lawyer to draft orders for the judge to sign? Can lawyers be trusted to do this?

# 10

# Arraignment

It took a few days for Jack's parents to get a certified real estate appraiser to come over to their house and ultimately write a report to the court verifying the equity in the home. Once done, the clerk of court registered a lien on the house in the office of the county recorder of deeds. This lien would pop up in any title search done on the property, effectively preventing the Mahans from selling the property until the court lifted its lien. Once Rick's case reached final disposition, the lien on the house would be lifted, regardless of whether Rick was found guilty or not guilty in the process.

Rick's release on bail was a cause of joy for Rick and his parents. Yet, this joy did not last long. Relief soon turned to worry as Rick began to fret unceasingly about his future. Rick also mourned the deaths of the two victims in the car crash. He was not against being punished to help atone for his having fallen asleep behind the wheel. However, he was scared to death of serving many years in state prison. School thugs had picked on Rick during his junior high years. He imagined prison to be that experience all over again, with the pain and danger multiplied many times over. Rick began having periodic nightmares.

About 10 days after Rick's release on bail, Rick received notice from the courthouse that he was to appear on the coming Friday morning at 9:00 a.m. in Courtroom #1 for "arraignment." Since Rick was now back in school attending classes (another condition of bail that Judge Wood had wisely inserted into his court order), he stopped by Jack's classroom to ask him what arraignment would entail.

"Yeah, Rick, I received the same notice," Mr. Day said. "No worries, I will meet you there on Friday at 9:00 a.m. Don't be late and wear a tie."

"Is arraignment something big?" asked Rick.

"Not at all. Do not give it a second thought. It's nothing."

"Well," responded Rick, "It is stressing me out not knowing what to expect. Could you tell me what I can expect?"

Suddenly, Jack realized that Rick needed some basic explanation to calm his soul a little bit. Lawyers are used to going to court and learn to take some things easily in stride. Uninformed laypeople do not have the luxury of understanding and can wind up worrying over even minor steps in the process. "I guess every court appearance is a big deal to someone like Rick," thought Jack.

Jack invited Rick to take a seat in a desk at the front of the empty classroom. Sitting behind his teacher's desk, Jack announced to Rick, "arraignment class is now in session."

"Arraignment," began Jack, "has its roots in the Middle Ages when virtually everybody was illiterate. The court would have a piece of paper outlining the charges against someone but could not simply hand that paper to the defendant. Someone had to read that paper to the accused. That person would be the judge. So, the **first purpose of arraignment** was to have the charges read to you, including a brief summary of the facts backing up those charges. These brief facts would include things like the date, time, and place of the alleged incident. The charges are what we now call the 'indictment' in grand jury states or the 'information' in states like ours that use preliminary hearing judges instead of grand juries. These charges were read verbatim to the defendant. The judge would then ask the defendant to enter a plea of guilty or not guilty. So, pleading guilty or not guilty was, in addition to having the precise charges read, the **second purpose of arraignment**."

"But I already know what the charges are," said Rick.

"I know," acknowledged Jack. "But once in a while someone goes home from the preliminary hearing shell shocked and unsure exactly what charges survived the hearing. Arraignment makes sure you know what the state plans to throw at you going forward."

"I should plead 'not guilty,' right?" asked Rick.

"Oh, yeah, yeah, yeah!" insisted Jack. "No lawyer would ever let a client plead guilty at this stage, even if the client had confessed and there were three eyewitnesses and a videotape of the crime. You see, Rick, if someone pleads guilty at the arraignment, then the judge can **move straight to sentencing.** As long as a defendant can plausibly threaten to take up court time with a trial, even a hopeless one, the state will nearly always try to buy off the defendant by offering a plea bargain. Almost everybody gets a plea bargain offer, even those whose case is a total **dead bang loser** for the defense. The bottom line is that if a defendant wants a plea bargain offer, he or she had better plead 'not guilty' at the arraignment stage. Of course, I am not suggesting that you have to accept a plea bargain offer. We can still go to trial if we want. But it is nice to have an offer on the table and go from there."

"What happens to the poor schmucks who come to arraignment without a lawyer representing them?" Rick asked.

"That is a really good question, Rick. If the person pleads 'not guilty,' the judge records the plea and instructs the district attorney's office to schedule the case for trial at a reasonable date to be determined by that office. If the unrepresented defendant wants to plead 'guilty,' then it depends on the judge what happens next. A judge could theoretically accept the guilty plea and schedule a sentencing hearing on the spot. However, most judges know that entering a guilty plea at this stage is a horribly foolish and uninformed thing to do since you will have no leverage whatsoever with the district attorney's office in getting them to make you a plea bargain offer. No threat of time-consuming jury trial for them, no offer. It is as darkly simple as that. So most judges will actually refuse to allow an unrepresented defendant to plead guilty even if they want to. They will tell the defendant that they either must plead 'not guilty' or else come back with a lawyer if they want to plead 'guilty.' I suspect that judges do this both to be fair to unrepresented defendants but to also avoid a messy appeal for allegedly having taken advantage of some vulnerable ignoramus."

"So, the only thing I need to do on Friday is plead 'not guilty,' nothing more?" Rick inquired.

"That's it. Class dismissed. See you Friday, Rick."

Friday came and Rick and his parents sat in the oversized, lavishly appointed, historic Courtroom #1 along with dozens of other defendants and their lawyers. Many of the defendants sat alone because they were being represented (at least for this hearing) by one of the two public defenders who had their own table in the front. At about 8:58 a.m., Rick's dad spotted Jack enter through the doors and waved to catch his eye. Jack came over to the bench where Rick and his parents were sitting and squeezed in with them. "Sorry, I barely got here on time," explained a flustered-looking Jack. "I had to bring my class down to a fellow teacher's room for her to combine our classes this morning. She was not amused, and I had to do some horse trading with her."

Before Jack could get in another word, one of the public defenders at the table up front stood up and started to address the entire room. "Hello," the public defender began. Some in the audience stood up thinking she was the judge. "Please be seated, I am not the judge. My name is Janet Murphy of the public defender's office. Many of you today are being represented by our office, and I want to give you some group instruction. The rest of you have private lawyers, or maybe are here representing yourself, but what I am about to say applies to everyone here for arraignment, so please listen up to what I have to say. The judge asks that I address each arraignment cohort before she comes in.

"Let me start by telling you all that the purpose of the arraignment is to have your charges read to you and for you to plead guilty or not guilty. If you refuse to enter a plea because you are angry, crazy, confused, or whatever, the judge will deem you to be **standing moot** and will enter a 'not guilty' plea on your behalf. Now, I know that almost all of you already know what your charges are. However, the court wants to make sure that you really know. Every once in a while, defendants are surprised to learn that some of the charges they initially were told about were not actually bound over for trial."

Assistant Public Defender Murphy took a brief moment to direct an upset defendant who had approached the table uninvited to go back, sit down, and listen. Mini crisis averted, Murphy continued her address by starting where she had left off.

"Another thing that will happen today is that your attorney, whether you have a private attorney or a public defender, will be asked to **enter an appearance** on your behalf so that the court and the district attorney's office will know who is defending you from this point forward." (This entry of appearance has more or less become the **third purpose of ar-**

**raignment** in many jurisdictions that use it as their chance to get lawyers to firmly commit to stay on a case.)

Seeing some confusion still on many laypeople's faces in the crowd, Assistant Public Defender Murphy thought that she should elaborate a little further regarding the consequences of an entering an appearance. "Some of you may have hired a private attorney to do your preliminary hearing and then ran out of money and applied for a public defender or else hired a more affordable, private attorney. The court needs to know exactly who will be representing you from here on out. Once an attorney enters his or her appearance today on a form he or she will sign, the **lawyer cannot withdraw** from the case without the judge's express permission. Since such permission is almost never granted, your lawyer will be 'married to you,' in a sense, from here on out unless you are the one who wants the 'divorce.'

"Now I would like to explain something that can speed things up for all of you. You have the right to have the charges read to you word for word by the judge. Since almost all of you know how to read and also have an attorney with you who knows how, there is really no point in wasting the judge's time in making her read the charges to you in open court."

At this point Ms. Murphy held up a blue sheet of paper above her head for all to see. She instructed, "This form will have the charges, what we lawyers call the 'information,' stapled to the back of it, which you can keep and bring home. There is a copy for both you and your lawyer stapled to the form. The blue form itself asks you to read the charges stapled to it. You will notice that there is a big space in the middle of the blue form with bold-print language that asks you to check off whether you wish to plead 'guilty' or 'not guilty' to the charges stapled to the form. There is also a space at the bottom of the blue form for you to sign and for your lawyer to enter his or her appearance by signing.

"Now listen up because this is really important. I want all public defender clients to plead 'not guilty.' You will do this by coming up front when someone at the prosecution table next to my table calls your name. There are like a jillion people here so we do not have time to discuss your case now, so just plead 'not guilty' even if you think you have no defense. We will discuss options with you later.

"You private lawyers here today can find the arraignment form for your own client on the other table in the front. A secretary from the district attorney's office is sitting there and has everyone's form. You can take care of signing the form with your own client while here in the room. Private lawyers, please return the signed form to the secretary from the district attorney's office who is sitting here up front. She will see that is if filed properly. Make sure that your client has signed the form, you have signed the form, and you have entered your appearance on the form. You will notice big language on the form that advises your client that he or she **waives formal reading of charges** by the judge. It is up to you, their attorney, to read and to explain the charges to them.

"If you are here without a lawyer, you cannot waive — that means voluntarily give up — a formal reading of the charges to you by the judge. You will just have to wait until the judge comes in when the rest of us are finished for your arraignment to take place. It should not be too long a wait. I know that I am not your lawyer, but since you do not have one, I would strongly advise you to enter a plea of 'not guilty' today for your own protection. Many of you without a lawyer will wind up becoming a public defender client eventually, and we public defenders do not want to be saddled with a plea of 'guilty' made by you today. Trust me on this.

"Now, I believe that the secretary from the district attorney's office will begin to call names. As you hear your name, proceed with your private attorney to the table where the secretary is sitting. You will notice that several prosecutors are also sitting at that table. One of them will raise their hand when your name is called. You and your attorney should proceed to that prosecutor who will have the form for you to sign, waiving the formal reading of the charges, etc. If you are being represented by a public defender, our attorneys will already be standing around the prosecutor's table and will grab you as you approach in order to help you with the forms.

"After you have signed the forms, you are free to leave. You will receive a notice in the mail when your next court day is. If you are a public defender client, you will also receive in the mail an appointment to come to the public defender's office to discuss your case and the next steps. Thank you for your attention."

At this point, names started to be called out. When the secretary at the district attorney's table called for "Richard Mahan," Rick and Jack walked over to the prosecutor, whose hand was raised. The prosecutor handed Jack the waiver of arraignment blue sheet and two copies of the Information stapled to it.

Jack and Rick hunched over the paper on the table while the prosecutor patiently watched them both read the Information stapled to the blue sheet. Jack asked Rick if he understood the charges. Upon receiving an affirmative reply, Jack then had Rick sign the blue sheet waiving an oral reading of the charges. Jack then signed next to Rick's signature agreeing to the waiver. Finally, Jack signed a blurb at the very bottom of the sheet in which he officially entered his appearance in the case, thus effectively committing himself to serve Rick until the very end.

Jack then returned all of the papers to the prosecutor, who then separated the blue sheet from the two copies of the information stapled to it. The prosecutor gave one copy of the information to Jack and the other to Rick.

"Thanks for agreeing to waive an oral reading," said the prosecutor to Jack. "We will send you and your client a notice of the prosecutor assigned for trial. He or she will be in touch about a possible plea deal but probably not until we get much closer to the trial date. You will get a notice from us as to that trial date, probably in about five or six months."

"Anything else?" asked Jack.

"Yes, please give me your business card so I can give it to the prosecutor who gets assigned the case."

Jack peeled a yellow sticky Post-it note from a small pad he found sitting near the corner of the table. He wrote down "Jack Day, defense attorney," along with his mobile phone number.

"Here you go," said Jack as he handed the yellow sticky to the perplexed prosecutor. "Have a nice day."

～

## Key Terms Found in This Chapter

| | |
|---|---|
| First purpose of arraignment | Enter an appearance |
| Second purpose of arraignment | Third purpose of arraignment |
| Move straight to sentencing | Lawyer cannot withdraw |
| Dead bang loser | Waives formal reading of charges |
| Standing moot | |

# Questions for Class Discussion

1. Why was Rick so worried about arraignment even though it is no big deal?
2. How did illiteracy in the Middle Ages help lead to the creation of arraignment?
3. What is the first purpose of the arraignment?
4. Which judicial official decides which charges will be presented at the arraignment?
5. What is the second big purpose of arraignment?
6. Who should plead "not guilty" at this stage of the process? What about defendants who have "dead bang loser" cases: should they just plead "guilty" at this stage?
7. What is meant by "standing moot" at one's arraignment? What are some types of defendants who choose to "stand moot"?
8. How does the court handle a case if someone "stands moot" and refuses to enter a plea?
9. Can unrepresented defendants "waive" a formal reading of the charges? Why not?
10. How do lawyers "enter their appearance"? Why do courts require this?
11. Why would it be smart for a privately retained lawyer to refuse to file an entry of appearance until a client has first paid for his or her services in full?
12. Why do you suppose that judges rarely allow a lawyer who has entered his or her appearance to withdraw from a case?
13. Other than not having been paid yet, why else might a lawyer wish to withdraw from a case after an entry of appearance has been made?
14. Can clients still fire their privately hired lawyer even after the lawyer has entered his or her appearance? What about public defenders? Should a client who fires one of them have the right to have a new public defender assigned to the case?

# Unit 5
# The Prosecutor and
# Pre-Trial Matters

This unit acquaints us more thoroughly with the prosecutor in this case, Kate Page, and in doing so also acquaints us with the office and duties of prosecuting attorneys. It then goes on to familiarize us with, yet more, important pre-trial matters: how a prosecutor sees to a suppression hearing and how defense discovery of what is in a prosecutor's file is accomplished.

# 11

## Kate Page, Justice-Doer

Jack was not the only attorney now taking a keen and long-term interest in the ultimate fate of young Rick. Now that Rick's arraignment had come and gone, his file landed on the desk of Assistant District Attorney Kate Page.

Like most assistant district attorneys, Kate was fairly young—just 33 years old. Though still in her early 30s, Kate had already seen a lot of life.

For starters, Kate was a widow and had been one for about a decade. Kate was only in her early 20s when she married Bill, who she had met during their third year together at the University of Colorado. Kate's dream was to graduate, start a career in sales (she was a marketing major), and at some point, not too distant, start having some children. Bill was planning to work as a meteorologist, hopefully with the federal government somehow. All of these plans came crashing down on the day Kate's father showed up unexpectedly at her Boulder apartment. "I have some terrible news, Kate," her father nervously stated.

"It is Bill isn't it?" Kate gasped.

"Yes, I am afraid he died in a skiing accident. He hit a tree."

"Where is he?" asked Kate.

"At a university hospital in Denver. I'll drive you there if you are up to it."

Kate took a semester off from school to mourn, but her life eventually started to move on. It was slow going at first, but her recovery gained

speed with each passing month. Kate did finally graduate in marketing but ultimately decided to go into a career as a lawyer instead. The
thought of doing jury trials, as she saw so often in movies and on TV,
excited her as few other things did. Kate made up her mind to become a
prosecuting attorney someday. One day, she even went over to the local
courthouse and sat down in a courtroom midway through a trial. Seeing
the drama, the pageantry, and the spectacle unfolding before her eyes
just confirmed to her that her newly formed career goal was indeed a
good fit.

Kate correctly sensed that she probably would make a good prosecutor for the same reasons she thought she would do well in sales. She was
"book smart," but much more importantly for prosecution work, she
was "people smart." Kate was good with people because she simply liked
being around them. When she was down, she sought out people to feel
better. When she was up, she sought out people to share the good times.

Kate was a very likable person whose company others naturally sought
out as well. She was one of those people who often smiled with their lips
and who always smiled with their eyes. Kate was confident. She was quick
at thinking on her feet. She was good at reading people. She was very
slow to anger. She had a thick skin and was very difficult to offend.

It was Kate's book smarts, though, that got her an offer of admission
to Columbia Law School in New York City. She chose Columbia over a
couple of other good schools because her aunt lived there and told her
she could live with her for no rent. Kate was just 23 when she showed up
for her first day of class.

In law school, Kate would confront many of the same challenges that
Jack had confronted a few years earlier down at Penn. Like Jack, she did
not always enjoy the endless reading of appellate cases. She found the Socratic method of endless, aggressive, in-class questioning to be needlessly
stressful. Yet, unlike Jack, she never thought about dropping out at any
point. She wanted to do criminal jury trials as a prosecuting attorney.

By her third year, Kate was barely in the top 50% percent of her graduating class but felt proud of that ranking. Students at Columbia were
universally brilliant and workaholics. Kate knew she belonged there,
though, since just over half of this select group was underperforming
her.

For her last semester, Kate decided to sign up for an elective course entitled "Criminal Trial Practice." It was a clinical course taught by an adjunct professor. She was surprised to see just three other students in the classroom on the first day of the semester.

"Why are there just four of us?" Kate asked the instructor after the first day of class.

"Because this is Columbia," responded the woman. "Except for the rare saint here and there who want to become champions of the poor as public defenders, Columbia grads don't do criminal law."

"But I want to become a prosecutor," Kate clarified. "Is that weird or something?"

"Not to me, but I am not sure most of your fellow students or tenure track professors would see it my way. Most Columbia graduates can get jobs in corporate law paying big money. Prosecutors do not make big money. Neither do public defenders. Neither do most private criminal defense lawyers. People all just want to follow the money."

For the first time, Kate's confidence in her decision to become a prosecuting attorney was shaken. "Am I wasting an Ivy League law degree by going into criminal law?" she pondered.

She spoke to the person who ran Columbia Law's career center. That "expert" certainly thought that Kate would be making a "big mistake that you'll regret" if she were to follow her dream. "Look at all the recruiters who come here each year. None of them are from public defender or prosecutor offices. There is a reason for that," the office manager noted. "Not enough interest for them to bother recruiting here."

Kate began more and more to second guess her old plan to become a prosecutor. After speaking to one her favorite professors, she made up her mind to at least interview with some of the prestigious civil law firms flowing in and out of the school's career office each semester. She was trying to be mindful of the all the advice people in the school had been giving her. "Don't waste your potential by working for government wages in some DAs office," the concerned mentors kept counseling her. "This is an Ivy League you are attending."

The objective fact is that there really are just **two types of lawyers** out there. The first group constitute the **elite lawyers** who represent the top 10% of the profession. They tend to work for firms having large institutions (typically deep-pocketed corporations) as clients. The second group is everybody else, the vast army of **nonelite lawyers** who form the "bottom" 90% of the profession and typically help individual human beings (like you and me) with their everyday legal problems. The elite lawyers only come out of top law schools (like Columbia) and work for law firms with clients such as Exxon, General Motors, Amazon, or Apple. These clients pay fees of about $500 for each hour of one attorney's time. Often there are several, if not dozens, of attorneys working simultaneously on a case or problem, with each lawyer individually billing out at the $500 per hour rate. Sometimes the elite lawyers will work for a corporation as **in-house counsel** rather than for outside law firms with whom the corporation temporarily contracts. However, it is pretty much the same thing. Lawyers from ordinary law schools, even those graduating at the tippy top of their class, will never become part of lawyer high society.

Mom and Pop back home needing help with a personal legal problem would be among those who use the services of the nonelite lawyers. These lawyers help actual people (not institutions) with **individual-level legal problems** that single human beings tend to have: divorces, child custody matters, probating of personal wills, personal bankruptcies, automobile accidents, medical malpractice claims, and criminal defense (and prosecution). Some of these nonelite lawyers get very rich, but most remain forever in the middle class. Their clients simply cannot afford to pay the multi-million dollar legal bills per case that the elite law firms can routinely expect.

Kate, like Jack a few years before her, was in a position to get rich working for an elite law firm while serving corporate masters. However, unlike Jack, she was unable to follow her own inner voice and resist the siren song of prestige and money. Upon graduation, she took a job in a skyscraper-housed law firm in Philadelphia that specialized primarily in two areas: mergers and acquisitions and large, complex corporate bankruptcies.

Kate liked the fact that her starting salary at the firm was just south of $200,000 per year. "Not bad for a beginner!" she told herself with pride. Kate was even promised bonuses if her **billable hours** exceeded certain minimums. Yet, her employer would tolerate no less than 40 "billable" hours or so per week just for her to keep her base salary and her job. (One must work about 70 hours per week to generate 40 hours that can ethically be counted as "billable hours." Not all work is considered by lawyers or clients to be "billable.")

Eventually, the big money Kate was earning did not seem that important to her. During one tearful telephone conversation with her father, Kate lamented, "My reward for attending a stellar law school is to get to work nonstop in a boring, legal sweatshop utterly void of all creativity and human contact. I churn paper all day, every day. I will never see the inside of a courtroom any more than I ever get these days to see the inside of a movie theater."

Kate spent three long years at the firm selling her happiness for a pot of money. Finally, she had enough. "I am going to just start living what I—Kate Page—thinks is the good life, no matter what other people all seem to think" she promised herself. "If I can find a job as a criminal trial attorney, I am out of here."

It took Kate about three months to land an interview with a district attorney's office. Working in a law firm in Philadelphia had required Kate to study for and pass the Pennsylvania bar exam. Hence, her search for prosecution jobs was limited to openings in Pennsylvania, the only state that had issued her a license to practice law.

Unlike snobby elite law firms whose lawyers mostly churn paper all day, prosecutor offices are not particularly impressed by Ivy League law school degrees. Such schools are no more likely than any other law school to produce graduates possessing the **soft skills** required of courtroom lawyers. The ability to keep one's cool, think under pressure, read people, sell deals, and woo juries are the traits that really count in practicing criminal law. Harvard and Yale types are no more likely than are the graduates of less stratospheric law schools to possess those kinds of talents (if anything, perhaps even less likely).

Kate did not know about any of this and so was quite surprised that it took three whole months into her job search to land just one job interview. After all, in her mind, she was a product of Columbia Law School who was nobly willing to take a huge pay cut to fight societal bad actors in court. Finally, she did receive an invitation to interview with the district attorney of a suburban Philadelphia county, in the same courthouse that Jack used to inhabit as a public defender. Kate did not know it, but the real reason the district attorney had offered her an interview was due to the DA's son now attending the same university where a younger Kate had spent her undergraduate years. Elected district attorneys are political animals after all and tend to be both loyal and tribal.

District Attorney Gus Owens was not impressed with Kate's fabulous law school pedigree, nor with her uppity, downtown, law firm experience producing and proofreading thick documents. Kate did impress Owens, however, with an apparent ability to project positive emotions while keeping all dark ones in check. In other words, she seemed to have high levels of **emotional intelligence**. "I can tell just by talking to you that you have what it takes to work around here," Gus Owens announced after the hour-long interview. "Welcome aboard."

One of the happiest days of Kate's life was the day that she walked out of the elite wonder firm for the very last time. It was 8:00 p.m. on a Friday night, and more than half of her colleagues were still on the job toiling away. For the most part, her colleagues thought she had lost her mind. Two or three of them though secretly admired her courage just to chuck it.

Soon enough, Kate picked up all of the tricks of the trade of being a good assistant district attorney. Various attorneys came and left, but she was sticking around. After just four years on the job, Kate was surprised one day when she suddenly realized she was already fifth in seniority among the 15 full-time attorneys in her office. Prosecution is like that. Like public defending, it tends primarily to be a **young person's game**. Though every district attorney's office has a lifer or two, most attorneys leave after just two or three quick years, enough time to get the courtroom experiences so valued by many higher paying civil litigation law firms. Of course, burnout also helps grease that revolving door. Practicing criminal law (prosecution or defense) is a life filled with constant conflict and drama. Victims, cops, witnesses, opposing counsel, and defendants all seem to be upset all the time. These upset folks let the attorneys know how they feel.

Kate could feel herself becoming more and more cynical with each passing month on the job. She noticed how more and more distrustful of people she had become since she took the job. **Cynicism**, she noticed, was a pathology that many prosecutors seemed to acquire. She figured that it had something to do with all the lies that most defendants, some witnesses, and even a few defense attorneys had told her over the past few years.

Such cynicism among prosecutors can be dangerous since it is well known that prosecutors, not judges, hold the most **day-to-day courthouse power**. Judges have more prestige, but prosecutors actually have more power. As U.S. Supreme Court Justice Robert Jackson said decades ago, "The prosecutor has more control over life, liberty, and reputation than any other person in America." The same things still holds true to-day. American prosecutors like Kate Page get to act as accuser, jury, and sentencer in the vast majority of cases resolved by way of plea deals.

What helped get Kate through her cynical days was the realization that her love of doing a jury trial was never too far away. Criminal lawyers do more trials by far than any other type of lawyer in the United States. Even the so-called **Trial Lawyers of America**, the professional organization for civil litigation attorneys, only typically do about one trial per year (99% of civil lawsuits are settled out of court). Kate did not get to do as many trials as she might have originally guessed when she had taken the job, but she did far more than one trial per year.

Of course, criminal defense attorneys, as well as prosecutors, get to do a fair number of trials. Nevertheless, Kate was glad that she was a prose-cutor and not a defense attorney. She had the honor of wearing a **white hat** rather than a gray one. Unlike defense attorneys, whose sole duty is to their clients (within the bounds of the law), she, like every other prosecutor, also had been given a **duty to do justice**. Sure, like defense attorneys, she had to ardently or **zealously represent** the interests of her client (the people), but she also was required by law to make sure that justice was done in every case she undertook. Defense attorneys do not have a duty to see that justice is done. They can represent clients they know to be guilty and even push for an acquittal if they can achieve one. However, prosecutors cannot prosecute someone whom they do not per-sonally believe to be guilty (even if their boss thinks they are guilty), and they must provide huge amounts of discovery to defense attorneys so that their opponent can better mount a defense against them. With rare exceptions, discovery in criminal cases is pretty much a one-way street, running from prosecutor to defense lawyer.

This concept of discovery is a huge one. It meant that Kate would have to turn over nearly her entire file to Defense Attorney Jack Day: police reports, lab reports, eyewitness statements, Rick's incriminating statements, you name it. As we learned in an earlier chapter, about the only thing in her file that she did not have to share with Jack was her own work product (recordings containing her opinions, thoughts, con-clusions, and strategies regarding the case).

Yes, Kate had to fight fair, but she did not mind. That was all part of the white hat thing. Besides, she knew that her boss, the elected district attorney, gave her huge amounts of **discretion** to get her job done. She alone decided how to run her caseload, including what deals to offer, which cases to push into trial, what sentences to recommend to judges, and even which cases she should simply *nolle prosequi* (drop entirely in the interests of justice). Sure, her boss could overrule her in any of her decisions, but this happened almost never. District attorneys hire their assistants and trust them to be the professionals that they are.

Yet, Kate realized that this Rick Mahan case had at least the potential of getting on her boss's radar. After all, there were two fatalities. Kate knew that it already generated a brief mention on two of the Philadelphia nightly news programs. Yet, it could generate some more interest before it was through.

Like most chief county-level prosecutors across America, **district attorneys** in Pennsylvania (sometimes elsewhere called **county attorneys** or **state attorneys**, depending on the state) obtained their job via elections rather than by way of appointments. This meant that they had to worry about politics and public relations once in a while, especially when it came to high-profile cases. "Is this a high-profile case?" wondered Kate. She concluded probably not; otherwise, her boss would have spoken to her more about it. He might even have elected to prosecute it himself. Publicity is a big deal to elected office holders.

Her boss aside, Kate knew that Jack had her on his radar by now. He would already know that she was the prosecutor assigned the Richard Mahan case. A letter to that effect would have gone out from her office even before she herself knew that she had been randomly assigned to the matter. Kate was hoping not to have to deal with this case for another half year or so, as was usually the custom in her office. She would review the file closely in five months and then ask the person in the office tasked with scheduling matters for court to assign an official trial date and judge. As the trial date grew very near, she would likely communicate a plea bargain offer to Jack. "**Just in time justice…** That works for me just fine," she said to herself.

Tired of just sitting there and thinking, Kate decided to spend a couple of hours speed-reading a pile of misdemeanor files theoretically scheduled for "trial" the next week. After making quick 10 minute or so assessments of the strength of the evidence, the seriousness of the current offense, and the defendant's prior record, she would email or, if necessary, mail out a handwritten plea bargain offer to the particular defense attorney assigned to the case. In her email or note she always told the attorney, "Call me," with his or her answer. Most of these cases involved offers of probation (for those with nonexistent or minor prior records) or short jail stays (for those with beefier rap sheets), and attorneys usually just rolled over and agreed to sell the deals to their clients. Kate had long ago overcome a new prosecutor's rookie tendency to be **unnecessarily adversarial** in wasting defense attorneys' time with initial highball offers, especially in cases involving routine misdemeanors. Defense attorneys knew that in such minor, routine cases, Kate's first offer was now her last, but the offer would always be very fair.

Kate reserved the right to be appropriately manipulative in cases involving serious felonies, especially those coupled with serious prior records. Such cases called for offers on her part for years, sometimes decades, in state prison. She would sometimes offer an unreasonably long sentence initially to the defense attorney, knowing that he or she would discuss it with the client (as the law required) before naturally rejecting it. Then, she would lower the sentence and give the defense attorney the real offer, which the lawyer would usually sell to the defendant without too much difficulty. In a way, this strategy gave defense attorneys more credibility in selling the deal to their many angry, antisocial, criminal-class clients. "I am doing the defense attorney a favor," she would sometimes soothingly tell herself when initially offering a less than generous deal. "When I make them my second offer, the fair one that is in the defendant's own interest to accept, the defense lawyer will look good to their suspicious client."

Kate had learned many skills on the job these past four years in addition to the art of being helpfully manipulative. She was now extremely comfortable with public speaking. She was better than ever at thinking on her feet. She knew how to stay poised and articulate while under heavy stress. She was even better at sizing up people than when she first started. Last, but not least, she was great at salesmanship, an old goal of hers that went clear back to her undergraduate business school days.

Kate had also learned to give up some of the naïve notions about criminal court that she had possessed prior to joining the district attorney's office. She no longer believed the official law school line that a dog-eat-dog **adversarial system of justice** is best. Clearly, she thought, cooperation is usually a better approach in getting most deals. Speedy trials no longer meant "speedy" to her. "Speedy" depends on court resources. Nor did Kate any longer think of jury trials as the default way to go in most cases despite her personal love of doing them from time to time. "They are not always virtuous," she now believed. "In fact, oftentimes jury trials just waste everyone's time." Before Kate became a criminal lawyer, she thought that plea bargains usually benefitted the bad people. "Plea bargains usually benefit everybody," she would now tell herself. Kate used to admire defense lawyers who were very thorough. Now she was more irritated than admiring of most such lawyers. Working in a busy arena, she now preferred lawyers who were efficient. Finally, Kate no longer believed the naïve opinion of nonlawyers that **factual guilt** is what matters (what really happened). She had come to know that it is **legal guilt** (what can be legally proven beyond a reasonable doubt) that counts in her world.

Kate had just finished electronically communicating a series of routine misdemeanor plea deals when an office clerical worker came in to her office and dropped some legal papers on her desk. "This just came in for you," noted the clerk. "It is a motion from some supposed defense attorney, Jack Day. I have never heard of this person. He just dropped it off with our receptionist."

"I wonder what he wants so soon," Kate complained to the clerk as she picked up the motion. "Oh great," Kate murmured as she started to read. "It is a motion to suppress that DUI killer's incriminating statements to the police. Oh look, Jack Day already got a hearing scheduled on it for next Tuesday before Judge Mancini. Who is this attorney 'Jack Day' anyway? He is already starting to get on my nerves."

"Like I said, never heard of him," repeated the clerk. "Have fun with it."

## Key Terms Found in This Chapter

Two types of lawyers                                         Duty to do justice

Elite lawyers                                                Zealously represent

Nonelite lawyers
In-house counsel
Individual-level legal problems
Billable hours
Soft skills
Emotional intelligence
Young person's game
Cynicism
Day-to-day courthouse power
Trial Lawyers of America
White hat

Discretion
Nolle prosequi
District attorneys
County attorneys
State attorneys
Just in time justice
Unnecessarily adversarial
Adversarial system of justice
Factual guilt
Legal guilt

## Questions for Class Discussion

1. What types of clients do the so-called elite lawyers represent? Who gets to become such lawyers? Who has no real chance to become such lawyers?
2. Would you rather be a rich elite lawyer representing corporations or a modestly paid nonelite lawyer doing criminal trials?
3. What sort of actual individual-level legal problems do the nonelite lawyers tend to deal with?
4. How many hours per week are elite lawyers expected to put in for their big salaries? In your opinion, is the pay worth the sacrifices they must make?
5. What are some of the various "soft skills" that prosecutors should possess?
6. Why is "emotional intelligence," or the ability to keep one's cool, so important a trait in the practice of criminal law?
7. What causes prosecution to be primarily a "young person's game"? Do you think you could be a "lifer" if you were to become a prosecutor? What types of coping mechanisms would lifers tend to possess?
8. Who are some of the liars that cause prosecutors to become cynical? What other professionals in society endure frequent lies and hence tend to become cynical?
9. How is it possible that prosecutors have more day-to-day courthouse power than judges?

10. How many jury trials do most noncriminal lawyers do in their lifetimes? Does the subset of noncriminal lawyers who specialize in civil litigation do many jury trials? Do elite lawyers do many jury trials?

11. Why can it be said that prosecutors get to wear white hats, while defense lawyers have to wear gray ones? How does the "duty to do justice" play into this? What duty to defense lawyers have? Would it be more fun to wear a white or gray hat?

12. Why do head district attorneys give so much discretion to their assistants? What would happen if district attorneys started to micromanage office caseloads? What sort of discretionary judgment calls are assistant district attorneys (who are often quite young) allowed to make?

13. What are some reasons why a prosecutor might choose to *nolle prosequi* certain cases?

14. Prosecutors go by different titles depending upon the state in which they live. What are prosecutors called in the state where you live? Do you happen to know what federal prosecutors are called?

15. How is justice in our courthouses "just in time" justice? Is "just in time justice" a good or bad thing?

16. Why are rookie prosecutors sometimes unnecessarily adversarial? Do you suppose new public defenders also suffer from this rookie mistake?

17. Is there really such a thing as being "appropriately manipulative" when it comes to negotiating plea bargains in serious cases? Is such conduct ethical? Good lawyering?

18. How do criminal lawyers distinguish "factual guilt" from "legal guilt"? Why do you suppose they have invented such a distinction?

# 12

## Suppression Hearing

Tuesday came. Kate had instructed the police officer who had dealt with Richard at the scene of the crime to come to court to be her sole witness at today's suppression hearing. Suppression motions always wind up forcing the state to be the one to call the appropriate witness to court, even though it is the other side's motion.

The way the process works is that first, the defense lawyer files the motion alleging that evidence (incriminating statements or physical evidence) was obtained illegally by the police; that same motion goes on to request that such evidence be **suppressed** (kept secret from the jury at trial). Next, it is the responsibility of the prosecutor to summon the police officer to court for the hearing. At the hearing, the prosecutor will be required to call the officer to the stand and ask the officer to explain his or her actions during the incident in question. After the defense attorney cross-examines the officer, the judge hears arguments from the attorneys. Finally, the judge renders a decision, either right away or else later after having taken the matter **under advisement**. If the judge really wanted to, he could also order the attorneys to submit **memorandums of law** (similar to appellate briefs only much shorter) to help him decide the issue while he has it under advisement.

Jack thought he had a fair chance of achieving suppression. Jack was particularly hoping to get rid of Rick's admission that he had read the drowsiness warnings on the medicine box. Getting rid of the statement about drinking beer would be nice too, but Jack knew that the blood test would prove alcohol consumption in any event. Yet, Jack figured that a jury would be more forgiving of a little beer drinking than it would of someone who read a box's warnings and consciously chose to blow them off.

Of course, even if Jack got what he wanted, it would not mean complete victory. Still, having some of the incriminating statements suppressed would detract from the huge pile of evidence against his client.

In his motion, Jack was not bothering to deny that Rick had told the officer that he had read stuff on the back of the cold medicine box. Jack's motion instead claimed that the police officer solicited this potentially incriminating statement in violation of Rick's **Fifth Amendment** right against self-incrimination. This was so because the cop had not properly addressed Rick's concern that "maybe I need a lawyer."

When it was time for the hearing, Kate trudged her way up the stairs to the courtroom of Judge Anthony Mancini, with Officer Steve Blake in tow. Kate did not engage in any small talk with the cop on the way up. They both were concentrating on the job just ahead.

As she entered the courtroom, Kate saw Jack already sitting at the defense table, next to an unusually young-looking defendant. However, Jack was a little older than she had expected. She had expected Jack to be a novice in his 20s, brand new to the practice of law. After all, she had never heard of this attorney and figured it must be his first case. She guessed that only about 5% of the lawyers in her county practiced criminal law in any significant way. Consequently, they all knew one another. Criminal law essentially constitutes a **bar within a bar**. Kate was surprised then to see someone about 10 years older than she had expected. "Is this some hot shot ringer they brought in from Philly?" she wondered.

All rose on cue when Judge Mancini, a late middle-aged judge with a handsome Italian American look, entered the courtroom. Mancini sat down and got straight to business.

"We are here on a defense motion to suppress some incriminating evidence given to the police. For the record, this matter involves the case of Commonwealth versus Richard Mahan, involving two alleged felony counts of homicide by vehicle while DUI, one misdemeanor count of reckless driving, and one misdemeanor count of underage drinking. Ms.

Page, as the **responding party** in this matter, please call your first witness."

"Thank you, Your Honor. Only one state actor was in any way involved in the acquisition of the alleged incriminating statements. That person is Trooper Steve Blake of the State Highway Patrol. I call Trooper Blake to take the stand."

Trooper Blake walked up to the stand in full uniform. He had chosen that look instead of civilian clothes in order to project a hoped for aura of gravitas. What a cop should wear to court is a matter of opinion. Some officers prefer to appear in uniform, thinking that it helps give them more authenticity. Others prefer to dress in suit and tie, thinking it helps diminish their image as state agents with an agenda. In any event, the bailiff swore the trooper in once he took his seat.

"Please state your name and occupation for the record," began Kate.

"My name is Steven Blake. I am a corporal with the Pennsylvania State Police."

"Thank you, Trooper Blake," acknowledged Kate, "I wish to call your attention to the evening of Wednesday, April 5 at about 10:15 p.m. Can you please tell us where you were and what you observed at that time?"

"Yes," responded the trooper. "I was on routine traffic patrol on State Highway 41, also known as the Whitehorse Pike, in the northwestern part of this county when I came upon an apparent two-vehicle collision. Since nobody was moving inside the vehicles, I immediately called for backup and two ambulances. I first approached the smaller vehicle, a late-model Ford Focus, and saw on the ground two people, a man and a woman, who apparently had been ejected from their vehicle. I felt for a pulse on each of them and could not detect any. I then checked for respiration but could not detect any. I then swiftly proceeded over to the larger vehicle, a jeep. I observed the driver still behind the wheel, conscious but still a little dazed. He was wearing a seatbelt, and his airbag had deployed."

"Is the driver of the jeep in the courtroom here today?" inquired Page.

"Yes, that would be Mr. Richard Mahan, sitting next to his lawyer."

"Thank you," replied Kate. "Did you ask the defendant any questions at that time?"

"Yes, but just to be careful — since this looked like a potential vehicular homicide case — I first read him his Miranda rights. I then asked if he understood. He said that he did understand. Then I asked Mr. Mahan what happened. He said he thought that he must have fallen asleep at the wheel. I asked if he had been drinking. He admitted that he had drank one beer. I then asked if he was on any medication or had taken any drugs of any kind, legal or illegal. He then admitted that he had taken some cold medicine. He also admitted that he had read the box the medicine came in. This box has warnings on it telling the reader not to drive after taking the pills since the pills can cause drowsiness. The box also warns the reader that drinking alcohol with the pills could make any drowsiness even worse."

Kate thought for a few seconds. She knew that Jack on cross would bring up the "maybe I need a lawyer" play, so she might as well beat her adversary to the punch. "Trooper, did Richard Mahan mention wanting to get a lawyer or anything like that at any time?"

"May I look at my notes?" the trooper asked Judge Mancini.

"Yes," responded the judge. "You may look at your notes to **refresh your memory** if you would like." (Technically, the witness is supposed to testify purely from actual memory after having his memory refreshed, rather than simply echoing lines found verbatim in the written report.)

Trooper Blake flipped through the police report he himself had written. Memory refreshed, he looked up from his notes and then said, "Mr. Mahan stated that, 'maybe I need a lawyer' near the beginning of my interrogation at the scene."

"This was before you asked him about the beer or the medicine box, correct?" asked the prosecuting attorney. Jack was about to object for her having led the witness but just let it go since there was no harm done.

The officer studied his notes a little bit more, looked up, and then replied, "Yes, first I mirandized him. Next, I asked him what happened, and he said he had fallen asleep at the wheel. Then I asked if he had been drinking. It was at that point before answering about drinking that he mentioned that maybe he needed a lawyer. I had not yet asked him about having taken medicine or other drugs yet either."

"Trooper, what, if anything, did you say in response to Mr. Mahan's statement that maybe he needed a lawyer?" Kate inquired.

"I said, 'Well, Is that what you want?' He responded, 'No, not really,' and he just answered the rest of my questions."

"Thank you Trooper," concluded Kate. "Your witness, Mr. Day."

To Rick's surprise, Jack rose and simply said, "No questions." Upon sitting back down, Jack whispered in Rick's ear that the trooper had said everything that Jack needed for him to make his legal arguments. "Everything the trooper just said was factually correct, right Rick?" Rick nodded his head in agreement.

Since it was a defense motion that generated the hearing, Jack was the first one invited by Judge Wood to present his argument. Jack pounded the idea that when Rick had said that "maybe I need a lawyer," it was the moral equivalent of a clear assertion of his right to have a lawyer present before answering any more questions. Jack reminded the judge that Rick was only 17 and was probably using the word "might" out of deference to an older adult. Jack also asked the judge to consider the power differential that existed between the officer and the scared teenager and how that would have added to an already inherently coercive atmosphere. Jack finished by reminding the court of Supreme Court rulings that once a person in custody asserts his desire to consult a lawyer, all **questioning must stop**, and the police are forbidden to try to talk the suspect out of his choice.

"Thank you, Mr. Day," Judge Mancini said. "Ms. Page, please proceed with your arguments."

Now it was Kate's turn, and she was eager to get started. Kate began by arguing passionately that Richard never actually requested a lawyer but rather that "maybe" he needed one. The officer did not try to talk him out of anything but merely asked in good faith for the suspect to clarify if he was actually invoking his right to a lawyer. There was no coercion, she argued, on the part of the trooper in words, mannerisms, or tone of voice. Kate suggested that Rick's response to "Well, is that what you want," by replying "No, not really," constituted a free decision to continue to answer the officer's questions. Finally, Kate asserted that even if the court were to reject everything she had just argued, suppression still would not be appropriate. This was so because Rick was not yet in custody. He had not been placed under arrest. The officer was still in his initial stages of simply trying to figure out what was going on. Kate concluded by reminding Judge Mancini that Miranda protections do not apply until after a suspect has been taken into custody. "Miranda only applies to **custodial interrogations**, not to precustodial questioning," Kate said in summary.

Judge Mancini thanked both attorneys for their "helpful arguments." He thought quietly for a minute or so while staying on the bench. Then he announced to the attorneys, "It is the decision of this court that the defense motion for suppression is hereby denied. All answers given by Richard Mahan on the evening in question are admissible at trial. The court finds that this was not a custodial interrogation, and even if it was, Mr. Mahan did not adequately invoke his right to speak to an attorney at any point."

Judge Mancini now looked at Jack with a very warm and affectionate look. "Now that's kind of weird," thought Kate.

"Jack Day, you old courthouse warhorse. Welcome back. How long have you been away? Five, six months?"

"Substitute the word 'months' with the word 'years,' and you'd come a lot closer, Judge Mancini," quipped Jack.

"Do you mean to seriously tell me that you've been gone that long!" exclaimed Judge Mancini. With a look of profound astonishment he remarked, "It seems like you have barely been away."

"I have been teaching math over at St. Francis High School. Maybe you should give teaching high school a try, Your Honor. It could rock your world."

"I have no doubt about that, Jack," agreed the judge. "Now that you have come back from your therapeutic exile, I hope you will not hold it against me for ruling against you on your first day back. Not exactly the best of homecoming presents was it?"

"It is what it is, Your Honor," Jack shrugged in nonchalance response. "You always had a reputation in this building for being fair. Of course, that does not mean that I agree with the result today."

Prosecutor Kate Page watched all of this warm banter with great interest. She glanced over at the defense table to see how Richard was reacting. Rick just looked back at his adversary with an unlikely expression of empathy as if to say, "Don't ask me."

The business of the court now apparently over, all rose while Judge Mancini left the courtroom.

"Well, that judge had to think really long about this one, didn't he," Jack gently complained to his client in a voice loud enough for Kate and the trooper to hear. Jack then smiled at Rick and gave him a confident look as if to signal that his attorney still had his back. "We gave them an exciting little run for their money today, and this is just our opening salvo. No worries, Rick."

"Well played, Mr. Day," said Kate, who as victor of today's contest had no difficulty being gracious. "I thought you almost had me there. Please don't scare me like that."

"Thank you, Ms. Page," replied Jack. "Now, how about a deal for unsupervised probation?" he sarcastically suggested.

"Not in the cards," Kate countered as she rolled her eyes at Jack's silly request.

~

## Key Terms Found in This Chapter

| | |
|---|---|
| Suppressed | Responding party |
| Under advisement | Refresh your memory |
| Memorandum of law | Questioning must stop |
| Fifth Amendment | Custodial interrogations |
| Bar within a bar | |

## Questions for Class Discussion

1. What happens when a judge suppresses evidence? Can the state still go to trial if a defense lawyer wins a suppression hearing?
2. What examples of illegally obtained evidence can you name that should result in suppression?
3. What did you think of the judge's decision in this suppression matter? Even though Jack lost, did his motion have at least some merit to it?
4. What is the difference between a "memorandum of law" and an appellate brief?
5. Which amendment to the Constitution is violated when somebody admits to a crime without his or her Miranda rights being honored? What other amendment do you suppose is frequently invoked during various suppression of evidence hearings?

6. Did it surprise you that the prosecutor has the duty to identify and summon the appropriate witness to be interrogated at a suppression hearing? Why do you suppose this burden falls on the responding party rather than on the moving party?

7. Is it fair that police officers are permitted on the stand to "refresh their memory" by looking at their police reports? What would happen if this practice were forbidden?

8. Is it your sense that most laypeople know that all questioning must stop (period) once a suspect invokes one of the Miranda rights? Does Hollywood know this? Why are police officers forbidden to try to get someone to change their mind about remaining silent or requesting a lawyer be present?

9. What is meant by a "custodial interrogation"? What would be some examples of noncustodial interrogations? What makes custodial interrogations so special that the police must first recite Miranda rights before asking any questions?

10. How might a lawyer use a yet pending suppression motion as leverage to help get a client an early attractive plea bargain? Should Jack have tried to get a deal before suffering defeat on his motion to suppress? If Jack had used the specter of potential victory in the suppression hearing as ammunition, what would he have had to sacrifice if his client wound up taking that early deal?

# 13

## Discovery

Jack was disappointed that Judge Mancini had sided with the state against Rick on his motion to suppress Rick's incriminating statements. Adding injury to injury, Jack learned that Judge Mancini would not probably serve as the judge on the case from here on out, including the trial.

Back in Jack's day as a practicing public defender, a secret trick that defenders would sometimes play was to decide which judge they would want to preside over the case going forward until final disposition. Then, they would wait until it was that desired judge's turn to do "motions court" in the coming week. Then the defender would file a motion, any motion, to get the case before the sought after judge in motions court. The defenders knew that no matter how the judge ruled on the motion, he or she would then be permanently assigned the case by the presiding judge. This mechanism took precedent over the normal routine where the district attorney's office selected the judge at the same time they scheduled the matter for trial. This alternative procedure was due to the presiding judge's view that the judge who ruled on the motion (e.g., the motion to suppress in the case of Rick) would already know a lot about the case and should just stick with it for purposes of efficiency. The only time this strategy did not work was when the pretrial motion was just a request for bail reduction. Due to its usual simplicity, a motion to reduce bail did not trigger an ongoing judicial assignment to the case.

Remembering this old practice, Jack was expecting Judge Mancini, whom he liked and trusted, to be assigned the case from here on out. What Jack did not know, when he had first lost his motion, but which he soon learned from Prosecutor Kate Page, was that the days of using this workaround to get a desired judge assigned to your case had ended. Apparently, a couple of years ago, someone in the district attorney's office finally caught on and complained to his boss, who then complained to the president judge. The ensuing scandal caused the judges and prosecutors to all look down on the public defenders as manipulators of the system. In fact, some discussion even ensued about bringing ethical violation charges against them all to the state's **board of bar examiners**. Yet, the defenders themselves felt little remorse, figuring that if the district attorney's office was permitted to select the judge in the course of ordinary business, it was only fair that defense attorneys indulged in judicial selection themselves at times, even if it involved some creative lawyering on their part.

So, Jack would not necessarily have Judge Mancini assigned henceforth to the case. The district attorney's office would decide when the case would be assigned a trial date and who the trial judge would be. Jack would have filed his motion to suppress anyway on its substantive merits, but he really had been looking forward to locking in Mancini as trial judge. Alas, such was not to be. This meant that Rick's case could be assigned to a fair and reasonable judge (like Mancini or several others), "law and order" Robert Price (known locally as "Maximum Bob"), or one of the remaining judges whose judicial philosophies seemed to waver between the two camps. Only time would tell.

Jack decided to deal with the disappointment of losing his suppression motion and the frustration of losing Mancini by doing some work therapy. "It's time I find out everything the state thinks it has against my client," thought Jack.

Jack decided to write a letter to Kate (who, unlike Judge Mancini, had been permanently assigned the case), requesting **discovery**. Jack was sure to ask for all police reports, lab reports, physical evidence, the substance of any statements his client made, eyewitness names and statements (if any), and any evidence in the district attorney's possession that might have **exculpatory value** (that is, evidence that somehow could suggest the possibility of innocence). Should Kate ignore Jack's request for discovery, Jack knew he could file yet another pre-trial motion with the court to **compel discovery**. However, both he and Kate knew that such motions irritated judges who had no choice but to always grant the motion. Discovery is a constitutional right that every criminal defendant has in the country. It is needed in order to help the defense lawyer mount a proper defense. It is only fair. Never mind that in criminal cases it is all a **one-way discovery street**. (In civil cases, both sides engage in massive discovery of the other side's evidence. However, criminal defendants have the Fifth Amendment's protection against self-incrimination to protect them, not to mention attorney–client privilege.)

Jack knew that the only **defense-to-prosecutor discovery** in his state involved just two matters. One was the right of prosecutors to know if the defense was planning to put on an insanity defense at trial. The other had to do with a plan to put on an alibi defense. If either of these defenses were in the works, the defense not only had to give the state notice of this upcoming defense but also had to provide the names and contact information of those witnesses who would testify. Other than those two narrow exceptions, prosecutors could expect to get nothing in advance of trial from defense counsel, whereas defense counsel could expect to get nearly everything from its adversary.

Upon receiving Jack's letter requesting discovery, Kate wasted no time photocopying her entire case file and leaving the copies at the reception desk for Jack to pick up, per his specific request. Usually such **file sharing** is done electronically, but Jack preferred hard copies. Kate would essentially just share with him her entire file since she had not yet made any notes in the file as to her personal thoughts and strategies regarding the case, which she could have excluded as **work product**.

Jack appeared at the district attorney's office after school on the same day that Kate had telephoned him that the discovery was now available for his retrieval. The young receptionist, not recognizing Jack as a courthouse regular, asked him for ID before handing over the report-filled folder to a stranger.

Jack was so eager to see all that the state "had" against his client that he did not leave the courthouse without first sitting down on a hallway bench to take a brief peek. The peek turned in to a half hour worth of close reading and inspection. First, Jack read the police reports, most of which were written by Trooper Blake, who had been the first to arrive upon the tragic scene. The reports revealed that due to Rick's having been physically traumatized by the collision, no **field sobriety tests** were conducted, as is usually the case in a suspected DUI. Hence, there was no "heel to toe," no standing on one leg, no walking a straight line. The ambulance driver attending to Rick would not permit any such tests.

However, Trooper Blake was able to get the hospital to which Rick was transported to draw blood and perform a blood alcohol test. The police reports themselves did not contain the results of this blood work, but Jack knew it would be somewhere in the file. Before looking for that, Jack read everything else in the file. He wanted to make sure that there were no additional incriminating statements, civilian eyewitnesses, or other "got you" blind spots.

Now came the time for Jack to read the lab report, which would contain the highly anticipated results of the blood alcohol analysis. Jack nearly had an old style, apoplectic fit when he saw this scary number in italicized, upper case print: *BAC = 0.04.*

"BAC of 0.04!" Jack internally cringed. The old public defender in him instantly knew that a blood alcohol content of that level would only be possible if young Rick had consumed more than one beer. True, it was still well below the state's legal limit of 0.08, but it meant that Jack had lied to the police when he said he had only consumed one beer. As bad as that deception would look to a jury, Jack was even more upset that Rick had lied to him, his own lawyer.

Jack felt a wave of anxiety sweep through his inner core. He realized that a **blood alcohol content** (or **BAC**) of 0.04 would not be a big deal in most drunk driving cases. However, the state was going to argue that alcohol plus cold medicine equaled an inability to drive safely. Now, the state apparently could not only prove that Rick had drunk multiple beers but that he had also lied about the number. The state would portray this lying as a manifestation of Rick's **consciousness of guilt** in the matter.

"Here I go again," Jack thought. "I'll be representing someone yet again for a DUI who winds up killing someone, somehow." Up to this point, Jack had a near parental-like sympathy for his young student turned client. This sympathy had helped keep in abeyance the guilt he felt deep down in taking the case, even a case involving an alleged drunk driver. "I don't know if I can go through with this," Jack initially thought. "I might have to beg the court to allow me to withdraw my entry of appearance due to psychological unfitness." Jack could feel his sympathy for Rick and its associated prophylactic benefits melting away. "Multiple beers is a different story, especially with the pills," thought Jack. "And that lie to the cops and to me…"

Jack shut the file with the disgust of a brand-new parent desperately closing a dirty diaper. He decided on the spot to confront Rick immediately about what he had just discovered. Jack phoned Rick and asked him to meet him in the parking lot of the school. "I can't drive, remember?" Rick gently protested. "Then bum a ride," Jack insisted. "I will see you there in 20 minutes."

Jack drove to the school, stopping once on the side of the road to compose himself. "I can't stay on this case," Jack again told himself. "It is making me nuts."

Upon entering the school parking lot, Jack saw that Rick was already there, standing outside a car next to his mother. "Hello, Mrs. Mahan," Jack uttered. "Do you mind if I talk to my client alone for a few minutes?"

"Not at all," agreed Rick's mother. "I will just take a little walk and be back in 15 minutes."

Jack waited until Mrs. Mahan had rounded the corner of the nearby building before talking to Rick. "Rick, what the hell!" exclaimed the attorney. "You lied to me."

"About what?" Rick asked. The young man actually looked sincerely confused.

"How many beers did you have?" the lawyer demanded.

Rick was about to say, "Just one," but reconsidered when he saw an odd combination of betrayal and determination in the eyes of his lawyer. "Two beers," Rick softly confessed with his head lowered. "I drank two beers at the party."

"Are you sure it was not three?" asked a suspicious sounding Jack.

"It was two beers," Rick confirmed without the slightest hesitation. "On my word of honor."

Jack looked closely into Rick's eyes for several seconds before satisfying himself that "two beers" was probably the truth. He figured that two beers could match up well with a BAC of 0.04.

"Don't you ever, ever lie to me again, Rick. Do you understand?"

"Yes, sir. You are still going to stay as my lawyer, right?" Rick looked quite worried.

"I don't know. I may not have a choice. At this point, I cannot quit the case without a judge's permission. I already entered my appearance."

"Are you considering asking permission?" Rick needed to know.

"Maybe," related Jack. "I need to think about it."

"Who told you I drank two beers at the party?" asked Rick. "I did not know any kid there was keeping count."

"I figured it out from the hospital lab report on your blood work. It showed a BAC of 0.04. BAC stands for blood alcohol content. The only way a person could physically pull a 0.04 after drinking just one beer would be if they weighed under 100 pounds. How much do you weigh, Rick?"

"About 160 pounds," Rick noted.

Jack did some calculations in his head. "Yeah, two beers sounds about right. Of course, in order to know for sure, the state's experts will consider other factors when it comes to the BAC at the time of the actual crash. They will have to consider the alcohol content of the beers being served at the party, how much time passed in between your drinking the two beers, how much time between your last beer and the crash, and also how much time between your last beer and the time they drew the blood. Depending on all of that, plus your weight and sex, your BAC at the time of the accident could have been slightly higher or lower than the 0.04 reading at the hospital. It is the BAC at the time of the accident that is critical."

"When did you have your first beer at the party, Rick?"

"About 15 minutes before I left. I finished the second beer about 5 minutes before leaving to drive home."

Rick reflected. "The accident happened about 15 minutes into your drive, right?"

"Yeah, that's right."

"How long were you sitting in the crashed car before they put you in the ambulance?"

Rick thought a minute. "Okay, the cop came maybe 10 minutes or so after the crash, but I can't be completely sure on that. They put me in the ambulance as soon as it got there, about 10 minutes after the cop showed up. The cop had questioned me while we were waiting for the ambulance."

Jack did some quick head calculations. "According to the reports, the ambulance took about seven minutes to get to the hospital, and they drew blood as soon as you arrived."

"What does it all mean?" asked Rick.

"Well, the state will want to know if you were even higher than 0.04 at the time of the crash. Alcohol in the blood goes up and then down, depending on time passing. If the alcohol in your blood was already on its way down by the time they saw a 0.04, that would mean it could have been a little higher at the time of the crash, maybe 0.05 or even 0.06. I doubt it could have been above 0.06, but I'll need to see their report."

"That info wasn't in all the stuff you read already?" asked Rick.

Jack thought that Rick had made an excellent point. Jack walked briskly over to his car and pulled out the file. He flipped through it until he found a sheet stuck to the inside back cover. Peeling it away, Jack scanned what it contained. "Here it is," Jack announced. "The state blood expert estimates your BAC at the moment of the accident to be 0.05."

"Is that bad?" Rick looked bewildered. "What is the legal limit?"

"In most states, including Pennsylvania, the legal limit is 0.08," replied Jack.

"So, I was well below the legal limit. That is good, right?"

"Not necessarily, Rick. The so-called **alcohol legal limit** is simply what the state needs for an **automatic DUI conviction**. A jury could still convict you at a lower level if it decides you were **incapable of safe driving**. The only safe alcohol limit when driving is 0.00. Put another way, your driving skills get significantly affected well before 0.05. Therefore, a jury could find you guilty of DUI at any level. However, at 0.08 or above they must find you guilty. At least we do not live in Utah or in Europe. A BAC of 0.05 is the automatic conviction level in those places."

"But here in Pennsylvania I have a decent chance of beating this?" Rick looked as desperate as he looked hopeful.

"In a normal DUI case, especially one like ours with no field sobriety tests to nail you on, I would say, 'yes.' However, this is not a normal DUI case."

"Because I also took the cold medicine pills?" asked Rick.

"Yes," Jack acknowledged. "That plus the box with the stuff written on it, plus the fact that there are two dead bodies. Juries don't like it when there are dead bodies in a case."

"What's going to happen to me, Mr. Day?" Rick asked with an anguished tone of voice.

"Let me try to work a good deal with the prosecutor. That is our first step. We then go from there." With that statement, it suddenly dawned on Jack that he would be staying on the case after all, personal demons and/or Rick's lying be damned.

~

## Key Terms Found in This Chapter

Board of bar examiners

Discovery

Exculpatory value

Compel discovery

One-way discovery street

Defense-to-prosecutor discovery

File sharing

Work product

Field sobriety tests

Blood alcohol content

BAC

Consciousness of guilt

Alcohol legal limit

Automatic DUI conviction

Incapable of safe driving

## Questions for Class Discussion

1. What is the name of the body responsible for disciplining lawyers who act unethically? To what sort of punishments would you guess lawyers might be subjected?
2. Do you agree that discovery in criminal cases is essential for the development of a fair defense? Should both sides in criminal cases have to provide discovery to each other in equal amounts? Why should discovery in criminal cases be so one sided, whereas in civil cases it is fully two ways?
3. What should happen to a case if it is discovered after conviction that a prosecutor withheld some important discovery from the defense? What should happen to the prosecutor?
4. What are some examples you could give of potentially exculpatory evidence? Why might a prosecutor still want to move forward despite the presence of some arguably exculpatory evidence?

5. If you were a prosecutor, would you routinely require defense lawyers to ask courts to compel discovery before providing it? Why would this be such a bad idea?

6. What sort of things in the prosecutor's file should he or she remove before sharing the rest of his or her file with the defense? What specific examples of "work product" can you provide in, say, a drunk driving case?

7. What are some examples of field sobriety tests that you can identify? Do you think nervousness or accident injuries on the part of the defendant might interfere with the accuracy of any of these tests?

8. What is the automatic BAC cutoff limit for your state? Is it fair for the state to get an automatic conviction for DUI even if someone is sober enough to pass all the field sobriety tests?

9. How is it possible for the state still to prove DUI even if someone is considerably below the common legal BAC limit of, say, 0.08?

10. What is meant by the term "consciousness of guilt"? How might Rick's lying tend to help establish this? How might a criminal's flight from a crime scene help establish this? Does lying to cops conclusively establish guilt? Does flight from a crime scene?

# Unit 6
# Attempting to Settle

This unit delves into the system's reliance on plea bargains and the cooperative system of justice that it creates. We learn how a prosecutor and a defense lawyer go about actually negotiating a deal. The unit also introduces intrigue when a judge in the courthouse with a personal interest in the case convinces his friend, the chief district attorney, to veto the deal brokered by his assistant. Now that a judge takes center stage in the book, an opportunity is taken to explain how judges get their jobs and perform their duties.

# 14
## Let's Make a Deal

The founders who drafted our constitution probably never dreamed that our criminal judicial system would become one primarily based on plea bargains rather than trials. After all, the **Sixth Amendment** guarantees everyone charged with a crime the right to a jury.

For a long time, jury trials did seem to rule the day. Through much of the 19th century, almost everyone either plead guilty with no bargain or else opted for a jury to hear their case (with most choosing the latter). This **era of the jury trial** died a slow death long before mid-20th century America ever came along.

Plea-bargaining is now the dominant species in the man-made courthouse jungle. It is omnipresent. It is the expedient remedy that the Supreme Court (in the 1971 case of *Santobello v. New York*) ruled to be not only legal but also a practice that "is to be encouraged" in order to ward off institutional collapse.

"District attorney's office, how may I help you?" was the greeting Jack received after he dialed up the DA's office phone number.

"Hello, my name is Jack Day—Attorney Jack Day. I would like to speak with ADA Kate Page, please." The person with the pleasant voice told Jack to wait while she forwarded his call.

Kate was deep in thought while reading a medical report in an aggravated assault file when the sudden ring of her office phone slightly startled her. "Hello, this is Kate Page."

"Hi Ms. Page. This is Jack Day. Remember me? I am the attorney on the Richard Mahan homicide by vehicle case—"

"You mean homicides by vehicle case," Kate interrupted.

"What?"

"Homicides, as in more than one."

"Yes, of course," Jack agreed with no trace of defensiveness. Jack knew that he had to stay on this prosecutor's good side right now since he was about to request a meeting that normally takes place much later in the evolution of a case. "Listen, I would like to swing by later today if you are free to discuss some way for us both to resolve this case to our mutual satisfaction."

"I don't see the point," Kate objected. "Our office will not be listing this case for trial until months from now. We should talk more when it gets within a couple of weeks of trial. Besides, your client made bail, right?"

"Yeah, his parents were able to post their house, and Rick is home now."

"So, what's the rush?"

"Well, I remember when I had a huge caseload like you now have. If you are like me, you wind up not giving most of your cases a second thought until a fast approaching trial date forces your hand. Even so, there are always those three or four cases that haunt you from day one until they are resolved. I am guessing that the Mahan case is one of those worrisome cases. If we talk today, maybe you can resolve it right from the start and get it off your plate."

"Very well, Jack. I have some hearings in motions court this morning but will be in my office from 1:00 p.m. onwards. Just come in anytime then."

"You normally get off work at about 4:30 or 5:00, right? I'll pop in around 3:30 after I am done here at St. Francis."

"O.K."

At 3:30, Jack appeared at Kate's office door escorted by the receptionist. "Mr. Day to see you, Kate," the receptionist announced.

Without standing up, Kate invited Jack in, and he sat down in the middle of three chairs located in front of Kate's desk. "I appreciate your seeing me today," Jack began. "It means a lot to my young client who is freaking out." Kate shoved a huge pile of folders in the middle of her desk off to the side.

"Why is he freaking out? You got him out on bail."

"Wouldn't you be freaking out if you were a high school senior charged as an adult with serious felonies and facing unknown amounts of adult prison time?"

"I suppose I would," Kate admitted. "I guess your guy should be upset. He is in big trouble, Jack. As you no doubt know, the state legislature has listed homicide by vehicle while DUI on its list of offenses requiring judges to impose a **mandatory minimum sentence** if convicted. Your client Richard Mahan is facing two such mandatory minimum sentences of three years in prison, back to back. That comes out to be six years total, actual minimum time he will be spending incarcerated before he would get parole. Without a plea deal to protect him, a strict judge could give him much longer than six years. He could potentially serve 10 years of actual prison time followed by 10 more years on supervised parole." Kate squinted her eyes as she waited for a response.

"I know," Jack confessed. "However, judges only have to impose mandatory minimum sentences if the DA's office chooses to enforce them in a case. If you let my guy plead guilty to some other crimes in lieu of DUI homicide, the mandatory minimums will simply move off the field."

"Why should I let him plead to anything else? He drank beers. I have the BAC to prove that. He took cold pills, which he was warned not to take before driving. I can prove that. He knew that the drowsiness risk was enhanced even further if someone drinks alcohol while using the medicine. I can prove that. He fell asleep at the wheel. I can prove that. He crashed his car and two people died. I can prove that. It seems to me that two counts of homicide by vehicle while DUI is what I can prove, and so that is what your client should be punished for."

"Come on, Kate. He is just 17 years old. He has no priors. He is a straight-A student. He had at most two lousy beers at a party just like you probably did when you were his age."

"Yeah, but I didn't also take pills just after reading a bunch of drowsiness warnings on a box. I also never killed anybody."

"Two pills," Jack asserted. "Not half a box of pills, just two over-the-counter, legal pills. In any event, the bottom line in all of this is that this poor, young kid should never have been pushed out of juvenile court to begin with, and you know it."

"I do not know any such thing," Kate protested. "I have two dead victims here. What about them?"

Jack sighed, paused, and then looked Kate directly in the eyes. "I am not trying to avoid incarceration here. However, do you really think that this high school kid deserves six years in prison, maybe more? I will bet you that half a dozen or more of those kids at the same party drove home intoxicated that night. They just got lucky and made it home without incident somehow. Let us also not forget about all of those drunk drivers who are arrested every single day in this county. Nearly all of them spend 48 hours at most in jail. Even those with multiple DUI convictions who are caught driving drunk yet again, usually only spend months, not years, locked up. Is my 17-year-old client really so much more wicked than all of these other people that he should be thrown into hell for many long years? The intent of Rick Mahan who got in a crash that night was no different from the intent of all of his buzzed friends who made it safely home. Rick is no more mentally culpable than the dozens of motorists each year around here who drink themselves silly and who then just randomly crash into a tree rather than some other car."

"Yeah, but I have two dead people and their families who want justice," Kate insisted. "What are you proposing, Jack?"

"Let us amend the charges to include two counts of ordinary reckless vehicular homicide. I will not object to that amendment. Then, I will have him plead guilty to those two counts of ordinary reckless vehicular homicide, no DUIs. You will drop the counts of DUI homicide as part of the deal. That way the mandatory minimums do not come in to play. Then, let us agree to a sentence of two years of incarceration, one year consecutive on each count."

Kate remained calm and honestly told Jack, "I don't think that is enough time, not with two dead victims. Their families will kill me, not to mention the cops, my boss. I am not even sure this would survive the **judge's veto.**"

Jack noticed that Kate was employing a negotiation tactic commonly used by those who know how to bargain effectively. Prosecutors and defense lawyers portrayed on television go after each other's throats in shark-like fashion while negotiating bargains. Such aggressiveness does not work in the world of real courthouses. Most lawyers on both sides generally get better results by being likable and using a cooperative, **joint problem-solving approach.** The problem at hand was trial avoidance. Slamming fists on the table and exchanging insults does not move the ball very far down the field. That is why Kate was putting the blame for refusing Jack's offer on the victim's family, the cops, etc. She claimed that she could never sell it to them. What she really was politely saying to Jack (and he knew it) was that his offer was not acceptable to her. Her skill at saying, "No," while remaining merely **passively adversarial** was one that every good prosecutor and defender eventually must learn. After all, there is usually a **long-term professional relationship** to maintain.

Avoiding becoming too adversarial is a goal that few courtroom outsiders understand. The truth is that prosecutors, defense lawyers, and judges in our country are presented with the herculean task of processing endless numbers of criminal cases each month. The lawyers are supposed to do this by being highly adversarial with one another while a neutral judge acts as a referee. The truth is that an **adversarial system of justice** works well in a trial-based society but not so well in a society in which scores of cases must be negotiated each week. The **conveyor-belt court**, which has developed over the many years, has also led to the development of the "courtroom team." Defense clients come and go. Prosecutors' victims come and go. However, the small number of criminal defense attorneys and prosecutors in most jurisdictions do not come and go. There are always more cases rushing toward them on the conveyor-belt.

The members of the **courtroom team**, namely the prosecutor, defense lawyer, and judge, act indeed more as teammates than as opponents and referee because they come to realize that all three of them share the same important goals of reducing work and reducing stress. Jury trials create huge amounts of work and huge amounts of stress for all three members of the "team."

The cure for all of this is to negotiate cases away, whenever possible. This requires cooperation more than hostility. It requires a good "working relationship." It requires a courtroom team approach.

Normally, an outsider like Jack would not be thought of as a member of the intimate courtroom team. However, Kate recognized him as an honorary member given his years of service in the public defender's office. She would not be yelling at him or making personal attacks. Neither would Jack be taking such an approach with her. He was too much an old pro to go down that unfruitful path. This is not to say that he would let Kate destroy his client any more than Kate would give away the store just to get a deal. What it does mean is that both were willing to work hard, but ever so diplomatically, to achieve a **win/win outcome** if that were at all possible. If a win/win were not possible, both Kate and Jack were prepared to move on the **one winner/one loser** reality of a trial.

Both Jack and Kate regretted that this case was not one of the huge mass of routine cases that criminal defense lawyers and prosecutors deal with each month. These routine cases all come with **standard offers** that require no real bargaining between defender and prosecutor. When a case is of the type that comes with a standard outcome, a prosecutor is expected to offer it to the defense lawyer. The defense lawyer is supposed to accept it and sell it to his or her client. Expecting more or less than the normal offer in a standard, routine case is considered rude and "bad form." The problem for Jack and Kate in the case of Richard Mahan is that a case as serious as this one, coupled with an unusual blemish-free rap sheet in a felony matter, was hardly routine. There was no "standard offer" associated with it. Kate and Jack would have to figure out a proper bargain all by themselves.

Jack knew instinctively that getting a deal from Kate was in Rick's best interest if a fair one could be had. Judges do not like doing trials. One trial alone can easily take up two full days of their time. To help avoid the hassle of too many trials, judges learn to impose at sentencing what might be thought of as a type of **trial luxury surcharge.** This extra penalty is imposed on defendants who "selfishly" create the long, hard, stressful ordeal of a trial when most defendants "play nice" and take deals. Jack did not want young Rick to face the possibility of a heavy penalty surcharge. He wanted a fair deal to protect him from some judge who at any time might very well feel that "since you took up so much of my time, I'll take up a lot of yours."

Kate had a counteroffer for Jack. "Two years is just not possible," she calmly, but firmly, assured him. "I might be able to consider double that."

"I do not think I could sell four years to the kid's parents," Jack responded. I know I am supposed to have **client control,** but I do not see how I am supposed to have 'parent control.' Even if I could get my client to agree, his parents would have a fit. They fear for his life in prison."

"What if we split the difference then, Jack?" Kate suggested after taking some time to flip through the file some more. You say you want two years. I think I should have at least four. Maybe we just have to split the difference and go with three years total. If that sentence is agreeable, I will amend the complaint and have him plead guilty to one count each of ordinary reckless vehicular homicide with 18 months consecutive on each. If he pleads to those, I will then move to drop the DUI vehicular homicides along with their mandatory sentences. To clean things up, I will be nice and drop the two misdemeanors on his information as well."

Now it was Jack's turn to flip through his file. Three years in prison would be rough on Rick, to say the very least. Yet, this was the best offer he would ever get, and Jack knew that. It was much better than a decade or more that a judge might want to give him post-trial.

"All right, Kate," Jack finally agreed. "I will try to sell three years to Rick and his parents."

"Will that be a problem, Jack?" asked Kate.

"Of course, and a big one at that," replied Jack. "Just like you will have a problem convincing the family of the two dead people that justice is being served. I guess we'll both just have to find a way somehow to get it done."

$\sim$

## Key Terms Found in This Chapter

| | |
|---|---|
| Sixth Amendment | Adversarial system of justice |
| Era of the jury trial | Conveyor-belt court |
| Santobello v. New York | Courtroom team |
| Mandatory minimum sentence | Win/win outcome |
| Judge's veto | One winner/one loser |
| Joint problem-solving approach | Standard offers |
| Passively adversarial | Trial luxury surcharge |
| Long-term professional relationship | Client control |

## Questions for Class Discussion:

1. Which amendment to the Constitution guarantees the right to a jury trial? How serious should a criminal matter be to trigger this right? Should traffic offenses give you the right to a jury? Any misdemeanor? Just felonies?
2. The "era of the jury trial" was made possible by the fact that jury trials were very short (one jury might hear eight different cases in one day). Would you prefer a system that has many trials that are

of short duration or our modern system that has very few trials but each take a very long time?

3. Do you agree with the Supreme Court in the *Santobello v. New York* case when it said that not only are plea bargains lawful but they also ought to be encouraged?

4. What do you think the reaction of the founders would be to our post-jury trial era of omnipresent plea-bargaining?

5. In what ways can mandatory minimum sentencing schemes sometimes lead to consequences unintended by the legislatures who created them?

6. Do you agree that judges should have the right to veto plea bargains agreed upon by the lawyers, defendant, and maybe even the victim? Why would most judges be reluctant to use this power every time there is a deal they do not personally like?

7. What are some reasons why a joint problem-solving approach works better in deal negotiations than a "winner-take-all approach"?

8. Why do prosecutors and defense lawyers worry so much about retaining a strong professional relationship?

9. Who forms part of the "courtroom team"? What shared goals do they have in common?

10. What is a conveyor belt? How is criminal court like a conveyor belt? What, if anything, can be done to reform such a system?

11. Why do jury trials force lawyers to become adversarial? How does the one winner/one loser concept play into this?

12. Why is it rude for prosecutors to offer something other than what is "standard" in a routine case? Why is it rude for defense lawyers to expect something other than what is standard in such cases? What types of factors can make a case to become nonstandard in terms of plea bargains offered?

13. Is it just for a judge to punish someone extra for taking up her or his time with a jury trial? Should trials be considered "luxuries" that properly come with surcharges?

14. What is meant by a lawyer having "client control"? What do you imagine judges think of a lawyer known for an inability to achieve "client control"?

# 15

## Old Friends

District Attorney Gus Owens and his best friend, Court of Common Pleas Judge Stephen Hyde, had a lot in common. Both were in late middle age. Both were staunch Republicans. Both had achieved their lofty positions by way of elections. Each of them made a good living, per state statute. Judge Hyde, like all judges in the state, received $180,000 per year, while his district attorney friend received exactly (and intentionally) $1,000 less.

Gus and Judge Hyde had known each other since high school. Judge Hyde was a senior, while Gus was a junior. They became good friends when each served in student body government and as officers in the school's honor society.

In their early years as local attorneys, both helped the other integrate themselves deep into Republican Party politics. They paid their dues for years helping others be elected to various county and state offices. Then the day finally came when it was their turn to call in all of the favors. First, Judge Hyde was elected as judge. Then the electorate chose Gus to become the new head DA just three years later. For newly elected Judge Hyde, it meant liberation from his position as an assistant public defender. For Gus, it meant advancement from his hireling position as an assistant district attorney to his elected office as the district attorney (at well over twice the pay).

Judge Stephen Hyde had one career advantage over his friend Gus, besides the $1,000 of higher pay. Judge Hyde served the people for 10-year terms, whereas Gus had to worry about being reelected every four years.

Obtaining their jobs by way of elections is the **common chief prosecutor selection pattern** across the country for district attorneys like Gus. Luckily, for him, his suburban county was traditionally a Republican stronghold. Absent losing the backing of the party, and as long as he did not make a huge blunder while in office, his reelection every four years was fairly secure.

As was noted, Judge Hyde also obtained his job by way of election. Judicial elections are common in the United States. However, they are nowhere near as universal as elections involving chief county prosecutors. Judges in many states are appointed (by the governor or legislature) rather than elected. Some of these are **merit-based judicial appointments** (a blue ribbon panel of local citizens screens resumes of applicants and picks the judge). Others are **political judicial appointments** (the governor or legislature picks a judge without having to run it by any meddling citizen panel). It just depends on the state.

Judge Hyde was glad that he lived in a state that elected its judges. Working his way up in the local party machine had come naturally to him. Now that he had been elected, he knew he essentially had a *de facto* **lifetime elected position**. Sure, he still had to stand election once every 10 long years, but uninformed voters, not knowing one judicial candidate from another, always just voted along party lines. How could it be otherwise? People seeking judicial office are not allowed to make campaign promises or advertise agendas since that would be unbecoming of a future neutral judge.

Judge Hyde was indeed something of a political animal, but he also actually made a fine judge. Unlike appointed judges in other states who often come to the bench after much success helping rich people or rich institutions, Judge Hyde's pre-bench experience all involved helping ordinary people with their legal problems. Judge Hyde understood struggling people well, having grown up in a row house as the son of a supermarket butcher and a cosmetologist mother. Hyde attended a local law school at night while working 30 hours per week in a South Philly oil refinery. He understood ordinary people, including those in trouble with the criminal justice authorities, because he had grown up with such people.

Judge Hyde did not forget his working class roots when he rose to the bench. He did not see criminal defendants as evil losers. He understood how someone could do drugs. He understood how someone might steal from an employer. He even understood how someone could become an alcoholic. None of this is to say that he went soft on defendants in his courtroom. Yet, known as being firm, he was also very fair and even empathetic at times.

During his first few months as a judge, Hyde became quickly competent. This was saying quite a lot since judges get very little training for their job. Like many new judges in the United States, the only training he received was his county-funded stay for several weeks at the **National Judicial College** in Reno, Nevada. Those crash courses, along with his common sense notions of right and wrong, served him well when first on the job.

Stephen Hyde's duties as judge seemed much more expansive to him than his former duties as one of the local public defenders. For starters, criminal court was only a subset of what he now faced. He also had to become expert in divorce, child custody, adoption, probate, and civil law suits of all kind (those over $7,000 that were not the jurisdiction of small claims court).

Then, of course, there were all of the criminal court matters as well. Now, Judge Hyde had the privilege of presiding at criminal trials rather than his former lawyer's job of orchestrating them. **Presiding at trial** meant that he now ruled on objections rather than asserted them. He ruled on pre-trial motions rather than advanced them. He accepted guilty pleas rather than negotiated them. Finally, he sentenced people post-trial rather than made sentencing arguments to the judge. In carrying out all of these various judicial duties, Hyde always tried to remain firm but very fair.

Unlike Judge Hyde, who grew up in humble circumstances, Gus had been raised in an upper middle class home. Gus's father was a dermatologist, and his mother worked part time running her own dance studio. Owens was taking piano lessons while Hyde played stickball in the street. It was odd that two boys from such differing backgrounds would find close friendship in school.

Gus did not mind his friend Stephen Hyde's rather empathetic approach to criminals appearing in their courthouse. He did not have the depth of understanding of the criminal class that his friend Hyde seemed to possess, but Gus felt no particular hatred toward the class of people who tended to get into trouble. Rapists, thugs, and wife beaters would arouse the chief prosecutor's wrath, but the vast multitude of petty drug dealers, petty thieves, and drunk drivers did not particularly summon his moral outrage.

As far as managing his office was concerned, Gus personally made it a point to prosecute the occasional, select case of extremely high visibility but otherwise let his assistants run their own caseloads as they saw fit. His **hands-off supervision approach** to his subordinates' cases was more a situation of trust, professional courtesy, and a desire to not to micro-manage than one of laziness or lack of interest.

Given their friendship, Judge Hyde made sure over the years never to become involved in a case that Gus was personally prosecuting. If by chance Gus were personally prosecuting a case that somehow wound up before Judge Hyde, Hyde would never hesitate to **recuse** himself (vol-untarily step down). Presiding over a case being prosecuted by his close, personal friend would not only create the **appearance of impropriety** (which all judges know they must avoid) but might also create an actual, bona fide **conflict of interest**.

Imagine, then, Gus's surprise when Judge Hyde asked to discuss a "case of particular sensitivity" as they were finishing their usual bi-weekly round of golf one sunny Friday afternoon. "Sure, Steve," the DA said. "Let's discuss it in the clubhouse over a beer."

Judge Hyde and Gus were regulars at the posh country club in the western reaches of the county. Some of the other judges belonged to the club too, as did most members of the local political establishment. It was a good place to network and keep up on political gossip. Judge Hyde and Gus both felt a little sorry for the assistant district attorneys and assistant public defenders who worked with both of them on a daily basis but who could never afford to join.

As they took their seats in the clubhouse lounge, Judge Hyde wasted no time getting down to business. "Gus, your assistant Kate Page is pros-ecuting some guy named Mahan for causing a car crash that killed two people in another car. It was a DUI-type crash. Apparently, this bad actor had fallen asleep at the wheel after drinking beer and taking cold pills. Apparently, the cold pills cause drowsiness just by themselves. They make someone even drowsier when someone takes them along with drinking alcohol. The box even had a bunch of warnings."

"Okay, Steve, where exactly are you going with this?" Gus suddenly looked anxious.

Judge Hyde slowly took a sip of his drink. He then stalled for a few seconds more, looking as if he were about to call the whole discussion off. Then clearing his throat he finally said, "It has come to my attention that Kate Page has offered the defense lawyer a plea deal involving just three years total in prison. I am asking you to veto that deal as her boss. It is way too lenient."

Gus looked at his friend with astonishment. "What is this case to you, Steve? Do not tell me you are the judge assigned to it. You know the rule against a lawyer meeting alone with a judge without the other side present also, the rule against *ex parte* communications. Plus, there are at least two or three other rules I can think of that we would be breaking just discussing this case out of court."

"I am not here discussing the case with you in my capacity as a judge. If it makes you feel a little better, I have not been assigned the case and will recuse myself if I ever am."

"Then in what capacity are you approaching me? This all seems very inappropriate and probably illegal. I am really surprised at you, Steve."

"I am approaching you in my capacity as a father. There is nothing wrong about a prosecutor getting input from a homicide victim's parent before deciding on a plea offer, is there? Your assistants do that sort of thing as a matter of course."

"Wait," Gus responded. "You mean one of Mahan's crash victims was your child? Am I hearing this right? A father! You and Alice do not even have any kids, Steve. What do you mean, 'as a father'?" Gus was simply flabbergasted.

"When we were in high school, I got Judy Orsay pregnant during my senior year. You remember Judy, don't you Gus?"

"No, who was she again?"

"She graduated the year I did. She was not very popular, but I liked her. She was smart and super funny, witty actually. She and I went on three dates, and things just happened fast on the third date. We went too far. I did not ask her out again after the third date because I did not trust myself anymore to be alone with her. You know when we were young I was always relatively conservative about sex."

"Yeah, so you mean she got pregnant after just one sexual encounter."

"That's right. She told me the news around March, and she delivered the baby the fall after we graduated. There was a paternity test so I know for sure the kid was mine. We both signed papers allowing a young local couple to adopt our baby. It was mostly a closed adoption. I say, 'mostly,' because the agency allowed Judy to pick the parents, and I agreed with her choice. I have watched from afar all these years as my biological daughter grew up, got married, etc. Nobody knows about this except my parents, Judy, and Judy's parents. Even the adopted couple do not know that it was Judy who picked them."

"Whatever happened to Judy?" asked Gus.

"She and her parents moved to California about a year after the birth. I lost track of them after that."

"Wow, gee, Steve, I have to tell you this is some pretty heavy stuff!"

"I know," Hyde agreed. In a voice crackling under emotion, he then said, "I know my daughter's actual parents are the loving adopting couple who raised her, but I feel like I owe it to her to see that her killer does not get off easy. It's the least I can do."

"I don't know if I feel right about interfering in one of my assistant's cases out of a personal favor, Steve."

"Again, Gus, I am not asking you to veto this bargain in my capacity as a judge or even as a friend. I am asking as the father of a dead victim to reconsider your assistant's deal. Two people died that night, my biological daughter and her husband. The offer is for three years total. That's not right." Hyde looked like he would completely break down at any moment.

"Maybe it's right, and maybe it's not," Gus suggested. "I would not know without learning why Kate made the offer she did. She is no push over, and if she makes an offer in a case like this, she would have her reasons."

"Will you just look into it?" Judge Hyde pleaded. "Please."

"All right, Steve. I will look into it. But I can't make any promises."

⌖

## Key Terms Found in This Chapter

Common chief prosecutor selection pattern

Merit-based judicial appointments

Political judicial appointments

De facto lifetime elected position

National Judicial College

Hands-off supervision approach

Recuse

Conflict of interest

Appearance of impropriety

Presiding at trial

Ex parte communications

## Questions for Class Discussion

1.  What are the pros and cons of the common practice of electing our chief local prosecutors in this country? Is it a good or bad idea that, unlike elected judges, chief prosecutors must rerun every few years for office?

2.  Do you like merit-based or political judicial appointments more? If you were on a blue ribbon citizen, judicial selection panel, what sort of characteristics would you most favor in hiring a new judge?

3.  Why do we allow those judges who get their jobs by way of elections to serve typically for very long terms, e.g., 10 years or more?

4.  What are some reasons that judges who are elected often have essentially lifetime jobs despite having to stand for reelection now and then?

5.  What restraints do people running for judge face in campaigning that people running for most political offices do not have to worry about? Given these restraints, is it really a good idea to elect rather than appoint judges?

6.  In France, judges go to school for years to qualify to sit on the bench. How much training do American judges typically receive? Is it enough?

7.  Judges are said to "preside" at trials, while lawyers are said to "orchestrate" trials. What are some of the duties that judges have in presiding at trial?

8.  Why is a "hands-off" supervision approach probably a good idea for chief prosecutors to adopt? How can chief prosecutors make sure their assistants are doing their jobs well without resorting to micromanaging them?

9. What does it mean for a judge to "recuse" herself? What are some specific examples of when a judge should do this?

10. Why is it so important for judges to avoid even the mere appearance of impropriety? What other criminal justice officials can you name that share (or should share) this ethical standard?

11. What is so sinister about *ex parte* communications? How would you feel as a lawyer if you learned that your opponent had been discussing a case alone with the judge assigned to your case?

# 16
## Not So Fast

Kate was speaking on her desk phone when she noticed her boss quietly enter her office and take a seat.

"Let's plan on that, Sarah," Kate abruptly told the public defender on the phone. "Thanks for calling."

It was not at all rare for Gus to stop in the offices of his assistants to discuss various items of business but unusual enough for Kate to wonder what the district attorney wanted. "Hi Gus. What's up?"

"Hi, Kate." Gus looked a little grim. "I need to talk to you about one of your cases. It's Commonwealth v. Richard Mahan, a case of two counts of homicide by vehicle while DUI."

"Yes, I have been working on that case recently. I think I have it all worked out for a guilty plea. The defense lawyer and I have come to an agreement."

"Have you run your agreement by the family of the victims yet?" asked Gus.

"Not yet. However, I did tell Jack Day to give me some time to sell the deal to the family before considering it to be final, final." Kate knew that there was no such thing as **victim veto power** in plea deals, but common courtesy (and sometimes politics) compels prosecutors to consult victims (or their surviving family members) in very serious cases. (This same courtesy of **victim consultation** often does not apply in relatively nonserious cases due to the conveyor-belt nature of courts.)

Gus looked modestly pleased. "That's good you haven't run things by the family yet because I want to talk to you about this case first. Could you tell me about the current offer you have out there with the defense attorney? Who is the defense attorney, by the way? Is it the **public defender** himself, or has he farmed it out to one of his assistants?"

"No, it's some private attorney named Jack Day. He used to be an **assistant public defender** here years ago."

"Jack Day!" Gus looked genuinely surprised. "He is back?"

"I guess so," Kate acknowledged. "He is doing this case *pro bono*, apparently as a free service to the young defendant who is one of his students at the high school where he is now working."

"You have to really watch that lawyer, Kate," Gus admonished. "Jack Day is no feather weight. When he is not having a mental breakdown he can be a real force of nature."

"He has mental breakdowns?" Now it was Kate's turn to look surprised.

"Yeah, that's why he stopped doing criminal defense and ran off to that school to teach math."

"I had no idea," Kate said. "I just figured he must have become bored and wanted to do something else."

"Who gets bored doing criminal law?"

"Good point," Kate had to acknowledge. "Boredom is something I actually fantasize about having around here. So, what happened to cause Jack Day to stop practicing law?"

"I remember the weird chain of events pretty well," Gus began. "Jack Day used some technicality to get a DUI client off scot free. The client then goes out and immediately drives again after quickly getting drunk. This time the jerk kills some folks. Jack found out, and it totally blew his mind. He started having a bunch of panic attacks, including right in the middle of court hearings sometimes. He wound up leaving the public defenders soon thereafter. I guess feeling bad about enabling some creep who kills is as noble a reason as any for someone to go a little crazy."

"Who got killed by the client?" Kate asked.

"A dad, kid, and grandpa. The mom survived but is still in a wheelchair all these years later. I hear she hates Jack Day's guts. I mean she really hates the guy."

"Oh wow!" Kate exclaimed. "I cannot say that I blame Day for losing it. I am not sure I'd have the strength to still defend people after something like that."

"You and me, Kate," Gus concurred. Gus stopped talking and began staring at his shoes. After an awkward 10 seconds of silence, Gus eventually looked up and said, "Kate I need to ask you about the deal you made with Jack Day on the Mahan case. Could you tell me about that?"

"Okay, Gus. This is a case where a 17-year-old boy fell asleep at the wheel and plowed into a much smaller vehicle occupied by a married couple. Neither of the folks in the smaller vehicle were wearing seat belts. They both were ejected and died. The defendant, who was wearing a seatbelt, came out hurt but okay. The kid admitted to having drunk some beer and the hospital blood work revealed a blood alcohol content of 0.05. That level means he must have drunk at least two beers, though he told the cop at the scene he had drunk just one. The kid also admitted to having taken some cold medicine that the box warns causes drowsiness, especially in combination with alcohol. The kid admitted to the cop that he had read the box."

"Does the kid have any priors, juvenile or otherwise?"

"No priors whatsoever," Kate explained. "Apparently he is one of Jack Day's straight-A students and very well-liked by all his teachers and peers. He sounds like a real nice young man, at least when he is not out killing people."

"What was your offer?" Gus did not let on that he already knew.

"A total of three years' incarceration."

"How are you getting around the six years total of minimum mandatories?" Gus knew that was not hard to do but was curious enough about the details to ask anyway.

"With no objection from the defense, I will **amend the complaint** to include two counts of ordinary reckless driving, no DUIs. Mahan will plead guilty to those instead. Then, I will move to drop all of the remaining charges."

"I see," Gus said. Gus stared at a painting on the wall for a few seconds. He then looked at Kate and in a strangely gentle voice asked, "How do you justify just three years for two dead victims, Kate?"

Kate found the question embarrassing. Trying hard to avoid sounding overly defensive she asserted, "Well, the defendant is only 17 years old. He has no priors. He is an honor student in high school. He did drink and drive, but so did probably many other kids that night from the same party. His BAC was 0.05, which is well below the legal limit for an automatic conviction for DUI. There were cold pills but just two of them. They were legal and over the counter. I would add that this is the first person under 18 years of age I have ever had to prosecute in adult court in my career. To be honest, I am not even sure that he belongs in adult court. I guess I felt like three years in prison seemed like enough punishment to satisfy the demands of justice."

"Kate, as the district attorney, I am going to have to veto your offer. We are going to offer six years in prison, not just three. If Jack Day and his client cannot agree to that, then it will be a trial."

"Are you taking over the case, Sir?" Gus looked at Kate and could tell that she was hoping he was.

"No, Kate. I want you to stay on the case. Communicate my veto to Jack Day along with the new offer from this office. If this offer is rejected, I want you to take the case to a jury."

"How do I explain withdrawing a nearly done deal once it has already been made?" Kate's tone was one of seeking advice rather than one of raising any objection. "I cannot blame it on the victims' surviving family members since I have not even met with them yet."

"Blame it on me, your boss," counseled Gus. "Tell him I was not okay with just three years." Kate was about to ask her superior exactly why he was so interested in this case anyway. Some instinct warned her away from going down that path.

"Very well, Sir, I will let Mr. Day know right away. I hope he has not spoken to his client yet about our earlier agreement. I have a feeling this case might be going to trial."

Gus nodded his head in sympathy as he rose to his feet. "Thanks for all that you do in our office," he said as he walked out the door.

～

## Key Terms Found in This Chapter

| | |
|---|---|
| Victim veto power | Assistant public defender |
| Victim consultation | Pro bono |
| Public defender | Amend the complaint |

# Questions for Class Discussion

1. Do victims have veto power in plea bargain offers? Why do you suppose this is the case?
2. Why is it that prosecutors do not always consult victims first before offering a deal to the defense? If you were in charge of your county prosecutor's office, are there certain broad categories of "serious crimes" that you would always require your assistants to consult victims first about before offering some deal to the defense?
3. In some counties, the local head public defender is elected, while in other counties she or he is appointed. Should head county public defenders be elected or appointed? Can voters be trusted to select the best candidate for the job? Can appointing officials be trusted to select the best candidate? What characteristics should we want in our local public defender?
4. Should assistant public defenders be allowed to represent private paying criminal clients in addition to the clients they have as public defenders? If not, should public defenders be allowed to have private paying clients who hire them for purely noncriminal matters?
5. Should assistant district attorneys be allowed to represent people in civil legal matters as a way to earn extra income? Does your answer depend at all on how much they get paid in way of public salary?
6. Was the district attorney in this chapter "out of line" for vetoing Kate's plea bargain offer? Was he acting unethically? Illegally?
7. Should all lawyers do some legal cases now and then *pro bono* (at no charge)? Should this be a requirement of keeping a law license?
8. Do you think it is okay that scheming prosecutors and defense attorneys can apparently thwart the will of the legislature by simply agreeing to amend the charges to avoid triggering a legislatively desired mandatory minimum sentence?

# Unit 7
# Heading Toward Trial

### Chapter 17: Bad News

### Chapter 18: Deal or No Deal?

### Chapter 19: The Courthouse Scheduler

This unit explains how the prosecutor, forced to withdraw her plea offer to the defense attorney, uses third-party blame to mitigate the breach of etiquette that she causes. Defense Attorney Jack Day meets with his client, and they go over options, including a possible theory of the defense should they decide to take the case to a jury. With the decision made to proceed to trial, someone must now find a slot for the case in the busy courthouse. The courthouse scheduler thus is introduced, and a portrayal is made of her nearly impossible task of avoiding a situation of justice delayed becoming justice denied.

# 17

## Bad News

Kate was politically aware enough to avoid getting into a face-to-face conflict with her boss regarding his veto of her plea arrangement with Attorney Jack Day. That did not mean that she agreed with his doubling of the sentence offer. Nor did her reticence mean that she was not personally offended by a superior questioning her professional judgment in a case. However, Gus Owens was the elected district attorney, and she kept her appointed position at his pleasure. She knew that as an assistant district attorney, she had no **civil service protections** nor **due process entitlements** whatsoever. She also knew that, unlike police officers and teachers in her state, she had no union with whom to file grievances when being summarily dismissed. Assistant district attorneys are mere hired help, and their boss, like a business owner, is free to fire them at will.

In addition to feeling personally offended by the veto, Kate dreaded the task that now lay before her in having to be the one to offend the defense attorney on the case. She and Jack had pretty much made a deal. Kate had never gone back on a deal before. To keep good working relationships in order, all prosecutors and criminal defense attorneys have a strict code among one another that **one's word is one's bond**. How would Jack take the news that the deal he had negotiated with her in good faith was now defunct? Kate only hoped that Jack had at least not yet communicated their earlier agreement to his young client.

Kate decided to plunge in and take care of the nasty business right away. She took a deep breath and slowly began dialing Jack's phone number. She was shaking her head from side to side as she punched in each number. Kate was almost relieved to get Jack's voicemail. "I guess he is still teaching one of his last classes for the day," she reasoned. Kate hung up without leaving a message of any kind. "I'll try again after 3:00," she promised herself. "His teaching day should be over by then."

In the meantime, Kate went about trying to review some of the files of minor, new cases recently assigned to her. However, she could not get the Jack Day problem out of her mind. "I'm going to drive over to that school and talk with Jack in person," she finally determined.

Kate's drive to the school took a little longer than she expected due to some road construction on the way. The traffic aggravation only compounded the level of stress she was experiencing. She arrived at the school at 3:15. "I hope he is still here," she told herself as she parked her automobile in the mostly empty lot.

Kate walked into the school and felt strangely at home. Between elementary school, middle school, high school, university, and law school, Kate had spent about 20 years as a student—well over half of her entire life. As she entered the front doors, a passing teacher told her that she would need to check in at the office. "Where is that?" she asked. She was told it was just 25 feet to her right down the hall.

Kate found the office and explained her desire to speak with Mr. Day about a legal matter.

"Who are you?" the office secretary asked.

"I am with the district attorney's office." Kate flashed a shiny badge housed in a small leather case. The secretary, impressed, handed Kate a map of the school and circled the classroom where she could find Mr. Day.

Kate was not particularly good at reading maps, and this one seemed particularly confusing. After making a wrong turn or two, she thought she was now starting to get the sense of the school's layout. "Jack's classroom should be just ahead," she told herself. A rushing female student passed her along her side.

"Excuse me," Kate called out. "Is Mr. Day's classroom near here?"

"Are you his girlfriend?"

"Um, no. I am working with him on a project of sorts. Is his classroom just ahead?"

"It is right there," said the girl while pointing at a door just 10 more feet away.

As Kate approached Jack's classroom door, she saw the teacher working through a large stack of papers in what seemed to be some sort of exercise in grading. Kate stood there silently for a few seconds feeling sorry for him — and for herself. She knocked twice on the wooden doorframe. Jack took a couple of seconds to look up as he quickly finished marking a paper. He had expected to see a student at his door. Imagine his surprise to see an assistant district attorney.

"Ms. Page, come in," a startled Jack requested. "Please have a seat." Kate sat down in one of the student desks near the front of the classroom.

"Jack, I thought I should come by in person to discuss a snag in the Richard Mahan case."

"Oh no," Jack sighed. "What do you mean?"

"I am afraid the offer of three years is off the table."

"I thought we had a deal!" Jack exclaimed.

"Have you communicated the offer yet to Richard Mahan?"

"No. I was going to drive by his house on my way home today."

"Well, I am at least grateful that you have not discussed our agreement with him yet."

"What's going on, Kate?" Jack's tone was now more one of deep disappointment than one of anger.

"Gus Owens, my boss, has vetoed the deal. He says it is too sweet a deal for a double homicide case. He says our office cannot offer anything less than six years minimum incarceration."

"Six years! Are you kidding me? For a kid getting in an accident?"

"I think we both know that this matter is more than just a mere accident. Two lives were taken by your client."

"Yeah, but not intentionally, and my client is a child. Do you really mean to tell me that sending this kid to prison for six years is the right thing to do here? It will kill him. You know what prison does to defenseless people like Rick."

"Listen Jack," Kate responded sympathetically. "If it were up to me, we would still go with the three years. However, my boss has the final say. There is nothing that I can do. I am really sorry."

Using **third-party blame** is a standard device that attorneys like to employ to keep their professional relationships intact. Defense lawyers often reject prosecution offers by **blaming "unreasonable" clients**. Prosecutors refuse defense offers by **blaming "upset" victims** or **blaming "outraged" cops**. However, in this case, Kate was not diplomatically shifting blame for an awkward situation on some supposed third party. Her boss really was forcing her hand.

Kate silently watched Jack as he walked over to a window and started to stare at the massive evergreen tree just outside. "Do you think you could sell six years to Rick and his parents?" she finally inquired.

Jack did not respond. He just kept staring out the window. After a half minute or so, he turned around and bitterly asked, "What is so special about this case anyway that your boss would take such a personal interest in it?"

"Honestly, I do not know. I have been wondering the same thing."

"Didn't you ask him?"

"Well, no. He is my boss, and I could tell he was not in the mood for me to interrogate him on his motives. He simply said that three years for two dead people was not enough time. He essentially ordered me to revise the offer to six years. I could tell this was not something to debate with him."

"I had heard a rumor from Agnes that some judge in the courthouse might be related somehow to the two dead accident victims," Jack countered.

"Agnes, as in the secretary for Judge Wood?"

"Yes, she told me this when I was there getting a hearing date on my petition for a bail reduction a few weeks back. She did not know what judge it might be, other than it was not Judge Wood himself."

"Okay, that is disturbing, Jack. Do you think that there is anything to it?"

"I don't know," lamented Jack. "I followed up again on it later by asking Agnes where she had heard this rumor. I could tell that she honestly could not remember who might have told her this. She was not even sure if she had actually heard what she thought she might have heard. It's all a blur to her at this point."

"Well, no trial judge is assigned the case yet. Let's see who gets assigned and see if he or she has any familial relation to the two deceased victims."

"I have already run checks on every judge in the courthouse," Jack countered. "I could not find any familial links between the dead victims and any of our courthouse judges."

"How did you accomplish that?" Kate seemed impressed.

"Family history websites, tools in Facebook, a bunch of other re-sources on the vast internet. I have my ways."

Jack and Kate stared at one another, neither of them being in a par-ticular hurry to say anything else for the moment. They then simultane-ously shifted their gaze to the big evergreen outside the window. A bird had landed on the tip of one of the branches, and watching it had a mild therapeutic effect on them both. Finally, breaking the short peaceful mo-ments, Kate reluctantly asked, "Do you think your client will take the six years, Jack?"

"No."

"Why not?"

"Because I will strongly advise him against it."

"But he could do 10 years minimum if he gets a tough judge," Kate protested.

"Six years or ten years. Either way, prison would destroy him. Rick Mahan is a gentle, sheltered kid from suburbia with no street skills whatsoever. I doubt any prison gang will take him under it's wings for mutual protection. He will come out of prison a mere shadow of his former self. Even three years was probably too much for him to take. But, six years…"

"Then I should expect this to be a trial." Kate declared. She bowed her head and softly asked, "Do you even have a theory for your defense when this goes before a jury?"

"Maybe," Jack suggested.

"Would you care to share it with me?"

"If I told you how Rick could possibly be acquitted, would that change your office's latest sentence offer?" Jack asked.

"No." Kate's voice was firm.

"Then why would I share any of my potential trial strategy with you?"

"I guess you wouldn't," Kate confessed. "I hear you used to be a terrific trial attorney, Jack. Trials always make me nervous."

"Me too," Jack stated.

The thought of actually doing a jury trial suddenly started to play in Jack's head. "What will happen if I have one of my old panic attacks in open court?" Jack asked himself. The very idea of an embarrassing panic attack during a trial started to trigger a panic attack in Jack in the present moment. Kate noticed that Jack started to look pale and seemed to be breathing heavily.

"Are you all right?" Kate asked as she excitedly rose out of her chair. She became more and more concerned the closer she got to Jack.

Jack could barely talk. "I am fine," he managed to blurt out.

"You don't look fine, Jack. You are scaring me. Is it your heart? Are you having a heart attack?" Kate frantically pulled out her phone with the intent to call 911.

"Stop!" Jack commanded. Kate looked confused until it suddenly occurred to her what might be really going on.

"Are you having a panic attack?"

Jack nodded his head in agreement. He decided to cope by bending over and placing his hands on his knees.

Kate waited patiently while Jack slowly recovered. "Feeling better?" she asked once Jack had stood back up.

Jack's pale face had blushed into a red one. He was embarrassed. "Sorry you had to witness that. I think I am just about through it though."

"I'll follow you in my car as you drive home in your car," Kate suggested. "I want to make sure you get home okay."

"Not necessary, but thanks. I am not going home anyway just yet. Where I am going you cannot come."

"Where is that? Rick Mahan's place?"

"Yes. I am heading straight over there right now," Jack confirmed. "I am required to **officially communicate any offer** you have made me to my client and have him officially reject it. I think you can pretty confidently plan on it going to trial, though."

Jack walked Kate to her car and tried to project a confident smile while waving to her as she drove away. "She must think I am a real nut-job," Jack painfully thought as he slowly walked toward his own vehicle.

$$\sim$$

## Key Terms Found in This Chapter

Civil service protections — Blaming "unreasonable" clients
Due process entitlements — Blaming "outraged" cops
One's word is one's bond — Blaming "unreasonable" victims
Third-party blame — Officially communicate any offer

# Questions for Class Discussion

1. What is meant by "civil service protections"? What sort of jobs can you think of that have such protections?

2. What is meant by "due process entitlements" in terms of losing one's government job? What would be an example of a due process right in this context? Why are assistant district attorneys exempt from such entitlements?

3. Should chief prosecutors be allowed to fire an assistant prosecutor "at will"? Why do we put up with this? In what sense do chief prosecutors think they "own" the office?

4. Would it be a good or a bad idea for a newly elected chief prosecutor to "clean house" by firing everyone hired by a defeated predecessor?

5. Why do prosecutors and defense lawyers put so much emphasis in keeping promises and deals? Should orally communicated plea offers be honored to the same degree as those put in writing?

6. Why do prosecutors and defenders love to put the blame for refusing one another's deals on other people? Why do they continue to do this even though their opponent knows what they are doing?

7. What would be an example of how a defense lawyer might blame an "unreasonable" client for a refused offer?

8. How might a prosecutor pretend to blame an "upset" victim for rejecting a defense offer to plea bargain? An "outraged" cop?

9. Should defense lawyers communicate all plea bargain offers to their clients even when they know they are lousy offers?

10. Is it a good idea for defendants generally to be present while their lawyer negotiates a plea bargain with the prosecutor?

# 18

## Deal or No Deal?

Jack was still quite upset, to the point maybe of outrage, as he drove over to his client's home. Jack put on some music to try to calm himself down. When he got to the house, Jack parked in the street even though the driveway was empty. He did not want to be noticed until he was sure he was ready.

The house of young Rick's parents was a large, older rancher with a big old-fashioned yard. Jack started walking up the driveway, which was very long but oddly narrow. As he neared the house, he was not sure if he should knock on the nearby side entrance or walk across to the front of the house to the formal main entrance. He decided to do the latter.

As Jack approached the front door, it suddenly opened. Rick's mother greeted Jack and warmly invited him inside. "My husband is not home, but I'll go get Rick," Mrs. Mahan said. "Please, have a seat wherever you'd like." Jack sat down on a rocking chair but switched to a less exciting chair as soon as Mrs. Mahan walked upstairs to fetch her son.

Jack stood as Mrs. Mahan and Rick entered the room in single file together. "Hi, Rick," Jack began. "The state has made a plea bargain offer that we should discuss." Rick and his mom sat down on a couch, and Jack too took his seat.

"What exactly is the offer?" Mrs. Mahan inquired.

Jack looked at Rick. "The state says you can avoid a trial and possible stiffer sentence if you would agree to serve six years in prison, three years apiece for each of the deceased accident victims."

Rick sprung to his feet as if he had been sitting on a hot stove. Mrs. Mahan remained seated but started to cry softly.

"Six years!" Rick shouted. "Rapists don't get six years. No, I do not agree to that deal."

Mrs. Mahan stood up as well in order to be next to her son. Jack decided he should stand also. For a few seconds it almost got a little awkward. Then Jack looked Rick straight in the eyes and calmly said, "Rick, my advice is that you reject this offer and we take this case to trial. I agree with you that six years is unacceptable."

"What are my chances at trial, Mr. Day?"

Jack nodded his head as if to acknowledge that Rick had just asked a good question. "Rick, nobody can predict what a jury will do in a criminal case. There is a rule of thumb among criminal lawyers that there is a **jury conviction rate** of about 75% regarding cases that go to trial. Of course, some cases are slam-dunks for the prosecution, while others are real toss-ups going in. Most cases fall in between, with it looking like the prosecution will probably win, but that it is not going to be a sure bet. If I had to assess your case, I would say that you come fairly close to that 75/25 figure."

"Meaning, that there is a 75% chance they'll convict me?" Rick asked.

"Yes. Those are not great odds but a whole lot better than 0%. which is what you will be getting if you accept their offer of six years."

"What kind of sentence will I get if I go to trial and lose with no plea bargain to protect me?" Jack was impressed that Rick knew how to ask all of the right questions. "This kid is really smart," Jack figured.

Jack raised his shoulders ever so slightly before letting them fall back into place. "Impossible to say for sure, Rick," Jack confided. "In our state, homicide by vehicle while DUI carries what they call a minimum mandatory sentence of three years in prison for each deceased person. Since there are two deceased victims, the judge, by law, would have to give you at least six years in prison. However, the judge could give you more than the minimum mandatories. In fact, the judge could give you the max for the crime. He or she could give you a sentence of 10 to 20 years in prison. That means you would probably serve 10 years before the parole board let you out to spend 10 more years on parole. If the judge really wanted to whack you, he or she could potentially even give you 20 years in prison followed by parole. The judge would do this by giving you 10 years actual incarceration per deceased victim and make both of these sentences consecutive rather than concurrent. My best guess is that you'd get much closer to 10 years total prison time rather than 20, but it would be up to the judge."

Rick sat back down on the couch to think this all through. Jack and Rick's mom remained standing.

"So, let me get this straight," Rick finally said. "I can do six years in prison by taking their deal, or I can go to trial and maybe have to do 10 years or even maybe 20 years actual lockup time, or I can go to trial and maybe win flat out but only a 25% chance of that."

"Yep. That's about the size of it," Jack concurred. "There is also a chance that a jury might acquit you on the homicides but find you guilty on one or more of the misdemeanors they are charging you with. So they might say not guilty on the big stuff but guilty on underage drinking, for example. That's the least likely outcome in my opinion, but it is a possibility."

"What can a judge give me for a conviction on a misdemeanor?" Rick was curious.

"**Misdemeanor punishments** are capped at something less than 12 months in the county jail," Jack replied. "**Felony punishments** allow for 12 months or longer in state prison. So 12 months is the boundary between a misdemeanor and a felony—that and county jail versus state prison."

Rick started thinking again on the couch. Mrs. Mahan looked at Jack and said, "This is some complicated stuff, Mr. Day. What is your thinking behind your recommendation that Rick takes this to trial?" Rick stopped thinking and looked up at Jack to see what he had to say.

"Well," Jack began. "For starters, six years is a lousy offer. Three years would be more appropriate if they really were serious about our giving up our trial rights. If their offer had been three years, I would tell Rick to take it. I cannot tell him to just sign away six long years of his life without a fight." Rick paused and let what he said sink in a little bit. Then Jack continued. "Rick, if you have to serve many long years in prison anyway, you'd be much happier with yourself if you knew you put up a fight first. Besides, there is a chance—not a big one but a decent one—that we could win. As I said, juries are unpredictable. It is your decision, Rick, and I will totally respect any choice you want to make. I am your lawyer, and I give you my best advice. But you have to decide for yourself since it is your life."

"Any chance that you can get them to offer me three years?" Rick wondered.

"No, I already tried. Believe me, I really tried. This is their final best offer, for what it's worth."

Rick bowed his head to give himself a tiny bit of privacy while he thought some more. "If we went to trial, what would be your defense, Mr. Day?"

Jack took a long breath and gathered his thoughts as he slowly exhaled. "Juries **think with their hearts** as well as with their heads," Jack began. "They love **convicting people they hate** and **hate convicting people they love**. We would have to put you on the stand and get them to like you. The state is portraying you as some kind of killer. We would have to get them to see that you are in fact a good person who is just like them. I do not think getting the jury to like you would be too hard. You are likable just the way you naturally are. Therefore, we would put you on the stand. We also would put a couple of character witnesses on the stand to tell the jury what a responsible person you normally are."

Mrs. Mahan interrupted Jack by saying, "Rick is a great kid. He's been good all his life."

"Yes, I know," Jack agreed. "However, getting the jury to like Rick in their hearts is just step one. We then have to **appeal to the jurors' brains**. That is step two. By this, I mean we have to give them an intellectual basis—a **legal theory for acquitting** Rick—upon which they can hang their hats. Most likely this will take the form in our particular case of our raising doubts about intoxication and doubts about causation."

"How would that work, Mr. Day?" Rick almost seemed like a curious student asking a teacher a question in class.

"Well Rick, the state has to first prove that you were in fact intoxicated. We would suggest to the jury that two beers, even in combination with two cold pills, might have made you unsafe to drive, but they cannot be sure. Quite honestly, Rick, my job at garnering jury sympathy would be a lot easier if you had not told the cop at the scene that you had read the warnings on the box not to drink alcohol after taking the pills and especially not to drive. I don't think that will endear you to the jury very much."

"I never read any such warnings!" Rick protested.

"The cop says that you did. The cop will claim that you told him that you did."

"No, I told that cop that I had read the box. I did not mean that I read the entire box. I just read enough to know what kind of pills I was taking and make sure they were for someone who had a cold."

"I get that," Jack replied. "However, the cop will tell the jury that you told him you read the actual drowsiness and alcohol warnings."

"Well, the cop is a damned liar!" Rick protested.

"More likely the cop simply is remembering it wrong," Jack explained. "Lying and faulty recollection can be **two different forms of mistruth.** Nevertheless, I believe you when you tell me you never read the warnings. I hope that we can convince a jury of that too."

"Is not reading the warnings a defense to intoxication?" a cynical sounding Mrs. Mahan inquired.

"No, it is not. However, it makes Rick a lot less disagreeable in the minds of the jury than if he had actually read the warnings and just flippantly blew them all off."

"And the causation defense thing that you also mentioned?" Rick asked. "How does that play into all of this?"

Jack responded, "We would have to suggest that your falling asleep at the wheel might have been caused by everyday drowsiness and not necessarily by your drinking a little beer and taking a couple of pills. We could bring up the fact—like you told me before—that you had fallen asleep while driving once before without having taken any intoxicants. It is an uphill battle, but if the jury likes you enough, it could work."

Rick looked at his mother. She looked at Rick and smiled a mother's smile. "Let's go to trial, Mr. Day!" Rick announced. "Tell them to take their six years and… Well, you know."

Jack laughed. "Okay, Rick, just sit tight for now. This thing won't be scheduled for court for at least four or five more months."

"You're kidding!" Mrs. Mahan interjected. "Why so long?"

"This is the government," Jack reminded her. "Moving at a **glacial pace** is what courts do."

## Key Terms Found in This Chapter

| | |
|---|---|
| Jury conviction rate | Hate convicting people they love |
| Misdemeanor punishments | Appeal to the jurors' brains |
| Felony punishments | Legal theory for acquitting |
| Think with their hearts | Two different forms of mistruth |
| Love convicting people they hate | Glacial pace |

# Questions for Class Discussion

1. Why do you suppose that prosecutors win most criminal trials? Is it because they are better lawyers than are defense attorneys? Could prosecutors sneakily boost their personal conviction rate higher than the office average by the way they plea bargain cases? How?

2. Other than the length of incarceration, how else would pleading guilty to a felony have much more serious life consequences compared with pleading guilty to a misdemeanor?

3. What does it mean that juries "think with their hearts" as well as their brains? Is that what we want juries to do or not?

4. Why is it so important for a defense lawyer to get a jury to "like" their client? What are some ways a defense lawyer might go about doing that? How might a prosecutor get a jury to "hate" a defendant?

5. Why do lawyers have to appeal to the jurors' brains and not just their hearts? Though an appeal to both jurors' hearts and brains are important, is one more important than the other is? Which would be important in your particular case if you were serving on a jury?

6. What are some examples of how a defense lawyer might go about appealing to the jurors' brains in a case involving (for example) a critical prosecution eyewitness?

7. What is an example of a "legal theory for acquitting"? Does the theory have to be as strong in a case regarding a very likable defendant as it would in case involving a defendant who is not very likable at all?

8. How is it possible that a witness is not telling the objective truth while at the same time not lying? Why are such witnesses so dangerous in a trial?

9. What is it about government that causes its workers to move at a glacial pace sometimes? Is that even a fair characterization of government agencies and government workers in general? Do court workers hold any of the blame for a criminal case process that can seem so slow?

10. If you were Rick, would you have turned down the offer of six years and let your case go to trial? How short a sentence would you have to be offered before agreeing to forego a trial and plead guilty?

How would the lawyer's estimation that you only have a 25% chance of victory at trial factor into any of your calculations?

# 19

## The Courthouse Scheduler

Just as Jack had predicted, it took about five more months for the case of the Commonwealth v. Richard Mahan to come out of a deep **procedural hibernation**. If truly **justice delayed is justice denied**, Rick certainly was far from getting his full measure of justice. However, he was not alone. Virtually nobody in modern America can expect his or her case to be called to trial without waiting and waiting. Rick just had to sit, endure, and try to go on with his life as best he could until the district attorney's office got around to scheduling the matter for trial. The person working for the district attorney assigned the task of scheduling trials for court was none other than Sallie Rogers.

Sallie Rogers was not an attorney, so she never dreamed that one day she would work in the office of the district attorney. Yet, here she was. After graduating high school, Sallie opted to attend one of the dozen or so smaller state colleges sprinkled throughout the state. She majored in social work. Upon graduating with her bachelor's degree, she returned to her parents' house in suburban Philadelphia and started to look for a job. A cousin eventually told her about an opening in the county's adult probation office. She applied and they hired her. The working conditions were great. Sallie loved the combination of paper work and field work. She enjoyed the strange characters she had the opportunity either to help (her social work role) or have thrown into jail (her policing role).

What Sallie did not like was the pay. In Pennsylvania, there are two sets of adult probation/parole officers: those who work at the state level (paid well) and those who work at the county level (not paid well). Sallie was one of the latter. Unlike state parole officers, she mostly supervised misdemeanants or minor felons who were out on probation or parole after having served a brief county jail sentence. She did not have to manage a caseload of serious felons that were out on parole after serving years of hard time in one of the state penitentiaries. Unlike state parole agents, Sallie did not even carry a gun.

Sallie often told herself that if it were not for the low pay, she would love keeping her job in community corrections for the rest of her working life. Nevertheless, because of her dissatisfaction with her salary, she was always looking out for opportunities to improve her standard of living.

It was during her third year with the county that she read with great interest the lunchroom flyer advertising the position of "court scheduler" in the local district attorney's office. It was the pay that first caught her attention. The position paid nearly double her current salary. She was a little discouraged when she read that the preferred qualifications included a law degree. Yet, she took courage that nonlawyers would be considered if they had significant criminal justice agency experience, especially if they also had a good working knowledge of the local court system. Sallie sensed that her vast experience hauling probation and parole violators in and out of court might give her a shot at the job. She was right. The DA was impressed with her familiarity with the local judges and offered her the position (not a single person with a law degree had applied).

It was not long into her new job as court scheduler that Sallie realized why none of the local members of the bar had been interested in applying for the position. The work was insanely intense.

As the **court scheduler**, Sallie was essentially the courthouse version of a busy airport's air traffic controller. Hundreds of cases had to be scheduled for court each month and losing track of a single case could spell disaster.

Sallie knew how easily things could get out of hand. Shortly after being hired, Sallie leaned that her predecessor had failed to schedule dozens of cases for trial that were now very stale and very old. They had slipped through the cracks somehow, and neither the defendants nor their lawyers were about to complain. Sallie did not know at first what to do to fix this problem. If she were to start calling all of these old cases for trial, local defense lawyers would scream bloody murder. She decided to just create a "bad bank" of files and put them all in it to rot away, hopefully into oblivion. It was a lousy solution, but she did not know what else to do.

Sallie was determined that she would not make the same mistakes as her predecessor. This required that she become neurotically obsessive about tracking cases through her office. As is the case in many jurisdictions, cases in her county typically did not get resolved by way of plea bargain until the matter had a firm trial date that was about to come up. Miraculously, 90% of the cases would be plea-bargained away within just a day or two of the scheduled trial date. Most of the remaining 10% would find resolution within a few hours (sometimes minutes) before the supposed trial. Most of the rest actually went to trial.

The problem for Sallie was there was no way to know if a specific case that appeared heading for trial would actually wind up going to trial. Sure, one could take educated guesses on many of the cases, but the **just-in-time resolution** that lawyers like to engage in caused fits for schedulers like Sallie. She had to schedule four or five "likely" trial cases to start at the same time on the same day before the same judge, knowing that only one of them would probably not be successfully negotiated at the very last minute.

During criminal court weeks in the courthouse, Sallie would come to work hours before the prosecutors arrived and leave hours after they had left for home. She had yellow stickers obsessively posted all over her desk in some sort of spatial arrangement that made sense to nobody but her. She had her mobile phone alarm ring at odd times all during the day for various enigmatic reasons. She even had various cryptic messages written in ink on her hands and forearms. She looked like a frantic mess to any outside observer. Somehow, she managed to get all of the cases processed on time without defense attorneys or prosecutors complaining very much. She was a hero really, though nobody saw her as such with the exception of her ultimate boss, the elected district attorney.

Sallie's system for scheduling a case for "trial" involved a basic rule of thumb she came up with that involved a hierarchy of priorities. Sallie would schedule cases involving felonies within five or six months of arrest and those involving misdemeanors within seven or eight months of arrest. She chose which judge would preside over the case in a relatively random manner. There were exceptions, however. For cases involving serious violent felonies, Sallie would sometimes ask the prosecutor assigned to the matter if he or she had any judicial preference. If they did (they always did), she would strive to see that the case landed before the preferred judge. Usually, this meant a judge who had a reputation for giving out "no nonsense" sentences and a natural "law and order" inclination.

Sallie could see nothing wrong with a **contestant choosing the referee** to the point that she would occasionally ask the prosecutor "what judge do you want" even in the presence of various defense lawyers circulating around the office. Prosecutors eventually educated Sallie regarding the importance of being less audacious and more circumspect.

Sallie remembered noticing the case of Richard Mahan needing to be scheduled for its possible trial day and judge. Since this was an important case involving two deceased victims, she stopped Assistant District Attorney Kate Page in the office hallway one afternoon to discuss options. Sallie told Kate that the case was being assigned a trial date the week after next, and asked her if she had any preference for a judge. To Sallie's surprise, Kate said, "Not really, you decide." Sallie used her own judgment to assign the case to one of the more tough sentencing judges, though not to the judge local defense counsel had long ago nicknamed "Draconian Dan."

Sallie figured that she must have made a proper choice in judge selection for the case when District Attorney Gus Owens himself casually asked her one day which judge she was going to select to **preside** over the Richard Mahan homicide by vehicle trial. When Sallie answered, "Robert Price," her boss simply nodded and walked away.

Sallie deduced that her boss probably liked judges like Robert Price because they were tough on criminals. Sallie liked him for that reason too but especially because he was hard working and cleared his docket. Cases assigned to his court were processed, and Sallie felt relief getting them off her plate. Sallie wished that the other judges in her courthouse were as efficient as was Judge Price. He certainly was no fan of courthouse delay.

The truth is that much of the delay in getting cases disposed of in criminal court in a timely fashion is not due to lack of resources but to the **human desire for delay**. True, there are probably too many cases with too few judges, prosecutors, and public defenders to get them all done quickly. However, Sallie came to learn that the professionals in her courthouse seemed to like delays. To the frustration of victims and defendants, the truth was that defense lawyers, prosecutors, and judges all had their reasons for not being very bothered by delays.

Private criminal defense lawyers often like delay in the hopes of being fully paid before the case goes to trial. They know that once a case reaches final disposition, the likelihood of their ever being paid largely evaporates. If they win the case, the attitude of their client is "Why should I have to pay if I did not do any crime?" If they lose the case, the attitude is, "Why should I pay you if you lost my case?" Either way, the private defense lawyer will not be paid if the case is over.

Public defenders do not have to worry about being paid. However, like private defense lawyers, they often like delay in the hope that prosecution witnesses will move away, become lost, or lose interest in the case and not show up for court. They also like the idea that prosecution witnesses will forget important details of a case with the passage of time. Additionally, sitting in jail for many months might qualify their many clients who do not make bail for an easy-to-sell "time-served" plea agreement offer from the DA's office.

Like defense attorneys, prosecutors also like delays when they **soften defendants up** for time-served pleas. In addition, prosecutors do not mind delays when they might help crime victims to mellow over time, thus minimizing their objections to what initially might have struck them as being overly generous plea bargain offers.

Finally, work avoiding, **trial-averse judges** often like delays, knowing that cases eventually tend to be resolved one way or the other if the attorneys are only allowed enough time to work things out. Of course, this might require a judge to grant a defense or prosecution motion for a **continuance**, that is, a postponement.

Judges in Sallie Rogers's courthouse did not seem to mind granting motions for cases to be continued, especially if there was no objection from opposing counsel. Sallie knew that opposing counsel usually were reluctant to object because they themselves might soon need a continuance in a future case. If they object too readily at prosecution motions for a continuance, prosecutors would start retaliating by opposing their future motions.

Lawyers constantly seek continuances for a variety of reasons. Sometimes it is simply a matter of their inability to be in two different courtrooms at the same time. Sometimes they need more time to locate a key witness or adequately prepare a complicated case. Sometimes they need time off work to take care of personal matters or family obligations. Sometimes (in the case of private defense attorneys), they announce in court their desire for a postponement due to mysterious **Rule 1** (lawyer code in Sallie's courthouse meaning that the defense lawyer needs more time to get paid). Whatever the specific reason, judges in Sallie's courthouse did not mind granting continuances, and lawyers usually refrained from objecting too strenuously, if at all. To do otherwise would go against the prevailing courthouse norm **to go along to get along** when it came to tolerating court delay.

Defense requests for continuances (as opposed to prosecution requests) are especially nonproblematic for the courthouse work group. This is so because defense continuances **stop the clock** for any possible speedy trial concerns that might otherwise potentially develop. For this reason, prosecutors and judges who desperately want a trial to be postponed sometimes privately ask the defense lawyer to do a them a favor and put the request for a continuance on the defense.

Sallie knew that judges and lawyers did not seem to mind continuances, but she hated them. Such postponements only caused her to have yet that many more cases to have to continue to keep on her radar. That is why she liked Judge Robert Price so much. In her opinion, he was the only judge in the courthouse who did not excessively grant motions for continuances. "I wish all judges were like Price," she would tell her husband incessantly. "He really knows how to move the court's business."

## Key Terms Found in This Chapter

Procedural hibernation

Justice delayed is justice denied

Court scheduler

Just-in-time resolution

Soften defendants up

Trial-averse judges

Continuance

Rule 1

Contestant choosing the referee                    Go along to get along
Preside                                                          Stop the clock
Human desire for delay

## Questions for Class Discussion

1. What is meant by the term "procedural hibernation"? Why does this phenomenon occur? How long does such hibernation last?
2. What are some ways that "justice delayed is justice denied"?
3. Why is the job of court scheduler so stressful? Would you be willing to do this job? In what ways is it compared to the job of air traffic controller?
4. What problem did new courthouse scheduler Sallie inherit from her predecessor? How did she deal with this problem? Would you have handled it any differently?
5. Why are so many cases disposed of in a "just-in-time fashion"? What are the pros and cons of resolving cases "just in time"?
6. Unlike courthouse scheduler Sallie, do you see anything unethical in allowing a member of your office to choose the trial judge in a case? Is there anything potentially unconstitutional about such a practice? If you were a local defense lawyer, would you likely raise a stink about this practice?
7. Why are judges said to "preside" at trials? What sort of things does "presiding" entail?
8. How much of the delay in criminal case processing can be attributed to the idea that courthouse actors like delays? What are some reasons that prosecutors like delays? Defense attorneys? Judges?
9. Why do some defense attorneys like it when their clients who cannot make bail are "softened up" for a time-served deal? How does this "softening" occur?
10. Why are some judges so averse to doing trials? What do you think of such judges? Would you likely be "gung ho" for trials if you sat on the bench?
11. What is meant by a "Rule 1" defense request for a continuance? Would you likely object to such a defense request if you were a prosecutor? A judge?

12. Why do lawyers (defense and prosecution) feel the need to refrain from objecting too often and strenuously to the other side's continuance requests?

13. Which side's successful continuance request will stop the speedy trial clock? Why does the clock not stop when the judge grants the prosecution a continuance? Is there any circumstance whatsoever that you, as a defense attorney, would ever agree to put a prosecution need for a postponement on the defense, just in order to stop the clock?

# Unit 8
# Judge, Lawyer, Juror

**Chapter 20: The Trial Judge**

**Chapter 21: An Interesting Affair**

**Chapter 22: A Juror's Call to Duty**

This unit provides some character development regarding the judge, lawyers, and jury foreperson who will eventually become key players in the jury trial of young Rick Mahan. In reading their personal stories, we also will learn about how such people get such jobs and/or what is it is like to serve in these various roles.

# 20
## The Trial Judge

Judge Robert Price was notified before just about anybody else that the court scheduler working in the district attorney's office had selected him to be the trial judge for the upcoming case of Commonwealth v. Richard Mahan. The case, scheduled for trial early in the week after next, immediately caught his attention due to the word "homicide" appearing in the summary list of charges.

Judge Price knew that he had a reputation for being something of a pro-prosecution judge, no doubt because of the many tough sentences he had given out over the years. However, the veteran judge did not like the label of being "pro-prosecution." He took his duty to be neutral and impartial very seriously.

In fairness to Judge Price, he almost never favored one side or the other during trials in his courtroom. Nevertheless, a casual observer might not think so given the fact that he did probably express annoyance more frequently toward grandstanding defense lawyers than he did toward prosecuting attorneys. However, this was due more to the reality that defense lawyers, so often lacking truth on their side, simply resort to **grandstanding** more often than do assistant district attorneys. Defense attorneys in his jurisdiction often seemed to subscribe to the old adage that "when the facts are on your side, pound the facts; when the law is on your side, pound the law; when neither is on your side, **pound the table**." Judge Price did not like it when lawyers "pounded the table."

As for handing out tough sentences, that was only partially true. Judge Price tended to give out sentences of ordinary severity, with one exception. He did not like people convicted of crimes of violence. Hence, thieves, minor drug dealers, drug possessors, and even burglars convicted in his court fared no worse during post-trial sentencing than they would in nearly any other courtroom in the local courthouse. However, rapists, armed robbers, child molesters, and those convicted of aggravated assault could expect to be heavily stung if they landed before Judge Price without the protection of a plea bargain. Prosecutors and defense lawyers all knew this, and lawyers defending those charged with violent crimes worked extra hard to sell deals offered by prosecutors once they learned that it would be Judge Price who would be doing the sentencing if their client went to trial and lost.

Judge Price usually saw drunk driving matters as crimes calling for "middle of the courthouse bell curve" type sentences. However, this was not the case when a drunk driver caused serious bodily injury. The more serious the injury, the more closely Judge Price saw the offense as one of "violence." Homicides by vehicle while DUI were absent of all ambiguity in the mind of Judge Price: they were unarguably crimes of violence. He would punish the perpetrator of any such crime very robustly.

The Honorable Robert Price began his judicial career under rather humble circumstances. After graduating 72nd out of 148 of his graduating class from Dickinson School of Law (a good law school that nobody ever heard of), Robert Price, Esq. began work doing collections for a large collection agency. He hated this work for obvious reasons. Robert sensed an opportunity to "move up" a bit when he learned that one of the small claims court judges (before whom he often appeared as a collections attorney) was planning to retire. "Why don't you take over my job, Rob," the petty court judge suggested. "You live in my jurisdiction, and I will endorse you if you choose to run for the position."

Robert realized that he would have a decent chance at getting this job if he wanted it. Robert grew up in the area and had a lot of name recognition. The pay was low enough that few lawyers sought the position (in fact, the position did not even require admission to the bar). Add to all of that the current position occupant's endorsement, Robert just might be able to pull off an election victory. Rob decided to run for the office, humble though it was. After all, it was better than what he was doing now. After a low budget, simple campaign (consisting mostly of getting out his friends, relatives, former friends, former schoolmates, and various acquaintances to vote), Robert became Pennsylvania's newest "district court judge."

Lower court judges (generically known as **magistrates**) — the officials who take care of small claims, traffic, and other petty matters — exist all around the country. They go by different names depending on the state where they work. The traditional term for such judges is **justice of the peace**. Many states still use that title, while others prefer calling these lower court judges by other names: justice court judge, district justice, etc. Robert was now known as a "district justice" since he worked in what was locally known as "district justice court." (It is interesting that even among those states who have ridded themselves of using the traditional term "justice of the peace," the word "justice" seems somehow often to survive in whatever might be the current moniker.)

After his election, people started calling Robert Price "Judge," but he never could quite bring himself to think of himself that way. Many of his fellow district justices did not have law degrees. Often, they were small business owners who supplemented their business with the steady income and medical insurance benefits that this job brought in.

The county was carved up into 12 "districts," with each district presided over by a district justice just like Robert. Each district was designed to have about the same population as every other district. Hence, some districts covered a small, but densely, populated area (e.g., one town or even half of a town), while others (more rural) were huge in geographical size. This population-based attempt at equality was supposed to make things fair in terms of workload for each particular district justice. Of course, such was not the case since certain areas contained many more deadbeats and petty law violators than did others.

"Judge" Robert's duties were not highbrow, but he chose to find meaning in them. On the civil side of things, he presided in bench trials (no juries) involving lawsuits in which the amount in controversy was under $7,000. Most contestants in such suits showed up without a lawyer, and the rules of evidence were relaxed to the point of being nearly nonexistent. Judge Price dealt with the constant flow of such things as tenants not paying back rent, damage caused to personal property, dishonored minor contracts, and (his old favorite) unpaid consumer bills of all stripes. In addition to such small claims court matters, Judge Price also had the honor of performing civil marriage ceremonies, a function he performed once or twice per week.

In addition to civil matters, Judge Price also attended to various minor criminal law matters. He preferred the criminal law side of things to the civil side.

First, Judge Price and his ilk were the judicial officers that the police typically came to in order to obtain search warrants and arrest warrants. The main thing he concerned himself here was whether the person or place was "particularly described" and whether the petitioning cop could provide him with adequate "probable cause." To tell the truth, Judge Price, like most of his magistrate peers around his county, rarely sent an officer seeking a warrant away empty-handed.

Judge Price also handled "traffic court." This usually involved a quick two-witness "trial." The police officer would take the stand and testify as to why the motorist broke the law, and the motorist would testify as to why he or she thought they did not. He nearly always decided in favor of the police officer if the police officer showed up to testify. The problem was that many officers simply failed to appear. In those situations, Judge Price would either dismiss the charges out of hand or else convince the motorist to plead guilty to a less serious offense, generating a much lower fine and lower points posted to one's driving record.

Not all of the "criminal" cases appearing before Judge Price involved traffic offenses. Some involved very serious misdemeanors and even major felonies. His role in these serious matters was limited to conducting preliminary hearings. The purpose of such hearings was to determine whether probable cause existed that a crime had occurred and the defendant was the one who had committed it. This is a check by a neutral judicial officer that the arresting police officer's earlier determination that probable cause existed was in fact correct. If after hearing a skeleton case Judge Price determined that probable cause indeed existed, he would declare the establishment of a prima facie case. The matter would then be bound over for a jury to decide if there was also guilt beyond a reasonable doubt. If the state's few brief witnesses during a preliminary hearing could not establish probable cause, he would dismiss the case **without prejudice.** This meant that the state could try again later in a new preliminary hearing if it developed new evidence.

Some states (though not the one in which Judge Price worked) also allow their lower court judges to do actual trials (not just preliminary hearings) for lower level misdemeanors (e.g., Class C, but not Class B nor Class A). The problem here is that many lower court judges are not graduates of law school and preside over cases involving such true crimes (transgressions more serious than mere traffic violations) even though the Constitution guarantees a "law-trained judge." Such states get around this hurdle by allowing the lower court judge to do the bench trial but then also providing a universal right to appeal in the form of a **trial** *de novo* before an actual law-trained judge. Given this right to appeal and to get a brand new trial from scratch, lower court judges often feel the need to walk the fine line of not giving unnecessarily harsh penalties to those they convict.

Seven years went by while Judge Price toiled away in his lower court. Sometimes, he felt the indignity of working in obscurity. Other times he convinced himself that his job was of vital importance since it is in these **people's courts** where most of the day-to-day justice is actually meted out in this country. Eventually, nearly everyone winds up in such petty courts at some time in one's life.

Toward the end of the seven years serving on the lower court bench, magistrate Robert realized that if he had won an election once, he could perhaps do it again. This time, he could go for the big job of becoming a "real judge" in the Court of Common Pleas. After all, he wisely had spent his years in district justice court working hard for the dominant local political party and its various candidates and causes. It might just be his time to have the party return the favor.

**Real judges** (as Judge Price mentally considered the law-trained, jury trial-level judges to be) were indeed oddly called judges of the "Court of Common Pleas" in his home state. Other states prefer to call them by less archaic terms, such as "superior court judges" or "district court judges" (not to be confused with "district justices" of which Judge Price was one). Whatever they go by, and however chosen (elections in some states, appointments in others), these folks certainly have many **benefits of being a judge** that any lower court magistrate could envy.

One big benefit of being a jury-trial level judge is, of course, the pay. In Robert's state, they made $180,000 per year. The judges often did not feel like that was a lot of money (medical doctors, some corporate executives, and even lawyers working in corporate law often make much more). However, the judges conveniently forgot to factor in the number of hours they had to work for their pay (probably about half the hours of doctors, corporate executives, and corporation lawyers). Try to find a judge in a courthouse on a Friday afternoon.

Another big benefit of the job that attracted Robert was the prestige. Being a judge is the **last remnant of aristocracy** in our society. Just as it was a crime in the Middle Ages for a commoner to refuse to tip his hat to a passing lord or lady, so too is it even today an actual offense to fail to rise when a judge enters a courtroom or to fail to address a judge with sufficient deference. Judges finding a person disrespectful in their very presence can immediately punish, with a fine or with jail time, such a brazen courtroom visitor for **direct criminal contempt.** (They also can punish a person with fines or jail for **indirect criminal contempt** for failing to obey a court order while outside of their presence.) It may be true that prosecutors have more day-to-day power than do judges but (like the prime minister of England versus the monarch) have nowhere near the same level of prestige.

Robert also liked the fantastic amount of job security that all trial-level judges enjoyed in his area. Once you were in, you were in. Robert knew that he would have to stand election every 10 years, but once elected, he knew that party-backed judges in his county almost never lost reelection. Of course, in some states, judges are appointed rather than elected. However, there too, job security is typically impressive. Appointed judges either officially serve for life or else practically do so by only having to run once in a while in bogus **retention elections** in which there is no opposing candidate. Voters either vote "yes" to retain the sitting judge or "no" to fire the judge. The vast majority of voters, not wanting to ruin the professional life of someone they know nothing about, vote "yes."

Robert also looked forward to what he would be doing if elected to this higher office. Rather than doing small claims trials, he would preside over big claims trials. Rather than doing preliminary hearings in serious criminal cases, he would preside at the actual trial. Rather than sentencing people for their traffic violations, he would often be sentencing people for their major felonies.

Robert ultimately did secure the backing of his party and was delighted when the voters elevated him to the office of "real judge." His early life of doing collections work and more recent years as a mere magistrate were now behind him. Finally, law school would pay off. The new job did teach him that there were some **drawbacks to being a judge**: the loneliness of being on a pedestal, boredom as a figurehead rubber stamping endless streams of plea deals negotiated by others, and sitting on the bench during trials watching the lawyers having all the fun creatively scripting, acting in, and producing the show. Yet, Judge Price was pleased with where he had arrived.

It did not seem to take long for 25 years to pass by since he was first elected as a judge in the Court of Common Pleas. Now, as he had done so many times before, Judge Price would preside over yet another homicide by vehicle while DUI. In fact, the Richard Mahan case involved two homicides, he noted. The jurist knew that he would be very fair if negotiations fell through and this case actually went to trial. He would be neither pro-prosecution nor pro-defense. He would do his duty and be an impartial referee. "Yet heaven help any drunk who kills two people and expects much sympathy from me come sentencing," the Honorable Robert Price thought as he finished his initial perusal of the Richard Mahan trial file.

≈

## Key Terms Found in This Chapter

| | |
|---|---|
| Grandstanding | Benefits of being a judge |
| Pound the table | Last remnant of aristocracy |
| Magistrates | Direct criminal contempt |
| Justice of the peace | Indirect criminal contempt |
| Without prejudice | Retention elections |
| Trial de novo | Drawbacks to being a judge |
| People's courts | |

# Questions for Class Discussion

1. Do prosecutors or defense attorneys tend to "grandstand" more often during jury trials? Why is this the case?
2. When do lawyers feel forced to figuratively "pound the table" during a trial? Would you want your lawyer to do this on your behalf?
3. What are some ways that magistrates are considered a "lesser form" of judge than are judges who do jury trials?
4. What is the traditional term in this country for a magistrate? What is the term used for them in the state in which you live? Should we require such officials to have law degrees? College degrees?
5. Why can it be unfair to "equalize" magistrate workloads by merely making sure that the same number of people live within each of a county's magisterial districts? Does the county in which you live have areas that would generate more work for a magistrate than other areas? Which ones?
6. Is it fair that when a magistrate dismisses charges against a defendant after a preliminary hearing, he or she does so "without prejudice" to the state's interests? Why do you suppose that it does not violate the guarantee against double jeopardy if the state amasses new evidence and then requests a new preliminary hearing?
7. In what ways are the lower courts (magistrate level) the people's courts? Have you ever landed in such a people's court? If not, do you know anyone who has?
8. Why did magistrate Robert Price not consider himself to be a "real judge" yet? Do you consider magistrates (e.g., justices of the peace) to be "real judges"? As a lawyer, could you easily give sufficient deference to a magistrate who had far less education than you did?
9. What are some of the benefits that you can you identify that come along with the job of being a law-trained, jury trial-level judge?
10. How is it that some people think of judges as being the last remnants of aristocrats in our American society? Can you get away with being more disrespectful to your state governor in public than you can to a sitting judge?
11. How does "direct criminal contempt" differ from "indirect criminal contempt"? What can judges do to people who are contemptuous of them?

12. Some states require their judges to undergo occasional "retention elections." Why does the author apparently consider them as "bogus" elections? Do you agree?
13. What are some of the drawbacks to being a "real judge" that Robert Price discovered after being elevated to that position? Can you think of any other possible drawbacks not mentioned in the book? Do the benefits of the job outweigh the various drawbacks?

# 21

## An Interesting Affair

Father Joseph Skelly was staring out his office window at St. Francis High School when he noticed Assistant District Attorney Kate Page walking toward the building's front door. "She looks too young to be a mother of one of my students," the principal thought. "I bet she is applying for the opening we have for a new biology teacher. She looks intelligent."

Skelly thought he should make a good impression by personally greeting the woman as she entered the school office area. Hiring science teachers for the wages he could offer was no easy trick to pull off.

As Kate walked into the school office, Father Skelly stood a few feet away and warmly welcomed the visitor to St. Francis. "Hello, I am Principal Skelly. I have a feeling you might be here to learn more about our fabulous biology faculty position opening."

"What?" the confused visitor asked. "My name is Kate Page. I am a prosecutor with the district attorney's office."

"Why would someone like you be coming here?" Now Father Skelly expressed confusion.

"I was hoping to see one of your teachers, a Mr. Jack Day. Would it be all right if I dropped by his classroom for a chat?"

Father Skelly's face registered sudden understanding. "Oh, you must be the prosecutor assigned to Rick's case."

"Yes, I am in charge of the Richard Mahan prosecution."

"I will walk you over to Mr. Day's classroom. He should be finishing up his last lecture for the day since school ends in a few minutes."

"No need to escort me, Father," Kate replied. "I think I know the way. I met with Mr. Day in his room once before to discuss the case."

"Oh, I have nothing better to do. It will be my pleasure to escort you," Skelly countered. Skelly was not merely being polite. He wanted to **lobby** on behalf of young Rick Mahan while he had a golden chance.

As the pair walked down the hallway toward Jack's classroom, Father Skelly filled Kate's ears with every good thing he could remember about young Rick Mahan. He told her his stellar GPA — his exact GPA. He told her about his popularity among his fellow students, especially among the unpopular ones. He told her about his many hours of service as a student body officer, including how he and his fellow officers had raised more funds for school charities than anyone else in school history had. He even delicately threw in some hints about Rick's piety as a faithful Catholic.

"I get it, Father," Kate acknowledged, smiling. "Richard Mahan is a good kid. Still, I have a job to do. It is nothing personal."

"I know, I know," Kelly affirmed. "I just want you to see the whole person here in Rick and not just a dark snapshot of the **worst day of someone's life**."

"Understood." Kate and the principal suddenly stopped talking now that they had arrived at Mr. Day's classroom. The door was wide open.

"I think he is almost done," Father Skelly whispered. "Let's wait here quietly outside while he wraps things up."

The two of them moved away from the door but could easily hear Jack finishing his lecture. Kate was impressed by what she heard. Jack sounded masterful as he bantered back and forth with the class. "Was this the same guy who had a nervous breakdown the last time I visited him here?" she marveled. Jack was joking and calling on students at random by name, asking them various math questions. The student responses sounded as warm and enthusiastic as Jack's questions. "Father Skelly, you have a great teacher here," Kate whispered. Father Skelly smiled as he nodded his head in affirmation.

Suddenly the bell in the hallway sounded, startling Kate. "School's over," Skelly announced. Kate and Skelly put their backs firmly against the hallway wall as scores of students suddenly flooded into the corridor from various classrooms. After the rush had died down a bit, Skelly motioned Kate to follow him into Jack's room. Jack was talking with a student at his desk. Skelly and Kate decided to wait patiently until he was done. "Mr. Day," Father Skelly eventually announced as the exiting student walked by them, "A Ms. Page is here to see you."

"Thank you, Father. Ms. Page happens to be the assistant district attorney over Rick's case."

"I know," Skelly replied. "I'll leave you two alone to chat." With that said, Father Skelly was about to leave when he suddenly remembered something. "Ms. Page, is your boss Gus Owens?"

"Why, yes. Do you know Gus?"

"Indirectly," Skelly replied. "His daughter, Sandra, attends our school. She is in the 9th grade, I believe."

"Oh, I did not know that," Kate responded.

"Me neither," said Jack.

"Well, she is a great kid," Father Skelly remarked. "Have a good chat, you two." With that, Father Skelly left for good.

Finding themselves alone, Kate thought she should begin by telling Jack the purpose of her visit. "I was in the area and thought I'd drop by and give you an update on **where things are procedurally** with the Richard Mahan case. We have a trial date and judge now."

"Oh really," Jack replied with genuine interest. "Do tell."

"Do tell?" Kate joked. "Are you teaching Shakespeare these days in addition to algebra?"

"Sorry. When is the trial date?"

"A week from Tuesday, 9:30 a.m., in Courtroom #6, up on the third floor."

"Is that Judge Archer's courtroom?" Jack asked hopefully. Judge Archer was an old defense attorney favorite.

"No, Archer is next door in Courtroom #7. Courtroom #6 belongs to Judge Robert Price."

"Oh crap! The pro-prosecution judge!" Jack exclaimed with some frustration.

"I don't think he is pro-prosecution at all," Kate protested. "That reputation really is unfair."

"Would you want Judge Price if you were me?" countered Jack.

"Sure, I would have no problem with that."

"Who picked Price to be our judge in this trial, you?" Jack gently shook his head as he asked the question.

"No, he was chosen by the official courthouse scheduler, Sallie Rogers."

"Who just happens to work in your office," Jack cynically quipped.

Kate was offended. "Listen, I drove over here as a professional courtesy to fill you in about the case. I like to do **professional courtesies** so that people I am confronting in court realize that I hold no personal animosity toward them. I must say that I do not appreciate this cross-examination. For the record, I gave no input whatsoever to Sallie Rogers about which judge to pick. She picked him on her own. By the way, if I really wanted to nail your client, I would have picked someone else entirely."

Jack could see that he had hit a nerve. He bowed his head slightly and said, "I am sorry, Kate. Please forgive my paranoia. I guess it is an old occupational hazard that we former lawyers never quite get over."

It only took a few seconds for Kate to calm down. She was used to **passions igniting** in her line of work. She lost her cool on a regular basis as well. Every criminal lawyer (prosecution and defense) does. The important skill was the ability to cool down and not hold a grudge. That was all part of the **emotional intelligence** that every good criminal lawyer possesses. Lawyers forgive passions igniting. What they do not like are the petty lawyers who hold a grudge.

"Apology accepted," Kate said, followed by a chuckle. "I see that you still have some fire in your belly, teacher man."

"Thanks… I guess," Jack said with playful hesitation.

"Jack, Father Skelly and I listened out in the hall a few minutes ago as you were wrapping up class. You are a very good teacher. I had no idea."

"Thanks, I really like my job. The kids here are fantastic. They make it easy."

"I appreciate your humility, Mr. Day," Kate asserted. "Are those lecture notes on your desk? You know, I spent nearly two decades of my life in school and never once managed to see what those things actually look like."

"Yes, they are indeed marvelous to behold," Jack responded as he motioned Kate to come take a closer look. Kate came over to where Jack was standing, and the two stood inches apart, side-by-side, as Jack pointed at some of the highlights in his lecture notes on his desk. Kate pointed at a weird geometric figure and asked Jack what it was. Jack could not help feeling a bit turned on as he saw Kate's delicate finger next to his own on the paper. Kate was in no apparent hurry to lift her finger back up. Jack was in no hurry to lift his either.

Meanwhile, in a different part of the school, Father Skelly was surprised to see District Attorney Gus Owens in the school office just a short while after the principal had returned from Jack's classroom. Apparently, Gus had come to the school to discuss some absences he wished to have excused on behalf of his daughter, Sandra.

"Mr. Owens, would you like to hear about a weird coincidence," Skelly remarked upon first noticing Gus talking to the attendance secretary. "I was just talking about you with your assistant, Ms. Page, a few minutes ago."

"Page is here?" Gus looked surprised.

"Yes, she is talking with one of my teachers who just happens to be acting as defense counsel in one of her cases."

"Which case?"

"Richard Mahan. He was charged with…" Gus cut Father Skelly off before he could finish the sentence.

"With two counts of homicide by vehicle while drunk driving," Gus announced in an oddly authoritarian tone.

"Yes," the principal confirmed. "One of my faculty has a law degree and is taking care of the defense."

"Might that person be a certain Mr. Jack Day?" asked Gus.

"Yes, Jack Day. He teaches math here."

"Jack Day!" Gus exclaimed while somberly shaking his head from side to side. "Well, he was pretty good back in the day."

"He is still pretty good, I bet. I would rate him as one of my top teachers. The guy has some real people skills."

"Just please tell me where I could find Ms. Page."

"I'll escort you to her," Father Skelly offered in a suddenly subdued tone of voice.

Father Skelly walked in awkward silence with Gus as they headed toward Jack's classroom. Skelly considered lobbying Gus on behalf of young Rick Mahan as they walked but sensed somehow that it would be better not to do so. As they came within a few yards of Jack's door, their journey was interrupted when Gus noticed his daughter talking to a friend nearby. He went over to greet his daughter while Father Skelly continued on to Jack's classroom door. Skelly thought it strange that Jack's door was completely shut. Unlike some teachers, Jack never shut his door, not even during his lunch break.

Father Skelly gently knocked and slowly cracked the door. A look of concern swept across Skelly's face as he saw Jack and Kate passionately kissing. Skelly was about to say something when he sensed the presence of someone just behind him. Turning around, the priest saw Gus standing there waiting patiently for Skelly to usher him into the room. Skelly had to think fast.

"Mr. Owens, before we go into Mr. Day's classroom, I wanted to say how highly we all think of your daughter, Sandra." Father Skelly said this so loud that Gus stepped back a step in startled response.

"Why, thank you, Father," he replied with eyes wide opened.

"Now, let us see if your assistant Ms. Page is still here. Hopefully, she has not left already." Skelly was continuing to speak excessively loud. Seeing the look of puzzlement on Gus Owen's face, Father Skelly pointed to each of his ears in turn and said, "Sorry, I forgot to put in my hearing aids today. I keep forgetting how loud I must sound."

"No worries, Father," Gus sympathetically replied.

Father Skelly then slowly swung open the door all the way, making sure to cough twice as he did so. He then walked into the room with Gus in tow. Both of them immediately noticed Jack's hair all mussed and his shirt all tucked out.

"Hello, Jack," Father Skelly said as he subtly scanned the room with anxious eyes. "Guess who I happened to run into back at the office? This is Ms. Page's boss, who just happens to be here to clear up some attendance matters regarding his daughter, Sandra. I mentioned that Ms. Page might still be here discussing Rick Mahan's case, and Mr. Owens just wanted to drop by and see her."

Father Skelly noticed that Jack was trying hard to look nonchalant. Jack cleared his throat and straightened his hair a little bit. "She was here, but she just left. I am surprised you didn't see her in the hallway."

"Good to see you again, Jack," the district attorney said. "I heard that you were teaching school somewhere, but I suppose I had forgotten that it was at my own daughter's high school."

"Yes, this is my gig now," Jack confirmed. "I bet your daughter is one of our smarter students. I look forward to perhaps one day teaching her."

Gus smiled as if to say, "Thanks." Father Skelly was smiling too until he noticed the shoeless foot of Kate sticking out from behind Jack's big wooden desk. Skelly figured that if he could see her foot, Gus could as well—at any second.

"Mr. Owens!" Skelly shouted as he suddenly spun the man toward the door. "I think we left your daughter waiting patiently out in the hallway. The buses might have left by now. Let's see if she needs a ride home."

Jack knew that Father Skelly must have seen something amiss but did not know exactly what. He looked back at his desk to make sure all looked well when he too noticed Kate's naked foot. Jack moved his body and then shuffled his feet tightly together in order to block any potential view should Gus suddenly look backward while he was in the process of leaving. In fact, Gus did turn around briefly to smile at Jack as he started to pass through the door.

As Gus disappeared into the hall, Jack immediately walked over and stuck his head out into the hallway to confirm that Gus, Father Skelly, and Sandra were walking away. Pulling his head back inside, he quietly announced to Kate, "The coast is clear." Kate sprung up and started to tuck in her blouse and straighten her hair. She looked quite upset with herself.

"I better go," Kate summarily announced. As she passed Jack on the way out the door, she stopped, looked deeply into his eyes, and firmly whispered, "Let's just pretend this never happened."

"I concur, counselor," Jack replied. "See you in court."

## Key Terms Found in This Chapter

Lobby

Where things are procedurally

Passions igniting

Worst day of someone's life

Professional courtesies

Emotional intelligence

## Questions for Class Discussion

1. Was Principal Skelly "out of line" for trying to lobby a prosecutor on behalf of a defendant? Would he have been "out of line" if he had tried to lobby a sentencing judge outside of court?

2. To what degree did Principal Skelly have a valid point when he suggested it was unfair to judge someone by what happened on "the worst day of their life"? Do you have much sympathy for someone who does a bad thing but only on "the worst day of their life"?

3. What did the prosecutor mean by the phrase, "Where things are procedurally"? If you were a defendant, how interested would you be in always knowing "where things are procedurally" with your case?

4. Are professional courtesies important in the practice of law? Why or why not? What are some types of professional courtesies that one lawyer can extend to another without being unfaithful to the side that they represent?

5. What might be some possible reasons why "passions ignite" frequently between opposing counsel in criminal cases? Why do lawyers forgive these when they are so reluctant to forgive grudges?

6. What does the term "emotional intelligence" mean to you? How did ADA Kate Page and Defense Attorney Jack Day demonstrate emotional intelligence in this chapter?

# 22

## A Juror's Call to Duty

Jane Morgan was a busy woman. She worked full time as the principal of a public junior high school. She was the mother of two teenaged daughters (and one grown son). She was wife to the busy owner of a home construction business. She managed her Alzheimer-stricken mother's finances and health care. The last thing on earth that Jane needed right now was to be summoned for jury service.

Jane could blame the Magna Carta for the frustration she now had to endure upon opening the summons she had just received in the mail. American juries have ancient roots that trace back to England, ultimately to the year 1215. It was back then that King John reluctantly signed the **Magna Carta** (a sort of early, 13th-century constitution). Nobles at the time were keenly interested in increasing their power by reducing that of the king. They got together and drafted a lengthy document that accomplished just that. The king was told to sign or else prepare for armed conflict. He signed. Among the rights that the king signed away was his right to have everyone (including even nobles) tried before either himself or his appointees. The Magna Carta put an end to that. From 1215 onward, all "freemen" would henceforth be tried only by a jury of their peers. Of course, **freemen** only consisted back then of landowning nobles. **Peers of the freemen** consisted of the same. Landless people neither received jury trials nor were allowed to serve as jurors. Nevertheless, granting noble owners of "real" property jury trials was a huge step forward in breaking the absolutism of the monarch. Eventually, as the centuries ticked by, the right to a jury of one's peers spread to every English person.

The British colonies in America inherited this tradition of juries of one's peers. Still, some evolution had yet to take place. In the beginning, only **White Christian, land-owning males** could serve on juries. Blacks could not serve. Native Americans could not serve. Jews and atheists could not serve. Women could not serve. Eventually, non-Whites, non-Christians, and nonlandowners received the right to serve. Then, finally, deep into the 20th century, after many typical all-male juror films, such as *Twelve Angry Men*, had come and gone, females (lastly) received the right.

This brings us to Jane who had the opportunity to serve on a jury but who, right now, was not appreciating that long delayed right. "I don't have time for this crap," she muttered to herself upon reading the summons. The summons "commanded" her to put all business aside and appear at the county courthouse at 9:00 a.m. this coming Monday morning for up to five days of jury duty. "**Failure to appear**," the letter advised, would constitute a "criminal offense," resulting in this jurisdiction in an automatic $700 fine.

Jane noticed the name and telephone number of the official who had sent her the notice. Taking the cynical attitude that juries consist only of those people who are too stupid to get out of jury duty, Jane decided to call the official and ask to be excused from service.

Some people actually like jury service. Retirees like it because it gives them something stimulating to do. Many government workers like it because they get out of the routine of their normal jobs while still being fully paid. However, busy people like Jane (whose work at the school would only pile up anyway) usually hate being drafted for jury service.

Jane made the phone call to the official listed in the letter. She was surprised that the person who answered the phone was the very same person whose name appeared in the letter. "Hello, my name is Jane Morgan. I just received a summons for jury duty starting this coming Monday. I really need to be excused."

The official did not seem very friendly. He very coldly asked, "Are you a lawyer, medical doctor, police officer, or firefighter?"

"No."

"Do you have a felony record?"

"Of course not," Jane protested.

"Do you have a serious illness or handicap that would make it extremely difficult for you to serve as a juror?"

"Well, no," replied Jane.

"Then could you please tell me the nature of your request?" the jury official asked.

"Well, I am really busy," Jane began. As she said it, she realized how common and unoriginal her excuse must sound. "I know you must hear that a lot but I am really busy. I am principal of a school. Also, as a mom, I take care of my two younger kids…"

"How old are the kids?" the voice asked.

"Teenagers."

"Go on," he mechanically said.

"I also manage my mother's affairs. She has dementia. I simply cannot take a week off to serve on a jury. My family needs me. My girls especially need rides to teams and clubs. In addition, I am indispensable to the school I lead. Nobody else can do my job there, especially right now with the teachers' union threatening to strike."

The man on the phone was not impressed. "I am sorry. Your reasons fit none of the legal bases for a lawful excuse. You must comply with the **summons**. It is a court order for you to appear as directed. Failure to comply will result in your being charged with contempt of court, a misdemeanor. You will be fined $700 plus have a criminal record going forward in life."

Jane angrily slammed the phone down. "I just won't show up," she reasoned. "I will call their bluff."

Many people drafted for jury service "**call the summons' bluff**" or otherwise fail to show up. This can cause great problems from time to time for the smooth administration of justice. Once, in the county where Jane lived, so few people showed up to the courthouse for jury service that gridlock resulted. The president judge, using an old **roundup law** still on the books, ordered a bewildered police officer who had merely showed up to testify in some trial to "go downstairs and bring me three people for jury service; do not take 'no' for an answer." The police officer went downstairs and grabbed three courthouse visitors (including a mail carrier). "You are to come with me to serve on a jury," he directed them. All of them laughed as they thought he was joking at first. He was not joking. All three wound up serving on a jury that day.

Some jurisdictions really are bluffing when it comes to supposed consequences for someone who ignores a summons for jury service. If one fails to appear, absolutely nothing will happen. Unfortunately, other jurisdictions are quite serious and will impose serious penalties on those who ignore the command (Jane's jurisdiction was now one of the latter).

In addition to living in a nonbluffing jurisdiction, Jane had the misfortune of having to deal with a tough jury selection official. Some of these officials are "soft touches." They will excuse almost anybody just for the asking. The people who try to dodge jury service are legion. They include busy professionals facing important deadlines, small business owners who would have to close up shop, students who would miss important projects, dairy farmers whose cows would go unmilked, nonsalaried workers who only get paid if they show up for work, stay-at-home mothers of preschool children, elderly people who care for their frail spouses, etc. Officials who are generous with granting excuses often do so under the theory that angry jurors would make lousy jurors anyway. On the other hand, perhaps they are simply one of those extremely polite people who really just dislike saying "no."

Jane's official had no problem saying "no." True, the law required him to excuse certain people who fell within **statutory jury-service exemptions**. Lawyers could refuse because they might be needed to conduct court business elsewhere. Cops could refuse because it is assumed they would side with the prosecution. Extremely ill folks could refuse due to their incapacity. Doctors could refuse because they had patients relying on them for treatment. Firefighters could refuse since they were essential for public safety. Felons were simply forbidden to be on juries even if they wanted to serve. However, since Jane fit into none of these categories, she was out of luck. "Being too busy" or "being indispensable" was not going to cut it in her county. "Put all business aside," the summons commanded. The jury official took that statement literally. "We all have excuses," he figured.

Jane wondered how they had targeted her in the first place. "How did they get my name?" she asked herself. Jane guessed it might be from the list of registered voters. That is not a bad guess. However, jury officials in her area learned that reliance solely on voter registration lists was a bad idea. The idea is to try to get a fair **cross-section of potential ju-**

**rors.** Voter lists come close but tend to exclude certain people more than others, especially young adults and the poor. Most criminal defendants also tend to be young and poor so using voter lists filled with wealthier, older folks do not produce a fair result for them. Other jurisdictions use other methods, e.g., driver license lists, utility records, tax rolls. All have their merits and debits. Jane's county (the one with the no-nonsense jury summons official) was clever. It first merged all of the above lists (and even threw in welfare rolls). It then excised duplicate names before randomly selecting individuals to receive a summons.

In the end, Jane decided to show up in obedience to the summons. In doing so, she became part of the *venire*, meaning the group of people who actually physically assemble at the courthouse in response to their summons. She was apparently "too stupid" to have avoided jury service after all.

Jane's choice to comply and become part of the *venire* was more consequential than she ever contemplated during her bitterness stage. Not only would she actually wind up serving on a jury the coming week but on a big case worthy of her precious time: a case alleging two counts of homicide by vehicle while under the influence of intoxicants. Furthermore, Jane would not only serve on this particularly important case as a juror but would also wind up serving as this **jury's first among equals:** the jury foreperson. Jane, so worried about being disrupted from her everyday routines, was about to have an experience of a lifetime.

## Key Terms Found in This Chapter

| | |
|---|---:|
| Magna Carta | Call the summons' bluff |
| Freemen | Roundup law |
| Peers of the freemen | Statutory jury-service exemptions |
| Venire | White Christian, landowning males |
| Failure to Appear | Cross-section of potential jurors |
| Summons | Jury's first among equals |

# Questions for Class Discussion

1. Why did the nobles force the King of England to sign the Magna Carta? What "big picture" were they trying to change?

2. Who were the "freemen" of 13th-century England? To whom did they ask the right to a jury of one's peers be given? How was that a positive step toward democracy?

3. Who were the peers of the freemen? Why would they only want such people serving as their jurors?

4. What characteristics in colonial America did a person have to possess in order to qualify for jury service? Would you qualify?

5. Who was the last group of Americans to be granted the right to serve on juries? How long ago did this change take place? Why do you suppose these people were last?

6. Is "failure to appear" for jury service a crime? Should it be? Would you be more concerned about a fine or a blotch on your record should you fail to appear?

7. How do you feel about the ability of the government to summons you for work you do not want to do? Is this similar to or different from being drafted?

8. What kind of people tend to "call the summons' bluff"? Are you that sort of person? Do you think that a summons in your area is merely a bluff?

9. How does a roundup law work? Why did the people in the lobby laugh? Should judges still have this power?

10. Why is it so critical to have a fair cross-section of potential jurors? What are some ways that jury officials attempt to achieve this? What are some pitfalls with merely using voter registration lists?

11. What is meant by the *venire*? Do you happen to know what the word *venire* means in the French language?

12. Who is the jury's "first among equals"? In what way is this a fair description of their status?

# Unit 9
# The Trial Gets Underway

This unit describes the beginnings of the actual felony trial. Oftentimes, trials are won or lost by either who gets on the jury in the first place or else what the jury learns during the opening statements. Jury selection and opening statements, if done right, can constitute a sort of "game over" before the first witness even testifies.

# 23

## Jury Selection (Part I)

Defense Attorney Jack Day was actually relieved that the long-awaited day for young Rick Mahan's trial had finally arrived. "Let's get this ordeal over with," he told himself. Jack was ready — sort of. Early in the morning, Jack had made sure to take one of the anti-anxiety pills that his family practice doctor recently had prescribed. He also had been practicing deep breathing exercises on YouTube, which he now had down to a near art form. The old panic attacks that had driven him away from the practice of courtroom law years ago were hopefully now in check. Yet, Jack could not be certain of that. Like former stutterers, panic attack survivors often suffer from constant fear of a possible future humiliating relapse.

Jack met Rick Mahan in the hallway outside of Courtroom #6 on Tuesday at 9:15 a.m. Court was scheduled to begin at 9:30. Jack told Rick's parents that the first stage of the jury trial would be *voir dire*, a fancy term meaning jury selection. Only Rick would be accompanying Jack into the courtroom for this initial stage of the trial. Once the jury was picked (a process that should not take more than about an hour), there would be plenty of space available in the courtroom for the parents and general public to come in and observe the rest of the trial.

Jack, pretending to be a bit more confident than he actually was, winked at Rick and said, "Let's roll." With that, Jack escorted Rick into the courtroom.

Rick could see why Jack had told his parents to wait outside for now. The courtroom was full with bodies. "Who are all these people?" Rick asked his attorney as they sat down at one of the two tables in the front of the courtroom.

"These are all potential jurors in your case," explained Jack. "Twelve of them will wind up serving on your jury."

"Which ones?" Rick asked.

"That is up to me and the prosecutor. Just sit tight and watch for now."

Out of the corner of his eye, Jack noticed Assistant District Attorney Kate Page quietly taking her seat at the table next to him and Rick. He glanced over and nodded a silent "Hello."

"Good morning, Mr. Day," the prosecutor vocally stated in the courteous, but cold, professional tone of an adversary.

The lawyers, Rick Mahan, and the crowded courtroom of prospective jurors all sat there quietly awaiting for the trial judge to enter the room. "All rise," commanded the bailiff as Judge Robert Price briskly entered from a side door. "You may be seated," announced the same bailiff once the judge had taken his seat in the large leather chair high on the judge's stand.

"Ms. Page, you may begin your *voir dire*," Judge Price instructed the prosecutor. Kate stood up with pen and notepad in hand. Prosecutors always get to go first in *voir dire.*

"Good morning, ladies and gentlemen," began Kate. "Thank you for your service this week in court. I know I speak on behalf of the judge and defense counsel when I express to you our appreciation for the sacrifices you all have made to be here today in fulfillment of a very critical responsibility of citizenship. My name is Kate Page. I am the assistant district attorney who will be prosecuting this matter. Seated at the table next to me is Mr. Jack Day, the defense attorney, and his client, Mr. Richard Mahan. You may remember the judge just instructing me to begin my '*voir dire*.' Those are French words meaning 'to see' and 'to say.' What we will be doing for the next hour or so is indeed a sort of 'show and tell' in which I first will be asking you a series of questions to which you will raise your hand should the situation I describe apply to you. If you raise your hand, I may ask you a follow-up question or two, as might the judge. When I am finished asking all of my questions, Mr. Day, the defense attorney, will then ask you a series of questions, again with the understanding that you will raise your hand should the matter asked about apply to you. When we are done with all of our questions, we will select 12 of you to serve on the jury in this case. Those of you who are not picked to serve on this particular jury will return to the jury waiting room where you just came from. It is very possible that you will be picked to serve on another jury very soon.

"The **purpose of jury selection** is to make sure that both the defendant and the Commonwealth of Pennsylvania have not just any old jury of 12 people but a fair and unbiased jury of 12 people. That is why both Mr. Day and I will be asking you a series of questions this morning. We both are only trying to make sure that whoever serves on the jury today can be unquestionably fair to both sides. As an extreme example, suppose that my sister had received a summons for jury service and was sitting among you here today in this courtroom. I suspect that Mr. Day would not want her to serve on his client's jury.

"So, let me begin my questions by first asking if any of you know Trooper Steven Blake of the state police, or Kate Page — that would be me — of the district attorney's office, or Defense Attorney Jack Day, or the defendant Richard Mahan who is sitting next to Attorney Jack Day?" A potential juror seated in one of the rear benches raised her hand.

"I see a hand up in the back," Kate noted. "Mary, would you like to explain to the court how we know one another?"

"Yes, Ms. Page," a young woman acknowledged. "You and I play on the same team in community soccer."

"Yes, we do," the prosecutor readily agreed. Kate looked over at Jack. He dutifully rose to his feet, turned toward the judge and said, "Your Honor, the defense challenges this potential juror for cause."

The judge looked at Kate, who had nothing to say. "Challenge granted," Judge Price ruled. "Ma'am, you are excused from serving on this jury. Please return to the jury waiting room for possible use in another jury. Thank you for your assistance." With that, one of the bailiffs walked over to the end of the bench in which the woman was sitting and motioned her to follow him out of the courtroom. The rest of the audience watched as she awkwardly scooted her away over to the bailiff, who then escorted her out of the room.

The lawyers and judge knew that there were two types of "challenges" during *voir dire*: challenges for cause and peremptory challenges. **Chal-**

**lenges for cause** are used when one of the attorneys believes that a prospective juror has demonstrated potential bias by responding to a question. The expectation is that the opposing side will assert the challenge for cause as soon as the potential for bias is revealed. The judge then makes a ruling either granting or denying the challenge on the spot. If the challenge is granted, the prospective juror is asked immediately to leave the courtroom. There is no limit to the number of challenges for cause. If a potential juror is biased, he or she absolutely cannot serve. If the *voir dire* process results in so many successful challenges for cause that fewer than 12 prospective jurors remain, more prospective jurors will be sought from the central jury waiting room.

The second category of challenge is limited in number. These so-called **peremptory challenges** allow an attorney to get rid of a prospective juror for any reason or no reason whatsoever. The attorney need not satisfy the judge of any potential for bias. (There are, however, two **exceptions to exercising peremptories**: getting rid of prospective jurors based solely on their race or getting rid of them based solely on their sex. The judge will watch carefully for **suspicious strike patterns** to develop and call an attorney up to the stand to explain things should a pattern of race- or sex-based peremptory challenge choices emerge.)

In any event, the thinking behind allowing peremptory challenges is that sometimes an attorney has only a hunch that a juror will be biased (e.g., hostile body language, eccentric dress or grooming, etc.). Thanks to peremptory challenges, an attorney who cannot actually prove bias can nevertheless strike a juror who gives them a very bad vibe.

The **allowed number of peremptories** depends upon the seriousness of the charges and is set by statute. For example, a felony in most states will typically call for about seven or so peremptory challenges per each side, with misdemeanor cases only providing for about four. A capital murder case would allow many more, perhaps as many as 20 (depending on the state). Capital murder cases (as well as perhaps other super serious cases) typically also involve **individual *voir dire*** rather than group *voir dire*. In individual *voir dire*, each prospective juror is brought into the courtroom one at a time and individually asked the questions (and challenged) out of the hearing of the rest of the potential jurors. This slow process can take one or two full days all by itself. This is why judges, exercising their discretion, choose to go with **group *voir dire*** (i.e., "raise your hand if the question applies to you") rather than individual *voir dire* in all but the most serious of cases.

Unlike challenges for cause, peremptory challenges are not asserted right away. They are strategically decided upon and exercised by both of the attorneys at the end of the entire *voir dire* process.

In any event, *voir dire*, in the present case, had barely begun. There could yet be a few more successful challenges for cause before Kate and Jack would have to start deploying their precious peremptory challenges.

Kate was ready to ask her second question. "Ladies and gentlemen, I might as well tell you that this trial will involve two counts of homicide by vehicle while driving under the influence. Have any of you been convicted of drunk driving or have relatives who have been convicted of drunk driving?" No hands went up.

"Have any of you been convicted of a felony at any time of your life or of a misdemeanor in the last five years?" A man in his mid-20s sitting in the front row raised his hand and admitted to Kate that he had been convicted of public drunkenness four years ago. "I challenge this juror for cause," Kate said to the judge.

"I object to that challenge," Jack asserted. "There is no proof of bias."

Judge Price looked at the prospective juror and asked, "Sir, would the fact that you were convicted by the district attorney's office four years ago cause you to be unable to remain neutral in a jury trial here today?"

"Not at all," the man protested. "I can be fair."

"Your challenge for cause is denied, Ms. Page," Judge Price remarked.

"Very well, Your Honor," Kate acquiesced as she subtly scribbled the word "peremptory" next to the man's name on the list provided to her at the start of *voir dire* by the bailiff. (The name of each prospective juror brought to the courtroom is on a list given to the attorneys at the start of *voir dire*. Each juror is seated by the bailiff in a precise order corresponding to the place of his or her name on that list. Thus, attorneys can use this courtroom seating chart to match names with faces when it comes time to exercise their peremptory challenges.)

Kate was ready to ask her next question. "Do any of you have any philosophical or emotional reasons that might make it difficult for you to convict a fellow human being of a very serious crime?" Again, nobody answered. However, Kate noticed a middle-aged woman take a deep breath and nervously scratch her right ear. She looked on her list to see the name that corresponded with that person's seat and jotted "peremptory" next to her name. Jack knowingly smiled to himself as he witnessed the prospective juror's body language and Kate then responding with a scribbling.

Kate next asked, "Do any of you disagree with our drunk driving laws?" Nobody raised his or her hand.

"Or our homicide by vehicle laws involving drunk driving?" No hands went up.

"As long as I establish proof beyond a reasonable doubt, would anyone here have trouble upholding any of our criminal laws, even ones they might not personally agree with?" Still, no hands went up.

"Would any of you be tempted to acquit someone merely to avoid the unpleasant duty of convicting someone?" Not a hand went up.

As we see from the above, not all questions put forth in *voir dire* are advanced solely to expose biases. Smart lawyers also use *voir dire* to **educate the jury** on trial norms and rules beneficial to their side. Toward this end, Kate asked yet a couple of more questions.

"It is true that the state must prove guilt beyond a reasonable doubt. Yet, this does not mean that it must prove guilt beyond all doubt or to a mathematical certainty. Would any of you require me to prove the defendant's guilt not just beyond a reasonable doubt but beyond all doubt whatsoever?" Just as Kate had expected, nobody raised his or her hand. Still, Kate had taught the future jury members an important concept going in and simultaneously had received a public commitment of sorts from each one of them not to require her to produce an impossible level of proof.

Kate was ready for her last question: "It is also true that your job as a jury will be to only decide guilt or innocence and not to consider what possible sentence may or may not result should you produce a verdict of guilty. Would any of you be tempted to refuse to find someone guilty because of what sentence the judge might ultimately impose?" Again, no hands went up. However, Kate thought she had made the point she had been seeking. She was trying to **obtain a public commitment** and thus cutoff any such improper, speculative sentencing discussions during jury deliberations. Such discussions seem only to help defendants.

Kate sat down. Now it was Jack's turn to play *voir dire*. He had not played that game in quite a few years. He hoped he would not be rusty.

## Key Terms Found in This Chapter

Voir dire

Purpose of jury selection

Challenges for cause

Peremptory challenges

Obtain a public commitment

Exceptions to exercising peremptories

Allowed number of peremptories

Individual voir dire

Group voir dire

Educate the jury

Suspicious strike patterns

## Questions for Class Discussion

1. According to the chapter, what do the French words "voir" and "dire" mean? How do the literal translations of these words aptly describe what takes place during jury selection?

2. Why even allow lawyers to "pick a jury"? Why not just bring 12 random people into the room and let them serve? What are some specific examples of people who should be disqualified from serving on a jury?

3. What is a challenge for cause? How many of these are given to each side? Why is this the case?

4. When should a lawyer challenge a prospective juror for cause? Why not wait until questioning of everyone is completely over?

5. What is a peremptory challenge? How many of those do the lawyers get?

6. What are the two exceptions to the "anything goes" practice of exercising peremptory challenges? How can a judge go about making sure that inappropriate use of peremptory challenges is not taking place in the courtroom?

7. When do lawyers exercise their peremptory challenges? Why not just do it as they go along, as is the case with challenging prospective jurors for cause?

8. How does individual *voir dire* differ from group *voir dire*? What sort of cases call for individual rather than group *voir dire*?

9. What are some examples of Kate using *voir dire* to "educate the jury"? How might the defense lawyer "educate the jury" when it gets to be his turn?

10. How can attorneys use *voir dire* to obtain a public commitment from soon-to-be-picked jury members? What are some examples of this in the chapter?

# 24

## Jury Selection (Part II)

Defense Attorney Jack Day had not forsaken the practice of criminal law so long ago as to have forgotten the critical importance of *voir dire*. He knew that cases are sometimes won and lost at the stage that the jury is picked, even before the lawyers make their opening statements or the first witness testifies. Often, verdicts are determined more by who happens to land on the jury than by any other factor in a trial.

"Good morning," Jack began as he rose to his feet and flashed a friendly smile at his audience of prospective jurors. "I too wish to thank you for your service in coming here to the courthouse. I know that many of you are very busy people, and I thank you for your sacrifice. Like Ms. Page, I also get to ask you some questions. I agree completely with Ms. Page that both the state and the defense deserve to have a jury of fair and impartial members. Please just raise your hand if anything I am about to ask applies to you personally.

"Let me begin by asking all of you if any of you are or have in the past been members of Mothers Against Drunk Driving or Students Against Drunk Driving or any similar organization?" Nobody's hand went up.

"Have any of you been the victim of a drunk driver or had a family member hurt by a drunk driver?" An old man on one of the middle benches raised his hand. "Yes, Sir," Jack responded. "What happened?"

The old man stood and with lowered eyes told the room that his grown daughter had spent two weeks in a hospital last year after being involved in an accident caused by a drunk driver. "Thank you for your honesty, Sir," Jack responded in as deferential a tone as he could credibly muster. "I imagine that such an ordeal involving a loved one would cause you some difficulty in remaining neutral in a trial involving harm to people involved in an alleged DUI matter?"

"Yes, I think you are right," the citizen agreed.

Jack looked at the old man sympathetically before slowly turning to Judge Price and stating, "Your Honor, I feel that this good man should be excused for cause."

"Motion granted," Judge Price announced without even waiting for a possible objection from Kate. "Bailiff, please escort this gentleman back to the central jury waiting room."

Jack waited for the man to exit the room before he asked his next question. "Do any of you have any religious or philosophical issues with drinking alcohol?" At this point, Jane (the busy school principal who had earlier telephoned the court in the futile attempt to be excused from jury service entirely) came very close to raising her hand. She was a teetotaler all of her life ever since she saw her father drink himself to an early death. She even forbade her husband to ever bring alcohol into their home. "This may be my best chance to get out of serving on a jury," she realized. "I bet that if I am not picked today or tomorrow, I'll be done with it all and can go back to my life." Yet, she was not sure if Jack's question really applied to her. "I really don't have anything against other people taking a drink," she always told her family. "But for me and my family, we will always be abstainers." Jane was about to raise her hand to allow Jack to ask some inevitable follow-up questions when Jack had suddenly moved on to his next question. "Oops," Jane thought. "Too late now."

Unknown to Jane, Jack had noticed her shift in her chair twice after he had asked his last question. He wrote the word "peremptory" next to her name but followed it with two question marks.

For Jack's next question, he asked, "Are any of you employed in law enforcement or previously employed in law enforcement or related to someone employed in law enforcement?" Two hands shot up. One of the two told Jack that she was married to a local police officer. The other admitted that he was himself a retired police officer. Jack decided to ask follow-up questions before challenging either for cause, with the thinking that he could perhaps get them to **admit bias freely** and therefore not have to use some of his very precious peremptory challenges on them.

As to the woman who was married to a police officer, Jack asked, "Does your husband often discuss DUIs he encounters while at work?" After the woman responded in the affirmative, Jack then asked, "Would your being a sort of insider with regards to cases involving drunk driving cause you to have some difficulty not siding with the state in a case like the one we are dealing with today?" The woman responded that she definitely would lean toward backing the state in any criminal case, let alone one involving drunk driving somehow. Jack thanked the woman for her honesty and challenged her for cause. The judge granted that challenge.

As to the retired police officer, Jack tried to pull pretty much the same thing but this time had no luck. The sophisticated retired cop adamantly maintained that he could remain neutral in the present trial despite his having personally processed dozens if not hundreds of DUIs during his long career. "I can indeed be very fair and neutral," the cop insisted. "That is the law, and I devoted my life to upholding the law." When Jack challenged the ex-cop anyway for cause, the judge denied the motion. "The gentleman said he can be fair and neutral," the judge explained. "He stays." This time Kate was doing the smiling as she watched Jack scribble something. She knew he was no doubt writing a reminder to exercise a peremptory challenge against this potential juror.

Jack next asked the people if any one of them thought that he or she would have any trouble remaining cool and rational in a case involving two dead bodies. Nobody raised a hand, but Jack noticed a woman looking angrily at his client, young Rick Mahan. He knew that to challenge her for cause would probably be futile and perhaps give other people some bad ideas. Instead, he wrote a private reminder to later use one of his peremptory challenges against her.

Jack decided to finish his questions with his own attempt at "educating the jury." First, he explained to the jury the concept of "innocent until proven guilty" and asked the jury if any one of them would require him "to prove his client's innocence even though the state had the heavy burden all alone of proving guilt." Of course, no hands went up, but that was okay with Jack. Jack then told the jury about guilt beyond a reasonable doubt, "the highest standard of proof known in our courts of law," and asked them if they would be tempted to convict someone whom they thought was probably guilty even though they had a reasonable doubt. Again, no hands went up. With his educating done, Jack thanked those in attendance for their time and sat down.

Now that Jack had sat down, one of the bailiffs knew that it was her job to help the lawyers start to exercise their peremptory challenges. After first seeking and receiving an approving nod from the judge, the bailiff rose from her seat and first approached Kate sitting at the prosecutor's table. Kate watched as the bailiff handed her a sheet of paper with a listing of all of the prospective jurors. The listing was true to the seating chart used in the room. Kate took 30 seconds or so as she scanned the sheet of names, looking up at the faces of the prospective jurors to make sure she understood the geography of the seating correctly. Confident that she knew which face corresponded with each name, Kate drew a line through the name of the man in his mid-20s who had been convicted of public drunkenness by her office four years ago. Kate then wrote "C-1" next to the stricken name, which stood for **Commonwealth Peremptory #1**.

Now it was Defense Attorney Jack Day's turn to strike his first name. Jack knew that he, like Prosecutor Kate Page, would be given seven peremptory challenges given that this trial was a felony-level matter. Like Kate, Jack made sure he understood how the seating chart worked. He then took joy in using his very first peremptory challenge to strike the name of the retired cop who insisted that he could remain fair and neutral. "Goodbye, liar," Jack thought to himself, and he wrote "D-1" (for **Defense Peremptory #1**) next to the name he had just crossed off. Jack handed the sheet back to the waiting bailiff standing next to him.

The bailiff solemnly returned to the table of Kate and handed her the sheet. Kate looked to see whom Jack had chosen as his very first peremptory strike. "No surprise there," she told herself. "That guy would have been poison for the defense." Kate took a few seconds looking for the name of the middle-aged woman who had taken a deep breath and nervously scratched her ear when Kate asked the group about any potential philosophical or emotional problems anyone might have in convicting a fellow human being of a very serious crime. Having located what she thought was the correct name, she looked up at the audience to make sure the name on the list matched the face of the correct woman. Kate knew better than to look first directly at the woman since that would be too obvious. Instead, she scanned the entire room while being sure to notice exactly where the woman in question was sitting. "That's the right name," she told herself after scanning the room. She took no time to cross off the woman's name from the list and write "P-2" next to the scratched out name. Kate handed the list back to the waiting bailiff.

The bailiff, like a dinner servant waiting next to her English Lord's table, was making sure to mind her own business by averting her eyes during the striking of the names by each attorney. The bailiff extended her hand to receive the list only after Kate first reached out to her. List now back in her hand, the bailiff quietly walked back to Jack's table and handed him the sheet.

Jack smiled as he saw whom Kate had just scratched. He could not resist glancing at that woman in the audience. The woman noticed Jack's gaze and realized immediately that she would not be serving on this particular jury that day. The woman looked more relieved than offended.

Jack now used his pen to strike the name of the woman who never raised her hand but shot his client an angry look during questioning about remaining rational in a case involving two dead bodies. "D-2" Jack jotted next to his scratch.

Now it was Kate's turn again. Kate had already got rid of the two people she was sure she did not want on the jury. There was nobody else that it was obvious she should strike. Yet, she still had five peremptory challenges left and (like nearly all attorneys in such situations) did not want to waste challenges by **leaving peremptories on the table**.

This is the point where attorneys resort to personal **peremptory challenge prejudices** and superstitions in exercising their remaining challenges. Kate scanned the waiting group of prospective jurors looking for people who "looked" either like pro-prosecution or pro-defense types. For example, all other things being even, she preferred conservative dressers to casual ones. She preferred people who groomed themselves conventionally to those who went for styles that are more rebellious. She liked old people more than young people and people who looked rich to those who looked poor. She definitely did not like men with long hair or flamboyant dressers. These were her personal prejudices, and she was allowed to use such prejudices in striking jurors peremptorily.

Kate used her third peremptory challenge to get rid of a long-haired man with a beard sitting in the very back row. Now the list was back in Jack's court.

Jack still had one more peremptory challenge in mind before totally resorting to his personal prejudices. There was the name on the list of that woman who never raised her hand but who had shifted twice in her chair when Jack asked if anyone had any religious or philosophical issues with drinking alcohol. Jack looked on the list to match the name with the face of that woman. "Jane Morgan," Jack thought to himself. Jack was about to strike her name when he noticed that he had earlier jotted down two question marks after the word "peremptory." Seeing these two question marks caused Jack to scan the audience "casually" to subtly take one last look at the woman during the scan. Jack noticed the woman looking almost maternally at young Rick sitting next to him. Jack moved his pen away from her name and instead struck the name of a middle-aged man wearing a very expensive suit and silk tie. "I don't want too many Republicans on my jury," Jack thought, even though he himself was a registered Republican. Jack wrote "D-3" next to the crossed off name and handed the sheet back to the dutifully waiting bailiff.

The bailiff continued going back and forth between the two attorney tables, facilitating the standard **alternating method of striking**, until both lawyers had finished scratching off seven names apiece. Both Kate and Jack ultimately wound up striking enough names to use up all of their seven peremptory challenges apiece. Ironically, Kate almost used her last peremptory challenge to strike Jane Morgan's name from the list, just had Jack had nearly done. Kate thought she looked a bit too "social work" somehow. She did not like "bleeding heart" types on juries if she could help it. On the other hand, Jane looked highly intelligent, a trait that prosecutors often shoot for. Some defense lawyers prefer stupid people when they can get them to smart ones, under the theory that stupid people are more likely to get confused during a trial. Confusion often winds up eventually crystalizing into reasonable doubt. In any event, Kate allowed intelligent-looking Jane to stay. This is thus how the reluctant Jane, the school principal who had phoned the courthouse the week prior in a failed attempt to be excused from jury service entirely, wound up surviving the **striking pens** of both Prosecutor Kate Page and Defense Attorney Jack Day.

With the peremptory challenges all exercised, the bailiff approached Judge Robert Price and handed the sheet up to him as he sat high on his bench. The judge reviewed the sheet and was relieved to see that no obvious pattern of race-based or sex-based strikes seemed to exist. Since that was the case, he would have no problem with any of the peremptory challenges as exercised by the two attorneys. (Nor legally could he have any problem with them.)

"The following people have been selected to serve on the jury," Judge Price began. "As your name is called, please take a seat in the jury box on the right side of the courtroom." He pointed at the dark wooden jury box filled with plain wooden chairs. A mural of a young beardless Abe Lincoln arguing a case to a jury hung on the wall above the box.

"I will call 12 names, then a 13th," Judge Price continued. "This 13th juror will also sit in the jury box in the seat in the rear corner that is a different color than all of the other seats. You will serve as an alternate in case someone gets sick or otherwise cannot serve for the duration. If nobody gets sick or otherwise has to leave before the end of trial, you, the **alternate juror**, will be excused when the jury is ultimately dismissed to start its deliberations."

At this point, the judge read off 12 names plus the 13th. In doing so, he simply began with the first name on the list that had not been stricken (either peremptorily or for cause) and continued in order down through the unstricken names on the list, until the 13th juror had heard his name read. Bailiffs made sure that each person whose name was read took a seat in the jury box; they also made sure the person whose name was read last took a seat in the specially colored chair reserved for the alternate juror. All of the prospective jurors still in the room were then asked to return to the **prospective juror waiting room** for possible use in another trial. A bailiff assisted them by escorting them back to that area.

After all of the unchosen prospective jurors had left, Judge Price turned to the chosen ones and said, "Thank you for your willingness and ability to serve as fair and impartial jurors. I shall now administer to you the juror oath. All please rise and raise your right hand."

Kate and Jack watched as the jury members took the oath. Young Rick was more interested in watching the courtroom front door in hopes to see his parents. He was not disappointed. Mr. and Mrs. Mahan were among the very first of spectators now flowing into the courtroom and taking their seats.

Kate glanced over toward Jack. He smiled back. It was not the cold, professional smile of an adversary. It was the smile of a friend. It threw her for a loop. Yet, she liked it. It made her remember the awkward encounter she almost had with her boss in Jack's classroom during the unprofessional, passionate "conflict of interest" she and Jack engaged in there.

Now it was the turn of Judge Price to look at Kate. He did not smile. However, he did nod at her as if to say, "Let us begin."

"It is showtime," the assistant district attorney thought to herself as she rose to her feet. "Time for me to get this party started."

## Key Terms Found in This Chapter

Admit bias freely

Commonwealth Peremptory #1

Defense Peremptory #1

Leaving peremptories on the table

Peremptory challenge prejudices

Alternating method of striking

Alternate juror

Prospective juror waiting room

Striking pens

## Questions for Class Discussion

1. Do you agree that verdicts are often determined more by who happens to land on the jury than by any other factor in a trial? How can this be true?

2. If lawyers have peremptory challenges, why do they try hard to get prospective jurors to admit bias freely? How might you phrase your questions to maximize such an admission? Would your tone of voice play a role?

3. What were the two concepts that Jack used *voir dire* questioning for in order to do his own version of "educating the jury"?

4. If the defense had a lot of money, would it be worth hiring a jury consultant to sit and watch during *voir dire* and then help the lawyer decide whom to strike using peremptory challenges? If you were such a consultant, what sort of specific signs would you be looking for during questioning of prospective jurors?

5. When the prosecutor struck her first name on the list, what did she write down next to her strike? What did the defense lawyer write down after he had struck his first name?

6. Why do lawyers hate to "leave peremptory challenges on the table"? Would you bother using up all of your peremptory challenges if you ran out of nonprejudicial reasons to continue to strike names?

7. What were some of the personal prejudices that Prosecutor Kate Page exhibited in exercising her later peremptory challenges? What were some of the prejudices exhibited by Defense Attorney Jack Day? Do you share any of these prejudices when it comes to picking a jury?

8. Why do defense lawyers sometimes prefer stupid people to smart people to serve on juries? All other things equal, would you prefer stupid jurors if you were a defense lawyer? How might a lawyer guess as to someone's intelligence? Would you resort to potentially unfair guesses about intelligence if you were an attorney?

9. How does the "alternating method of striking" potential jurors work during the exercise of peremptory challenges? Why not just let the prosecutor make all of her strikes at once, followed by the defense making all of his?

10. Why is it necessary to select an "alternate juror"? How long do they sit and serve during a trial? Can you think of a situation where a judge might want to have more than just one alternate juror?

11. Would you rather serve as a mere alternate juror or spend your service time sitting days in the prospective juror room without ever serving on a jury at all?

12. How would you feel if you were rejected and sent back to wait in the prospective juror waiting room? Would you take the rejection personally? Would you be upset if you did nothing during your service but wait in such a room, only to go home after?

13. How many days should we ask those called up for jury service to serve without being picked before we let them go home?

# 25

# The State Makes Its Opening Statement

As Assistant District Attorney Kate Page rose to her feet in response to the trial judge's nod, she looked straight at young Rick sitting at the defense table. She was in the habit of doing this at the start of each of her jury trials to show the criminal defendant, and the jury, that she was there to bring the scoundrel to justice. This time, however, her staring look backfired. Rick suddenly looked young, very young to her (a "look" orchestrated and amplified in no small part by his defense attorney). The defendant's boyish appearance made Kate feel a little bit guilty. "Maybe Jack was right," she told herself in a brief moment of doubt. "Maybe this case should have stayed in juvenile court." Then Kate looked down at the notes on her legal pad in which she had outlined her prosecution case. The names of the two dead innocent people leaped off the page. Feeling righteous once again, Kate was now ready to make a genuine and robust opening statement to the jury.

Kate knew that just as picking the right jury during *voir dire* often goes a long way in determining the ultimate outcome of a trial, so too can the opening statement almost produce the same result. Members of her office had long ago taught Kate that some jurors permanently make up their minds as to guilt or innocence after hearing opening statements. For them, it is **essentially "game over"** from that point onward. Kate needed to be sure to get this right.

Kate positioned herself to stand front and center before the jury box.

She glanced up at the mural of young Abe Lincoln in front of her on the wall for inspiration. She imagined him being a prosecutor but was not quite sure if he ever even worked as such. Lowering her gaze, she now smiled and looked briefly into the eyes of several members of the jury. They all smiled back at the moment her eyes met theirs.

Kate felt nervous, but you could not tell that by the air of confidence and competence she was projecting. It was not an arrogant type of confidence but rather the type all of us hope for in those whose job it is to defend us from bad actors.

Kate subtly took a deep breath to relax. It helped. She now was ready to present her opening.

"Ladies and gentlemen of the jury, you have a solemn duty today to decide the guilt or innocence of a man named Richard Mahan. Richard may be a young man, but he is old enough to be capable of doing some great harms. Specifically, the commonwealth has charged this defendant with four crimes: two felony counts of homicide by vehicle while driving under the influence of alcohol and/or drugs, one misdemeanor count of reckless driving, and a misdemeanor count of underage drinking.

"I would love to start making some impassioned arguments to you right now as to the facts of this case and to the law. However, that is the purpose of closing arguments. Right now, I will be making a statement rather than an argument. The **opening statement's purpose** is to outline for you what the state's witnesses will be testifying about during the trial. I give you this **trial outline** because without seeing the beginning from the end, you could easily lose track of where the trial is heading. Trials are put together one witness at a time. A trial is a **piecemeal presentation**. I know that before I put together a big jigsaw puzzle, it helps me a lot to see first the completed picture on the box. I know that before I put together a piece of exercise equipment that came unassembled from the store, it helps me a lot to see a sketch in the instructions of what the final product will look like. This helps me from getting lost as I begin, piece by piece, to assemble a nice finished product.

"So it is with my opening statement. I will now quickly walk you through **witness-by-witness** and give you a sort of heads up as to what I expect each of them will tell you. That way, when they actually do take the stand to talk to you, you will know how they are each meant to fit in to the final picture. Of course, what I am about to tell you now is not evidence. The **sole source of evidence** is information delivered by the sworn witnesses. However, I will try to paint as accurate and helpful picture as I can to give you an advanced look at the presentation that lies ahead.

"Let me focus primarily on the two felony counts of homicide by vehicle while driving under the influence and how and through whom I intend to prove those two crimes. The same evidence that establishes guilt of those two crimes should simultaneously prove the lesser included offense of reckless driving. Underage drinking should also be established at the same time, especially since the defense attorney has **stipulated** or agreed to in advance of this trial that his client is under 21 years of age, which we all know is the legal age for drinking in our society.

"So, how shall I prove homicide by vehicle while driving under the influence? First, I must prove to your satisfaction that the defendant was operating a vehicle on a public road or byway. Next, I must prove that he was doing so while under the unsafe influence of alcohol or drugs or an unsafe combination of the two. Finally, I must prove that someone died because of the defendant's substance-induced, unsafe driving. Of course, I must prove that two people died since there are two counts of this offense. Let me now **link witnesses to evidence**, that is, connect a witness to each essential element of proof that I must present.

"The first witness the state will produce is Trooper Steven Blake of the Pennsylvania State Police. He is the officer who first arrived at the scene of a two-car accident, a little after it happened. One person involved in the accident is the defendant Richard Mahan who was found alone in his parents' car. He was hurt but conscious. The passengers in the other vehicle, a middle-aged husband and wife, were both ejected from their small Ford Focus and found dead at the scene. Trooper Blake will testify that Richard Mahan admitted to him that he had been falling asleep at the wheel and must have caused the crash. Richard Mahan smelled of alcohol. He was too hurt to do any field sobriety tests like 'heel to toe' but was instead transported to the hospital. Before being taken away in the ambulance, however, the defendant admitted to Trooper Blake that he had drunk some beer and taken some cold medicine at the party he had just left 15 minutes earlier. Trooper Blake will also confirm that the defendant had told him that he had read warnings on the cold medicine box that drowsiness can result and driving a vehicle must not be under-taken; also, that these pills should never be consumed along with alcohol since that combination only makes the drowsiness worse.

"The second witness I will call before you is Nancy Foley. Nancy will testify that on April 5th of this year, she was attending a drinking party at the home of one of her high school classmates. The parents who owned the house were out of town. Nancy will testify that the defendant, Rich-ard Mahan, was also at the party. Nancy knows Richard Mahan from high school where they are both seniors. Nancy will tell you a couple of important things. First, she will tell you that she saw the defendant drinking a bottle of beer as she spoke with him about 45 minutes or so after the party had started. The party started at about 9:00 p.m. While she was talking to the defendant who was drinking the beer, she noticed him starting to cough quite a bit. She offered him some medicine she had in her purse that she had been taking for a cold. There was nothing wrong with this medicine. It was over the counter and legal for anyone suffer-ing a cold to take. Nancy will tell you that Richard Mahan took two cold pills, and she in fact watched him swallow them with a gulp of beer. Very importantly, Nancy will tell you that before taking the pills, the defen-dant Richard Mahan took the time to read carefully the back of the box. The box—and I will produce this box during the trial—has clear and bold warnings that say under no circumstances should a person drive a car after taking this medicine since the medicine causes drowsiness. The box also states that alcohol taken with these pills makes the drowsiness even worse and should not be consumed with the pills. Nancy will tell you that Richard Mahan took the pills after reading the box and while drinking his beer.

"The state's next witness will be Dr. Roger Knight. Dr. Knight runs the pathology lab at the hospital to which the defendant was transported for treatment. Dr. Knight will tell you that his lab analyzed blood drawn from the defendant at the hospital. In the blood, they found evidence of Benadryl—that would be the cold medicine—and alcohol. Dr. Knight will also testify that the blood alcohol content of the defendant's blood came out to 0.04 percent. Dr. Knight will testify that it would require the defendant to have consumed no less than two beers to register a result that high, not just one beer as the defendant claimed when he answered the trooper's questions at the fatal crash scene.

"The state's next witness will be the county coroner who will testify as to the cause of death of the two dead victims at the scene. In short, the crash is what killed them, not two heart attacks out of the blue.

"Finally, the state will call Dr. Wanda Grant to the stand. Dr. Grant is a PhD biochemist who works at the State Crime Lab in Harrisburg and is an expert regarding the interaction of alcohol and drugs like Benadryl. Dr. Grant will express to you her expert opinion that feeling extremely sleepy was a highly likely outcome if someone were to take two Benadryl pills while also drinking two beers.

"After you hear from all of these witnesses, it is my contention the state will have proven all four of the counts as charged beyond a reasonable doubt. I will be asking you to return verdicts of guilty on all of them. Thank you for your service on this jury."

$\sim$

## Key Terms Found in This Chapter

| | |
|---|---|
| Essentially game over | Witness-by-witness |
| Opening statement's purpose | Sole source of evidence |
| Trial outline | Stipulated |
| Piecemeal presentation | Link witnesses to evidence |

## Questions for Class Discussion

1. How can a trial be "essentially game over" merely at the end of the opening statements and before the first witness is even called? What is said during them that is so important?
2. The state gets to go first in giving opening statements. Is there any way around this? Does going first give the state something of an unfair advantage? How can having the first word in a matter give someone an edge?
3. What exactly is the main purpose of the opening statement? Why is it called a "statement" rather than an "argument"? How would you expect the tones of voices to differ during opening "statements" as opposed to closing "arguments"?

4. How can trials become and stay very confusing to jurors without opening statements?
5. In what way is the opening statement something of a "trial outline"?
6. Are statements made during an opening statement considered evidence? What is the sole source of evidence during trials? Would you guess the closing arguments to be evidence or nonevidence?
7. What is meant by a "stipulation"? Why would an attorney ever agree to stipulate to anything during a trial? What sort of things can you think of that could be handled by way of stipulation?
8. What is meant by "linking a witness" (or witnesses) to each essential element of proof? How does doing so in advance help a prosecutor to draft the opening statement? How does preparing the opening statement help the prosecutor organize the entire trial?
9. How important is it for a lawyer making an opening statement to seem likable to a jury? What other positive traits should an attorney try to project during the opening statement? What negative traits should the attorney attempt to avoid projecting?
10. Does it matter how the defense attorney and defendant are appearing while the prosecutor is giving her opening statement? How should the defense lawyer appear while his adversary is presenting her opening? Should the defense lawyer coach his client to project a certain attitude while sitting and listening?
11. How likely is it for members of the jury actually to look at the defendant during certain moments of the prosecutor opening statement? What are some of these likely moments?
12. Where should Rick's parents be seated during the opening statements (and the trial)? Should they be coached to act in a certain way right from the start?

# 26

## Defense Opening Statement

Most laypeople do not know it, but defense attorneys have a choice when it comes to the timing of their opening statement. A defense attorney can deliver his or her opening statement immediately following the opening statement of the prosecutor. On the other hand, the defense attorney can wait until midpoint in the trial and make the statement after the prosecutor rests and just before the defense starts presenting its own case and witnesses.

Defense Attorney Jack Day knew that there were advantages to doing an **opening at trial midpoint**. If he were to do that, he would be able to see how the state's case actually evolved during the battle and adjust his war strategy—and opening remarks—accordingly. He also could adjust a plan as to whether or not call a particular witness for the defense, most particularly his own client. Nothing can turn around a case going well for the defense faster than a lawyer putting his own client on the stand who goes on to ruin everything.

Despite the benefits of waiting, criminal defense lawyers generally choose to make their opening statements sooner rather than later. This is so because of their idea that they need to get their **rhetorical punches in early**, before the jury already makes up its mind. Waiting until midway through the trial to start suggesting a different side to the story is a dangerous game to play.

Jack decided to play it safe and make his opening statement right away.

As soon as ADA Kate took her seat, Jack was out of his. As he approached the same spot on the courtroom floor from which Kate had addressed the jury, a dark thought suddenly crossed Jack's mind. "What if I were to start having a panic attack, right now?" Jack asked himself. "What would I do?" The thought of possibly having a panic attack started making Jack actually have one. Jack could feel his heart starting to race out of control. His breathing had become rapid and shallow. He knew that if he began to speak, his voice would be quivering. Jack seriously thought he might even faint.

Jack tried to buy some time by returning to his table to pick up a piece of paper that he was pretending he had forgotten. As he next walked slowly back to the jury box, Jack realized that this brief delay had just made matters worse. Now, the rustling paper in his hands was only helping to put on full display the degree to which his hands were uncontrollably shaking. After pretending to take note of its contents, Jack folded the paper up and slipped it into one of his slack's front pockets.

ADA Kate Page was watching this spectacle with a mixture of fascination and horror. She wanted to win her case but not this way. Kate liked Jack as a person. Maybe she even felt some emerging deep affection for him. Kate could only imagine the humiliating trauma that Jack was about to endure, the pains of which might last his lifetime. As a prosecutor who liked finality to her victories, Kate also was concerned with a potential claim of **ineffective assistance of counsel** that could result in a new trial even if she got a conviction. "What would be the point of winning if I have to do this all over again with some other defense attorney?" she reasoned.

Kate looked up at the judge who was sitting there oblivious to what was going on. The jury too seemed to have not yet caught on. "How can they not see this?" Kate wondered in awe. Of course, Kate had the advantage of having watched Jack break down once before in his school.

Kate did not know what to do to help Jack out of his crisis. In desperation, she decided to create a crisis of her own in order to create a diversion. Kate intentionally knocked over the metal pitcher full of water on her table. The pitcher's contents immediately flooded the table, and Kate jumped to her feet. "A little help here, please," she shouted to Jack, who happened to be the closest person to her table. Jack rushed over, grabbed some tissues from a box on the table, and began to sponge up the mess. While Jack was doing this, Kate made a joke to the jury that got them all laughing. As Jack was just about finished cleaning up the mess, Kate whispered some advice in his ear. "Jack, your breaths are too quick and shallow. Your body thinks you are suffocating and is causing you to panic. I promise you that you can trick your body out of the panic by now taking three long, deep breaths and slowly exhaling. It will work, I promise."

"What if it does not work?" Jack asked.

"Then, just tell the jury you changed your mind and will be reserving your opening statement until the prosecution rests its case."

Jack subtly did what Kate had suggested. He took three deep breaths and slowly exhaled. He did this as he slowly finished at the table and repositioned himself before the jury. Kate's breathing trick was working! Jack felt nervous but no longer panicky. He could do this!

Like Kate had done before him, Jack nodded to the jury and smiled. "Good morning!" his voice boomed. "There are always two sides to a story. Let me tell you what the defense plans to show once we have the chance to start calling our own witnesses later in the trial. However, as a matter of housekeeping, let me begin by asking you a favor. Please do not make up your minds about this case until you hear completely from both sides. Will you be willing to do that for my client?" Jack took turns looking at the faces of the jury members who all nodded their willingness to withhold judgment until the end.

Jack had one more matter of educating the jury he wished to attend to before going any further. Jack wanted to preach the importance of proof beyond a reasonable doubt. Sure, he could do this during closing arguments, and the judge would no doubt do this during his instructions to the jury at the trial's end. However, this concept is so critical that many defense attorneys wish to saturate the trial as much as they can with the principle. The burden on the state to prove guilt beyond a reasonable doubt is the **criminal defendant's best friend.**

"Ladies and gentlemen of the jury, one more very important item I wish to bring up at the start of my opening is the duty we all have in America to never convict someone unless we have no reasonable doubt whatsoever as to guilt. The state has to prove every element of every count against my client beyond a reasonable doubt. Beyond a reasonable doubt is higher than the standard used in civil trials. It is the highest standard of proof in our legal system and for good reason. Please do not assume that where there is smoke, there must be fire. I know there is smoke in this case. Every single criminal trial has smoke. As you are hearing all of the evidence from the various witnesses today, please remember this: mere probability is not enough, not even close. It is not even remotely close."

Jack was now ready to introduce his theory of the defense by giving a brief preview of what each defense witness would contribute. Every defense attorney should establish a **theory of the defense** during a client's criminal trial. The defense needs to give the jury a theme that the jury can use to help acquit someone whom they wish to acquit. The defense needs to come up with some plan and stick to it. In some cases, the theory can be based on consent. In other cases, that they got the wrong person (e.g., an alibi exists, or there is foggy eyewitness memory). In still others, the theory might be one of self-defense or even insanity. It is true that the prosecution has the full burden of proof, and the defense does not have to suggest a possible alternative. However, having a theory of the defense, hopefully with some decent facts to back it up, can sure grease the skids toward a finding of reasonable doubt.

Jack knew that he could not seriously cast much doubt on certain undeniable truths. His client had drunk more than one beer (the BAC would prove that). His client took some Benadryl cold medicine pills (a witness plus his own client's admission would prove that). The box the pills came in had warnings not to drive a vehicle or drink alcohol, and even if Rick had never actually read those warnings, he was still legally responsible as if he had read them. Jack knew the state could also prove that Rick fell asleep while driving a car that led to a crash that killed two people. Jack decided he would not insult the jury's intelligence by coming up with a defense theory that would deny any of those facts. Instead, Jack decided to go with "causation." For homicides by vehicle while DUI, the state would not only have to prove that Rick fell asleep causing the fatal crash, but that his falling asleep was caused by his intoxication. Maybe Rick just dozed off as he had done while driving before when he had not even taken any intoxicants. With his theory of the defense in mind, Jack was ready to present his opening statement to the jurors.

"Members of the jury, let me keep this simple. The defense plans to call four witnesses to the stand. They will paint a picture that will be quite different from that painted by the prosecution.

"My first witness will be my own client, Richard Mahan. He will tell you that he did drink beer, just two of them, and did take two legal cold pills for his cold. He did not guzzle beer, nor stuff his face with pills. When he left to drive home from the gathering to his parents' house — Rick is still in high school — he felt fine and completely sober and in control. He had no reason to doubt his abilities to drive since he only had two beers. He had read about the correct dosages on the box but had not read the warnings about drowsiness on the box. Rick will admit to you that he felt sleepy some time into his drive and must have crashed his car before he could find a place to pull safely over. However, this was not the first time he fell asleep at the wheel. Just two or three months earlier, Rick also fell asleep at the wheel without having taken any alcohol or cold pills. Rick will testify to this. So will another witness, defense witness number two.

"Defense witness number two goes by the name of George Franklin. George is a friend of my client. George will tell you that he was a passenger in Rick Mahan's car a couple of months before and at about the same time of night as the incident that Rick was involved in that resulted in the fatal car crash. During this earlier episode, Rick completely fell asleep at the wheel and drove off the road into a field before coming to a stop. George will testify to you that he and Rick had been together for several hours and neither he nor Rick had consumed any alcohol or drugs whatsoever. There was no beer, and there were no cold pills. Rick just fell asleep while driving, just as many of us do or nearly do at some time or another in our lives. Rick drove his car into the field, woke up, and then pulled back on to the highway."

Attorney Jack Day had two more witnesses he wanted to mention to the jury. These would be character witnesses. **Character witnesses** can be very important in a criminal trial. They vouch for the bona fides and relevant, positive attributes that a defendant possesses. Jack knew that juries love to convict people they hate and hate to convict people they love. Part of Jack's defense would be to get the jury to like young Rick Mahan and feel compassion for him. If he could accomplish that, the jury would be much more likely to "buy" his theory of the defense. If they hated Rick, they would be aching to convict him instead. Jack knew that Rick was a very likable and responsible young man. He was not your typical criminal. Jack could make the jury see Rick as one of them, or even better, not too different from one of their own kids. This was one of the reasons Jack decided to call the defendant himself to the stand despite it being risky business. Jack knew that Rick did not have to pretend to be a nice guy on the stand. He was a nice guy. The jury would sense that. Rick did not have to pretend to be a responsible person who follows rules; he was a kid who followed the rules. Jack was hoping the jury would see this and be reluctant to convict him.

Jack was now ready to tell the jury about those two remaining witnesses. Jack suddenly smiled to himself when he realized that not only was he no longer in panic mode but he was also not even particularly nervous anymore. He really owed Kate a lot for her sense of fair play and goodness.

"In addition to my client and his youthful friend," Jack announced, "the defense will have a third and a fourth witness." Jack was now making sure to look into the eyes of every juror at least once as he was summing up his opening. "They will both be full-blown adult character witnesses who deeply know my young client and can fill you in about what type of person he is. I want you to get to know my client. People who drive while intoxicated are not normally models of responsibility and integrity. However, Father Joseph Skelly, who is Rick's high school principal, and Mrs. Amy Johnson, who is Rick's Honors English teacher, will both give you insights into Rick's highly responsible nature and unquestionable integrity."

With that, Jack gently bowed his head to acknowledge he had finished. As he walked back to the defense table, he suddenly stopped halfway and spun around to face the jury once again. "Please remember to not prejudge this case and require guilt beyond a reasonable doubt," he called out. "I'll shut up now."

Jack's little post-script amused Judge Price who could not help to let go a mild chuckle. Judge Price thanked both attorneys for their opening statements. Looking directly at ADA Kate Page, he was about to tell her to call her first witness. However, Judge Price noticed that it was already 11:00, and he needed an early and extended lunch break to attend the funeral of a retired county commissioner. "Ladies and gentlemen of the jury, it is nearly the normal lunch hour. I have a funeral to attend that starts in a half hour. Let us take our lunch break now. It will be a solid break since I will not be reconvening court until 2:00 p.m. So, please reassemble yourselves in this courtroom at that time, 2:00 p.m. While you are on break, you must not discuss this case with anybody, including family, friends, fellow jury members, or anyone else. To do so will result in a **mistrial**, which means we will have to pick a new jury all over again and start this trial from scratch, most likely on some other day. We would have to reassemble the attorneys all over again. We would have to reassemble the witnesses all over again. Whoever would cause such aggravation would be guilty of contempt of court and face some jail time. I especially caution you to avoid all contact whatsoever with the attorneys conducting this trial and with the potential witnesses. Stay clear of all of them. In the meantime, have a good lunch, run some personal errands, and be back here just before 2:00 p.m. I will see you all then."

"All rise," commanded a bailiff. "This court is in recess until 2:00 p.m."

The jury watched as the judge walked through his side door. Then they slowly started to file out themselves. Rick and his parents asked Jack if it would be okay if they left for home for an extended lunch. "No problem," replied Jack. "See you at 2:00."

Jack tried to say "so long" to prosecutor Page. However, she was already on her phone jabbering with someone. The conversation seemed very intense and animated. Jack decided just to take his leave. Looking over his shoulder as he walked toward the exit door, Jack noticed that Kate was now screaming at whomever she was on the phone with. "Geeze," thought Jack. "Kind Kate can have a real edge to her. It looks like I may yet be facing someone all pumped up and in the mood for combat today."

## Key Terms Found in This Chapter

| | |
|---|---|
| Opening at trial midpoint | Theory of the defense |
| Rhetorical punches in early | Character witnesses |
| Ineffective assistance of counsel | Mistrial |
| Criminal defendant's best friend | |

# Questions for Class Discussion

1. What are the advantages to a defense attorney of reserving his or her opening statement until the trial's midpoint? Given these advantages, why do most defense attorneys in most trials choose not to wait?

2. In what way is the defense opening statement similar to the opening statement of a prosecutor?

3. How did Jack use part of his opening statement to preach values to and thus "educate" the jury? Cannot the attorney just ask the judge to take care of this during standard jury instructions at the trial's end?

4. What legal result was Kate worried about if she won her case after Jack had gone through a public panic attack? Can you think of any other behavioral states a lawyer might be in during a trial that would clearly render the attorney "ineffective"?

5. Appeal concerns aside, do you admire or disrespect Kate for helping her adversary out during a crisis? Did she have a moral duty to help him? A legal duty?

6. According to the chapter, who or what is the "criminal defendant's best friend"? Why is this so? Is it fair to say that the same is also the prosecutor's worst enemy?

7. What is a "theory of the defense"? Why is it so important to have one? What might be a common "theory" used in a rape case? A domestic assault case? A shoplifting case?

8. What was Jack hoping to do by promising character witnesses? Why did he pick these two?

9. Why did the judge so sternly warn the recessing jurors not to talk to each other about the case during the lunch break? What would happen if a juror were discovered to have disobeyed the judge's warnings?

10. What would be an appropriate amount of punishment for a juror who speaks to one of the lawyers or witnesses during a break and causes a mistrial early in the trial? Late in the trial?

11. What would you, as a juror, do if one of the lawyers or witnesses started a conversation with you in a restaurant during lunch break? Would it depend on what they wanted to discuss? Would you bother telling the judge about an innocent encounter even if "no harm was done"?

# Unit 10
# The State Lands Its Blows

This unit begins with a light chapter, which teaches about the unexpected bonds of loyalty that can develop between opposing lawyers just trying to do their jobs. We then swiftly turn to three critical chapters, which detail how a prosecutor goes about the heavy lifting of actually proving a state's case to a jury.

# 27

## Recess Misadventure

Jack spent the first hour of the extended three-hour lunch break from court eating a packed lunch while he sat on a bench in a nearby park. He had no appetite but forced himself to eat anyway. The last thing he needed now was to get a hunger headache. The air was cool, but Jack liked it that way. He knew it was harder to become nauseated when one is too cool rather than too warm.

Finishing his sandwich, cookies, apple, and Dr Pepper, Jack decided to kill some time by taking a walk around downtown. He planned to walk in a wide circle down city sidewalks, hoping to get back to the court-house parking garage in plenty of time to sit in his car and just breathe peacefully while meditating. Maybe he might even listen to some soft music on the radio. Jack's main concern was remaining calm and relaxed and to avoid worrying about getting anxious.

Jack's long walk was nearly over when he suddenly realized he was getting thirsty. The morning chill was rapidly evaporating, and the day was warming up fast. Jack stepped into a tavern to purchase a soft drink. As Jack took a seat at the bar, he could not help noticing a very well-dressed woman, head down on the bar, who obviously had too much to drink. "Drunk in the middle of a work day—that woman's a real class act," thought Jack.

Jack ordered a ginger ale and started to snack on some free pretzels. He stared at himself in the mirror behind the bar. He was not used to seeing himself wear a suit and tie anymore. He thought he looked like his father, which actually was not a bad thing. Jack looked down at his hands on the bar and studied them in deep thought.

"Buy me a drink, sailor?" asked a soft voice. Jack winced to himself as he suddenly realized that the well-dressed drunk must have moved over to where he was sitting.

"Well, okay, I guess," Jack responded as he very reluctantly spun his body around to face the pest. To Jack's utter shock, the drunk was none other than Assistant District Attorney Kate Page!

"Oh, Kate, it's you! I can't believe it!" Jack exclaimed. "You are…"

"Drunk!" Kate responded in a voice so loud that everyone in the bar took notice. Kate burst out into laughter. Jack's eyes grew wide open, and he pulled his head back a little bit.

The bartender was not amused. "You know this lady?" she asked Jack. "You need to take her home. She is over her limit."

"I'd like that very, very much," Kate suggested, using a flirty voice while batting her eyes. "Do you want to take me home, Jack?" Jack's surprised face made Kate laugh some more, this time even harder.

"Come on, Kate. Let's go," Jack commanded. Jack took Kate by the arm and escorted her out into the sunshine. "Where are we going?" Kate asked, now with a voice that sounded much more annoyed than flirtatious.

"To my car. I parked in the courthouse garage two blocks from here. You need to sit there, and we need somehow to get you sobered up fast. Let's get some food inside you. Did you eat anything at the bar?"

"Nope," Kate admitted. "In my defense, counselor, you were hogging all the free pretzels."

Jack gazed around until he noticed a street vendor in front of the garage. He bought Kate a soft pretzel, some chips, and a banana. Arriving at Jack's car, Jack helped Kate get into the passenger seat. "Wait a second," Kate requested as Jack was about to close her door. Jack froze as Kate poked her head outside the door and vomited inches from Jack's shoes.

"I guess that's good," Jack said in reaction as he handed her one of the many napkins he had taken from the street vendor's dispenser. Kate pulled her head back into the car and started wiping her mouth as Jack shut the door.

"How many drinks did you have?" Jack inquired.

"Four shots of vodka," Kate answered. "I am pretty sure it was four. I know it was vodka."

"Well, it is now 12:20 and **court resumes** post-recess in an hour and 40 minutes. Let's see if we can get you functional by then."

"You are such a prude, Jack Day. I am not going to drive a car. Calm down."

"Well, I am defending someone accused of driving a car while drunk and killing two people. Imagine the reaction of the judge and jury in such a trial when the prosecutor returns from lunch drunk herself."

"I see your point," Kate said. With that, Jack started slowly to feed Kate the food he had just bought her. He wished he had some coffee to give her but had none. He did have some Dr Pepper that she sipped on from time to time, at first spilling quite a bit of it on his dashboard.

After an hour of eating, brief napping, eating some more, and sitting, Jack thought he saw signs of rationality starting to return. "Kate, what is the matter with you? You cannot be getting drunk during a court recess. The DA will fire you for sure if they catch you. You might even receive **professional discipline**: letter of reprimand, censor made known to the legal community, license suspension, or maybe even full-blown disbarment."

Kate stared at Jack intensely for a little while. She looked beautiful to Jack, even drunk. Then she spoke. "Do you remember seeing me screaming on the phone at someone as you left the courtroom?"

"Yeah, what was that all about?"

"That was my boyfriend."

"You have a boyfriend! What about our fling in my classroom?"

"That was an accident, Jack. Nothing more. Okay, maybe something a little bit more, but I quickly came to my senses. Having my boss show up and almost catch us certainly didn't hurt with me coming to my senses."

Jack felt a little bit hurt that Kate could kiss a guy like him so passionately even though she had a boyfriend. He decided to avoid bringing up his feelings on that matter just right then.

"Okay, so why were you yelling on the phone?" Jack waited patiently for her response, which was less than immediate.

"Well," Kate finally began as she turned her head to look out the passenger window. "My so-called boyfriend just told me that he could not meet for lunch. It is his wife's birthday, and he has to take her out."

"You are dating a guy who is married to a wife he still likes to take out on a date?"

Kate shook her head in frustration. "That's just it, Jack. I did not know he was married. He chose that time to tell me on the phone. Just out of the blue, he explains in a matter-of-fact tone of voice that he cannot keep our lunch date as planned since, after all, it is his wife's birthday. He did not want to hurt his wife's feelings on her big day. I was so upset that I went out and started drinking. I guess that was far from being the smartest way to cope with the news. Now I not only lost my so-called boyfriend but maybe my career as well."

Jack announced it was time for them to go for a walk. Kate liked that idea. Jack got out of the car, and Kate pulled herself out of the car as well. They walked out of the garage and onto the sidewalk. Jack made sure they headed away from the nearby courthouse. As they began their walk, Jack noticed in horror as Judge Price was fast approaching them on the sidewalk from the opposite direction. Jack knew that there is nothing wrong with **opposing counsel** talking with one another during a court recess. Yet, that was not what had him worried. Kate's professional future was hanging delicately by a thread.

"Good afternoon, Your Honor," Jack said as they all got within close proximity to one another. The judge nodded a greeting to both of them without saying a word. He just seemed to want to keep walking without getting into a conversation of any sorts. That suited Jack just fine. Then Kate blew it.

"Hi there, Judge!" Kate whispered in a voice so quiet that neither Judge Price nor Jack had any idea of what she had just said. Judge Price stopped suddenly in his tracks. He fiddled with his hearing aid, thinking it was not working correctly. "Pardon?" he asked Kate. "This stupid hearing aid must be on the blink again."

"Hello Judge!" Kate now shouted so loud as to cause Jack to turn red with embarrassment. Once again, Judge Price adjusted his hearing aid, this time trying to turn down its amplification. After getting the setting to where he thought might be the right place, the judge again turned to Kate and smiled.

"Hello, Ms. Page," he said. "You and Mr. Day are both fine attorneys. I look forward to observing a great contest. See you both soon back in court."

Kate was about to say something again, but Jack shoved her forward before she could utter her thoughts. Judge Price was just glad to be able to continue on his way again and took little notice.

Jack and Kate spent the next 15 minutes or so walking a wide circle on the sidewalks surrounding the expansive courthouse. Kate and he walked in silence as Jack held her by the arm. To strangers they must have looked like a romantic couple. That caused both Jack and Kate to worry a little about what colleagues might think if they were spotted. As they neared the front doors of the courthouse, Jack asked Kate how she was feeling.

"Almost sober," Kate prognosticated. "I think I am back on line, sort of."

"Well, here is some advice," Jack counseled. "I will bring you up to the courtroom, and you will sit down immediately at your table. I will go to my table. When the judge comes in, he will tell you to call your first witness. You will call Trooper Steven Blake to the stand."

"No kidding!" Kate snapped. "I know how to **run a case**."

"Okay, okay," Jack acknowledged. "Just stay sitting. No need to stand, ever, while you ask your questions."

"I have to go," Kate announced.

"Yeah, it's time. Let's go up to the courtroom."

"No, I mean I have to go to the restroom."

Jack escorted Kate to the restroom and waited outside for her to return. Five minutes went by, and he was about to go in. Kate emerged, no longer looking disheveled but rather professional. Jack was relieved for that. It was one thing for him to dress and groom his criminal clients for court. He did not want to have to do the same thing for his adversary.

"Shall we go, Ms. Page?" he asked. Without answering, Kate quickly marched over to the elevator and pushed the button. Jack scurried after her.

"Um you pushed the 'going down' button," Jack gently pointed out.

"Oh, right," Kate acknowledged as she now pushed the button to "go up."

"Remember, Kate, if you get a little stuck, just keep asking the trooper to tell the court 'what happened next.' That **boilerplate prosecution prompt** is all that a **professional witness** like a seasoned cop will need to be repeatedly asked in order to get your team ball into the end zone."

"Got it." Kate said. "With all the rules about leading a witness during direct examination, that's about all I ever ask a cop on direct any-way—even when I am feeling normal."

With that, the elevator's doors opened, and Kate and Jack walked in. Kate pretended to stumble and fall against the wall. As Jack reached out to help her to regain her balance, she suddenly sprang upright and admitted to Jack that she had been "just kidding."

"Not funny, Kate," Jack replied as he rolled his eyes and slightly shook his head from side to side. "You can be worse than my students. Speaking of which, it is time for me to get in there and defend one."

∾

## Key Terms Found in This Chapter

Court resumes

Professional discipline

Opposing counsel

Run a case

Boilerplate prosecution prompt

Professional witness

## Questions for Class Discussion

1. How do you think you would spend your time during a lengthy recess if you were a defense attorney doing a jury trial? What works for you?

2. Would you probably have an appetite during the lunch break of a jury trial if you were an attorney? Would eating make you feel better or worse?

3. Did Jack have a moral duty to help Kate out when he discovered her drunk in the bar during recess? Did he have a legal duty? Was helping her out a betrayal of his client?

4. If you were in charge of disciplining attorneys for professional misconduct, which penalty (if any) would you give Kate for getting drunk during a trial recess: private letter of reprimand, public censor (made known to all members of the bar), temporary suspension of her law license, or full disbarment?

5. If the disciplinary authorities found out that Jack had tried to help Kate cover up her lunchtime indiscretion, should he also be subjected to professional discipline? If so, to what degree?

6. What do attorneys mean when they say they "run a case"? How could Jack, a defense attorney, know how to tell a prosecutor like Kate how to run a state's case?

7. Did Jack betray his client when he told Kate what question to ask her police witness repeatedly if she got into a jam? How would Rick and his parents feel if they knew Jack had done this?

8. What does Kate helping Jack out during his crisis followed by Jack helping Kate out during her crisis say about the power of the court-room work group? Could you imagine yourself developing such loyalty?

9. How is a cop a "professional witness"? What is meant when the chapter suggests that this cop would know how to get the ball into the end zone with some minimal promptings?

# 28

## The State's Case (Part I)

Defense Attorney Jack Day followed Assistant District Attorney Kate Page from the elevator to the courtroom, where the trial was being conducted. As they entered the room, Jack noticed that the jury was already in their seats. Judge Price had not yet made his entrance. Everyone and everything was so quiet!

Jack thought that Kate looked good, meaning very professional as opposed to looking drunk. Except for her slightly bloodshot eyes, there were few visible hints that she had been drinking during the break. Jack did not know it, but all of his efforts in helping Kate during lunch to avoid a professional fiasco actually distracted Jack in a way that minimized his own anxieties about having to do a jury trial. Karma happily works that way, sometimes.

As Jack followed Kate down the center aisle toward the interior wooden fence that separated the lawyers section of the room from that of the spectators, Jack allowed Kate to first cross the bar (fence) by passing through the gate (thus gaining **admission to the bar**). Big mistake. Kate was still tipsy enough to have trouble swinging the gate open properly. Jack announced in a voice loud enough for all on the jury to hear, "Yeah, that gate has been sticking a lot lately. Here, let me try." With that, Kate stepped aside and watched as Jack swung the gate open correctly. Both lawyers passed through and took their seats at their respective tables.

Now that the jury and the lawyers were all assembled, one of the bailiffs approached the side door leading directly into Judge Price's chambers. The bailiff knocked three times on the heavy wooden door and then took his seat on the side of the courtroom opposite that of the jury box.

Thirty seconds or so passed until Judge Price, in full **judicial regalia** (clothing reminiscent of medieval clerical robes) passed through the door and emerged into the courtroom.

"All rise," went out the command. All rose. Judge Price took his seat on the bench, and everyone else sat down as well.

Judge Price ignored the lawyers and smiled at the jury. "I hope you had a nice, long break. Let us begin." Turning to prosecutor Kate, the judge said, "Please call your first witness, Ms. Page."

Kate hit her knee hard on the table as she rose to her feet. She tried to hide the pain as she said, "The Commonwealth calls Trooper Steven Blake to the stand." Per custom, as the main investigating officer in the case, Trooper Blake was already now sitting at the prosecution table, right next to Kate. She could consult with him from time to time during the trial as need be.

Trooper Blake rose from the prosecution table to walk to the witness chair. He was dressed in his recently pressed state trooper uniform. Blake had the option of wearing a civilian suit and tie instead. As noted before, there are differences of opinion as to which outfit is better for a police officer to wear to court. The uniform can give an air of authority, but the civilian clothes can project a handy aura of neutrality. Trooper Blake elected to wear his uniform this day. He was proud to be a trooper and thought his uniform made him look more competent.

The police witness is perhaps the most common witness to appear in criminal hearings and trials. Victim witnesses are less common because many crimes are victimless (drug possession, most DUIs, etc.). Defendants often do not testify because their lawyer knows they would be lying or would otherwise make a dangerous witness. Eyewitnesses are great, but criminals usually make it a point to do their misdeeds in private. Yet nearly every case involves an investigating officer of some kind. Officers are routinely called upon to identify physical evidence found at crime scenes, relay the details of a defendant's incriminating statements, testify as to what they saw and heard at a scene, identify a suspect they saw fleeing, debunk an alibi defense, establish the chain of custody of physical evidence, etc.

In fact, police officers testify so frequently in court that they must consider it as a central duty of their jobs. In a sense, the police witness (as mentioned earlier) is a **professional witness**. As such, they should know better than ever to come to court unprepared. They need to read all of the police reports and refresh their memory of the details of the case just before the trial starts. Otherwise, a defense attorney could use his or her skills to make forgetfulness seem like incompetence (which it is). The lawyer can find success in putting words in the officer's mouth or catch them making statements that contradict what they may have written in their reports. Who can trust an incompetent or unsure cop?

Unlike some rookies, Trooper Steve Blake was prepared today for court. This preparation would help him to appear more relaxed and more confident. In a word, it would help him to look very truthful.

After Trooper Blake was sworn in, he sat down and waited for Kate to get the ball rolling.

"Please state your name and occupation," Kate requested. Trooper Blake gave his name, occupation, rank, and number of years on the job. He knew Kate would be asking for such information next anyway.

"Trooper Blake, I wish to draw your attention to the evening of Wednesday, April 5 of this year at about 10:00 p.m. Did anything unusual happen at that time?" Trooper Blake ran with this invitation to launch into a long narrative. He began by explaining how he was on routine patrol on the Whitehorse Pike, State Highway 41, in the northwestern portion of the county, when he came upon a two-vehicle accident. He spoke of how he first approached the smaller vehicle, a Ford Focus, and found two dead people (no pulse or respiration) on the ground nearby who he determined to have been ejected from their car. He then quickly checked on the jeep and observed Richard Mahan still behind the wheel, dazed but conscious. He was still in his seatbelt. Trooper Blake paused at this point to allow the prosecutor to take control should she so wish. Kate did not so wish.

"What happened next?" Kate simply asked.

Trooper Blake launched once again into his **testimonial narrative** of long uninterrupted monologue. The professional witness knew just what to say to hit all of the necessary buttons and levers. Kate checked off various boxes on a list she kept on the table as the officer addressed each element of the crimes via his testimony. Prosecutors always worry that while they are presenting their various witnesses, they will forget to ask some witness or another to cover some indispensable point of proof. When a prosecutor messes up in this way, the defense attorney will wait until the state rests its case and then will announce to the judge that "the defense demurs." A **demurrer** is a motion by the defense that the defendant be found not guilty because even if the jury believes everything testified to by the various state witnesses, some **key element of proof** was never covered. As a matter of law, the state utterly failed to meet its burden to establish guilt. Kate was making sure that this was not going to happen in her case.

The trooper continued through the case, hitting all of the buttons. He established that the defendant had been driving a vehicle. He spoke of how the defendant had admitted falling asleep at the wheel and causing the crash. He testified how the defendant had the smell of alcohol on his breath and admitted to drinking beer, supposedly just one beer. The trooper spoke of how the defendant also admitted to having consumed two Benadryl cold pills along with the beer, shortly before he left his friends' party to drive home. Trooper Blake also spoke of how the defendant had admitted to him that he had read the Benadryl box before taking the pills. This box, which the officer later recovered during his investigation, had all sorts of warnings written on it for the consumer to not drive or operate machinery since the pills can cause drowsiness. The box also warned against drinking alcohol along with taking the pills since that only makes the drowsiness worse.

Kate picked up a Benadryl box on her table. It was now her intention to have it admitted into evidence. As customary, she approached the defense attorney and provided him the **courtesy of first examination**. Jack was sure to read the various warnings on the back of the box, noting their prominence or lack thereof on the box. Satisfied that he was familiar with what was on the box, Jack handed the item back to Kate and nodded his head. Kate then asked the judge for **permission to approach** the witness. The judge granted his permission, and, box in hand, Kate walked up to the witness stand. On the way to the witness stand, Kate stopped at the workstation of the court reporter and whispered to her to "mark this please as '**Commonwealth Exhibit One**.'" The stenographer wrote "C-1" on a little white sticker and stuck it on the box.

Kate took the box, finished approaching the trooper on the stand, handed him the box, and said, "Trooper, I show you what has been marked as Commonwealth Exhibit One. Do you recognize it?"

"Yes, that is the box of Benadryl that I got from its owner during my investigation. It is the same box that the defendant used as his source for the cold medicine he took during the party."

"How do you know that it is the very same box?"

Kate was asking a critical question. Like guns, knives, masks, and other tangible objects, a box would be classified as **real evidence**. Unlike testimonial evidence, real evidence is no good unless the prosecutor can establish an unbroken link (called a **chain of custody**) that proves that the object is the very one taken earlier by the police into evidence. A chain of custody (usually a sheet attached to the tangible object on which an investigator must sign in and sign out as he or she handles the object before trial) is not strictly necessary if the object is so unique as to obviously be one of a kind. In this case, the box was hardly unique. Rather, it was **fungible**, meaning there were many more in the world just like it. Fungible items always require the establishment of a chain of custody in court before being admitted.

In order to prove it was the same box from the party, Trooper Blake held up the box of cold pills. "Here on the top of the box that I had retrieved from the owner, I had written the letters, 'TSB,' standing for Trooper Steven Blake. I did this as soon as the girl from the party gave me the box." Trooper Blake pointed the initialed and hence nonfungible box toward the jury, then toward the judge, and then toward the attorneys to make sure they could all see his markings.

"Objection, Your Honor," Jack Day interjected. "This is all well and good, but how do we know that the owner gave the trooper the very box she had at the party? She has not testified about this. Maybe she gave the trooper the wrong type of box entirely for him to write initials on."

"Your Honor, I will be calling the girl who had brought the box to the party as my next witness. I will be able to tie it all up then."

"Very well, I will hold you to your promise," Judge Price announced. "Defense objection overruled."

Kate next asked the trooper to read all of the warnings on the box to the jury. He did so. Jack tried to look very bored as the trooper read some very damning warnings about not driving and not drinking. Jack was anything but bored. When the trooper had finished his reading, Kate addressed the judge and said, "The Commonwealth moves that this Benadryl box be admitted into evidence as Commonwealth Exhibit One."

"No objections," Jack conceded without even waiting for the judge to ask him.

"Very well, the box is admitted into evidence and will be available for the members of the jury to inspect during their deliberations at the end of the trial."

With that, Kate looked down at her **prosecutor checklist.** Trooper Blake had covered all of the elements of the crimes of homicide by vehicle while DUI as well as the misdemeanor of reckless driving. It looked like he had failed to cover all of the necessary elements of underage drinking. She could fix that.

"Trooper, were you able to establish the age of Richard Mahan as of last April 5, the date of the incident?"

"Yes," the trooper answered. "The defendant produced his driver's license as I processed the accident scene. He was 17 years old back on April 5 of this year."

"And what is the legal age in our state for drinking alcohol?"

"The defense will **stipulate** and agree without further proof that the age for that is 21," Attorney Jack Day chimed in.

"Very well," acknowledged Judge Price. "Ms. Page, do you have any more questions of this witness?" Kate took a few seconds to scan her checklist one more time. "No more questions, Your Honor."

"Very well. Mr. Day, you may cross."

There are two types of examination involving witnesses. The first type is known as "direct examination." This is the type of examination that just took place when Kate asked questions of Trooper Blake. **Direct examination** occurs when an attorney is asking questions of his or her own witness that the attorney has called to the stand. Since such a witness is usually on the attorney's side, there is a general rule against leading a witness during direct examination. (Though, it is conceivable that a lawyer may wish to call a witness hostile to his or her case to the stand. In this case, the lawyers requests permission from the judge to **treat as hostile.** If permission is granted, the attorney may then begin to lead the witness even though the attorney was the one who called that person to the stand.)

An attorney has posed a **leading question** when the question explicitly telegraphs the exact answer desired. Leading questions are usually easy to recognize because they typically can be answered in a "yes" or "no" fashion. Leading a witness is forbidden during direct examination because the attorney is not the one who should be testifying but rather his or her witness. For example, an attorney on direct could not ask a witness, "Was the person fleeing the scene a super tall, skinny white guy in his 20s?" Instead, the attorney should ask, "Can you please describe the person who you said you saw fleeing the scene?"

Not being able to lead a witness can be frustrating for a prosecutor presenting evidence, but police officers are usually very skilled at hitting all of the necessary evidentiary levers in their testimony with minimal prompts. Such was the case today with Trooper Steve Blake.

The second type of examination is known as "cross-examination." **Cross-examination** follows direct examination and is done by the attorney on the competing side who has no desire to engage in friendly fire. It this case, the attorney on the other side was Jack Day. Jack knew that he was allowed to lead a witness on cross-examination. This is because enemy witnesses usually do not let a hostile attorney put words in their mouth. Since Jack Day could lead Trooper Blake, he knew he always should. Day would structure his cross by using "yes/no" style questions that would box the enemy in. If Jack were to make the mistake of asking an open-ended style of question such as "what happened next?," Trooper Blake would then have the floor to launch into a lengthy, and potentially harmful, narration.

Jack decided to concentrate his cross-examination of the trooper on the medicine box and a lack of personal knowledge that his client was drunk.

"Good afternoon, Trooper Blake."

"Good afternoon, Counselor."

"Trooper, you testified that my client, young Rick Mahan, read the box that had the warnings. Is that correct?"

"Yes."

"Is it not correct that my client never actually said exactly what warnings he read?"

"He told me he had read the box. There are warnings on the box. I just read them to the jury. The defendant used the word 'warnings' when he told me what he had read on the box. I have that word, 'warnings,' in my notes from the scene."

"Yes, but can't the word 'warnings' refer to other things besides a caution not to drink or to drive after taking the medicine? For example, doesn't the box warn about correct dosage?"

"Yes, but I would not characterize that as 'warnings.'"

"Oh really? Is it not possible that a 17-year-old boy might consider dosage information a type of warning?"

"I don't know."

Kate decided to try to interrupt this exchange. "Your Honor, I do not see the relevancy of this line of questioning. The defense attorney knows full well that, as a matter of law, a user of medicine is responsible for using the product safely, whether or not he or she bothers to exercise good judgment in reading the warnings associated with the product. Mr. Day also knows that, as a matter of law, a driver is always responsible to not drive while impaired, no matter what."

"How do you respond to that, Mr. Day?" asked the judge.

Jack Day glanced at the jury and gave them a "look" with his eyes as if to say, "See what they are trying to pull?" Attorney Day then turned his head toward the judge to respond to his question. "Your Honor, the state made a big production about the box, the warnings on the box, how my client read the warnings on the box. By bringing it up first, they **opened the door** to my covering this matter now on cross-examination."

"Quite so," declared the judge. "Objection overruled. The testimony will be considered by the jury and given whatever weight they deem appropriate."

"Thank you, Your Honor." Jack made sure that the jury saw him give a dirty look to that agent of the state, Kate.

Jack figured his point about the box had now been adequately made, so he was ready to ask his next question. "Trooper, you said you smelled alcohol on my client's breath. You could not tell how intoxicated he was just by that, right?"

"That is correct."

"Also, I did not hear you mention conducting any field sobriety tests, like walking heel to toe, standing on one leg, etc. I bet that is because the ambulance people would not allow it." Jack already knew from the police reports what the answer would be. If he did not know the answer in advance, he never would have asked the question. One **unofficial rule**

**of questioning** is that a lawyer should never pose a question to a witness unless he or she already knows the answer.

"Yes, there was a concern about possible injuries, so I was not able to administer any field sobriety tests at the scene."

"Or anywhere else," Jack quipped. He knew Kate would not bothering to object to that. Jack looked sympathetically now at the officer and asked, "Field tests sure help establish whether or not someone is too drunk or high on pills to drive safely. I bet you wish you could have done the field tests."

"Well, of course I do. However, there are other ways to prove intoxication."

"Oh, you must mean things like blood alcohol content in the blood," Jack countered. "Officer, what is the legal limit again for BAC in Pennsylvania? Last I heard it was 0.08. Yet, correct me if I am wrong, but your police report citing the hospital lab will put by client's BAC at 0.04, or maybe 0.05 at the most. Is that not true?"

"Yes, however, there were pills as well, plus falling asleep just like the box warned about."

"Well, you are not an expert on pills and their interaction with alcohol, are you?"

"No, but my police report discusses someone who is and will be testifying."

"No doubt true. But as far as you personally are concerned, you cannot state with certainty—personally—that my client was too drunk to drive safely or too high on pills to drive safely or too high on pills combined with alcohol to drive safely, correct?"

"Me personally, all alone? No."

"Thank you," no further questions.

Judge Price looked at the prosecutor and asked, "Any redirect?" An attorney is allowed to engage in **redirect examination** by asking a few follow-up questions after cross if he or she so wishes. Any questions on redirect are **limited in scope**, however, to those questions covered during the cross-examination. In other words, no new territory can be covered.

"No redirect, Your Honor."

"Very well," concluded Judge Price. "The witness may step down."

As the trooper joined Kate at her table, she thought about whom she should call next. "I guess I better call that girl from the party," she thought. Rising from her chair, Kate announced, "The state calls Nancy Foley to the stand."

## Key Terms Found in This Chapter

| | |
|---|---|
| Admission to the "bar" | Fungible |
| Judicial regalia | Prosecutor checklist |
| Professional witness | Stipulate |
| Testimonial narrative | Direct examination |
| Demurrer | Treat as hostile |
| Key element of proof | Leading question |
| Courtesy of first examination | Cross-examination |
| Permission to approach | Opened the door |
| Commonwealth Exhibit One | Unofficial rule of questioning |
| Real evidence | Redirect examination |
| Chain of custody | Limited in scope |

## Questions for Class Discussion

1. Where does the term, "admitted to the bar" come from? What does it have to do with the traditional physical layout of a courtroom?
2. What sort of clothes constitutes a judge's regalia? What connection is there with this outfit and medieval authority figures? Should American lawyers also wear such clothes as lawyers appearing in court do in the United Kingdom?
3. Why was the trooper referred to as being a professional witness? What should police officers do prior to trial to get ready for court? How does this make them a better witness? How should they dress while in court?
4. How did the trooper know how to drone on in long testimonial narrative? Why did the prosecutor let him testify in such a narrative style? Could most witnesses be trusted to testify in such a way?
5. What is a demurrer that makes prosecutors so careful in covering all of their bases? What things do prosecutors have to make sure they

cover to avoid the successful granting of a demurrer? How does a prosecutor checklist factor into all of this?

6. What is real evidence? What is meant by "courtesy of first examination" concerning real evidence? What is a chain of custody, and when is it required?

7. How does an attorney go about getting a piece of real evidence admitted into evidence? What becomes of such evidence at trial's end?

8. How is direct examination different from cross-examination?

9. What does it mean to "lead a witness"? Why is there a general rule against leading a witness during direct examination? Why does this rule not apply to cross-examination? How often should lawyers lead a witness during cross-examination?

10. What is a lawyer asking when he or she asks a judge permission to treat a witness they have called to the stand as "hostile"? Why might an attorney call a hostile witness to the stand in the first place?

11. How does the argument that the other side had "opened the door" sometimes allow an attorney to pursue a line of questioning normally not allowed? Can you give an example of the other side "opening the door"?

12. What is the "unofficial rule of questioning" that lawyers tend to follow when asking questions of a witness? Why would you be scared as a lawyer to deviate too frequently from following this rule of thumb?

13. When does redirect examination take place? What sort of matters can be addressed during redirect examination? Why not just allow anything to be raised during redirect?

# 29

## The State's Case (Part II)

Young Nancy Foley walked to the witness stand in obedience to the prosecutor's summons. Nancy had been sitting in the benches behind the prosecutor's table. Trials are like weddings. Just as the groom's guests sit on one side of the aisle and the bride's guests on the other side, so too do prosecution witnesses seem instinctively to sit behind the prosecutor's table, while defense witnesses sit behind the defense attorney's table. Not only do witnesses obey this unspoken seating chart, so do all of those rooting for one side or the other.

Nancy and the other prosecution witnesses were lucky to be sitting at all in the courtroom during the trial rather than waiting out in the boring hallway for their turn to testify. In many trials, defense attorneys, concerned state witnesses may taint each other's recollection of events, move at the start of the trial for the state's witnesses to be "sequestered." A judge always grants such a motion when advanced. Nancy was able to sit in the courtroom and listen to Trooper Blake's testimony because Attorney Jack Day did not worry about the need for **sequestration of witnesses** in this particular trial. What each witness had to add to the body of evidence was quite independent, one from another.

Nancy, being only 17 years old, had never been inside a courthouse in her life before, let alone asked to testify in a criminal felony trial. As she sat down, she thought she would die of fright. Her hand shook vigorously as she lay it on the Bible and took the witness oath to tell the truth.

When she finished that task, the prosecutor winked at her and smiled. That did not help calm Nancy down very much, but she still appreciated the kindness.

"Please tell us your name and age," began Kate.

"I am Nancy Foley. I am 17."

"Back on April 5 of this year, were you at a party of high school friends?" Since this called for a "yes/no" response, it was technically a leading question and forbidden on direct. Yet, only a stupid defense attorney would bother irritating the court in objecting to a **time-saver leading question** like this one on such a technical ground.

Nancy looked only at Kate and said that she indeed had attended a party on that date.

"When did the party start?" Kate asked.

"About 9:00 p.m."

"Were you and others drinking beer?"

"Yes. The parents of the kid who lived there were out of town."

"Did you encounter the defendant, Richard Mahan, at some point during the party?"

"Yes, he was there. I started talking to him about 45 minutes into the party. He had a bad cough."

"Was he drinking beer?"

"Yeah, he was." Jack was finally getting impatient with so many leading statements and was thinking of objecting on those grounds unless Kate started to alter her ways soon.

"Tell us about what happened between you and Richard Mahan from that point onward," Kate requested. Jack was glad that he would not have to object to the form of the question. It was no longer leading.

"Well," Nancy began in a quivering voice, "Rick was standing by himself by the fireplace drinking a beer. He looked lonely, so I went over and started talking to him about school stuff since we both attend the same high school. While I spoke with Rick, he started to cough really badly. I had some Benadryl cold pills in my purse because I had a cold too. I asked Rick if wanted to take a couple. He said, 'yes' so I handed him the box."

"Then what happened?" Kate asked.

"Rick took the box and started reading it."

"What parts of the box did you see him read?"

"First he read the front and then the back of the box."

"Did he read it fast, slow, or what?"

"Slow. He spent a lot of time reading the back of the box where all the warnings and stuff are. I remember because I thought it was a little weird. It is not like I was giving him heroin or something."

"How long would you say he spent reading the box?"

"Like a whole minute. That is why I thought it was kind of overkill. He spent almost all of that time reading the back of the box where all of the warnings are."

"Where is this box now?" Kate inquired.

"I gave it to the cop when he came to my house and asked for it."

"When was that?" Kate asked the girl.

"The morning after the party. It was still in my purse."

"Is the officer you gave the box to in this courtroom?"

"Yes, ma'am," Nancy said as she pointed directly at Trooper Steve Blake.

"Let the record reflect that the witness pointed at Trooper Steven Blake, thus identifying him as the officer to whom she gave the medicine box."

"What?" the young girl asked, appearing confused.

"No, that was meant for the **court stenographer** to record so that it appears in the trial transcript," Kate explained. (The **trial transcript** is a verbatim, shorthand recording of the spoken word. The stenographer, a sworn court officer who is still actually used today despite a world flush in technological change, uses a method known as "chording." **Chording** breaks words down into their basic phonetic syllables that later get reconstituted back into full English words. The machine a stenographer uses during chording, called a stenotype, only has phonetic, piano-like keys and thus does not have a way to record gestures or give context. For this reason, trial lawyers or judges at times make comments—such as Kate's "Let the record reflect"—so that a future transcript reader will know what had just happened.) Young Nancy, of course, did not understand any of this but lost interest when she correctly sensed that none of it apparently concerned her anyway.

"What did you see Rick Mahan do after he finished taking forever to read that box?" Kate next asked.

"Objection," Jack interjected. "The witness never said that anything took forever."

"Sustained," Judge Price ruled. "Ms. Page, please rephrase."

"What did Rick Mahan do after he finished looking at the box?"

"He took two pills and washed them down with some beer. He then handed me back the box."

"Thank you, Nancy," Kate said. "Your Honor, the Commonwealth has no further questions of this witness."

Young Nancy started to rise from her seat when the judge used his hand as a signal for her to keep seated. "Mr. Day," the judge then said, "Your witness."

Jack knew that cross-examination allowed him to do a number of things. He could of course lead the witness, which he had every intention of doing. He also could try to make the witness look stupid, ignorant, irrational, biased, or incompetent. Often, in trials past, he had made it his goal to do just that. Juries do not like to reward witnesses they do not like with verdicts the witnesses would like. Moreover, juries simply do not like witnesses that are stupid, ignorant, irrational, biased, or incompetent. They also do not like prosecutors who present them with such witnesses. Jack knew all of this yet decided to be gentle with this child witness. Bullying a young girl would not score him any points today.

Jack also knew that the jury would just think him a charlatan if he were to try to cast doubt on the fact that Rick Mahan had drunk beer or that he had taken cold pills. Rick himself had admitted such to the police. Jack decided instead to pursue those angles where he could perhaps gain some traction.

"Ms. Foley, is it not true that you only saw Rick drinking one beer that night?"

"Yes," Nancy responded nondefensively. It was obvious to Jack (and he guessed to the jury as well) that this girl had no agenda against his client.

"He was not acting drunk when he spoke to you, was he?"

"No, he seemed fine."

"How he did seem after he took the pills?"

"Fine."

"In fact, you never saw Rick drunk or high at any time during that evening, correct?"

"Yes, that is correct."

"These pills do not require a prescription do they? Anyone can legally take them, including Rick Mahan?"

"They are just the sort of stuff you pull off the store shelf," Nancy explained.

"Did Rick read the box out loud or silently?" Jack already knew the answer from the police reports or else he would never have asked a question as dangerous as this.

"Silently."

"So, you cannot say for sure that he read all of the warnings on the box. You just do not know, right?"

"Well, I assume that…"

"Please don't assume. Just tell the jury what specific things you know for sure that Jack spent time on while reading the print on the box."

"Well, I can't say for sure what he read."

Jack received the answer he wanted and knew to **quit questioning while ahead** on this particular point. A big mistake rookie lawyers sometime make is to follow up on a subject when they already achieved their objective. "No further questions, Your Honor," Jack told the judge.

"Any redirect, Ms. Page?" asked the judge.

"Just two questions, Your Honor. Nancy, when you say that you did not see Rick Mahan drinking more than one beer, what did you mean by that?"

"Just that I personally did not see him drink more than one beer while I was talking to him. I do not know how much he drank that night."

Kate had just one more question, something she actually had planned to ask during her direct examination but messed up and forgot to ask. She was grateful that she could sneak it into the trial by way of redirect. "Nancy, Mr. Day asked you if you observed Rick read the box out loud or silently. You said Rick read the box silently. However, did you see Rick do anything unusual with his beer bottle while he was reading the box?"

"What?" Nancy asked before she quickly realized what the prosecutor was getting at. (Nancy and Ms. Page had gone over all of Nancy's potential testimony earlier by way of standard witness preparation. Attorneys may **prepare witnesses pre-trial** by suggesting what might be asked of them during a trial and how they might effectively answer a question in terms of style. However, attorneys are forbidden to coach witnesses substantively by suggesting the actual content their answers should include.) Remembering her pre-trial preparation, Nancy now responded.

"Oh yeah, when Jack was reading the back of the box, I saw him look at his beer bottle and shake his head from side to side."

"What do you think Rick was reading about when he reacted by shaking his head at the beer bottle like that?"

This last question caused Jack to leap from his seat with indignation (part real, part exaggerated). "Objection! **Calls for speculation**."

"I will sustain that objection," Judge Price ruled.

Kate took the ruling in stride. She had made her point in any event. "Thank you, Nancy," Kate simply concluded. "I have no more questions of this witness."

The judge looked at Jack and asked if he had any re-cross. Just as redirect questions cannot cover any new material but rather are limited to material brought up for the first time during the cross, so too are questions on **re-cross** limited in scope to fresh matters narrowly brought up on redirect. Jack had no follow-up questions about the number of beers Nancy saw Rick drinking. However, he could not just let Nancy's testimony during redirect about Rick shaking his head at his beer bottle go unchallenged.

"Just one question," Jack told the judge. "Ms. Foley, there could be a dozen meanings to Rick shaking his head at the beer bottle after he read the box, is that not true?"

"I guess so," Nancy admitted. Having got the response he sought, Jack knew that he should now just shut up. "Exactly," he said. "No further questions."

The judge told Nancy that she was excused. Nancy left to retake her seat in the audience.

Judge Price looked at the big ornate clock on the back wall and noticed the time. "Ladies and gentlemen of the jury, since we got off to a late start this afternoon due to the funeral and our consequently long lunch break, I suggest we call it a day. The court stands in recess until 9:30 a.m. tomorrow morning. Once again, I exhort you not to discuss this trial or the testimony with a single soul, including your family members. To do so would get us all in trouble, especially you. In addition, just in case this matter is mentioned on the television news, on the radio, in social media, in a newspaper, or in any other forum, you are under strict obligation to refrain from listening or reading about it. Avoid doing this at all costs. Both the defense and prosecution have the right to have a jury free from all outside influences and opinions. With that, I will see you all again here tomorrow morning when we will likely hear from the rest of the state's witnesses. Have a pleasant evening."

The judge stood up and the bailiff announced for all to rise. The judge exited the room while everyone else watched in quiet deference. (Judges really are the last vestige of aristocracy in our country.) After the judge was gone, a bailiff signaled the jury members that they could now leave as well.

Attorney Jack Day, his client Rick, ADA Kate Page, and Trooper Blake all stood respectfully and quietly until the last juror had left the room. Kate then nodded farewell to Jack as she walked away with Trooper Blake toward the exit doors. After they had left, Jack turned to Rick and offered him words of encouragement. Rick's parents also told their son that they thought things seemed to be going reasonably well. Young Rick seemed distraught, however. That made his attorney feel bad.

"Rick, I cannot say for sure, but I think we could win this," Jack assured him. "Just try to relax tonight and distract yourself by doing something you enjoy."

"I don't know about all of this," Rick said. "Is it too late for me to get that plea bargain?"

"Well, I don't know," Jack said with surprise. "It is never too late until the jury returns with an actual verdict, assuming I could still get the prosecutor and judge to agree. Is that what you want me to try for?"

Rick thought about that for a little while. "No," the teenager finally replied. "I am just really scared. I'll see you tomorrow, Mr. Day."

⌇

## Key Terms Found in This Chapter

| | |
|---|---|
| Sequestration of witnesses | Chording |
| Time-saver leading question | Quit questioning while ahead |
| Court stenographer | Prepare witnesses pre-trial |
| Trial transcript | Calls for speculation |
| Re-cross | |

# Questions for Class Discussion

1.  Why do lawyers have the right to have trial witnesses sequestered? How does this work? What would be an example of when a lawyer would want to do this?
2.  What would a judge think of a lawyer who objects to a leading question that is merely asked that way to save time? What example did the chapter give of such a leading question?
3.  What is a trial transcript? Who creates this? What is it used for? What useful trial happenings does it not contain?
4.  Why do you suppose that courts continue to use stenographers in an age of artificial intelligence and advanced technologies? What might a desire to have an ultimately responsible, sworn court officer have to do with the reason? Who would be responsible should outside noise, ambiguous sounds, equipment failure, etc. cause any such hypothetical "advanced" technologies to fail?
5.  What is meant by the idea that a lawyer should shut up and quit while he or she is ahead? Why do rookie lawyers sometimes refuse to stop pursuing a line of inquiry when they already got the answer they desired? Could you see yourself making that mistake?
6.  Do attorneys have the legal right to prepare witnesses pre-trial? What sort of things are they allowed in way of witness preparation? What sort of things are they forbidden to help a witness do?
7.  What is so wrong with a witness speculating about things during their testimony? Whose job is it ultimately to connect all of the major dots in a trial? What is the difference between a lay witness speculating and an expert witness rendering an opinion?
8.  What type of examination directly precedes re-cross examination? Why does re-cross usually involve just a very small number of questions, if it occurs at all?

# 30

## The State's Case (Part III)

The next morning came quickly enough. Jack asked his client to meet him at the courthouse a half hour before court was to resume so that he could update young Rick on the progress of the trial, from a lawyer's viewpoint. Jack told Rick that things were not going badly, and, overall, he thought that an acquittal was not a foolish thing to hope for. Jack encouraged Rick to stay hopeful but made sure to make no promises. Jack wanted to be optimistic enough to keep Rick's hopes firmly alive (he would eventually need him to make a confident defense witness, not to mention the desire to spare him unproductive suffering and worry). Yet, Jack also wanted to stay realistic. The truth is that nobody can confidently anticipate what any one jury will do. Every prosecutor has lost what he or she thought to be a virtual "slam dunk," and every defense lawyer has lost a case that the defender was sure was saturated in reasonable doubt. Juries are rascals. That is just one more reason that courthouse professionals are so enamored of plea bargains.

So far the state had produced two witnesses in the case against Richard Mahan: Trooper Steven Blake, who was the first to respond to the crime scene, and young Nancy Foley from the drinking party. Both the trooper and the girl could be categorized as **eyewitnesses**, people who saw relevant evidentiary events with their own eyes. Juries love eyewitnesses because if they believe what they are telling is truthful and accurate, they usually do not have to make any inferences or guesses. The thinking is over. Who likes to think?

Eyewitnesses thus often give what is known as "direct evidence." **Direct evidence** is evidence that, if believed, requires no further inference or guess to be made. Juries just have to decide if the witness is accurately telling the truth. Both of the state's witnesses delivered some circumstantial evidence in addition to their direct evidence. **Circumstantial evidence** is evidence, which, even if believed by the jury, requires the jury nevertheless to make an inference. For example, Nancy Foley testified that Rick Mahan had shook his head at the beer bottle in his hands while reading the print on the back of the box of cold pills. Even if the jury believes that this happened, it would still have to make an inference—a guess—that Rick shook his head in recognition of the fact that he should not be taking the cold pills along with the alcohol he had consumed. Circumstantial evidence is fine as long as a jury can make its guess beyond a reasonable doubt or if the guess, along with all of the other building blocks of the state's case, enables it to overcome collective reasonable doubt.

Eyewitnesses are great, and the state and juries love them. However, other witnesses are needed in a case involving alleged intoxication causing death. Assistant District Attorney Kate knew that she would also have to call a couple of expert witnesses to render opinions about alcohol and drug interactions and causes of crashes and death.

Expert witnesses are curious creatures indeed. Their testimony flies in the face of the usual rule of evidence that witnesses should never express opinions but instead stick to delivering just the facts. In other words, the job of a witness is to present the "data" to the jury, but it is the job of the jury to "analyze" that data. When witnesses attempt to analyze what the data mean—to draw conclusions—they are wrongfully encroaching into the jury's exclusive turf.

One exception to the general rule that witnesses should never express opinions is testimony being presented by so-called **expert witnesses**. Only the expert witness may express an opinion. One of the brilliant things about juries is that they usually are very good at drawing conclusions themselves. However, sometimes juries are just plain incompetent to draw conclusions given the esoteric complexities of the information being presented to them. In these situations, an expert is needed not only to present them with the facts but also to give them some analysis. Expert witnesses are allowed to express an opinion during their testimony regarding matters **outside the ken of ordinary knowledge**. There are many different types of expert witnesses in court: fingerprint analysts, forensic accountants, handwriting analysts, psychiatrists, automobile accident reconstruction experts, ballistics experts, voice print identifiers, blood typists, coroners, and many more. All of these witnesses can lawfully be used to render an opinion about something within the area of their expertise.

Now that the trial was about to reconvene, Kate was ready to call her next witness. It would be an expert witness.

Attorney Jack Day, his client Rick, Prosecutor Kate Page, and her state trooper sidekick were all sitting and waiting for the show to recommence. The jury too was now seated in its box. As usual, all rose when the judge came in and walked to his chair.

"Good morning," Judge Price cheerfully said to everyone. The judge was in a good mood. The trial was moving along at a nice speed, and he felt confident that no big appellate issues had yet developed. "Ms. Page, please call your next witness."

"The Commonwealth calls Dr. Roger Knight to the stand." An intelligent-looking bald man in his early 60s rose from one of the benches behind Kate and walked quietly up to the witness chair. Upon arriving at the chair, the witness did not even bother to sit down but instead raised his right hand without even waiting for a prompt to do so. It was obvious that he, like police officers, was no stranger to court.

Everyone watched as Dr. Knight finished taking the oath and took his seat. "Good morning," Kate said. "Good morning," the gentleman responded. Kate asked the man to tell the court his name, which he did.

Kate knew that this witness, being an expert witness, meant that she could not simply start asking substantive questions as she could a regular witness. Because she would be asking this witness not just for what he had observed but for an opinion as to what these facts meant, she would have to first **qualify the witness as expert**.

The attorney who wishes to qualify a witness as an expert must first **lay the foundation** by calling this person to the stand and establishing that he or she possesses special knowledge and expertise not held by ordinary people. In order to accomplish this, Kate would have to ask the witness about his credentials, training, and experience. (Jack would also be given a chance to cross-examine.) If after this foundation is laid, the judge accepts this witness as an expert, then Kate would be allowed to go about questioning him in such a way as to ultimately lead to the expression of an opinion.

Kate knew what she needed to ask to qualify Roger Knight as an expert. "Dr. Knight, could you tell us about your education," she began.

"Yes, I have a medical degree from Rutgers University in New Jersey. After medical school, I did a 4-year residency at the Hershey Medical Center in Hershey, Pennsylvania in the area of pathology. I am a board certified pathologist and for the last 20 years have run the pathology lab at the local county hospital."

"Very well," Kate noted. "How often have you analyzed blood for alcohol content during these past 20 years in the hospital lab?"

"I would say that a week does not go by when I do not personally run or closely supervise others who run such a test."

"Are you familiar with how to calculate the exact percentage of alcohol in the blood?"

"Yes, of course. That is a routine part of my job at the hospital. Attending physicians, as well as anesthesiologists, rely heavily on such information."

"Thank you, Doctor." Judge Price could see that Kate had finished. He asked Jack if he wanted to undertake cross-examination of the proposed witness' credentials. Jack indicated that he had a question.

"Dr. Knight, I have not heard any testimony about specific expertise regarding an ability to calculate BAC at the time of the accident, as opposed to the time the blood was drawn at the hospital. Will you be getting into any of that?"

"No," replied Knight. "I will only be testifying as to the BAC at the time blood was drawn. I can also testify about how many beers typically produce a BAC like that in a man the weight of the defendant."

"Thank you, Sir. No further questions." Jack was done.

Kate now spoke up. "Your Honor, the state moves that this witness be accepted as an expert in the area of BAC in the bloodstream and closely related matters." Judge Price glanced over at Jack who shook his head indicating that he had no objections.

"Very well. The court accepts this witness as expert in the area so described. Members of the jury, as an expert, this witness will be permitted to express opinions about various matters within his expertise. You are required to give careful consideration to any opinions expressed but are not required to agree with them. You should give them the weight you feel that they deserve." Looking now at Kate, the judge told her that she could begin her direct examination of Dr. Knight.

"Dr. Knight, I want to call your attention to the date of April 5 of this year. Did your hospital lab analyze a sample of blood from someone named Richard Mahan?"

"Yes, just before midnight my staff extracted blood from Richard Mahan for testing. This was done at the request of the emergency room physician and the state police. I was called in from home given the serious nature of the situation. It is my policy that any blood work done in connection with any fatal automobile accidents be done by me personally. I arrived at the hospital at about 12:15 a.m. on April 6 and did the lab work on the blood myself. All findings were set down in my report per standard protocols."

"Were you able to ascertain the blood alcohol content of the blood that was drawn?"

"Yes," replied the doctor. He took a second to look down at his official lab report. "My lab notes indicate a BAC of 0.04." Jack was listening to all of this with great interest but raised no objections. He knew that medical records were not subject to any hearsay or similar objections, especially when it was the very person testifying who also had created the record.

"Dr. Knight," the prosecutor continued, "What do your records say was the weight of Richard Mahan at that time?" The doctor responded that Richard Mahan's weight was "160 pounds."

"Could a man of that weight drinking just one beer achieve a BAC of 0.04?"

"No, that is not possible. The defendant would have consumed at least two beers to arrive at that result. Maybe three beers depending on the brand of beer. But there is no beer that I ever heard of sold in this country that could get a 160-pound man to a BAC of 0.04 after having just drunk one can or one bottle of beer."

"So, if Richard Mahan told the state trooper at the accident scene he only had one beer to drink, he would have been lying?" Kate wondered if Jack would let her get away with such a question. It never hurts to try.

"Objection!" Jack protested. "This question calls for an opinion that is not part of this witness' unique training and expertise."

"Objection sustained," Judge Price ruled. "The jury can form its own conclusions about such matters without the assistance of this witness." Both Kate and Jack knew that her provocative question was getting them to do just that right now.

Kate went on to ask the witness one more question. She wanted to know if any drugs other than alcohol were found in the defendant's blood sample. The witness confirmed that a small dose of Benadryl was also in his system. Satisfied, Kate indicated that she had no further questions of this witness. Judge Price told the witness he could step down.

"The Commonwealth now calls Dr. Caroline Holland to the stand." Kate had been turning around and nodding at Dr. Holland as she was uttering those words. A tall, skinny woman in her 50s stood up and walked to the stand.

Kate had no problem qualifying Caroline Holland, who was the official county coroner, as an expert capable of testifying as to the cause of someone's death. In fact, Jack did not even waste his time in cross-examining this witness as to her qualifications. Kate went on to get this witness to testify that the cause of death of the two victims at the car accident scene was blunt traumas caused by their being ejected from their automobile upon impact with the other vehicle. Their deaths would have been instantaneous given the level of force that they experienced. With that, Kate was finished with this witness. It was time for Jack's cross.

Though Jack earlier had no questions about this witness' qualifications as an expert on death causation, he did have a question he wanted to ask the expert now. He had to be clever though about how he asked the question he wanted to pose. His goal was to get the jury thinking that there might have been some fault on the part of the two deceased people for not wearing seat belts. Jack did not want to be so blunt though as to anger the jury against his client by directly "blaming the victims." Neither did he wish to draw an objection from the prosecutor on the grounds of relevancy since Pennsylvania law held a drunk driver responsible for vehicular deaths whether or not the victims had buckled up.

"Doctor, help me to understand," Jack began. "How could the force of impact be so great as to not only kill two people but kill them instantly when my client, in another car, was not even seriously hurt?"

Kate was about to object but could not immediately come up with a basis for her objection should the judge ask. She hesitated long enough that the doctor already began her response. "Your client was buckled up; the two decedents were not and got ejected."

"Oh, I see. Thank you, Doctor," Jack uttered. "No further questions." The judge gave Kate a dirty look for not having had the sense to object when she had the chance. All Kate could do now was to think to herself, "Well played, Jack. Well played."

Kate had just one more witness for the state to call. She too would be an expert witness, perhaps the most important of them all. "The Commonwealth calls Dr. Wanda Grant to the stand." Dr. Grant was qualified as an expert PhD biochemist who worked at the state crime lab in Harrisburg. Her specific areas of expertise involved, among other things, alcohol absorption rates in general as well as the way alcohol can interact with other drugs to aggravate intoxication. Jack fought tooth and nail to prevent her from being qualified on the "interaction with other drugs" aspect of her supposed expertise but to no avail. She just had attended too many seminars over the years on that very subject to give the judge any pause in accepting her purported expertise. After the judge had accepted her as an expert and instructed the jury to consider her as such, Kate was ready to begin her questioning.

"Dr. Grant, prior to this trial, did you have a chance to review all of the medical reports from our county hospital as well as statements made by the defendant at the accident scene as noted in the police reports?" Dr. Grant indicated that she had studied all of these reports quite thoroughly. She added that she had also studied statements written down by Trooper Steven Blake as well which documented various periods, including the time it took for an ambulance to arrive, the time it took for the ambulance to get to the hospital where blood was drawn, etc.

"Dr. Grant, we have heard testimony from the hospital pathology lab director that the defendant's BAC at the time blood was drawn was 0.04. However, what really most interests us is what his BAC would have been at the time of the actual accident. We want to know the degree of his intoxication then, at the moment the alleged crime had occurred. Were you able to do an analysis of that?"

"Yes," the doctor affirmed. Using the defendant's own statements to the police, times logged in to the police report by Trooper Blake, and times noted on the pathology lab report, Dr. Grant told the jury what she could safely conclude. She confirmed that she was able easily to put together an accurate picture of how much time had passed from the time of the defendant's first drink to his second one. She also could determine the exact amount of time between the defendant's last drink to the time of the actual crash. Furthermore, she was able to figure out the amount of time expired from the crash to the time the blood was drawn at the hospital. After going through a bunch of technical explanations, which nobody else in the courtroom totally could understand, the doctor then got to the bottom line, which even the most confused jurors could comprehend. "The BAC at the time of the accident would have been slightly higher than the BAC at the time the blood was drawn. This is so because, in my expert opinion, the defendant's blood alcohol content was already on its way down by the time he arrived at the hospital. I calculate that at the actual time of the collision, the defendant's BAC would have been 0.05 rather than 0.04."

Jack did not like this testimony but would like what the expert was about to say next even less. "Dr. Grant," Kate asked, "What did you ascertain regarding possible interaction with the cold medicine named Benadryl?"

The doctor then went into an extensive narrative about how Benadryl combined with alcohol usually aggravates the side effects of drowsiness. She finished by expressing her "professional opinion" that Richard Mahan's sleepiness that night behind the wheel was almost certainly caused by the "powerful" interaction of Benadryl with alcohol. She also stated that given his two beers plus two pills, he would have been utterly incapable of safe driving that night. He was a "menace on the highway," she told the jury.

On cross-examination, Jack decided to attack Dr. Grant first on the 0.04 versus 0.05 BAC distinction. "Dr. Grant," he began, "Is it not true that many people are capable of operating a vehicle safely whether their BAC is 0.04 or 0.05?" Dr. Grant admitted that this was true. Jack was then able to get Dr. Grant to admit that though the law makes 0.08 an automatic DUI conviction, there are actually some people capable of driving relatively sober even at that higher figure. Jack then went on to establish that many people could take two Benadryl pills and not be a "menace on the highway." It took some prodding on the part of Jack, but Dr. Grant finally conceded that point as well. Jack next launched into a series of intentionally long, complicated questions regarding time frames and alcohol absorption rates in the blood. Jack knew that none of the answers would be on his side but asked the endlessly boring questions anyway hoping that the jury would become confused and bewildered in the haze. "Sometimes, confusion can be **reasonable doubt's best friend**," Jack figured.

Jack wanted to finish by trying to get the expert to admit that her alcohol/cold medicine interaction theory was sketchy, but he decided not to go there. He had read enough scientific reports on his own in preparation for this trial to know that the doctor was exactly right in testifying about the scary interactions of combining alcohol with the cold medicine. Just having scored a series of smaller body blows to this witness, he decided to quit while he was a little bit ahead.

"No further questions," Jack finally announced. To Jack's surprise, Kate had no redirect. "Maybe she is just tired?" Jack thought. "Or, maybe she thinks she has won?" That last thought scared Jack, a lot.

The judge excused Dr. Grant, and she took her seat in the audience. The judge waited patiently while Kate silently studied her checklist one last time to make sure she had covered every element of every crime charged, via one witness or another. Kate eventually rose to her feet and announced, "The Commonwealth rests."

Both Judge Robert Price and ADA Kate Page looked over at Jack. Would he demur? Was there some essential thing that Kate had forgotten to cover that would enable Jack now to ask for an acquittal on all or some of the charges? Jack knew that Kate had crossed all of her T's and dotted all of her I's. Jack had been keeping a checklist of his own throughout the trial. Knowing that making Kate squirm would score no points anyway with the unsuspecting jury, Jack decided to be merciful and let her off the hook quickly. "The defense is ready to present its witnesses," Jack merely announced.

"Very well, we shall take a 15-minute recess," the Judge instructed. "Members of the jury, continue to refrain from discussing this case with anyone during the break. I will see you all back here in 15 minutes."

Rick Mahan whispered to Jack that he was very grateful for the break. "I have really got to go to the restroom," he told his attorney. "Me too," Jack confided. "Let's use the one in the basement. It may not look dignified if some of the jury members see us. Besides, with all of the judge's constant admonitions to not discuss the trial, they are probably so freaked out that they might think we are trying somehow to influence them if they even accidently encounter us during a break."

## Key Terms Found in This Chapter

| | |
|---|---|
| Eye witnesses | Outside the ken of ordinary knowledge |
| Direct evidence | Qualify the witness as expert |
| Circumstantial evidence | Lay the foundation |
| Expert witnesses | Reasonable doubt's best friend |

## Questions for Class Discussion

1. Why do juries love eyewitnesses so much? Do you love eyewitnesses? Do we tend to put too much trust in eyewitness testimony? Why or why not?

2. In what way does eyewitness testimony meet the definition of direct evidence?

3. How does circumstantial evidence differ from direct evidence? Is circumstantial evidence always inferior to direct evidence? Can a case be proven using only circumstantial evidence? What would be an example of that?

4. What can an expert witness do that no other type of witness is permitted to do? Why do we allow this in the case of experts? Does a jury have to accept the expert's testimony?

5. What must a lawyer do to "lay a foundation" before the judge will accept a witness as an expert? What are some examples of experts that testify in criminal cases?

6. What is meant by expertise "outside the ken of ordinary knowledge"? Do you possess any such knowledge that would qualify you as an expert in court?

7. How can boredom and confusion become the friend of the criminal defense attorney during a trial? What did Jack do to help bring this about?

8. Is it ethical for Jack to hope that the jury will become confused about all of the technical material? Is it ethical for him to try to exacerbate the problem by delving deeply into highly boring and technical matters? Would it be ethical for a prosecutor to attempt to confuse the jury about some technical defense strategy?
9. What did Kate make sure to do before she finally rested her case? What was she so neurotically worried that she had maybe failed to do?

# Unit 11
# The Defense Hits Back

This unit details how a defense lawyer takes care of the second half of a trial: the presentation of the case for the defense. The three chapters in this unit teaches us the "ins and outs" of how one goes about punching back.

# 31

## The Case for the Defense (Part I)

Before returning from break with Rick Mahan to the upstairs courtroom, Attorney Jack Day took five minutes on a bench in the basement to do a quick "final prep" of Rick, his intended central defense witness. Even though attorneys who coach and prepare their witnesses in advance of their testimony add extreme value toward their goal of favorably influencing jurors, lawyers often have **excuses for witness nonpreparation** in many criminal cases. This is so for several reasons.

First, the big majority of people accused of crimes in the United States are represented by public defenders or other types of government-financed "free lawyers." These lawyers typically have massive caseloads that leave little time for witness preparation.

Second, even if a public defender wanted to prepare witnesses in a case headed for trial, there is no sure way of actually knowing which of the many cases scheduled for a particular criminal court week will actually result in a trial. Sure, defense attorneys can narrow the range of possibilities down to maybe a half dozen or so cases. Yet, for which of these half dozen should the attorney prepare the witnesses? It is likely that only about one of them will actually go to trial in the end, as tentatively anticipated. Most cases, even those that appear to be unalterably heading for trial, wind up resulting in a guilty plea at the last second when the client finally comes to his or her senses and takes the deal.

Third, even private criminal defense attorneys tend to do little preparation of their potential trial witnesses. True, unlike public defenders, private criminal defense attorneys typically have too few cases at any one time to rob them completely of spare time. Therefore, they have plenty of time to prepare all of their witnesses in every case for possible trial. Yet even many of them are reluctant to do much witness preparation. This is because they get sick of preparing witnesses repeatedly for trials, only to see the cases wind up being plea-bargained in the end, frequently due to last minute changes of mind on the part of their fickle clients. In addition, private lawyers often feel that they are being underpaid for their services since most people hiring private lawyers do not have much money. The underpaid private lawyers resent having to go to trial in the first place, so they do not have much desire to "donate" time beyond that for which they think they are being fairly compensated.

In some twisted way, the fact that defense lawyers often spend little time in preparing their trial witnesses for court is all right since their professional adversaries often behave similarly. Like public defenders, prosecutors too have crushing caseloads. Like public defenders, they can never be sure which of their many cases scheduled for criminal court week will actually go to trial. Like public defenders, they often wind up frantically spending the few spare minutes they do have for last-minute preparation engaging in attorney self-preparation rather than attending to the "luxury" of getting witnesses prepared. Jack, as well as every criminal lawyer in this courthouse, could remember several instances in which they witnessed frazzled prosecutors frantically preparing opening statements in the elevator for a sudden, unexpected trial.

Like a small minority of criminal lawyers, Jack had the ability and desire to take the time to prepare his witnesses for testifying. He had met with all four of his witnesses several days before the start of the trial. He had given each of them a "heads up" on what he would be asking each of them, and what he anticipated the prosecutor would be asking each of them. He particularly spent quite a large amount of time preparing his own client, Rick.

Preparing Rick involved much more than merely cluing him in as to what questions he would be asked. Jack also wanted to make sure that he himself knew what answers his client planned to offer. This area of ascertaining prior to trial what answers a particular witness plans to give is a delicate one for attorneys; attorneys must tread very lightly to stay on the right side of the law and attorney ethical standards. In coaching witnesses, attorneys may give **tips on style** (allowed) but cannot **suggest content** (forbidden). They can rehearse and roleplay to help witnesses appear more relaxed, confident, and credible. They can coach witnesses on which tone of voice to use, when to make eye contact with jurors at critical times, how to avoid being rattled during cross, and even what clothes to wear. Jack was sure to do all of these things with each of his four intended witnesses but made especially certain to do a good job with Rick.

Prosecutor Kate Page had also prepared her witnesses more than usual because this was a double homicide case and she sensed this was a unique case that was undeniably going to trial. Yet, unlike Jack, she had a mountain of other cases to attend to and could only invest a fraction of the time Jack could toward these endeavors. Of course, Kate, like all prosecutors, still possessed the huge one-sided advantage of having the assistance of state-paid investigating police officers like Trooper Steven Blake, not to mention the scientist from the state crime lab. These helpers provided Kate with a lot of *de facto* **trial preparation** by organizing her entire case for her, complete with handy police reports in her file providing natural templates for what to cover during trial.

Even though Jack was using 5 of the 15 minutes of recess preparing Rick to testify, this was hardly the full extent of the trial preparation to which Rick had been subjected. This was apparent to any trained legal eye just by how Jack had "dressed" his client for court. He helped Rick select a suit and tie combination that somehow simultaneously made Rick, the alleged killer, look respectable and innocently youthful. Thanks to Jack and his clever stylist friend, Rick's new haircut also seemed to project the same desired image.

Jack's specific witness preparation during these last few minutes before his client took the stand mainly involved just trying to calm Rick down and help him to relax. "Take deep breaths," Jack urged him and rightfully so — the kid was a bundle of nerves. "If you get into trouble, look at me," Jack advised him.

Jack Day was so busy trying to help his young client avoid becoming overly anxious that he had totally forgotten about his own dreaded fears of personal panic attacks. Without even giving it much thought, Jack was managing to hold his own anxieties at bay through his drive to help save the future of one of his favorite and brightest students.

When time for the break was up, Jack told Rick that they "probably should be getting back now to the courtroom." Jack was shocked when Rick's knee buckled as he rose to his feet. "Geeze," thought Jack, "this poor kid really is scared."

Jack decided to tell Rick a joke to help distract him as they took the elevator up to the third floor. The joke was silly to the point of being embarrassingly corny, but it made Rick laugh hard anyway. This helped ease Rick's tensions a little bit and gave him the ability to look somewhat at peace as he and his lawyer entered the courtroom and took their seats at the defense table in the front.

Kate and her ear-whispering trooper were already in their seats at their respective table. The jury had not yet entered nor would they for another five minutes. Nobody but the bailiffs knew what was taking the jury so long. The judge would not come out until the jury first did. Kate whispered to Jack across the room that some poky juror always seemed to hold up all of the others somehow. Eventually, the jury did come in. Jack took Rick by the elbow as they (as well as the prosecutor and her trooper) all stood to show respect. The lawyers soon stood once again as the judge entered the room in response to a bailiff's cue. For the first time, Judge Price did not take an opportunity to smile and greet the jury. Trials can be taxing on judges too.

"Let us get started," Judge Price instructed. He looked at Jack and told him to call his first witness.

Jack patted young Rick on the hand and announced to all, "The defense calls Richard Mahan, the defendant to the stand." Jack looked down at the hand he had just patted and noticed it was trembling on the table. He leaned over to the petrified client and told him to look backward briefly at his parents as he walked to the stand. Rick did just that. This accomplished two things, just as Jack had hoped. It gave young Rick enough courage to get out of his seat and start walking. It also helped the jury to realize just how very young this kid in adult court was.

Jack watched as Rick's right hand now started to tremble as he raised it to the square in preparation for the oath. Rick's left hand also trembled a little but less visibly so since it was firmly pushing down on the Bible held by one of the bailiffs. Kate was watching the trembling hands with an odd combination of maternal-like sympathy coupled with professional satisfaction. "Maybe I can use this witness's fear to my advantage,"

Kate found herself plotting. She felt quite ashamed at the thought, but her lawyer training would not permit her to purge the dark strategy from her mind entirely.

Having finished taking his oath, Rick sat down and simply stared nonstop at his lawyer. Jack saw the fear in his youthful client's wide eyes and gave him a smile. With his own eyes, Jack then guided Rick's eyes over to the painting of young Abraham Lincoln that hung on the wall above the heads of the jurors. Rick knew what his lawyer was trying to tell him. When Jack had prepared Rick to testify several days earlier, Jack told Rick a fabricated story of Abraham Lincoln's first time doing a trial as supposedly depicted in the painting. Jack told Rick that Lincoln was so frightened at the start of his first trial that he started to throw up in his mouth when it was his time to start speaking. Lincoln took a deep breath and slowly exhaled while looking at his kind father sitting as a spectator in the courtroom. This worked like a charm for the new young attorney, and it calmed him down. None of this was a true story, but Jack had told the white lie to his client anyway. He figured that this story might come in handy. Indeed it did. Rick looked at the painting and then looked at his own father in the audience. He then took a deep breath and exhaled slowly. He immediately felt much better.

Jack took a deep breath of his own. He knew that calling one's own client was fraught with peril. Jurors' attention becomes riveted when a defendant elects to testify in his or her own behalf. The defendant is often **the witness jurors most anticipate** hearing from during a trial. True, jurors often hold it against defendants who exercise their constitutional right not to take the stand, even when judges at a trial's end tell them not to. Still, defense lawyers always think long and hard before putting their client on the stand.

For one thing, lawyers are not allowed to **suborn perjury**. Though they are allowed to defend a client regarding a crime already committed, lawyers may not lawfully aid and abet a client in committing a new crime, in this instance the crime of perjury. If a lawyer knows for a fact that a client would be lying under oath by claiming innocence, the lawyer is forbidden from calling the client in the first place. (The lawyer may still hold the prosecutor to her burden of proof; he just cannot call the perjuring client to the stand.)

There are several other reasons why a lawyer might refrain from calling a client to testify. If a client has a prior criminal record, the record (previously inadmissible) suddenly becomes fair play in prosecutorial attempts to **impeach** (cast doubt on the truthfulness of) the defendant's testimony. In addition, lawyers have to worry about the degree to which their client might be unlikable. Jurors, most of whom come from the middle class, prefer witnesses whose diction, bearing, and mannerisms project middle class standing rather than lower class standing. Fairly or unfairly, if a lawyer has a client who cannot at least act as though he or she is from the middle class, it is usually wise to keep them off the stand. Finally, a rule of thumb known to all seasoned defense attorneys is that a lawyer should never put a defendant on the stand if the state is losing its case. Nothing can change victory faster into defeat than calling a defendant to the stand.

Jack thought about all of these matters and still chose to call his client as a witness. Rick had no criminal record that Kate could use to impeach his integrity as a witness. Additionally, Jack did not know for a fact that Rick was guilty. (In fact, he actually believed his client was not guilty — a rarity for a lawyer during a trial.) Thus, Jack did not have to worry about aiding and abetting the commission of perjury. Jack also knew that Rick could "pull off" coming across as middle class since he was middle class. The **jurors' tribal instincts** would be with him. In addition to that, Rick was young and seemed innocent. That would help get the jury to like him. Jack could not helping remembering, once again, that jurors hate to convict people whom they like.

Jack was now ready to ask Rick his questions. Jack gave Rick another very warm look (this time to communicate his fondness for Rick to the jury rather than to help him calm down).

"Could you please state your name for the record?" Jack requested. Rick replied by giving his name. "What is your age?" asked Jack. Jack wanted the jury to know that they would be sitting in judgment over a kid. Kate stood up and objected on the grounds of relevancy. Judge Price responded by saying, "No, I will allow it." Rick told the jury that he was 17 years old.

Before getting to questions relevant to the theory of his defense, Jack decided first to clear the air by getting his client to admit to facts that he strategically chose not to dispute. In doing so, Jack hoped that Rick would come across as an honest person who had nothing to hide. Jack made sure during witness preparation prior to trial that Rick would not beat around the bush with this first series of questions.

"Rick, I call your attention to the evening of April 5 of this year. We have heard testimony that you were at a party at a friend's house and you had drunk some beer. Is that correct?"

"Yes, I drank beer. Everyone there was drinking beer, so I did too."

"How many beers did you drink?"

"Two beers."

"Yet we heard testimony from the trooper that you drank just one beer, Rick. Did you tell the trooper you only had one beer?" Jack asked him this question because he knew Kate was eager to bring it up soon on her cross-examination anyway to make Rick seem like a liar. It always looks better for the defense to **air any dirty laundry first.**

"I was scared, so I told the trooper that I only had one beer."

"Why were you so scared?"

"Because the trooper told me that two people in the other car had died. He was very angry at me, and I got super scared."

"Why should the jury believe you now when you say you drank just two beers?"

"You got really upset with me when you found out that I had lied to the police about having had just one beer. I thought I had better just start telling the truth both to you and everyone else from then on. I should have just done that from the start. I was stupid."

"How many cold pills did you take?"

"Two, that was the dosage listed on the box."

Jack was glad that Rick had mentioned the box. "Speaking of the box, the trooper testified that you had told him that you had read the warnings on the box, all of the warnings. What exactly did you read?"

Rick leaned forward just as he had been coached by Jack to do when this question was asked. He also gazed intently at the jurors, again as coached. "I read some of the warnings but not all of them. I read what the medicine was used for; I read that it could be taken without a prescription. I read the dosage; I read that it was not habit forming if taken as directed. I read some other stuff as well but cannot remember all of it. There was a lot of fine print on the box. I know for sure that I never read any of the warnings about drowsiness or about not drinking alcohol while also taking the pills. I barely even wanted to take the pills in the first place even without having to worry about getting drowsy."

Jack looked over at the jury. Every one of them seemed to be trying to look into Rick's soul as he spoke. "Rick," Jack began again, "What about the testimony you heard from young Nancy Foley from the party that she saw you taking a whole minute to read the box? I guess she was insinuating that you had more than enough time to read everything on the box. How do you respond to that?"

Jack knew what Rick would say. They had rehearsed the best way to say it before trial.

"I did read the front of the box first. There were no warnings there. Then I read the stuff I specifically just mentioned on the back of the box. That took a while, I suppose. I read slowly because I was debating inside myself whether this medicine would do me any good. I knew that there is no cure for a cold and was trying to decide if my symptoms were bad enough to make it worth taking some medicine that really would not cure me anyway. I suppose I must have looked like I was carefully reading everything on the entire box, but I was not. I never read any warnings about drowsiness. I never read any warnings about not drinking alcohol while taking those pills. That is the truth!"

Jack let Rick's testimony sink in for a little while before asking his next question. "Rick, what I am about to ask you is very important…" Jack had prefaced what he was about to ask his client with those words so that he could be sure that the jury would know to pay strict attention now. "If you did not read the warnings about mixing pills with alcohol, then how do you explain Nancy's testimony that she saw you looking at your beer bottle and then shaking your head from side to side at the bottle as you continued to read from the box?"

Rick again leaned forward and looked at the jury. "I had a splitting headache while I was reading the box. I always get a splitting headache when I drink any alcohol in any amount. I get that from my dad, who always gets headaches from alcohol. Anyway, my headache was getting worse and worse as I was trying to read stuff on the box. I guess I was sort of showing my anger at the beer for making feel so bad while I just was trying to read the damn box!"

Jack was glad that Rick had remembered to call the box "the damn box," just like they had rehearsed. Rick had used that phrase with Jack when he first described this matter to him. Jack thought the phrase made Rick sound believable when he spoke about getting mad at the beer bottle and its contents for his headache. "Be sure to tell it the exact same way to the jury," Jack had told him. Rick had just done as advised.

Jack finished his direct examination of Rick by having Rick verify that he felt completely sober when he left the party. He had Rick describe how he started feeling sleepy during his drive home but was unable to find a place to pull over safely before the crash had occurred. Jack finished by asking him to tell the jury about his having fallen asleep once before at the wheel about two months before the fatal crash. Rick indeed told the jury about just that and swore he had nothing to drink that former night, nor had he taken any medicine or other drugs. He had just fallen asleep at the wheel because he was plain old tired.

"Thank you, Rick, for your testimony," Rick's defense lawyer concluded. "I believe the prosecutor may now have a few questions for you."

"Indeed, I do!" exclaimed Kate. "I most certainly do."

～

## Key Terms Found in This Chapter

Excuses for witness nonpreparation

Tips on style

Suggest content

De facto trial preparation

The witness jurors most anticipate

Suborn perjury

Impeach

Jurors' tribal instincts

Air any dirty laundry first

## Questions for Class Discussion

1. What are some excuses that busy prosecutors and public defenders have for not preparing all of their witnesses in cases apparently heading for trial? Are any of these excuses invalid?

2. What are some reasons that private defense lawyers, who typically have much smaller caseloads, have for not preparing witnesses pre-trial? Are these excuses valid?

3. What is allowed and forbidden in terms of preparing a witness for trial? How can this sometimes involve walking a fine line?

4. What would be a clear example of a lawyer giving a defense witness a mere tip on style? What would be a clear example of unethically suggesting content?

5. Do you think that pretrial preparation of witnesses really makes all that big a difference?

6. What does the chapter mean when it suggests that prosecutors, unlike defense attorneys, benefit from some "*de facto* trial preparation"? Who provides this service for the prosecutor? Is it fair that one side has such help, while the other side does not?

7. Would you be in favor of reducing caseloads among public defenders in your area if that would enable public defenders to better prepare for trial? Would you be in favor of funding an office investigator who can work at the behest of the public defenders?

8. Why do juries anticipate hearing from defendants perhaps more than any other witness? Would you hold it against a defendant for electing not to testify in a trial? What are some reasons a defense lawyer might have in keeping their client off the stand if they are supposed to be innocent?

9. What is meant by "suborning perjury"? How might a lawyer violate this rule in a trial? Why does the right to represent a client zealously not protect an attorney who suborns perjury during a trial?

10. Do you believe the chapter's assertion that jurors tend to be beholden to "tribal instincts"? Do such instincts truly exist? What are their roots? Are they always bad?

11. Why should defense attorneys air dirty laundry while they have the chance? How does doing this help make things better for their clients? What dirty laundry were aired in this chapter by Jack and his client?

# 32

## The Case for the Defense (Part II)

Kate was indeed eager for the opportunity to cross-examine Rick. She knew Rick was very nervous and very young. She considered immediately adopting a very aggressive, **confrontational approach** to her questions but realized that this could easily backfire. Kate wanted to get the job done of pulling any facts from Rick that would be favorable to her side. She also hoped to cast doubt on Rick's willingness to always tell the truth. Yet, she knew she would not help her cause if she were to **alienate the jury** by coming across as a bully. Given the huge differences between her and Rick in terms of age and education, coming across as a bully was definitely something she had to worry about.

Like Jack, Kate knew that since an attorney is permitted to lead a witness on cross-examination, the attorney almost always should do so. Effectively, she wanted to be the one doing the testifying, rather than the official witness, with Rick merely being a **trial puppet** answering "yes" to as many of her questions as possible.

Kate's desire that Rick become her mere puppet was not so easy to realize. Jack had anticipated Kate's approach on cross, even including her desire to come across as something other than a bully. He had coached Rick never to let Kate put words into his mouth, no matter how respectful or kind she might be pretending to be. "Remember, Rick, she is not your friend," he warned him many times over. "Do not take forever to answer questions so that the jury does not think you are making things up as you go along. However, do not answer so fast that you are letting her control and dominate you. Remember, she is trying to trap you with nearly every question she asks. Do not let her."

Kate looked Rick straight in the eyes as she prepared to throw out her first question to him. He looked back at first but Kate outstared him. Embarrassed by the prolonged eye contact, Rick looked down at his lap the way a dog looks away from an alpha. Kate was pleased with this reaction. It was what she was going for.

"You do not mind if I ask you a few questions, do you Mr. Mahan?" Kate's tone of voice was surprisingly respectful to Rick. He liked that she referred to him as "Mr. Mahan." She sounded almost deferential. What he did not realize was that Kate was trying to suggest to the jury that he was not just some young child she was going to be picking on. He was a young man, not a boy.

"You can ask me questions," Rick replied. He was nervously shifting about in his seat without even realizing it.

"You admit to drinking beer on the night you fell asleep at the wheel, correct?"

"Yes, I drank two beers."

"You lied to the trooper though and told him you had just one beer. You were worried that two beers would make you sound tipsy or buzzed, right?"

"I only lied because I was so scared. The trooper seemed really angry at me."

"So, you only lie when you are really scared?"

"Yes, I would say that is right," Rick responded.

"Are you really scared right now?"

Rick sensed a trap. "No," he replied.

"Didn't I see your hands trembling when you were sworn in?"

"I don't know what you saw."

"Your hands trembled, didn't they Mr. Mahan?"

"Maybe."

"Can you think of any reason why 'maybe' your hands would tremble, other than your being scared?"

"Well, I am nervous, I guess. Who wouldn't be?" Rick explained.

"I bet you are you nervous about having to speak in public," Kate suggested. Rick agreed with that suggestion. "I bet you are also nervous that you could lose this trial?" Rick had to admit that this was true also. "In fact, I bet right now is one of the scariest times of your life?" He agreed that it was.

"How many beers did you really drink that night at the party, one or two, or maybe more? Please do not lie." Kate asked the witness bluntly.

"Two beers," Rick insisted. "I would not lie."

"But don't you sometimes lie when you are really scared? You are really scared right now, right?"

"I sometimes lie when I am really scared but not this time."

"Oh, I see," Kate replied. "You just lie sometimes when you are very scared but not this time when you are very scared."

"Objection," Jack announced. "The prosecutor is harassing my client. She is **badgering the witness**." Judge Price simply told Kate to move on.

She looked at Rick intensely. "In addition to more than one beer, you also had taken two Benadryl pills, right?"

"Yes. I had a cold. Nancy Foley suggested they might help with that. She fetched a box of that cold medicine from her purse and handed me the box."

"We have heard testimony that the back of the box warns about not driving after taking these pills because the medicine can cause drowsiness; also, that drinking alcohol while taking the pills can make the drowsiness much worse. Yet, somehow you never read any of that stuff."

"That is correct," Rick agreed. "I only read about dosage and what the pills are for."

"Nancy Foley, the girl from the party, told the court that she saw you take a whole minute reading from the box. Was she telling the truth?"

"I doubt I took a whole minute."

"But you don't really know, do you Mr. Mahan?"

"No, not really."

"Nancy said you spent the bulk of the time that you spent reading the box by reading on the back of the box instead of on its front. Was she right about that?"

"Yes, if she says so."

"The back of the box is where the warnings are about drowsiness and also about alcohol, but you never read that part of the back. Is that what you would have us believe?"

"It is the truth."

Kate asked the judge for permission to gather the box from the court reporter and to approach the witness. Judge Price granted her requests.

She walked up to Rick with the box and handed it to him. "Mr. Mahan, I show you what had earlier been marked as 'Commonwealth Exhibit 1,' the Benadryl box. I now ask you to please read aloud to us what it is you read silently to yourself from the back of the box on the evening of April 5. The jury and I can watch the second hand on the big clock on the back wall of this courtroom as you do so. Just start when you are ready. Take your time first and look all you want at the box before you begin."

Rick did take about 15 seconds to study the back of the box. "I am ready to read now," he announced.

Kate spun around with her back to Rick. She looked up at the big clock on the back of the wall. She glanced over at the jury to make sure they were all looking at it too. They were. "Go ahead," Kate told Rick. "Read out loud what you think you had read that night on the back of the box, and nothing else."

Rick started reading information on the box about what the pills were for; he read about dosage; he read about the symptoms treated by the medicine; he read about how they were non-habit forming if taken as directed. Then Rick stopped reading. Kate told him that it was up to the jury to decide for themselves, but it looked to her that his reading took a total of 25 seconds and "not the bulk of a whole minute." She looked at Rick and gently asked, "Now, Mr. Mahan, read what comes next. Read the very next lines from the point where you just finished."

Rick once again read out loud to the jury: "Caution: this medicine causes drowsiness. Do NOT drive or operate machinery while taking any of these pills. Do NOT consume alcohol while taking this medication, as alcohol tends to aggravate the tendency to cause drowsiness."

"Thank you, Mr. Mahan. I am glad you are so very good at reading," Kate said. "I bet you can even read faster when you are not reading out loud. Let me ask you something else. Was Nancy correct when she said you started shaking your head at some point at the bottle of beer while still reading the back of the box? You did shake your head at the bottle, correct?"

"Yes, but it was because I had a bad headache from drinking the beer; the act of reading just made it even worse, so I looked up at the bottle of beer. I was sort of frustrated at the beer for giving me the headache and making it so unpleasant for me to try to read."

"Oh, right," Kate said in a sarcastic tone. "What do you suppose Nancy thought was the reason why you were shaking your head at the beer bottle?"

"Objection," Jack called out. "Calls for speculation." The judge sustained Jack's objection. Kate was not bothered by his objection or the judge's ruling on it. She just had wanted to remind the jury about the incident. In order to do that she was willing to commit a **strategic foul** and get called on it.

Kate now wanted to ask a series of questions that she considered went straight to the heart of Jack's defense of Rick. She knew that the defense was suggesting that Rick had just fallen asleep at the wheel for reasons unrelated to his drinking and taking cold medicine. In other words, the crash had nothing to do with the beer and the pills. Falling asleep behind the wheel was all just an unlucky coincidence.

"Mr. Mahan, you admit that you fell asleep on April 5 behind the wheel and crashed your car?" Rick Mahan admitted that this was true.

"You admit that it was the crash that caused two people to die." Rick bowed his head low and softly agreed that this was also correct.

"You fell asleep once before behind the wheel, a couple of months before the night of the fatal crash. Is that your testimony?" Rick agreed with this statement.

"I bet you fell asleep behind the wheel that first time because you were very tired. It was because you were tired that you fell asleep and not because of beer or cold pills?"

"Yes. That is exactly right. I was very tired that night. I drank no alcohol and took no medicine of any kind. I just fell asleep."

"I see," Kate noted. "Mr. Mahan, in your entire lifetime, how many times have you fallen asleep at the wheel?"

"Just twice," Rick answered.

"The first time was because you were very tired. Why do you think you fell asleep the second time, the time of the fatal crash?"

"I guess I must have been very tired then too," Rick explained.

"Yet you felt completely fit to drive when you left the party, correct?"

"Yes, I thought I felt okay at the time."

"And you remember Nancy Foley saying you seemed okay when you left the party? Her perception of that was accurate, would you not agree?"

"I do not disagree," Rick answered.

"In fact, all during the party you felt alert and fine, including up until the very moment you left?"

"You could say that," Rick agreed.

"So it was not until after you drank beer and took cold pills and allowed about 15 minutes to pass that you first felt sleepy that entire evening?"

Rick was unsure how to respond to that question. He sensed that the prosecutor was **setting a trap**, just as his attorney had told him she would attempt to do. Rick looked at his attorney, hoping he would object. However, Jack knew that there was no credible objection to field. If he attempted to assert one, it would make matters look even worse.

"The witness will please answer the question," Judge Price instructed.

"Yes, I first felt tired about 15 minutes into the trip," Rick confirmed.

"So," Kate continued, "the first time in your life you fell asleep at the wheel of a car was a time you were very tired; the only other time you fell asleep was when you were not tired but got tired only after first having consumed alcohol and cold pills. So…"

"Objection!" a now annoyed Jack shouted. "I would appreciate it if the prosecutor could refrain from **making a speech**."

"I will sustain that objection," Judge Price declared.

"Very well, Your Honor," Kate replied. "I have no further questions of Mr. Mahan."

"Any questions on re-direct, Mr. Day?" the judge asked Jack.

"Just a few, Your Honor. Rick, the first time you fell asleep behind the wheel a couple of months before April 5 — tell us when you first noticed yourself falling asleep."

"I never noticed myself falling asleep until I had run off the road."

"And tell us when you first noticed yourself falling asleep on the night of April 5."

Rick thought for an instant and reflected on his pre-trial rehearsal of his testimony with Jack. "Initially, I first felt sleepy about 15 minutes into the trip. I started looking around for a safe place to pull over. I felt alert again while looking, but the next thing I remember is having crashed."

"So the way you ultimately crashed your car on the fatal night was pretty much the same experience as the first time a couple of months before — the time you did not have any alcohol or cold pills? You felt alert one second and had simply crashed the next."

Now it was Kate's turn to get annoyed. "Objection, Your Honor. I would appreciate it if the defense attorney could refrain from making a speech."

"Sustained," the judge ruled trying to hide a smile. "Mr. Day, I believe there is a rule against **lawyers testifying**. That includes Ms. Page before and you now."

"No further questions, Your Honor," Jack announced. Kate told the court that she had no questions on re-cross. The judge therefore excused Rick, who gratefully took his seat back in the relative comfort of the defense table.

Jack was ready to call his next witness.

## Key Terms Found in This Chapter

Confrontational approach                              Strategic foul
Alienate the jury                                      Setting a trap
Trial puppet                                         Making a speech
Badgering the witness                              Lawyers testifying

## Questions for Class Discussion

1. The prosecutor in this chapter was concerned with taking a confrontational approach with the defendant. Why was that so? Under what circumstances would a jury be more tolerant of an aggressive, confrontational approach by the prosecutor while cross-examining a defendant on the stand?

2. ADA Kate Page was worried about alienating the jury. Should Jack also worry about that possibility during the trial? What might he do during the trial that could alienate the jury?

3. How do attorneys on cross-examination try to turn a witness into their trial puppets? Why do they want to keep the witness stringed up? What could happen if a prosecutor allowed a defendant to become a free speaker instead of just a puppet?

4. What do lawyers mean when they claim their opponent is "badgering the witness"? What is the difference between being blunt with a witness versus badgering?

5.  Is it ethical for a lawyer to commit a "strategic foul" by asking a question that they know they should not ask? How should a lawyer in such a situation react when the inevitable ruling against them is made by the trial referee? What analogy is there to this and intentionally fouling in a basketball game?
6.  How was the prosecutor in this case trying to set a trap by her questioning of young Rick? Are lawyers ethical when they try to set traps or just doing their jobs?
7.  Why do lawyers like trying to "make a speech" while questioning a witness? Are there any points in a trial when lawyers are permitted to engage in speech making?
8.  What did the judge mean when he reminded Jack that lawyers are forbidden from testifying? Do lawyers ever seem to testify during trials in fictional television shows or movies? What would you think of a situation in which a lawyer called himself to the stand in order to give insights to the jury about a case?

# 33

## The Case for the Defense (Part III)

Jack looked up at Judge Price, who was waiting patiently for him to call his next witness. The judge did not seem bored, and Jack took that somehow as a good sign for his side. This probably was not going to be a "slam dunk" for the prosecution as is sometimes the case with trials.

"The defense now calls George Franklin to the stand," Jack announced. A young man started to walk in a self-conscious manner toward the front of the courtroom. He was wearing the "business blue," dress shirt and purple tie that Jack had personally purchased for him to wear (no jacket — Jack had wanted him to look conservative yet young like Rick). George Franklin also sported the small U.S. flag pin that Jack had purchased himself and asked him to wear on his tie.

Arriving at the stand, George started to seat himself but reversed course mid-descent when he saw the bailiff approaching him with a Bible. After taking the witness oath, George finally took his seat. He looked at his friend Rick sitting at the defense table but dared not smile or do anything to make him look like a biased witness. Soon enough, his gaze naturally shifted to Rick's attorney since he knew that Jack would be the one about to pose his first question.

"For the record, please state your name," Jack requested.

"Um, my name is George Douglas Franklin." George thought he should include his middle name since this was such a solemn occasion to him. "My last name is spelled…" Jack cut George off and told him, "It's okay. We got that."

"George, how do you know my client, Richard Mahan?" Jack inquired.

"Rick and I go to school together. We are good friends. We hang out together, quite a bit. We have been friends at St. Francis since the first semester of ninth grade."

"Do you remember that night when Rick fell asleep while driving?"

"Do you mean the night he got arrested for driving drunk and stuff?"

"No," Jack clarified. "I am not talking about the night he drove home alone from the party but a night a couple of months prior to that when you were with him in a car."

"Yes, I was a passenger in Rick's car on that occasion."

"Tell us about what happened." Jack knew that George was an **eyewitness**, someone who was present during a significant event and could tell the jury exactly what he had witnessed on the spot with his own senses. Jack knew that juries put a lot of weight into what eyewitnesses have to say. Therefore, Jack had previously taken great pains to coach George, including teaching him to start looking at the jury when he was asked to "tell us about what happened." In his nervous state, however, George just continued looking exclusively at Jack, even after receiving the cue. As George was about to start talking, he noticed Jack pointedly turn his head and begin to watch the jury. George got the hint, and he too shifted his gaze toward them.

"Well, Rick and I had been playing ping pong at his house that evening," George began to explain to the jury. "When it was about 10:00 p.m., it was time for me to go home, so Rick and I got into his car, and he started to drive us toward my house. I live about 20 minutes away. We talked at first, but then I took out my phone and started checking out some social media stuff. Rick just drove silently. When we got within a couple of miles to my house, I suddenly felt the car leaving the road. I looked up from my phone at Rick and saw that he had dozed off! I screamed for Rick to wake up, which he did. He slammed on the breaks, and we came to rest in a field. Rick looked very scared. After a minute, Rick realized nothing was wrong, and so he just drove back on to the highway and finished taking me home."

"Thank you, George," Jack said. "How much alcohol, if any, had you seen Rick consume that night you were playing ping pong together?"

"None. His parents do not drink. They have no alcohol in the house, ever. I know because I have been in their fridge and cupboards a hundred times looking for stuff to eat. Rick had nothing to drink that night, except Dr Pepper. That's his thing."

"Did you see Rick take any medicine that night or drugs of any kind?"

"No, nothing."

"What about marijuana?"

"No, are you kidding? Rick is not that kind of guy. He is, like, the biggest square I know." Jack loved this response. Of course, they had rehearsed it before trial.

"So why do you suppose he fell asleep at the wheel?" Jack asked. "Could it be that it was because he was just plain tired even though he had not drunk any alcohol nor taken any type of medicine?"

"Oh, come on… Objection!" Kate called out, rising angrily to her feet. "Not only does this call for the witness to make a conclusion, but Mr. Day is also trying to lead this witness all over the place."

"Sustained," noted the judge. "Mr. Day, you know better than that!"

"Very well," conceded Jack. "I will be very content to allow the jury to draw its own conclusions. No further questions of this witness."

As so often is the case, the witness started to stand up when he had heard the phrase, "no further questions." "Please take your seat, young man," the judge instructed. "I believe the assistant district attorney wishes to ask you some questions now." Kate was grateful for this instruction from the judge but wished he had not referred to the witness as being a "young" man. It was her job now to grill the witness if she could, and she still was worried about looking like a bully.

"Mr. Franklin," (Kate made sure to avoid calling him "George") "have you ever before or after this car crash on ping pong night seen your friend, Mr. Mahan, fall asleep at the wheel?"

"No, that was the only time."

"I take it that you have driven with him before?" (Kate already knew the answer thanks to the police investigation reports in her file.)

"Yes, quite often," George agreed.

"In fact, he has driven you around so many times you cannot count the times."

"Well, yeah, I guess so."

"So, is it not fair to say that Richard Mahan falling asleep at the wheel is an exceeding rare thing to happen?"

"Yes, you could say that."

"A freak occurrence?" Kate asked.

"I would not say that," the witness countered.

"Why wouldn't you say that?" asked Kate. "In all your countless times driving with him, you personally witnessed Richard only fall asleep a grand total of one time, right?"

George looked at Jack for guidance. "Objection," Jack called out. "I believe the prosecutor is starting to badger the witness."

"Overruled," Judge Price announced. "The witness will answer the question."

Despite the judge's unfavorable ruling on the objection, Jack's assertion that this prosecutor was picking on George had sounded right to George. George was now determined not to play into his adversary's hands.

"What was the question again?" George heatedly asked. Kate liked this showing of anger on the part of the witness. Juries generally do not like angry people on the stand. Their anger suggests bias.

"Was your friend Richard Mahan's falling asleep at the wheel a freak occurrence?"

"No."

"Oh really?" Kate responded. "Yet, you do admit it has never happened before or after that one time among all of the countless times he drove with you somewhere."

"Who says it was countless times?" George protested. "That was your phrase."

"Oh, okay. How many times have you two driven together, rough estimate?"

"I have no idea," George countered.

"You have no idea because it was so many times, right?"

"I suppose so," George grudgingly admitted.

"Thank you, Mr. Franklin. I have no further questions." Before George could even begin to stand up from his seat again, the judge proactively motioned with his hand for him to remain seated. "Is there any re-direct from the defense?" the judge inquired of Jack. When Jack informed the court that he had no further questions, the judge told George that he could now leave the stand. As George walked to take a seat in the audience, he gave Kate a dirty look. "Thanks, good buddy, for that!" Kate thought as she imagined the jury seeing that look as well.

Jack just shrugged George's look off and was now ready to call his last two witnesses, both of whom would testify as to his client's character. He decided to call Rick's principal first and his honors teacher second, in conformity with Jack's philosophy that stronger witnesses should always go before those that are (even slightly) less strong.

Jack knew that **character witnesses** could be of great benefit to defendants charged with serious offenses. These witnesses can help a defendant who is a total stranger to the jury seem like a person who is honest, responsible, or nonviolent, as the defense need may be. Their use plays in to the rule that defense lawyers should always go out of their way to get jurors to like their clients whenever they can. However, defense attorneys must be very careful in using character witnesses. **Evidence of bad character** (which generally takes the form of a prior criminal record) is generally not admissible unless the defendant "opens the door" first by **putting one's character at issue**. Once a defendant places his or her character at issue in the trial, the prosecutor is then free to **rebut evidence of good character** with evidence of bad character, including the existence of any prior convictions. Jack knew that his client had never been convicted of anything before in his life. Hence, unlike defense attorneys in many, if not most, criminal trials, he could afford the luxury of "opening the door" to his client's character.

"The defense calls Joseph Skelly to the stand," Jack announced. Father Joseph Skelly arose and walked to the witness stand. He was dressed like the Catholic priest that he was. Jack hoped that having a priest testify for the defense would not backfire, given the bad press of late that a very small, but very infamous, minority of Catholic clergy had generated due to their abuse. Still, Jack figured that calling a priest to testify to someone's character was probably a good call, especially since this was a county (and hence probably a jury) heavily populated with Catholics.

Kate watched as the priest fervently swore on the Bible to tell the truth. "Oh brother," she cynically thought, "this guy is too much."

"Please state your name and occupation," Jack instructed.

"My name is Joseph Skelly. I am the principal of St. Francis high school here in the county. I am also a Jesuit."

"A Jesuit is a type of priest?"

"Yes, Jesuits are priests who typically choose either missionary or education work as their specific calling in the church."

"Father Skelly, as an educator, do you know my client, young Richard Mahan, who is on trial for two counts of vehicular homicide, among other things?"

"I most certainly do know Rick Mahan. I know him very well."

"How do you know him so well in such a big high school?"

"He is one of the top students in the school. He would be hard to miss. He is a known quantity among all of the faculty and staff, I imagine."

"So, not only do you know Rick, but you know many others at the school who also know Rick?"

"Yes, that is correct."

"Among the people whom you know that also know Richard Mahan, what is his reputation, if any, among them for honesty?"

"He is known for never cheating, never falsifying. He is above reproach in this area. He is known to be a young man of honesty and integrity."

"What about his reputation, if any, for responsibility?"

Joseph Skelly looked at Rick and smiled approvingly. "Rick Mahan is known within my school community as being in the top one percent of students in terms of responsibility. He has a 3.98 GPA. Teachers love it when they find out he will be in their class. He is a very serious and responsible young man, well beyond his years."

"Thank you, Father Skelly," Jack said. He looked over at Kate and said, "Your witness."

Kate stood up. "Mr. Skelly, I have just a couple of questions for you." Jack looked at the jury and saw one older woman seem to cringe at hearing a priest referred to as "Mr." "Way to go, Kate," Jack thought.

"Tell me, Sir," Kate continued, "is it responsible for a high school senior to drink beer?"

"Why, no," Skelly admitted.

"Is it responsible for someone to drink beers, take cold medicine, and drive like Richard Mahan has already told the jury that he had done?"

"No, I suppose not."

"So, is it fair to say that Richard Mahan, who has admitted to this very court to drinking underage and also to driving after drinking and taking cold pills, apparently is capable of acting irresponsibly?"

"Nobody is perfect," protested Skelly.

"I could not agree more," Kate responded. "What about honesty, Sir?"

"What about it?" asked Joseph Skelly.

"Is it honest for someone to lie to the police about the number of beers they had drunk?"

"No, but I think Rick Mahan cleared that up."

"But he is capable of lying, is he not?"

"Everyone is capable of lying, Ms. Page. Even you and me."

"No further questions." Kate sat down. The judge looked at Jack and invited him to call his last witness.

"The defense calls Amy Johnson to the stand." An intelligent and rather young woman walked up to the stand and was sworn in. Like Father Skelly before her, she was asked to state her name and occupation. She identified herself as Amy Johnson, Rick's Honors English teacher at the high school. Like Father Skelly before her, she testified on direct examination to Rick's reputation for being both very honest and responsible. In addition, like Father Skelly before her, Amy admitted to the prosecutor during cross-examination that drinking beer underage and lying to the police about the number of beers show that even Rick could act irresponsibly and dishonestly.

After Amy stepped off the stand, Jack announced that he had no other witnesses, and that therefore, "**the defense rests**." The judge asked Kate if there was anything else she wished to raise before they moved on to closing arguments. The prosecutor replied that she had no **state rebuttal witnesses** whom she wished to call to counter something or anything else raised at some point during the defense case. That being the case, the judge announced that it was growing late in the day, so the court would recess until 9:30 a.m. the next day. At that time, the court would reconvene to hear the attorneys' closing arguments.

After the judge and jury had left the courtroom, young Rick nervously asked his lawyer what he thought about his chances. Jack shrugged and told him it could go either way. Jack looked over at Kate talking to her trooper friend at the prosecution table. He could hear her whispering the same thing to him.

∾

# Key Terms Found in This Chapter

Eyewitness

Character witnesses

Evidence of bad character

Putting one's character at issue

Rebut evidence of good character

The defense rests

State rebuttal witnesses

# Questions for Class Discussion

1. Why do juries love eyewitnesses so much? Do they tend to put more trust in eyewitness accounts than is perhaps warranted? What sort of things might cause an eyewitness to have problems recollecting an event with accuracy?

2. To what sort of specific traits do defense attorneys hope that a character witness will attest? What trait would you want a character witness to verify in a case involving the alleged embezzlement of company funds? A case involving the alleged rape of an acquaintance?

3. Should prior criminal records of a defendant and other evidence of bad character generally be admissible during a trial no matter what? In what way might their value in ascertaining truth be outweighed by prejudicial effects?

4. What is meant by a defendant's "putting his character at issue"? How does this occur? What may a prosecutor do once this has happened?

5. Are character witnesses truly very helpful in ascertaining the truth? How much credibility would you as a juror give such testimony presented by the defense? Do jurors probably put too much (or too little) faith in such evidence?

6. Would you give more weight to character testimony offered by clergy (like Father Skelly) than by neighbors or teachers? Less weight?

7. Would you give any weight to character testimony offered by relatives or close friends of a defendant?

8. If asked to testify about the character of a close, but dishonest, friend, would you refuse the request? Would your best friend be willing to exaggerate qualities about your reputation for honesty and integrity if it would help you in court? How might this all depend on what the charges were?

9.  The defense often rests its case after using up much less time than the state used up before resting its own case. Why do you suppose this might be so?

10. Sometimes, a defense attorney will rest its case without even calling a single defense witness. If you were to do this as an attorney, what reason might you give in closing arguments to justify to the jury this unusual course of action?

11. The prosecutor in this case presented no rebuttal witnesses after the defense had rested its case. If the prosecutor were to call a rebuttal witness, to what matter(s) might she have had this witness testify?

# Unit 12
# Crossing the Finish Line

**Chapter 34: The Defendant Briefly Absconds**

**Chapter 35: Closing Argument: Defense**

**Chapter 36: Closing Argument: Prosecution**

This unit begins with some recess adventure through which we learn some things about failing to appear and the odd job of being a bounty hunter. Then, closing arguments for both sides take place, through which we learn of the importance and some of the rules of having one's last say.

# 34

# The Defendant Briefly Absconds

After saying goodbye to his young client and his parents, Jack drove home for some much needed rest. Tomorrow morning's closing arguments would come soon enough, and he needed to kick back. He was determined to spend the evening watching old movies. Jack just wanted to relax and get the trial out of his mind for one evening. He still worried a lot about having another panic attack before the trial was completely over. If he could just hold it together for one more round, he would be out of the woods.

Jack's client, the supposed highway killer, had other worries on his mind. He too went home but not to watch movies. He went home to fret endlessly about what Jack had just told him at the end of court that day: his case could go "either way." "What the hell is that supposed to mean?" Rick kept asking himself. Jack thought that "either way" was a good thing. He knew that prosecutors, smart or dumb, typically experience a **supermajority of trial victories,** so "either way" was not a bad position to be in. However, Jack was seeing this from his vantage point as a criminal defense lawyer and not from the perspective of a 17-year-old boy who was scared to death of imprisonment again, maybe this time for many long years in a dark, austere, violent, state hellhole for grownups.

The more Rick thought about doing hard time, the more agitated he became. By the time dinner was done, his parents found their son to be inconsolable. They suggested he lie down for a few minutes in his room, and they would talk some more after he got a little rest. Rick stormed up the stairs and slammed the bedroom door behind him.

It was around 7:00 p.m. when Father Skelly's phone rang at his rectory. Skelly ran from the stove and answered on the sixth ring. He was expecting a call from his elderly mother, so he was quite surprised to hear instead the voice of Rick's father on the other end.

"Father Skelly, this is Frank Mahan, Rick's dad. I am sorry to disturb you, but Rick is gone, and we were wondering if you might have some idea about where he could be. We have called all his friends, but he is not with any of them. We thought maybe he might have gone to see you since you have been attending his trial and all — I know this is a long shot."

Skelly sat down with the phone in his suddenly trembling hand. "No, I have not seen Rick since I left the courthouse today. I hope he is all right."

"Well, that's just it," Frank countered. "He is not all right. His mom found a note in his room telling us he has decided to run away. He said he would rather take his chances starting a new life somehow than to risk going to prison. I think he has flipped out and is not thinking rationally at all."

Father Skelly paused so long that Mr. Mahan asked, "Are you still there?"

"Yes, I'm here. Did your son take anything with him?"

"Yes," affirmed the distressed caller. "He took a duffle bag he uses when we go camping as a family and, I suppose, some clothes."

"What about money?" Skelly asked. Before Mr. Mahan could answer, Mrs. Mahan grabbed the phone and interjected, "I just checked my late father's collection of silver dollars that we inherited when my parents died. They are all gone. There were over 200 of them. Rick must have taken them."

"Did you call up Attorney Day yet?"

"No, should we?"

Father Skelly again paused before replying, "Maybe not. I have a friend who can maybe help us much better than Jack Day could. He is a bounty hunter."

"You, a priest, and you know a bounty hunter!" exclaimed Mrs. Mahan.

"Yes, he is one of my many former students. He lives in the area. Let me work with him and see what he might be able to do for us in getting Rick back before he gets himself into any new trouble."

"I don't know," replied Mrs. Mahan. "Bounty hunters sound like rough characters."

"That is exactly what we need right now, Mrs. Mahan. I will call you back within three hours. Just sit tight and wait for my call. Do not call the police or even Jack Day. Let me handle this."

With the parents' reluctant blessing, Father Skelly got to work. It took him just two minutes to get hold of Theo Blake, graduate (barely) of St. Francis High School and professional bounty hunter.

Father Skelly explained the matter to Blake, who actually laughed at hearing the story. Theo's flippant attitude irritated his former high school principal, but Father Skelly was shrewd enough to avoid conveying that off-putting emotion to the man whose help he was now seeking.

"What will happen if the kid does not show up for court tomorrow morning?" asked Father Skelly. Theo explained that the parents' $40,000 bail would probably be forfeited, and a bench warrant would be issued for their son's arrest. Once arrested, the kid likely would be charged with **failure to appear**, yet another crime to be added to his others.

"What about the trial?" asked Father Skelly.

"I'm not sure, but I think the judge would just put it on hold until your young friend is caught by the police and dragged back to face the music. The trial would be placed in recess until that happened. None of this delay in the trial would sit favorably with the jury, who is probably going to be told by the judge what is going on. It will not sit favorably with the judge either when he sentences Rick once he is convicted of the homicides, assuming that he is convicted of the homicides. Of course, the crime of failure to appear is also a way for some judge to slam the kid, and that is a 100% guaranteed conviction."

"Will you help me find Rick?" Father Skelly bluntly asked.

"No," Theo bluntly responded. "I only work for money."

"How much would you want?"

"As a **bounty hunter**, I usually ask for 10% of the bond that would be forfeited by the bail bondsman. That is my **standard bounty**. Of course, your case is weird since there is no bail bondsman here to hire me. I guess I would ask the parents to pay me the 10% since they—and not a bail bondsman — would be out the money. Since the bail posted was $40,000, I would want $4,000 to get the kid back to court on time."

Theo was right in explaining that bounty hunters usually work for the **bail bondsmen** who put up the bond money, and they typically receive a percentage of the forfeited bail if they can produce the defendant for court. Even if the defendant is brought days late to court, the forfeited bail will be returned to the bail bondsman who had posted it. Bail bondsmen typically do not bother hiring bounty hunters if the monetary stakes are low. In such cases, the bail bondman merely writes off the forfeited money as the **cost of doing business**. However, when the monetary stakes are high, it pays to hire a bounty hunter.

Bounty hunters can make a lot of money for little work. Oftentimes, people who fail to show up for court have not fled the jurisdiction but are very close by. A few simple inquiries can often help determine their current hiding place. Theo instinctively sensed that Rick's flight would be an easy case to solve. Therefore, when Father Skelly painstakingly reminded Blake of many elaborate past favors owed, Theo agreed to track the kid down for no charge as long as he could accomplish it in just one evening.

Theo figured that finding an inexperienced kid like Rick would indeed not be too hard for an old pro like him. Since Rick was facing a long prison sentence, the bounty hunter knew that his first course of action should be to play it safe by first making sure that a panicky kid was not about to flee the area entirely. He figured that if Rick were seeking to leave the area, he would almost certainly avoid an airport. He only had 200 silver dollars, after all. Theo elected to go straight to the town's intercity bus station. He knew that if Rick were there he would stand out from the crowd: a young, middle-class kid with a duffel bag. If Rick were not there, Theo would start shaking down Rick's local friends, who almost certainly would be giving him cover despite their assertions to Rick's parents otherwise.

Arriving at the bus station, Theo searched the place — including the restroom stalls — but found no sign of Rick. Theo next asked the sole worker on duty at the ticket counter if she had sold a ticket to a White teenaged male carrying a duffel bag that night. "He probably would come across as a real square," Theo explained. When she said that she did not think so, he asked if anyone — anyone at all — had bought a ticket that night using silver dollars. The woman said that she had sold someone a ticket for Harrisburg, and the young man paid the $60 fee using 60 silver dollars.

"Where is the customer now?" asked Theo.

"He is on the bus. It left 10 minutes ago." Blake thanked the woman and ran to his car illegally parked outside. He broke more than several traffic laws speeding toward Valley Forge, the town where the Pennsylvania Turnpike begins as it starts its long westward journey from eastern Pennsylvania to the western part of the state (with Harrisburg on the way).

"Why Harrisburg?" Theo pondered to himself as he drove faster than was prudent. "I bet the kid has some friend or relative there who he thinks will help him out." (In fact, Rick's favorite cousin had moved there last year to attend a nearby college.)

As he approached the long line of tollbooths marking the grand entrance to the eastern terminus of the Pennsylvania turnpike, Theo spotted a Greyhound bus. He pulled ahead of the bus and saw the word "Harrisburg" lit up in the marque above the large front windshield. Theo then made his bold move. He took out a portable siren and placed it on the top of his private vehicle. He then negotiated his car over to the driver's side of the bus, slowed down until the bus was parallel to his car, and signaled the bus driver to pull over. Believing Theo to be a cop, the bus driver did just that.

Theo got out of his car and walked over to the bus. The driver opened the door. Theo entered and flashed a fake badge. "I am a bail enforcement agent for the Pennsylvania court system," he announced to the perplexed bus driver. (Bounty hunters love referring to themselves using made-up titles such as **bail enforcement agent**.) "I believe that a fugitive from the courts may be on your bus. I have come to arrest him."

With that, the bounty hunter walked down the aisle reviewing each passenger. It took a matter of seconds before the hunter spotted his prey. "Are you Rick Mahan?" asked Theo. A frightened Rick confirmed that he was. "You are under arrest. Please come with me."

Theo's bold moves may seem outrageous to some but were far from being over the top in the strange world of bounty hunting. Unlike police officers and other public officials, private bounty hunters are given extraordinary **catch-and-return powers** in returning bail jumpers to court.

Since they are not really government officials or agents, but rather private business people working for themselves, the Constitution does not apply to them. Hence, bounty hunters do not have to concern themselves with such things as search warrants, arrest warrants, or formal extradition procedures. This incredible state of the law dates back a long time. In fact, little has changed since 1872, when the U.S. Supreme Court, in the case of *Taylor v. Taintor,* ruled that "Whenever they [bounty hunters] choose to do so, they may seize him… they may imprison him… They may pursue him to another state; may arrest him… And, if necessary, may break and enter his house for that purpose."

Theo stuffed poor young Rick into the passenger side seat of his car and drove him swiftly over to Father Skelly's rectory. Theo provided not a single word of explanation to Rick during the speedy trip. Upon arriving at the rectory, Theo marched Rick up to the front door, rang the bell, and waited for Skelly to appear at the door. When Skelly opened the door, Theo shoved Rick into the foyer, announced that all past favors were now "paid in full," and swiftly walked back to his car. Father Skelly and Rick looked with amazement as Theo laughed hysterically as he sped away into the night.

After shutting his front door, Father Joe Skelly escorted young Rick to his living room and the two of them sat down on two oddly large chairs. Rick tried to shake the disbelief from his head and then asked Skelly "who the flip was that guy?"

"He is a friend of mine, a bounty hunter," the kind, old man explained. "He owed me some favors, and I cashed them in for you and for your parents." Father Skelly looked at Rick and could tell that his young guest was about to become indignant. Cutting him off, Father Skelly scolded Rick so severely and incessantly that Rick could not get in even two words. Skelly told Rick how his parents would have lost the $40,000 in bail they had posted—all for nothing since Rick would have been caught anyway. When Skelly made Rick give an oral account of his imagined, long-range escape plans, Rick soon realized how foolish, hopeless, and temporary a life on the run would have been for him. Skelly then asked Rick if he believed in God. "Yes," Rick affirmed. Skelly asked him if he believed in the Bible. Again, Rick replied, "Yes." Picking up a Bible resting on his coffee table, Skelly instructed Rick to place his right hand on it. Rick did as ordered. Father Skelly then asked him to "swear before

God on this Bible that you will show up for court tomorrow morning if I take you back home right now instead of to the police." Rick capitulated and swore. With that, Father Skelly drove the young man home to his fidgeting parents. After many thanks from Mr. and Mrs. Mahan, he drove back home, exhausted, but satisfied, for having done his good deed for the day—and then some.

   Rick caused no more trouble that night. Just to make sure, his dad slept on the floor next to Rick's bed.

∽

## Key Terms Found in This Chapter

Supermajority of trial victories          Bail bondsmen
Failure to appear          Cost of doing business
Bounty hunter          Bail enforcement agent
Standard bounty          Catch-and-return powers

## Questions for Class Discussion

1. Why do you suppose that prosecutors win a supermajority of cases that go to trial? Is it because they are smarter than defenders?
2. Should "failure to appear" for trial be a misdemeanor or a felony? How common do you suppose it is for people to "fail to appear" for court as ordered?
3. For whom does a bounty hunter work? What qualities should someone possess in order to be a competent bounty hunter?
4. How are bounty hunters paid? When is it simply not worth it to bother hiring one?
5. Would you consider a career as a bounty hunter? What would be the pros and cons of such employment?
6. Would you consider opening up a bail bonds business? What, if anything, should we require of aspiring bail bondsmen before licensing them to open up shop?

7. Why do bounty hunters like to call themselves names like "bail enforcement agent"? How does that help them to do their job more effectively?

8. Is the bail bonds business a good thing or a bad thing for our society? Are they unavoidably necessary? Do bail bondsmen provide an honest service, or do they exploit people who are in a vulnerable state?

9. Is bounty hunting a noble profession? Should we ban them and leave their functions to publicly paid officials like the police?

10. Do bounty hunters have too much power as they go about their catch-and-return activities? Why do they not have to care what the Constitution says when it comes to respecting rights?

# 35

# Closing Argument: Defense

Jack was sitting all alone at the courtroom table assigned to the defense attorney. It was 9:20 a.m. on the last day of trial. He was passing the time by fidgeting with one of the new ties he bought for this trial. He had told his client to be in the courtroom by 9:15 at the latest for the 9:30 closing arguments, but young Rick and his parents obviously had not listened. "Where are they?" Jack wondered.

The door to the hallway creaked, and Jack turned his head to greet whom he thought would be his client. However, it was ADA Kate Page and her sidekick trooper. They each, in turn, greeted Jack with a perfunctory "good morning" and then took their seats at the prosecution table. Both of the attorneys and the trooper then quietly stared into space as the bailiff, courtroom security personnel, and court reporter inspected them closely.

Again, the door creaked. It was Rick, his parents, and Father Skelly. Rick came and sat down at the table next to Jack. His parents and Skelly took seats not far behind. A few other spectators gently ambled into the room and took their seats as well.

Jack turned to his client and said, "Did you have a good night's rest?"

Rick answered "Yes" but only after first hesitating long enough to suggest to his attorney that some weirdness must have transpired.

"What did you do last night to pass the time?" Jack inquired.

"Nothing special," Rick muttered. "I just watched some shows and went to bed." Jack turned around to look at Rick's parents and Father Skelly, who he knew were sitting close enough to have heard every word. All of them looked down at their laps in response to Jack's gaze. "I don't even want to know," Jack finally told young Rick. "Neither do I," quipped Kate, who also had been taking in the entire encounter from the neighboring table.

The awkward situation came to a swift end as the jury now entered the room. The two attorneys stood, as did young Rick and the trooper, until the jury had been seated. Almost instantaneously, Judge Price burst into the room so suddenly that the bailiff nearly fell out of his seat trying rapidly to stand. "All rise," the old crier commanded. All rose. The judge sat down, followed eventually by everyone else in the room.

"Good morning, ladies and gentlemen of the jury," the judge said by way of cheerful greeting. "Good morning," a few jurors said in response. The judge did not bother greeting the attorneys or anyone else. "I believe we are ready to hear closing arguments. Mr. Day, you may proceed."

In Pennsylvania, the state legislature by statute has designated the defense attorney to go first in giving closing arguments in a criminal case and the Commonwealth's attorney to go last. This is no accident. It expresses values held by the elected officials. They know that any attorney would prefer to have the **last say in trial**, for obvious reasons. Indeed, who gets to go last is a big deal to lawyers. Some state legislatures allow the defense attorney to go last under the theory that the state is the aggressor in the proceeding, and the defense should therefore have the last say. Other state legislatures believe that since prosecutors have the heavy burden of proof beyond a reasonable doubt, they should get to go last. Pennsylvania's legislature apparently took the later view. Jack would have to give his closing argument first, followed by his adversary.

Like cheerful Judge Price, Jack was also in a good mood despite the fact that he was very nervous. Closing argument was his favorite part of a jury trial. For one thing, it meant that the ordeal was nearly over — win, lose, or draw. For another thing, Jack knew that unless he said something spectacularly unlawful, Kate would just shut up and let him speak without advancing any more distracting objections. Objecting during someone else's closing is generally considered "bad form." Closing arguments (along with opening statements) are about as close as it ever gets in trials to being a **virtual objection-free time**. During this uninterrupted time, attorneys are not only permitted to outline the evidence but also (unlike the case with opening statements) go further and **engage in running commentaries**, suggest various interpretations, and even provide gentle mockeries regarding what witnesses had testified. All of this can be a lawyer's idea of having fun. At least, such was the case with Jack.

"May it please the court," Jack began as he rose to his feet and nodded deferentially to the judge. Jack nervously walked over to the same spot before the jury box where he had stood when addressing the jury the other day during his opening statement. "Ladies and gentlemen of the jury, good morning to you all."

Jack's personal view as an attorney was that he only had 15 minutes or so before the jury would begin to lose interest. He would strive to say what he had to say during that time. Jack's philosophy in closing was to avoid **endless summaries of evidence** by recounting in sonorous detail the accounts earlier given witness by witness. That would be boring. Other attorneys may elect to do that but not Jack. For the sake of his client, he wanted the jury to like him. Jurors do not like boring lawyers.

Jack also knew that it was important just to be himself while addressing the jury. He had to use his own manner to be effective rather than to ape some other successful lawyer. He would simply speak to the jury in his natural, conversational tone. Thus, Jack would talk more in the **casual register** rather than with the affectation of a sophisticate. He knew what the jury wanted to hear him explain: "How can we get out of convicting a decent and likable young man of major felonies who royally screwed up and killed a couple of innocent people?"

"Ladies and gentlemen, let me speak simply and openly to you," Jack began. "I am not going to waste your time or insult your intelligence by trying to suggest that my client, Rick Mahan, did not drink a moderate amount of beer or that he did not take a couple of nonprescription cold pills. He did do those two things. My client also drove his car and apparently fell asleep at the wheel, causing a crash that resulted in the tragic deaths of two human beings. Nobody is disputing that, certainly not my client nor me. However, I hope to convince you that at most, my young client Rick is maybe guilty of reckless driving and drinking underage—the two misdemeanors of which he is accused. I hope that you will acquit my client of all charges, but if you find you absolutely must convict him of something, please just convict him of one or both of those two misdemeanors and not of the two felony counts of homicide by vehicle while DUI."

Jack paused to let these statements sink in. Jack then walked back to the defense table and placed his hand on his client's shoulder. "This boy fell asleep at the wheel. The state has proven this. However, the state also has to prove that this boy fell asleep at the wheel due to his having drunk a small quantity of beer together with two tiny cold pills. I suggest to you that the state has utterly failed to link the falling asleep with somehow being intoxicated. Our defense is that of lack of causation. The state is not charging my client with the misstep of causing a fatal accident while naturally falling asleep. Sometime during our lives, many if not most of us will fall asleep—if only briefly—at the wheel while driving. Accidents, including tragic accidents involving falling asleep while driving, are regrettable but not nearly as damnable as the felony of homicide while DUI. The key phrase here is 'while DUI.' My client fell asleep because he was naturally tired. It was not the first time. It had happened once before. Perhaps, at most, my client was a bit reckless while driving while becoming sleepy, though he did not have a place where he could immediately pull over. It should be noted that he felt perfectly fine when he left the party. In any event, I suggest to you that by no stretch of the imagination was Rick Mahan ever proven to be under the influence. Maybe he was DUI, or maybe he just naturally fell asleep while he was sober. Who knows? Can you honestly and without hesitation say that you do?"

Jack again paused, this time though to collect his thoughts. Back on track, Jack took up where he had just left off. "The state put on a hospital doctor, a pathologist named Roger Knight, who runs the hospital lab. He said that Rick's blood alcohol content was only 0.04 at the moment the blood was drawn. That is not enough to prove the DUI part of homicide while DUI. It is well below the state's threshold of 0.08 for automatic proof.

"Oh, but wait. Another type of doctor, a PhD biochemist named Wanda Grant, drove over here from her far away office in the state capital to tell us ordinary folk that in her opinion, the BAC at the time of the actual crash would have been more likely to be 0.05 instead of 0.04. Still not proof enough though, is it?

"Oh, but wait again. The same expert, we are told, is capable not just of computing likely BAC back in time at the precise moment of the actual accident but is also supposed to be an expert on alcohol/cold pill interaction and their effects. Therefore, even though she admits that many people are capable of safely driving with a BAC of 0.04 or even of 0.05, that really does not matter because of the supposed interaction of the two small cold pills with the small amount of beer. Indeed, the good doctor tells us that Rick would have been 'utterly incapable' of safely driving, and his sleepiness was 'almost certainly' caused by the alcohol/cold medicine interaction. I seem to recall that this doctor of philosophy even philosophized at one point that Rick was a 'menace on the highway.' Hey, but no bias there, right? Are you comfortable finding guilt beyond a reasonable doubt based on the 'opinion' of one biased expert with a state agenda? She does work for the state, after all. The same state that seeks a conviction here today."

Jack sheepishly looked over at ADA Kate Page who was giving him a dirty look. "Say anymore," Kate was thinking to herself, "and I am going to object, closing arguments or no closing arguments." Jack knew what Kate was thinking. He probably had crossed the line a little with those state agents in collusion quips.

During this pause, Jack also took the opportunity to look over at the audience before resuming his argument. He wanted to get a sense from them of how he was doing. He first noticed the friendly faces of Rick's parents and Father Joe Skelly. "That a boy," they seemed to be thinking. Scanning to the other side of the audience aisle, Jack next noticed the face of an elderly woman beset with grief and rage: the woman Jack knew to be the elderly mother of one of the victims his client had killed. Jack was instantaneously stricken with a profound sense of guilt and shame. Was he using his talents to get yet another DUI killer acquitted? Was his defense moral? Was he the cold-hearted, verbal gunslinger that the mother in the audience believed him to be? Was it correct that Kate, the trooper, and the experts all had truth on their side? Jack felt like he was about to vomit. He had suddenly plunged into full panic attack mode.

Nothing can be worse for a defense attorney making closing arguments to display anything other than full confidence. True, the public can be sympathetic to an ordinary public speaker who is nervous and scared. However, juries do not consider attorneys to be ordinary public speakers. Juries expect attorneys who are asking them to return a fa-vorable verdict to be **zealous advocates** who forcefully and without the slightest discomfort or reluctance advance their clients' righteous causes. A panic attack would not sit well given these unalterable expectations.

Jack turned his gaze from the deceased crash victim's mother and looked straight at Kate. She knew from the look of anguish on her oppo-nent's face what must have been happening. She was in full adversarial mode and considered just letting Jack fall apart. However, her kindness as a human being, her feelings of camaraderie to a fellow member of her profession, and her concern about a future, successful, verdict-erasing claim of "ineffective assistance" all combined to cause her to come to the rescue of the wretched man. Kate knew that a claim of **ineffective assistance of counsel** could be successful if a reviewing court believed that a lawyer's botched representation was so bad that one simply could not have confidence in the soundness of the guilty verdict. Jack complet-ing falling apart during his grand finale could certainly constitute that. A crisis that had presented itself during Jack's opening statement was repeating itself once again during closing.

"Your Honor, may we approach the bench?" Kate finally blurted out as a voiceless Jack was attempting (but failing) to begin speaking to the jury again.

"Excuse me?" a shocked trial judge responded.

"I would like to approach the bench," Kate reiterated. Still shocked, the judge looked over at attorney Jack. Jack just looked back at the judge with a weird, lost expression.

"Very well, you and Mr. Day may both approach." With that, Kate started walking toward the judge's stand. On the way, she motioned for a bewildered Jack to follow her. He complied with her will.

Arriving at the bench, Judge Price turned off his mic, looked at Kate and Jack, and whispered, "What the hell?!"

"Your Honor," Kate asserted, "I am not 100% certain, but I think I may have noticed a man in the audience handling a gun in his slack's pocket."

"What!" Judge Price exclaimed. "Where? What man?!"

"The freaky looking, skinny guy sitting in the back by the door. He is wearing a bright green shirt with mushrooms printed on it."

"The guy with the stubble all over his chin and cheeks?"

"Yeah, that's the one. I am not sure that I saw a gun but kind of think that I might have. I don't want to take a chance."

"Neither do I!" insisted the judge. With Kate and Jack still at his side-bar, Judge Price informed the jury that they would need to take a brief, five-minute recess. The judge told them not to discuss or speculate about this break among themselves, and he assured them it had nothing to do with the lawyers or their presentations. After the jury had been escorted from the room, the judge motioned for one of the deputy sheriffs, posted in the courtroom for security, to approach the bench. The judge informed the deputy of Kate's suspicions. The deputy then pretended to walk toward the doors to exit when he pounced on the poor man and patted him down for weapons. Feeling something unusual in the man's slacks pocket, the sheriff reached in and retrieved a large, compacted pouch of marijuana.

Judge Price was watching all of this unfold with keen interest. Kate too had watched, in her case with guilty feelings. Seeing that no gun (of course) had been produced, she began to apologize to Judge Price for her misguided observations. Fortunately, he was very sympathetic. "No need to apologize, Ms. Page. You probably sensed something illegal in his pocket due to furtive gestures or something on his part. I can't fault you for your prosecutorial instincts." With that, the judge ordered the man from the room but told him he could leave without drug charges being filed against him. The man quickly left, leaving his stash behind with the hovering, indignant deputy.

The sideshow drama now resolved, Judge Price ordered the bailiff to fetch the jury back from their waiting room. Jack started to walk back to his table, and the prosecutor followed him, stopping him midway to his destination.

"Jack, can you finish your closing now?" she whispered.

It suddenly dawned on Jack what Kate had just done for him. "No, my heart is literally missing beats. If I did not know better, I would swear I was having a heart attack."

"Listen, to me Jack!" Kate ordered. "When the jury returns, just say a few words and sit down. You are finished with this trial. Can you say a few words?"

"Maybe," Jack responded as he and Kate watched the jury return to its courtroom box.

Judge Price was not sure what to tell the jury after they sat down. Seeing their puzzled looks, he decided simply to tell them the "truth," or at least what he believed to be the truth. Hearing about the apparent gun alert, the jury looked at an embarrassed-looking prosecutor and just smiled. She smiled back and lifted her shoulders, as if to say, "Oh well." Judge Price looked at Jack and invited him to resume where he had left off.

Jack once again approached the jury. On his way, he felt the urge to look yet again at the face of the mother of the car crash victim. Wisely, he resisted the temptation.

"Welcome back, ladies and gentlemen," Jack uttered with a strange squeak in his voice. Jack cleared his throat and took a deep breath. He sensed he had about 20 seconds left of decorum in him before he completely lost it again. "I think I have said enough for you to get my drift. Please think about what I have said. Please consider how honest my client seemed when he took the stand. That was no act. Please consider what his friend testified to regarding an earlier episode of falling asleep at the wheel without any alcohol or drugs involved. That was no lie. Finally, please consider the principal and teacher from young Rick's school and what good things they had to say about Rick." Suddenly, Jack could say no more. He wanted to plead with them not to convict this boy. He wanted to expound about reasonable doubt in all of its prophylactic glory. However, his tank was empty. He simply smiled at the jurors and nodded goodbye. Jack walked unsteadily to his table, pretending to have a leg cramp. Upon arrival, he sat down. He was so dizzy that he felt like he just got off a carnival ride.

"Good job," young Rick whispered to his attorney. Jack managed a wink, nothing more. Jack knew that for him, all speaking was now over. His only remaining lawyerly function was to sit there and look dignified while Kate made her closing. He thought he could perhaps manage at least that.

$\sim$

## Key Terms Found in This Chapter

Last say in trial

Virtual objection-free time

Engage in running commentaries

Endless summaries of evidence

Casual register

Ineffective assistance of counsel

Zealous advocates

## Questions for Class Discussion

1. What is so great about getting to do one's closing argument last? Who do you believe should get to go last: the defense or the prose-cution? Why?

2. Would you be all right if the prosecution got to go first and last? In some states, the prosecution goes first, then the defense attorney, and then the prosecution gets to say a few words to rebut anything the defense may have raised. If you favor giving the edge to prosecu-tors during closings, would you go so far as to let them go first and last?

3. Why do you suppose it is rude to raise minor objections during the closing arguments of one's opponent? Would the jury also consider it rude?

4. If both are used to outline the evidence of a case, how is the closing argument different from the opening statement? Why is the closing argument more fun?

5. How did Attorney Jack Day feel about using his closing argument to recount summaries of the evidence? Why did he think he only had about 15 minutes to make his pitch?

6. Why did Jack Day want to talk to the jury in the "casual register" during his closing argument? Would you prefer a lawyer to speak to you as a juror using a conversational manner or by adopting a more polished style? As a defendant, which way of speaking would you prefer your attorney to adopt during closing argument?

7. Is it ethical for a defense attorney to try to come across as a true believing, zealous advocate during closing argument even when the attorney is convinced of client guilt? Would it be unethical for such an attorney to advocate but not so zealously?

8. What is the difference between delivering a subpar performance as a defense lawyer versus being responsible for rendering "ineffective

assistance of counsel"? What happens when a reviewing court finds a trial lawyer to have been "ineffective"?

9. What do you think of ADA Kate Page's actions to help Jack out during his closing argument panic attack? Did she go too far? Do you admire what she did or condemn her for her fraudulent representations to the judge?

# 36

# Closing Argument: Prosecution

Assistant District Attorney Kate Page waited for Judge Price to nod at her before rising to her feet. As she walked over to the front of the jury box, she considered how much she had admired Jack's simple closing. "He cut out all the garbage and just went straight to his main points," she thought.

Now it was Kate's turn to address the jury. "May it please the court," she began while looking at the judge. After receiving a gentle smile in return, she spun around, looked at the jury, and nodded "hello" to at least three or four jurors. Kate did not do this out of artifice. She was by nature a very warm and friendly person. That was a large part of what made her such a great prosecutor.

Like Jack, Kate had learned over the years not to bore jurors with long, detailed closing arguments. She was not about to give them 50 different reasons why they should convict young Rick of what she believed to be his criminal homicides. Like Jack, she would strike only a few blows, but she wanted them to all land deep and hard. Kate figured that deep, hard strikes should not be too hard to do since she believed, as all prosecutors honestly do, that truth was completely on her side.

While considering her remarks, Kate reminded herself of a few basic rules that could get her into big trouble if not followed during her closing argument. The violation of any one of these rules could result in a **mistrial**, requiring her, Jack, and the judge to have to start everything over again from scratch before a brand new jury. In terms of **judicial economy**, mistrials are about the worst possible outcome imaginable in a case. She had to be mindful of three rules.

First, even though the jury expects some emotionality in her speech and would be okay with that, the judge would not permit her to go so far as to **inflame the jury's passions** (that is, to reduce them to irrationality). She knew, for example, not to show graphic, bloody pictures of dead bodies. She knew not to describe Rick's car as a 2,000-pound "deadly weapon" hurling at high speeds down the road. Kate would try to appeal to the jurors' emotions as human beings but would not go overboard. Jack had obeyed this rule during his closing and so must she.

Second, she knew there was a rule against attorneys **directly expressing personal opinions** as to the guilt or innocence of someone on trial. This rule applied to defense counsel as well as to the prosecutor. Courts have ruled that juries tend to give too much weight to the honest opinions and assessments of the lawyers when they should give none. This is why (as Jack had done regarding innocence) she would use mere **hypotheticals to assert guilt**. Hence, she could not flat out say something like, "I have reviewed many vehicular homicide cases during my career, and I assure you that the evidence in this case is more than sufficient to convict." However, she could lawfully make nearly the same point by saying something like, "Is it not so that the evidence here is not only sufficient to convict but rock solid?"

Finally, Kate knew that she (like the defense attorney) could not legally invite jurors to **consider future potential sentences** should a conviction result. The jury is supposed to decide only guilt or innocence. What a sentence might be is irrelevant to that determination. It is up to the judge alone to worry about a proper sentence. Just as the rules forbade Jack from scaring juries with revelations of long sentences, so too was Kate forbidden to comfort them with assurances of light ones.

With these rules in mind, Kate was ready to get going. She knew that Jack had scored big points with at least a couple of the jurors because she had studied the jurors' faces intently while Jack had made his pitch. She could identify two jurors who were likely now in Jack's camp and four who were likely in hers. The other members of the jury were poker-faced unknowns.

Kate had noticed that Jack had first got some real traction during his closing when he had walked over to his client's table and put his hand on young Rick's shoulder. She would begin her presentation with a similar show of humanity.

Before uttering a word to the jury, Kate took a moment to turn her head toward the grieving mother in the audience whose one look had caused Jack to spiral downwards. Kate nodded at her while simultaneously gently squinting her eyes, as if to say, "I have your back." The old woman burst into soft tears as did three or four other relatives of the two victims sitting near her. "Low blow, Kate," Jack thought to himself.

"Ladies and gentlemen of the jury," Kate finally called out, "you have the hard job today of seeing that justice is done. Your duty is not an easy one or a pleasant one. Nobody takes any pleasure in convicting a young man of homicide. Yet, we would not be here today if I were not asking you to do just that.

"First, let us take care of the easy business — the misdemeanors. Richard Mahan has been charged with underage drinking and reckless driving. As to the count of underage drinking, I suggest to you that it is a slam-dunk. The defendant drank beer while under 21 years of age. End of story. Nobody has contested that. As to the misdemeanor count of reckless driving, is it not clearly the case that the defendant drove while it was reckless for him to do so? Drinking beer while also taking cold medicine is acting irresponsibly and recklessly, whether or not the defendant read the box. We are responsible for reading the medicine box when we take pills, especially when we have been drinking and are planning to drive. I ask that you convict Richard Mahan of both of these misdemeanors.

"If it is okay with all of you, I would now like to spend the bulk of my time focusing on the main events: the two big felonies. In other words, the two counts of homicide by vehicle while driving under the influence of drugs and/or alcohol. I suspect it is the two felonies that will most concern you.

"Mr. Day has just argued some theory that even though his client drank beer, took cold pills that one should never take with alcohol, and fell asleep at the wheel, the state has failed to prove that his client's sleepiness was anything but a mere coincidence. His sleepiness had nothing to do with what he had irresponsibly and wrongfully just consumed. After all, according to his good friend, he had supposedly fallen asleep at the wheel once before in his life.

"Well, let us consider the facts. We know that the defendant had lied to the trooper about how many beers he had consumed. He told the trooper he had just one beer. Yet, by the time he got to the hospital, his BAC was dropping and it was still 0.04. We were told that it would be impossible for a man of Richard Mahan's size to get to 0.04 at any point after having just drunk one beer. So, why did Mahan lie to the trooper? Because he was afraid he would get into trouble. Mahan tells you that he was not intoxicated. Can you believe him? Is he afraid he would get into trouble if he told the truth?

"Mahan also tells you that the trooper got it all wrong when the trooper says Mahan had told him he had read the warnings not to drive and consume alcohol when taking the cold medicine. Are we to believe the trooper or Rick Mahan here? Who would have a greater motive to distort the truth? Troopers are trained to get such details right. I suggest to you that the trooper got this right.

"We also heard from the girl at the party who saw Rick Mahan read the box carefully and with intense interest. He even shook his head in disgust at his beer bottle as he read the box containing warnings not to mix alcohol with the pills. Oh, but Rick tells us he read the box — like forever — but never got to the part with the bold print warnings. Again, I would suggest to you that he was clearly being disingenuous. Do you remember the timing of it all when I actually had him take the time to read the print on the box while he was on the stand? I suggest that his saying that he never got to the part with the clear, bold print warnings about driving was just a dodge motivated by an ancient instinct for self-preservation. I suggest that this dodge along with other fabrications — like how he had only drunk one beer that night — shows a clear **consciousness of guilt**.

"We also heard from the biochemist who the defense mocks as the philosophizer. She studies DUI for a living, including the interaction of drugs with alcohol. She used words like 'almost certainly' in describing whether the alcohol/drug combination caused the defendant's sleepiness. In a few minutes, Judge Price will explain to you the concept of 'beyond a reasonable doubt.' I ask you to listen carefully to his lesson and then ask yourself whether or not 'almost certainly' squares with that. If you want mathematical certainty, I cannot give you that. However, I can give you guilt beyond a reasonable doubt and suggest to you that I have done just that.

"That same PhD biochemist, who has made it her life's work to study drunk driving, also testified that the defendant would have been 'utterly incapable' of safe driving. Again, in a few minutes you will hear the judge define for you the elements of homicide by vehicle while 'DUI.' See if 'utterly incapable of safe driving' squares with the definition he will give you.

"There is a reason why the company who manufactures Benadryl tells people not to drive after taking these pills. It is because they render driving unsafe. There is a reason the company tells people not to mix alcohol while taking their medicine. It is because such a combination causes even more drowsiness. Richard Mahan is responsible for his actions whether he read the warnings on the box, which by the way, I suggest to you he certainly did. Mahan drank alcohol. Mahan took the pills. Mahan drove a car. Mahan got sleepy. Mahan crashed the car. Mahan killed two people. Mahan is guilty of two counts of homicide by vehicle while DUI.

"I am asking you to convict Richard Mahan of everything with which he has been charged, especially the felonies. Hold him to the same standard to which all of us hold ourselves. You drive safely. You watch how much you drink and what pills you take before you get behind the wheel of a car. You do these things because you want to be responsible. Please hold this defendant to the same standards you do for yourself. Convict him and let justice be done. Thank you very much."

With that, Kate sat down. Like Jack, her sole professional role going forward was to just sit there and let the judge take control of the trial. As Kate took her seat, a wave of intense relief flooded her body. She now only had to sit there and look confident in her cause. No sweat.

∾

## Key Terms Found in This Chapter

| | |
|---|---|
| Mistrial | Hypotheticals to assert guilt |
| Judicial economy | Consider future potential sentences |
| Inflame the jury's passions | Consciousness of guilt |
| Directly expressing personal opinions | |

# Questions for Class Discussion

1. What happens when there is a mistrial? Does a mistrial mean that double jeopardy plays in, preventing any further prosecution? Should double jeopardy occur if a judge believes a prosecutor had caused a mistrial on purpose because the prosecutor was losing a case?

2. What does it mean that mistrials are terrible in terms of "judicial economy"?

3. Why do you suppose that defense lawyers often consider a mistrial to be a "win"? How do you imagine a defense lawyer using a mistrial to take a second stab at getting an attractive plea bargain?

4. What happens to a jury whose passions become inflamed? How does their thinking become handicapped? What are some examples in the chapter given for how a prosecutor could inflame a jury's passions? Can you think of any other examples on your own?

5. What is the line between creating righteous indignation for a defendant's dastardly acts and inflaming a jury's passions? Given the danger, should a prosecutor even attempt the former?

6. Why are lawyers (prosecution and defense) prohibited from directly expressing their personal views as to guilt or innocence to the jury? How does the use of hypotheticals help them get around this land mine? Why are hypotheticals allowed when direct declarations of opinions are not?

7. Why cannot juries consider potential future sentences in arriving at a verdict? Would you want to know such information if you were on a jury deciding a tough case?

8. What is meant by the term, "consciousness of guilt"? How does lying demonstrate the existence of such a condition? How would flight from the scene of a crime help suggest it? Does lying to authorities or fleeing the scene of a crime always establish a clear consciousness of guilt in your mind?

9. Why do lawyers in the chapter feel so relieved after closing arguments even though the verdict is yet to come? Would you feel better even though the verdict was not yet in? Would you feel as relieved, as the attorneys do after closing arguments, if you were the one on trial?

10. Why is important for lawyers who are finished speaking in a trial to continue to look confident and dignified after closing arguments are over? How might they go about looking confident? How might they go about looking dignified? How likely is it that a juror will look at the lawyers after closing arguments are over?

# Unit 13
# Judgment Day

This unit completes the coverage of the homicide jury trial by shifting the focus from the lawyers and witnesses to the judge and jury. These latter must now take the case to final resolution.

# 37

# The Judge Instructs the Jury

The time had now arrived for Judge Price to start running the show, all by himself. Up until now, he had been demonstrating the customary **passive judicial trial role**. His job primarily consisted of sitting there on his perch waiting for one of the two lawyers to raise the occasional objection on which he could make a swift determination. However, the lawyers were really in charge of the unfolding drama. Unlike in continental Europe where judges call witnesses, question them, and more or less micromanage the process, American judges do not run trials. Here, the lawyers are the ones who serve as actors, screenwriters, producers, directors, and prop managers. Yet, the moment had now come for Judge Price to take control of the pageant. He alone had the authority to teach the jury the law. In other words, it was time for him to **instruct the jury**.

"Ladies and gentlemen of the jury, before you leave to deliberate, I have a few instructions to give you," began Judge Price. "In order for you to do your job, you must know what the law is. You are to be **judges of the facts** but not the **judges of the law**. I will lay down the law for you. Your task will be to decide the facts (what happened) and then apply those facts to the law that I am about to provide you."

Judge Price opened a huge thick black book of canned **standard jury instructions** provided to all sitting judges by the Supreme Court of Pennsylvania. Price had earlier inserted sticky, yellow post-it notes on a variety of pages corresponding to an instruction that he deemed relevant and desirable to read to the jury. There were instructions in this big book about everything. If this had been a rape case, there was an instruction regarding the elements of rape. If there had been an insanity defense, there was an instruction in the book defining "insanity." These instructions take pressure off the trial judge since he or she merely needs to scan the table of contents in advance and decide which instructions would apply to the particular case of the day.

As a law trained individual, conversant in legalese, Judge Price admired the artistry that had gone into the drafting of these standard instructions by various committees of lawyers and judges. However, he realized that some of the instructions assumed abilities with language, especially legal language, that simply were beyond the comprehension of some lay jurors. Nevertheless, Judge Price, like most judges, was reluctant to deviate far from the careful wording of the texts out of fear that one lawyer or the other would raise the howl of judicial favoritism. To help avoid the look of bias on his part, he, as judges usually do, had also invited Kate and Jack to submit any jury instructions they wanted him to cover in advance. With just one exception, Judge Price promised to include the requested instructions. The sole exception? Price told Jack Day his request for an instruction regarding the psychological limitations associated with eyewitness testimony would not be explained to the jury. In Judge Price's opinion, eyewitness testimony was not central to the issues of this case, and such an instruction would be a waste of court time.

Judge Price decided to start his instructions to the jury by reading the various definitions of the crimes Richard stood accused of. Before teaching them about the various offenses, the judge explained to the jury that each of the three different crimes (one with two counts) would include several distinct elements or parts. In order for the jury to convict Richard Mahan of a particular offense, the jury would have to been convinced beyond a reasonable doubt of the existence of each of the **crime's statutory elements**. If they were so convinced, they must find Richard "guilty" of that offense. If they were not convinced that each separate element of a particular offense was satisfactorily established then they must find Richard "not guilty" of that offense.

With that introductory explanation completed, Judge Price chose to first define the elements of homicide by vehicle while DUI. "I might as well start with the big prize first," he thought. Judge Price told the jury that for them to convict Richard of this offense (on either one or both counts), they would have to find him first guilty of DUI. This was so because DUI was a **lesser included offense** of criminal homicide by DUI. (the same way that theft is a lesser-included offense of burglary). Judge Price then taught the jury that the elements of DUI included 1) driving or controlling the movement of a vehicle and 2) while one was incapable of safe driving because of impairment from either alcohol, drugs, or the combination of the two.

If the jury found Richard to have been DUI, they could go on to determine whether he was guilty of homicide by DUI. To decide that, they would have to be convinced beyond a reasonable doubt that Richard was not only DUI but also that 1) a death had occurred and 2) the death occurred as the result of the driving under the influence and not due to something else. Judge Price reminded the jury that the state had charged the defendant with two counts of this felony: one count for the male driver of the Ford Focus and one count for the female passenger.

Judge Price then went on to explain the elements for the two misdemeanors. In essence, he explained that "underage drinking" required proof of two things: that the defendant was under 21 years of age, and he had consumed or possessed any liquor or malt or brewed beverage. He explained that "reckless driving"—the other misdemeanor—required proof that Rick had "driven a vehicle" with "willful or wanton disregard for the safety of persons or property."

Having finished the relatively straightforward task of defining the crimes, Judge Price went about to tackle a much harder definition: "guilt beyond a reasonable doubt." This instruction is often the most important of all in a trial since deliberating jurors often become obsessed with the concept. The definition of "reasonable doubt" has been the cause of much anxiety for jurists and legal scholars for centuries. Just how sure should jurors be before taking away someone's liberty for an alleged criminal offense and stigmatizing them with the stain of a criminal record? Obviously, jurors should not expect mathematical certainty. That would not be possible. On the other hand, should jurors convict someone out of their mere belief that the person in probably guilty, even though they are not robustly confident?

In most civil lawsuits (slip and falls, medical malpractice, ordinary car accidents, etc.), one only needs to be convinced by a so-called, **preponderance of the evidence** that someone is responsible for the wrong in order to require restitution. That means that if the fact finder (judge or jury) believes that the defendant is probably culpable (more than a 50% chance), a judgment in favor of the plaintiff should be granted. Hence, if Johns sues Mary for conversion (wrongful taking) of his money, and a jury is convinced that Mary more likely than not did wrongfully take John's money, then Mary can be ordered to give John his money back. This payment to John would not constitute punishment of any kind. Mary is not being told to go to jail, have her liberty reduced by living under the rules of probation, or even pay a fine to the state. She is merely being asked to pay a debt she apparently owes John. If Mary is forced to pay restitution, which in reality she does not owe John, a harm is done to Mary. However, at least society never meant to punish Mary in any way — just to get her to pay what it thought was a debt owed. Mary does not suffer the stigma of being a criminal when she goes looking for a job. She never loses her liberty either, not even some of it, as probationers do.

On the other hand, if a police officer wishes to charge Mary with the "crime" of theft, the officer may arrest Mary based on a mere likelihood of guilt (what we call "**probable cause**" in criminal court, something akin to "preponderance of the evidence" in civil court). However, a final conviction in criminal court requires something much more than such mere likelihood. To convict, punish, and stigmatize Mary for a crime, the fact finder must be convinced of her guilt **beyond a reasonable doubt** (in other words, very firmly convinced and without significant hesitation).

As noted before, for a long time courts have struggled with a precise definition of reasonable doubt that judges should use to instruct juries. Some legal scholars have suggested not even trying to define it precisely for juries. They think the words should just be left alone to speak for themselves. However, Judge Price did not believe that the phrase "reasonable doubt" was self-explanatory. He wanted to explain it further and better than his *Pennsylvania Standard Jury Instructions* book provided. In that book, reasonable doubt was defined as "a doubt that would cause a reasonably prudent person to pause or hesitate before making an important decision in his or her own life." Judge Price was not sure what that even meant. Following a definition proposed by U.S. Supreme Court

Justice Ruth Ginsburg, he decided to take a small risk by deviating from the standard instructions and to instruct this jury with Ginsburg's definition as follows:

"Ladies and gentlemen, the state has the burden of proving the defendant guilty beyond a reasonable doubt. Some of you may have served as jurors in civil cases, where you were told that it is only necessary to prove that a fact is more likely true than not true. In criminal cases, the government's proof must be more powerful than that. It must be beyond a reasonable doubt.

"Proof beyond a reasonable doubt is proof that leaves you firmly convinced of the defendant's guilt. There are very few things in this world that we know with absolute certainty, and in criminal cases, the law does not require proof that overcomes every possible doubt. If, based on your consideration of the evidence, you are firmly convinced that the defendant is guilty of the crime charged, then you must find him guilty. If, on the other hand, you think there is a real possibility that he is not guilty, you must give him the benefit of the doubt and find him not guilty."

Following this instruction, and a similar one regarding "presumption of innocence," Judge Price explained to the jury that he had just a few more simple instructions before he excused them to go deliberate. He told them that their verdict needed to be unanimous (this is not required in all states, but it is in Pennsylvania). He told them that they should be polite and listen to one another's arguments with an open mind. He told them to elect a jury foreperson to direct their deliberations and tally the votes. He then excused them to deliberate.

As the jurors left the jury box, both lawyers stood out of respect. Young Rick did as well. Rick's fate was now in the hands of 12 ordinary, fellow Pennsylvanians. They were the only "government" that mattered in this case, starting now.

"Do you think they will be out long?" Rick asked his attorney. "I can't stand waiting too long."

"Let us hope that they are slow to return," replied Jack. "The rule of thumb is that **fast-returning juries** almost always convict. The longer the jury is out, the better. **Slow-returning juries** almost always involve some members having some serious reasonable doubt."

Kate observed this little discussion with amusement. "Oh, my guess is that they will be back fast," she told the trooper now standing beside her. She made sure to say this loud enough for everyone else still in the room to hear.

"Pay no attention to that woman," Jack reassured Rick. "Turn your phone ringtone back on, and I will call you once there is a verdict. In the meantime, I am going out to get a bite to eat. The bailiff will call the prosecutor and me once the jury is ready to return. When they call me, I'll call you."

"Where should I go until then?" asked Rick.

"That's up to you and your parents. Stay downtown. I will call you when there is a verdict. It might be 20 minutes or 6 hours. Let's hope for 6 hours—longer if we can get it."

⌇

## Key Terms Found in This Chapter

| | |
|---|---|
| Passive judicial trial role | Lesser included offense |
| Instruct the jury | Preponderance of the evidence |
| Judges of the facts | Probable cause |
| Judges of the law | Beyond a reasonable doubt |
| Standard jury instructions | Fast-returning juries |
| Crime's statutory elements | Slow-returning juries |

## Questions for Class Discussion

1. In what way are judges relatively passive creatures during a jury trial? Who are the main "movers and shakers" during trials? How so?
2. Do you imagine that judges sometimes have to guess when quickly ruling on objections during trials? How often would you imagine that this occurs? If you were a judge making a guess, would you tend to guess more often in favor of the prosecution or the defense? Why?
3. What does it mean for the judge to "instruct the jury"? When does this occur? Why is this necessary?
4. Who are the "judges of the facts"? Why is that same body not also the "judges of the law"? What is meant by the term, "judges of the facts"?

5.  Who provides judges with a set of "standard jury instructions"? Why not just let judges come up with their own? What are some topics covered in a set of standard jury instructions?

6.  Why are judges reluctant to deviate much from the standard jury instruction definitions regarding various topics? Should they be allowed any leeway at all to clarify and "ad lib"?

7.  What is meant by a crime's statutory elements? To what degree must the state prove the existence of each element? What would an example be of the elements for driving under the influence?

8.  What are some examples you can think of a crime that is a "lesser included offense" to a greater crime?

9.  What is the civil court's counterpart to "probable cause" in criminal court? If that counterpart concept is enough to achieve victory in civil lawsuits, why do we not use the similar concept of "probable cause" as our standard for convictions in criminal court?

10. How would you explain the concept of "beyond a reasonable doubt" to a family member or friend in a way that they would "get it"?

11. Would you consider it immoral of a society to permit criminal convictions on something less than "beyond a reasonable doubt"? Is it better that "10 guilty go free than for 1 innocent to be wrongfully convicted"?

12. If you were a defense attorney, would you prefer a jury that returns quickly with a verdict or one that is taking a long time? Why?

# 38

## The Jury Deliberates

"This will be your home until you decide upon a verdict," the bailiff announced to the jury as they took their seats around a very long and narrow conference table in a clean, but dated, deliberation room.

One of the jurors, Jane Morgan, took no time in dropping her body down into one of the cushioned seats. The busy school principal, mother of teens, and daughter to an aged parent had almost not even shown up for jury service in the first place. Now, she just wanted to get down to business fast so she could get the hell out of there. "How do we get word to the judge when we are done?" Jane asked the bailiff before any of the other jurors had even sat down.

"Just let the deputy sheriff know and he will alert me or one of the other bailiffs."

"The deputy sheriff?" Jane bristled. "How exactly would we find such a person?" With that, the bailiff walked over to the half open door, swung it wide open, and pointed to a deputy sitting in a chair in the hallway. Having just heard everything, the deputy leaned his head into full view, smiled, winked, and waved to the jurors. They all laughed. All, except Jane.

"You are now free to begin your deliberations," the bailiff said. "There is a bathroom behind that door in the corner, should anyone need it. If you need anything else, just tell the deputy in the hallway. Good luck."

The jurors nervously watched as the bailiff left. He took care to close the door completely as he exited the room. Everyone looked at Jane. She looked back. "What?" she finally asked them.

"What do we do next?" a timid-looking young woman asked her.

"How should I know?" Jane responded. "Maybe we should elect a jury foreperson. The judge told us we needed to do that."

"Okay, I nominate you," the same young woman countered.

"Me? I don't want the job."

Another jury member "seconded" the motion. A vote was taken, and it was unanimous: Jane would be their jury foreperson. It would be the job of this **jury foreperson** to keep discussions moving forward and tally up votes.

Jane dipped her head down, sighed, shook her head from side to side, and then looked back up again. "Very well," she announced. "It is no big deal anyway. My vote is the same as yours." Jane thought for a few seconds about where to go from there. "Maybe we can start by taking an initial vote on Mahan's guilt," she suggested. "We might get lucky and all agree."

Jane did not know it, but having her jury take an **initial vote** before any discussion was probably a big mistake, though one commonly made. Once people take a public position on something important, it is often hard for them to change positions quickly without their worrying about looking stupid or weak. Nevertheless, they all seemed to think that voting was a good idea, so that is what they now did. Jane led the effort by passing out some of the little slips of paper she noticed sitting inside a box sitting prominently on the table. She also passed out the pencils she noticed lying next to the box.

The results in, Jane saw that everyone had voted to convict on the misdemeanor charge of underage drinking and the misdemeanor charge of reckless driving. However, regarding the two felony counts of homicide by vehicle while DUI (one for each victim), the vote split almost down the middle, with seven voting to convict (both counts) and five voting to acquit (both counts).

"Swell," Jane cynically remarked after announcing the results. "The judge instructed us that the voting on any particular charge must be unanimous in order to count, and that applies to a finding of either guilty or not guilty. We need to all agree that Richard is guilty on the homicides or all agree that he is not guilty of them. The two vehicular homicides, much more so than the misdemeanors, is what is important here. We need to come to some sort of agreement on the felonies, not just on the minor crimes."

"What if we cannot ever agree on the big crimes?" someone asked.

"I don't know," Jane honestly admitted. "For now, why don't we just all explain to one another why we voted as we did? Maybe that will help change some minds. I will go first."

Jane had been one of the five to vote in favor of acquitting Rick on both counts of the alleged criminal homicides. She explained that she could not be sure that the beer and pills caused young Rick's sleepiness. "Maybe he just fell asleep on his own," she reasoned. "I just don't know. Since I don't know, I call that reasonable doubt."

Another juror jumped in and reminded Jane and the others, "We can have some doubt, just not reasonable doubt. The party dude drank beer, mixed it with pills, and fell asleep behind the wheel, almost as on cue. I think the state proved its case good enough."

"I agree," another asserted. "He almost certainly was driving under the influence. To some of you he might seem like a nice kid, but that has nothing to do with the law. Think of the two dead victims. We owe it to them to see that justice is done here."

"What about justice for the kid?" another juror protested. "I am on the jury foreperson's side. I have way too much doubt to convict on anything but the two misdemeanors."

Thus it went, back and forth, until everyone had at least one chance to speak his or her mind. In the meantime, a full hour had flown by, just like that.

"Let's take another vote," an older man suggested finally.

"Good idea," Jane replied. She passed out little slips of paper as she had done over an hour before. "No need to vote on the misdemeanors again," she suggested. Everyone seemed to agree with that. "Just vote on the two felony homicides: one for the man killed and the other for the woman killed." Everybody but the timid young woman quickly scribbled down his or her choices; she was staring into space deep in thought while the others passed their slips down to Jane. Finally, she scribbled down her vote and turned her slip in as well.

Jane silently counted the votes and recounted them a second time just to make sure. "The votes have changed. Before it was seven guilty on both homicide counts with five not guilty on both; now it is eight guilty on both and four not guilty." All eyes in the room immediately focused on the timid young woman who had been staring thoughtfully.

"Okay, it was me. I changed my vote to guilty." She then went on to explain that though she was not 100% certain, her doubts were not very large. "I think I now agree with whoever said that some doubt is okay to have," she concluded. "Beer plus cold medicine pills is supposed to put someone at serious risk of drowsiness. The big warnings on the box spoke all about that. Getting drowsy after drinking and taking the pills is exactly what happened here. Is there a chance that Richard Mahan fell asleep from merely natural causes? Of course. However, I think we are not asked to rule out every imaginable doubt. I am firmly convinced of his guilt, and that is all I need."

Those in the "guilty" camp nodded in approval. Those in the "innocent" camp gave the traitor their looks of contempt.

Jane could tell that it was not going to be a quick process getting to unanimity. Too bad that she and her fellow jurors did not live in one of the several states that no longer require unanimous verdicts. Although an ancient tradition that dates back to England, the U.S. Supreme Court eventually ruled that **unanimous verdicts** are not strictly required, even in criminal cases. In 1972 it decided (in a case called *Johnson v. Louisiana*) that, though convincing all 12 jurors in a 12-person jury would be nice, having a supermajority of **9 out of 12** was good enough. In its view, having a small minority of the jury disagreeing on a verdict would not in and of itself constitute reasonable doubt.

Unfortunately, for Jane and company, and despite the generous views of the U.S. Supreme Court, Pennsylvania held to the traditional view requiring unanimity. All 12 would have to agree in order to avoid a do-over on the two homicide counts. If even one juror held out, a **hung jury** and a consequential mistrial would result. From the point of view of judicial economy, hung juries are about the worst thing that could happen. A hung jury means that a new jury would have to be empaneled and the entire trial repeated all over again, from scratch. (Double jeopardy does not come into play since the "gun had simply misfired.")

The scary thing is that most juries are "hung" after the initial vote (whenever it is taken). It is quite unusual for 12 people to all agree on either guilt or innocence during the first balloting. Yet, most of the time, mistrials are eventually avoided. Jurors somehow come around and get the job done. However, it is not always a pretty process.

Certainly, calmly reasoning with one another is a pretty thing, and it does sometimes cause people to change their minds. Everybody can probably think of a situation in which he or she changed a strongly held view in the face of arguments not previously considered that seemed very persuasive. Jane thought that unanimity still could be achieved through a process of additional calm, rational discussion. Jane was wrong.

Jane began the additional discussion by trying yet again to explain her position that the state had failed to prove its case. She thought lack of proof beyond a reasonable doubt was a simple fact. Jurors who disagreed with her merely did so because she had not done a good enough job in explaining the truth to them. She now went about trying to fix that by telling the jury about a specific time she herself was sober but had fallen asleep at the wheel and ran off the road. "Surely, this has happened to some of you too," she suggested. Several on the jury admitted that they too either had fallen asleep at the wheel before or nearly had done so. "See!" she declared. "How do we know that Richard Mahan did not do the same, alcohol and cold pills be damned?"

Allies jumped in with their own intelligent reasons for having reasonable doubt. It all sounded so good to Jane. True, a couple of the members on the other side expressed their views that a little bit of doubt was okay and all they had. However, Jane was sure that even those making that case must realize how wrong it all sounded when actually spoken outloud. To drive this point home, she made sure to have rolled her eyes at the appropriate moments during their comments.

Jane thought it was time to take another vote. To her dismay, the results came back the same: eight guilty on both counts of vehicular homicide, with four not guilty. No movement whatsoever!

It was obvious to everyone that **rational argumentation**—using facts and logic to change minds—was not working so well. Fortunately, for the system, there are other tools to get a split jury to unanimity besides rational arguments. Normally, one of the best of these other tools is the marvel of **peer pressure**. Nobody likes to look like a fool, not even in a group as temporary as a jury. There is a strong human instinct to conform. As the Japanese like to say, "The nail that sticks up will be hammered down." The romantic notion that one heroic juror using only logic and reason can convert the other eleven to his enlightened ways propels the myth that sound reasoning can vanquish peer pressure, if given enough time. In the real world, it actually tends to work the other way: a lone juror nearly always is the one who ultimately caves. The same apparently holds true when there are just two or three disagreeing with a large majority. Peer pressure in such situations can be just the trick that gets the jury to an agreement. The courts are okay with that. They are simply not interested in knowing the ugly process of "how the sausage is made."

All of this said, the closer a jury is to being evenly split, the harder it is for peer pressure to work its magic. In the case of Rick, the jury began nearly evenly split (a very bad omen). Even after some lucky, initial movement resulting in one person converting to the opposing camp, the jury now appeared firmly stuck at eight to four (in favor of convicting on the homicides). Getting 4 people out of 12 to feel like fools can be a "hard sell." The minority is just not small enough.

Jane sensed that something else was needed. Perhaps another factor might play a role in achieving a consensus. During the arguments, she began to notice an interesting pattern developing. Not all of the jurors appeared to be created equal. **Jury leaders** had emerged. Only a couple of jurors in each opposing camp seemed now to be dominating the discussions: Jane herself plus some young man on her side versus the formerly timid woman (now with the zeal of a convert) plus an older man as the convert's staunch ally. The others on the jury seemed to be sheepishly looking for these four for guidance. Could it be that these four might be in a position to exert an influence disproportionate to their numbers? If so, the challenge for Jane would be to somehow get the four leaders to all agree on something. Then everyone else might just capitulate to the leaders' collective judgments.

Yet, how could Jane get four opinionated, strong-willed, apparently intelligent people to all agree on a verdict? Both sets of two now understood the other set's positions: all the rational arguments in the world would likely prove ineffective. Neither set could be bullied by peer pressure: both sides had their followers among the remaining jurors, with neither group able to claim the supermajority needed to crush the will of a tiny opposition.

At this point, Jane remembered something from her past. As a young woman, she had applied for a job with the U.S. Foreign Service. She had wanted to work for the U.S. State Department in faraway embassies around the world. After passing a written test, she had been invited to Washington, D.C., for oral interviews. Part of this interview process included a "leaderless group discussion." Jane was seated at a round table with five other candidates who were instructed to reach a group decision regarding how a fixed amount of money should be spent by a mythical government agency wishing to engage in charitable endeavors overseas. Six different charities were given as options to be funded. There was enough money to fund entirely two charities but not enough to fund six different ones completely. Jane and the five other candidates each argued for a charity that he or she thought was most deserving. Each argued his or her individual positions brilliantly for the entire hour allocated for the exercise, without ever agreeing to any particular course of action. Jane later learned that everyone in the group was deemed to have failed this exercise. It was explained to them, after the fact, that what the Foreign Service was really looking for was someone who could forge a compromise solution (e.g., to partially fund as many as possible). The Foreign Service was looking to hire people who knew how to build consensus. Compromise is the essence of any democracy. It is the grease that keeps democratic bodies humming. The American jury is a tiny democracy. Sometimes, compromise is the only way to get things done.

Jane decided that she would suggest that everybody consider what legal scholars would call a "compromise verdict." A **compromise verdict** is one in which juries agree to a middle position in order to reach a verdict that everyone can accept. Some civil libertarians condemn compromise verdicts as cop-outs that allow convictions despite the presence of reasonable doubt among some of the jurors. Such criticisms may reach a zenith when juries compromise in such a way as to return what is obviously an **inconsistent verdict** (one that is not logically possible). For example, finding someone charged with entering a home in order to commit theft inside not guilty of burglary while guilty of theft would be an inconsistent verdict. How could someone have stolen something from inside if he or she had not entered the home? Nevertheless, compromise verdicts—including even inconsistent ones—happen all of the time. The ends (a verdict) justify the means (a compromise).

Jane's grand "compromise" was for the jury to find Rick guilty of just one count of vehicular homicide while DUI while finding him not guilty of the other count. She suggested that the jury convict him of wrongfully killing the passenger in the other car but acquit him of wrongfully killing the driver. At first, the two leaders in the other camp scoffed at her idea. "How could he possibly have wrongfully caused the death of one but not the other?" they asked.

Jane explained that this would be "the compromise" that would get them to a verdict. The two leaders pushing for conviction on both felonies were intrigued but hesitant. "Is this even legal?" one of them bluntly asked.

"Are plea bargains legal?" Jane replied in defense of her idea. "Prosecutors compromise all the time to get their job done, so why can't we?"

The four leaders, two in each camp, took a few minutes to debate Jane's proposal while the other eight watched in relative silence. Finally, the four leaders all seemed to be on board. "Let's go for it!" Jane urged the group. The two leaders in favor of just deserts said that maybe they could go along since Rick would still be getting some serious punishment. The two in favor of mercy liked the idea that Rick's exposure to punishment would be cut dramatically. "Yeah, let's do it," another of the four leaders ultimately suggested. With that, the leaders had spoken.

A vote was taken: 11 now voted for conviction on one count of vehicular homicide while acquitting on the other homicide count. There was still one hold out though, favoring conviction on both homicide counts. That person was soon identified, and the **shaming and browbeating** began in earnest. "Do you want to be here all day?" said someone. "Be reasonable!" exclaimed several others. "Who do you think you are to hold up the group like this?" asked Jane. Peer pressure works fast when it is 11 against 1. Jane soon ordered another vote. It came back 12:0 for conviction on one — just one — count of homicide by vehicle while DUI (plus convictions on the small misdemeanors of driving underage and reckless driving).

The "deliberations" now seemingly over, Jane asked permission from the group for her to summon the bailiff. All gave their consent. Jane rose from her chair, walked solemnly to the closed door, and gave it four heavy raps. Five seconds later the door opened from the outside.

"Do you need something?" the young deputy sheriff asked.

"We have a verdict," Jane proudly announced. She was almost beaming.

## Key Terms Found in This Chapter

Jury foreperson                                      Peer pressure
Initial vote                                          Jury leaders
Unanimous verdicts                           Compromise verdict
Nine out of twelve                               Inconsistent verdict
Hung jury                                Shaming and browbeating
Rational argumentation

## Questions for Class Discussion

1. What are the duties of the jury foreperson? Why do you suppose they chose Jane to serve in this capacity? Would you like to serve as the foreperson if you were on a jury?
2. Why was Jane's decision to take an initial vote probably not such a good idea? What might you do first as jury foreperson other than to take an initial vote?
3. Do you like the traditional requirement of unanimous verdicts? What are its pros and cons?
4. What do you think of the "9 out of 12" rule used now in some states for arriving at legal verdicts? Does such a rule enable the presence of collective reasonable doubt within a jury? Would you be okay with a "7 out of 12" rule?
5. What is a hung jury? What happens next? Why is double jeopardy not violated if the case is retried?
6. If you were a prosecutor over a case that resulted in a hung jury, would you rethink your previous last plea bargain offer to the other side? Would it depend on how the votes stacked up?
7. In your view, is rational argumentation the most powerful tool to get a jury to arrive at unanimity? Why or why not?
8. Is peer pressure a lawful way for jurors to get one another to arrive at a verdict? Do you agree with that reality? What does it mean that appellate courts do not want to know how the "sausage was made"?

9. How does the emergence of jury leaders help return a verdict? Could you see yourself as a leader on a jury? A follower? Can you think of any other groups where this sort of dynamic occurs?

10. How does a compromise verdict work? What are some examples? How are they akin to plea-bargaining? Are compromise verdicts legal? Ethical?

11. Are inconsistent verdicts legal? What would be an example of an inconsistent verdict?

12. The chapter ends with the last hold-out being shamed and brow-beaten into submission. How realistic is it that a lone holdout would capitulate due to such pressures? Would you probably cave in under such circumstances?

13. When a juror switches sides, how likely is it that the juror will admit to succumbing to peer pressure or shaming? How likely is it for the juror to admit to being a sheep following the leaders? If a juror does switch, what likely reason will the juror claim to have?

# 39

# They Have a Verdict!

With no downtown (or other) law office to retire to, Jack had been killing time waiting for a verdict by reading a book in the county library two blocks from the courthouse. He was getting a little concerned because the jury had been out awhile, and it looked like the library was getting ready to close. He could not just go home since, like Kate, he was on **telephone alert** and expected to get back to the courtroom within a few minutes of receiving the bailiff's much-anticipated phone call. He was considering shifting his location to a downtown coffee shop when he felt his phone vibrating in his pocket. He pulled the phone out of his pocket so quickly that he fumbled it. The phone fell to the floor, and Jack hit his head on the bottom of the table as he tried to rise back to full sitting position after collecting the device. "Ouch!" he exclaimed so woefully that he caused the librarian stacking books nearby to smile rather than reprimand.

Phone now firmly in hand, Jack pushed a button and whispered, "Hello, this is Jack Day."

"Hi Mr. Day," the bailiff on the other end replied, "They have a verdict. The jury has a verdict."

"I will be there in five minutes," Jack assured the caller.

"Is your client with you?" the bailiff asked.

"No, but he is nearby. I have his phone number. I will make sure he gets to the courtroom right away."

Jack hung up and immediately called young Rick. The phone rang seven times before he finally picked up. "Mr. Day, is that you?" a scared voice uttered.

"Yes, Rick, it's me. They have a verdict. They want us in the courtroom within five minutes. Is that going to be a problem?"

"No, my parents and I are in the library near the courthouse. We were hanging out here since we had no place else to go."

A surprised Jack looked all around until he spotted Rick and his parents sitting in a far corner of the enormous room. "I see you, Rick! Look to your right." Jack stood up and waived until Rick spotted him. Normally Rick might have laughed at this situation, but he was too upset to do anything but wearily waive back at his attorney.

Jack walked over to Rick and his parents, who by then were all on their feet. "Shall we walk together back to the courthouse?" Jack suggested.

"That would be nice," his client's mother confirmed. "Do you know how the jury voted?"

"No. The bailiff who called me did not say. I doubt he even knows himself." With that, the small group left the library and started a swift walk back to the courthouse. As they reached the building's exterior stairs, young Rick stopped dead in his tracks. "I feel dizzy," he confessed.

"It is okay," Jack assured him. "Your breathing is probably too fast and shallow. Just take a couple of slow, deep breaths. It will help you get back on track. I know from personal experience lately."

Rick did as advised. Feeling better, he led his elders up the stairs and into the stately edifice.

"Let's take the elevator up instead of the stairs," Rick's dad suggested. Everyone agreed that would probably be for the best. As the elevator door was about to shut with them inside, Jack spied Kate walking up the nearby stairwell with her trooper friend. Jack realized that Kate must have moments before noticed the Mahans and him walking across the main floor since she suddenly took pains to look awkwardly over her shoulder toward the elevator. Jack nodded but dared not smile in consideration of the company he was keeping and the solemnity of the moment. Kate, however, managed to smile and wink at Jack before the elevator door entirely closed. Her friendly look reminded Jack that at this late point in the trial, she had become more of a comrade to him rather than an enemy.

The bailiffs watched attentively as both attorneys, as well as Rick and the trooper, took their respective seats. The audience section of the courtroom was empty, with the exception of Rick's parents and a few relatives of the deceased victims. Father Skelly was on his way from his rectory located near the high school. Having only just received a phone call from Mr. Mahan minutes ago, he would not be there in time to hear the verdict announced.

Satisfied that all the key players had assembled, the senior bailiff walked over to the deliberation room, smiled at the sheriff sitting in the hallway, and opened the heavy door. "Please follow me," the bailiff told the group. The jurors rose from their seats and marched behind their guide in single file over to the courtroom side entrance.

Once the last juror had taken a seat in the courtroom jury box, the bailiff crossed the carpeted courtroom floor to the door on the other side that led to the judge's chambers. Twenty seconds passed, then thirty. Jack noticed his client's hands trembling vigorously on the table before them. He then noticed that his own hands were very slightly trembling as well. "I wonder if Kate's hands still tremble at times like this," he thought. He tried to see if that were so, but Kate had placed her hands firmly on her lap under her table. Kate noticed Jack staring at her lap and gave him a curious look in return. Embarrassed, Jack turned his gaze back to his own hands.

"All rise!" The command shattered the stillness of the room. Everyone stood up as Judge Price entered and sat down on his judicial perch. "This honorable court is now back in session. You may be seated," instructed the bailiff.

"I understand that there is a verdict?" Judge Price asked the jury. Jane, the jury foreperson, stood and confirmed that this was correct. Judge Price directed his attention directly at her now. "Very well. Please hand your verdict slip to Mr. Anderson, the bailiff." Old Mr. Anderson walked over to that part of the front of the jury box nearest Jane and reached out his hand. She placed the official verdict slip in his hand. Mr. Anderson then walked over to the judge's bench, reached up, and handed Judge Price the slip. He received the slip with a slow nod.

The **verdict slip** was made of thick paper. It presented for the jury, in very bold printed type, the four charges against Richard Mahan: the two misdemeanors and the two felony DUI homicides. A check box appeared beside each of the four charges, where Jane could select either "guilty" or "not guilty" according to the unanimous decision of the jury. There was also a signature line for her to sign as foreperson.

Judge Price had his own personal beliefs as to guilt or innocence on each of the charges. He privately thought that Richard was guilty of everything. However, an acquittal on all charges would not have upset him terribly since he would then have the consolation of not having to design an appropriate sentence for someone so young and pitiful.

What would greatly upset Judge Price, however, would be to see one or more of the boxes remain unchecked on the verdict slip. Not returning a verdict on any of the charges would be unacceptable and probably require him at this point to deliver a dreaded "Allen charge."

The **Allen charge** gets its name from the 1896 U.S. Supreme Court case of *Allen v. United States,* which had first declared its legitimacy. Typically an "Allen charge" (also known as a **dynamite charge** because it breaks up the logjam) works as follows. A hopelessly **deadlocked jury** gives up any hope of ever reaching a consensus. The jury, ashamed of its inability to return a verdict, sends a note to the trial judge explaining that it is hopelessly deadlocked (or simply shows up with only a partial verdict as though that were all right). The judge then speaks to the jury in the courtroom. At this point, the jury typically feels defeated yet is greatly relieved that the ordeal is finally about to end. Believing that the judge is about to excuse it from any further deliberations, the jury learns to its horror that the judge is instead only going to reprimand it for its inability to get the job done. The judge stresses to the jury the importance of returning a verdict one way or the other, that it has a duty to do so if it possibly can, and that the jurors should reconsider their positions unless it would be doing **violence to their conscience** to do so.

Allen charges work quite well. After receiving one, most juries return fairly quickly with proper unanimous verdicts. Judge Price was happy to realize that none of these admonitions would be necessary with this jury today since all of the "guilty" or "not guilty" boxes had been checked.

In looking over the slip, Judge Price could not help immediately noticing the actual decisions of the jury in addition to merely whether or not some verdict on each count had been found. Both Jack and Kate now were studying the judge's face intensely for any signs of victory or defeat for their side. Judge Price knew better than to convey such information. His face remained completely nonreactive and emotionless.

The judge handed the slip back down to his bailiff and asked him to confirm the verdicts with the jury foreperson. "Ms. Foreperson," Mr. Anderson called out while looking down at the language on the verdict slip, "On the misdemeanor charge of underage drinking, how does the jury find the defendant, Richard Mahan? Guilty or not guilty?"

"Guilty," Jane replied. Jack stole a peek at his young client who did not seem upset. He told him earlier that he was going down on the two misdemeanors, but that it was no big deal. With no prior record, the worst Rick would get was a small period of probation on each of them. "It is the two vehicular homicide counts that matter here," Jack had taught his client. "Relative to them, the misdemeanors are background noise."

The bailiff was moving on to the next count. "On the misdemeanor count of reckless driving, how does the jury find Richard Mahan, guilty or not guilty?"

"Guilty," Jane announced.

The bailiff then got to the main events. "On the felony count of homicide by vehicle while DUI involving the death of the male driver of the Ford vehicle, how does the jury find Richard Mahan? Guilty or not guilty?" With that question now advanced, both Jack and Kate sat upright in their chairs. Young Rick's hands startled to tremble even more fiercely on the table. In the audience, Mr. Mahan was unconsciously biting his lower lip hard, and Mrs. Mahan looked as if she were about to burst out into tears.

"Not guilty," the jury foreperson declared. Jack noticed that his young client's hands had suddenly started to tremble noticeably less. "Thank God!" Rick whispered to his lawyer. Jack looked at him and whispered back, "We are not out of the woods yet, my friend."

The bailiff began to read the last charge. "On the felony count of homicide by vehicle while DUI involving the death of the female passenger of the Ford vehicle, how does the jury find Richard Mahan? Guilty or not guilty?" As the bailiff was reading this question, Jack got brave and decided to look over at the jury. He saw that nearly every member of the jury was in the process of shifting his or her gaze from his table to Kate's. "Oh crap!" Jack screamed inside. He knew that jurors like to place their eyes on those who they are about to reward. They avoid looking at those they are about to deny.

Before announcing the jury's decision on this count, jury foreperson Jane looked at some of her fellow jurors as if to draw courage from them. She then looked squarely at the judge. "Guilty," she softly declared. She then quietly sat down, crossed her arms, and began staring at her lap.

Young Rick instantly slumped in his seat, completely devastated. Back in the audience, Mrs. Mahan started to cry. Mr. Mahan tried not to but started to cry as well. Jack just sat there trying his best to look like a good loser, but he felt miserable. Over at the other table, the trooper was gently patting Kate on the back while she tried her best to look like a gracious winner.

Judge Price was the first to say something. "Mr. Day, would you like to poll the jury?"

"No, Your Honor, we will take a pass on that." In Jack's experience, **polling the jury** — asking each juror individually if they agree with the announced verdict — never works. It just repeatedly rubs salt in the client's fresh wound for no purpose. "However, I do ask the court to allow my client to remain on bail pending sentencing. His parents are here. He is a good kid. He is not going anywhere."

"Ms. Page, do you have a position on this?" asked the judge.

"The Commonwealth leaves this decision to the discretion of the court, without any recommendation on our part." Kate saw no point in looking like a jerk.

"Very well," the judge said. "Mr. Day, will you please stand with your client?" Jack stood and motioned for Rick to stand too. Rick got out of his seat, but his knees were shaking like those of the lion cowering before the great and terrible Oz.

"Mr. Richard Mahan, you have been found not guilty of one felony count of homicide by vehicle while driving under the influence. You have been convicted by a jury of your peers of one misdemeanor count of underage drinking, one misdemeanor count of reckless driving, and one felony count of homicide by vehicle while driving under the influence." Judge Price took a few seconds to look at his personal calendar on his desktop computer. He continued, "Sentencing on these matters will take place in this very courtroom at 9:30 a.m., exactly two weeks from today, on the 25th of this month. You will remain on bail until that time but are ordered to appear at 9:30 a.m. on the 25th. All rules previously explained as conditions of your bail will remain in effect. Mr. Mahan do you have any questions?"

Jack shook his head from side to side at his shell-shocked client helping him to know the correct answer. "No," Your Honor," Rick robotically responded.

"Very well. The court hereby orders the Office of Adult Probation and Parole to prepare a presentence investigation report for this court in this matter. This report is to be made available to the court and the attorneys on both sides at least three business days prior to sentencing. Mr. Day, please see to it that your client understands his duty to cooperate with the PSI unit in preparing this report for the court."

"Yes, Sir. I will explain everything to my client."

"Very good. I now excuse the jury from further service. On behalf of our courts and our government, I express my sincere thanks to all of you members of the jury for your good service. Without you, our criminal justice system simply would not function. Thank you so much for your wisdom and indispensable help. This court now stands in recess."

"All rise," the bailiff announced as the judge rose and left the room. The jury left next, being very careful to avoid looking at the distraught man they had just convicted, his attorney, or his parents. Kate and the trooper were the next to leave (Jack would congratulate her later, outside of the presence of his client). Finally, only Jack, Rick, and his parents remained in the large, empty room.

Suddenly, the front door to the courtroom flew open. It was Father Skelly. Skelly looked around the room, quite surprised that hardly anyone was still there. He looked at Jack and asked, "What did I miss?"

## Key Terms Found in This Chapter

Telephone alert                                    Deadlocked jury
Verdict slip                             Violence to their conscience
Allen charge                                      Polling the jury
Dynamite charge

# Questions for Class Discussion

1. Are you comfortable with lawyers and defendants waiting for verdicts to be put on "telephone alert"? If you were a bailiff, would you be worried about such a system?

2. If you were the young defendant in this trial, what sort of emotions would you probably be experiencing when you are first told that, "they have a verdict"?

3. Why does the chapter describe the relationship between Jack and Kate as they waited for the verdict news as now one more of "comrades" than "enemy combatants"?

4. In what ways might sitting in the courtroom waiting for the announcement of the verdicts be like waiting for the results of a field goal in the final seconds of a razor close football championship game? Have you ever had your heart race in such a situation?

5. What is a verdict slip? What information is on it? Who is the one who gets to read it to the court?

6. What is an Allen charge? Why exactly is it nicknamed the "dynamite charge"? Why do judges refuse readily to accept a jury's revelation to the court that they are "hopelessly deadlocked"?

7. How successful are Allen charges in getting the job done? Why do you suppose this is so?

8. What do they mean in an Allen charge when they use the phrase, "unless it would do violence to your conscience"? Why would words as powerful as those be used?

9. When did the defendant, Rick, start prematurely to take cheer during the announcement of the verdicts on each of the four different charges? Why would many lay people make the mistake of prematurely feeling relief like that? Why did his attorney probably know better?

10. What can lawyers guess by seeing who the jurors are watching as the verdicts are being announced? What is it about human nature that causes such behavior on the part of the jurors?

11. Why does it usually do more harm than good for a losing defender to ask the judge to poll the jury? Under what circumstances might you as the losing defender request that this be done?

12. Why did the judge not simply sentence Rick on the spot once the judge was aware of the verdicts?
13. In waiting for your sentencing day, what sort of affairs would you put in order if you were this defendant?

# Unit 14
# Down but Not Out

### Chapter 40: The Presentence Investigation

### Chapter 41: Sentencing

### Chapter 42: A Clever Idea

This unit introduces us to the job of the presentence investigator; it then teaches us all about the nuances associated with the actual determination of a proper sentence by the trial judge. Sentencing over, we then learn about how lawyers develop — hopefully — clever ideas for appeals rather than stiff their clients by advancing hopeless boilerplate issues.

# 40

## The Presentence Investigation

Presentence Investigator Maria Hernandez was eating her lunchtime hoagie sandwich on a park bench across the street from the county courthouse when she noticed Judge Stephen Hyde walking down a path in her direction. To her surprise, he stopped as he came to her bench.

"Good afternoon, Your Honor," Maria said by way of greeting. She wondered if she should stand up. To her huge surprise, Judge Hyde sat down instead — right next to her!

"Good afternoon," Judge Hyde said. "You work for the county probation office in their presentence investigation unit, do you not?" asked the judge. "Your name is Maria Gonzalez, right?"

"Maria Hernandez," the woman replied. "Is there something I can help you with?"

Judge Hyde knew that there was no possible way that Ms. Hernandez would know his biological connection to the deceased female crash victim in the case of Commonwealth v. Richard Mahan. The only person in all of county government who knew was his close friend, DA Gus Owens, of whom he knew would never talk. Still, he had to tread very carefully here not to raise any suspicions. Really, he was about to take a huge chance just talking to Hernandez at all about one of her pending cases. However, he could not restrain himself from putting in a plug for the deceased female that he and his temporary girlfriend had given up for adoption long ago while both were yet in high school.

Judge Hyde took a few seconds to gaze at some squirrels across the grass, smiled gently at Maria, and said, "I heard you are preparing the presentence investigation report for Judge Price on the Richard Mahan, DUI homicide case."

"Yes, I am," answered the woman. Judge Hyde could see the look of bewilderment on her face.

"Tough assignment, I bet," Judge Hyde continued. "We have such a problem lately with drunk drivers killing innocent people. I am glad that someone like you has been assigned such an important case. I'm sure you will do the right thing in this case."

"I don't know what to say!" Maria countered. "Are you taking over this case or something, Your Honor?"

"What? No! It would be highly improper for me to speak to you if I had anything whatsoever to do with this case. I simply find the case to be very interesting and am glad an intelligent person such as yourself is on it. I have heard good things about you in the courthouse. I enjoy watching rising young stars like yourself in county government. I am sure you have a bright future."

"Thank you," Maria replied. "I take my job seriously."

"I am sure you do, Ms. Hernandez. I will be interested to hear through the grapevine how this DUI killer is eventually sentenced, not that it is any of my direct concern. Anyway, forgive an old man of his ramblings. You have a good day, Ms. Hernandez."

"You too, your honor." With that, Maria watched as Judge Hyde got up and casually strolled away. She could not help but wonder what had just taken place. "Was Hyde trying to send me some kind of signal?" Maria keenly sensed that Hyde had just suggested to her that the "killer" Mahan should not be let off too easy in her report. "Should I report this encounter to my supervisor or the trial judge?" she asked herself. She was not even sure what exactly had just happened. Reporting a judge for impropriety was no small thing. It fact, it could play out to be a huge thing. No, Maria would just let it go. She rationalized her silence by concluding that maybe Judge Hyde had just wanted to engage in some courthouse chitchat about an interesting case. Not exactly proper, but no big harm done. Still, she felt a mix of pride in the judge taking notice of her career combined with some anxiety that he was vaguely linking his esteem for her with how she handled this very important Mahan case. "Very weird," she concluded.

Maria decided it was about time for her to get back to her courthouse office. She needed to get straight to work on the Richard Mahan case, of all things. Rick was scheduled to see her the next morning for an interview, and there were some preliminary matters with which to attend. One of the squirrels watched with interest as Maria threw away the rest of her sandwich in one of the park's open-top, trash baskets as she exited the small park. Maria noticed and hoped the animal would enjoy her bequest.

After making her way across the busy street and entering the courthouse, Maria walked over to the elevator and pushed the button for the sixth floor, the floor that exclusively housed the county adult probation and parole office. The **presentence investigation unit**, of which Maria played a part, was a specialized unit within adult probation and parole. Instead of supervising a caseload of probationers and parolees like most of her office colleagues did (and which Maria herself used to do), Maria and the small group of other agents assigned to the PSI unit now got to exclusively prepare presentence reports for judges. Their role was to help judges craft sentences involving people convicted of serious crimes who did not have a plea arrangement with the DA's office.

Before a judge sentences someone for a serious crime, the judge typically wants to become familiar with many important details. Sentencing is a critical stage of due process and should never become a mere game of chance. The judge will want to know about the circumstances of the crime, including the victim impact. The judge will also want to understand the defendant as a **whole person**. Hence, the judge is interested in various defendant characteristics, including age, education, employment history, family situation, prior record, and past attempts at rehabilitation, if any. In addition, the judge wants to learn of the defendant's version of the crime, the degree to which he or she accepts responsibility and shows remorse, and any medical conditions the defendant might have. Finally, and perhaps most importantly, the judge wants to know the state legislature's sentencing guidelines recommendations, as well as the investigator's own personal sentencing recommendations and reasoning.

Maria knew that she could get much of the above information for her report to Judge Price by reviewing the police reports on Richard, by reviewing the prosecutor's reports, by making a few phone calls, and by delving into some restricted governmental Internet sites. The data she needed for her written report to Jude Price started accumulating nicely, and the report almost began writing itself.

One of Maria's favorite exercises was to calculate the state's sentencing guideline recommendations for the given crimes. She liked doing this for the judge in her report because she herself would have to recommend a sentence and liked being "guided" by the legislature. She now turned her attention to calculating the "guideline" sentence.

Most states now use what are known as **sentencing guidelines**, developed by the state legislature to aid judges in meting out sentences. The idea here is that one's sentence should not be overly dependent on merely what judge one has but rather should reflect what is being generally implemented around the state for a similar offense, controlling for a similar prior record. Not all states use sentencing guidelines. Some states prefer to follow the traditional approach by giving judges almost complete discretion in creating an appropriate sentence (restrained only by the **statutory maximum penalty** for the offense). However, many states have decided to promulgate guidelines, believing that judges could use the help.

Sentencing guidelines are typically grids issued by the state legislature that reveal—as mentioned—the sentence deemed appropriate for a particular crime, given a particular criminal past history. Some female lawyers say that the grid reminds them of a pantyhose chart, used in selecting the right size of pantyhose. However, instead of the two criteria being a person's weight and height, a **sentencing grid** uses the two criteria of "current offense gravity score" and "prior record score." Picture a graph with an x-axis going horizontally (representing the **current offense gravity score**) and a y-axis going vertically (representing the **prior record score**). The x-axis moving left to right has 10 points numbered from 1 to 10 (with 1 being for petty crimes, such as misdemeanor theft or vandalism, while 10 would be for aggravated rape or attempted murder). Exactly how many points a particular offense gets is determined by the legislature and listed in a detailed list of crime scores published by the state. Once the presentence investigator has assigned an x-axis number to the defendant, they now must assign a y-axis number representing the prior record score. Typically, legislatures give one point for each prior felony conviction and one point for every two prior misdemeanor convictions, with a total y-axis score not to exceed six points.

Once having determined both the x-axis and the y-axis scores, the plotter will then see where on the grid the defendant lands. The grid is divided into many small cells, and each cell has a recommend sentence in it (expressed typically in months). For example, for crimes of average seriousness, the plotter might move five points to the right on the x-axis. Then, if the defendant has four prior misdemeanor convictions (and none else), the plotter will move up two points on the y- or vertical axis (since one receives a point for every two misdemeanor convictions). This plotting will land the person to be sentenced into a specific cell on the grid, with the cell containing a number reflecting the legislature's opinion of an appropriate sentence in a standard case.

In many states, such sentencing guidelines are not suggestions but are mandates (hence, the term **mandatory sentencing guidelines**). The judge must follow them. In other states, such guidelines are only strong suggestions (hence the term **nonmandatory sentencing guidelines**). True, the judge must calculate and at least consider the recommendation, but once having done this, the judge is free to do as he or she thinks best.

In Pennsylvania, where **PSI writer** Maria was working, the guidelines were merely recommendations; in other words, they were nonmandatory, rather than mandatory, guidelines. Still, Maria knew that most judges there found them very helpful in deciding what is right and wrong, sentencing wise.

In calculating the sentencing guideline figures for Richard, Maria would only have to move horizontally on the grid, since he had no prior record of any kind to rise him up vertically.

Rick's two current misdemeanor convictions (underage drinking and reckless driving) yielded just one point each on the horizontal axis (current offense severity), and Rick therefore landed in the extreme bottom left corner of the grid concerning each of them. The resultant guideline cell recommended "probation of 12 months or less" for both of these misdemeanor convictions.

Maria next went on to calculate the guideline sentence for the one homicide by vehicle while DUI conviction (remember, Rick was acquitted of the other homicide count). She knew that once again, Rick would not ascend vertically on the chart, but she wondered how far he would shift horizontally in light of the "current offense gravity" score. Maria knew it would be much more than a 1 like the two misdemeanors, but she doubted it would be a 10, the maximum. She was right. After looking through the detailed lists of offense gravity scores published by the legislature, Maria found the listing for various "homicides" under the letter "H" in the detailed list. Under the category "homicides," she skipped over the various types of murder, ignored the numbers associated with "voluntary manslaughter" and "involuntary manslaughter" and focused on the numbers under "homicide by vehicle while DUI" (which, technically, is a type of involuntary manslaughter but a crime of enough importance that the legislature chose to give it its own category). The number Maria saw in the listing was a 7, which was less than 10, 9, or 8 but still quite high. Maria held her breath as she looked for the specific number in the grid cell corresponding to the plot of seven over with zero up. It gave a range actually of not less than 36 months to not more than 60 months. This meant that the legislature thought that a crime like that should get someone with no criminal record at least 36 months in prison but probably no more than 60 months. The legislature, in giving a range, was leaving the judge to decide where in the range a defendant should land, given the judge's discretion and the particulars of the case. This does not mean that the legislature was recommending an indeterminate sentence of 36 to 60 months (with a parole board deciding when you get out) but rather a determinate sentence of either 36 months or 60 months or some specific, single number of months in between the two extremes, as the judge sees fit.

In addition to the guideline recommendation in the cell, Maria noticed an asterisk next to the number "36." She looked to see the meaning of this and learned that though sentencing guidelines in Pennsylvania are usually nonmandatory, the 36 months this time was a "statutory minimum sentence" that the judge had to impose by law for this particular crime. The judge could go higher but could not go lower. Homicides by vehicle while DUI in Pennsylvania carried 36 months as a **mandatory minimum sentence**.

So Maria knew even before meeting Richard that she would personally be recommending at least 36 months in prison for Richard, no matter how much she liked the guy. She might even recommend 60 months if he were a real dirt bag. She could even recommend more than 60 months since the guidelines in Pennsylvania were nonmandatory suggestions. She would just have to wait and interview him before deciding on her personal recommendation to the judge.

The next morning came soon enough and Richard appeared as instructed at 10:00 a.m. Maria came out to the reception area at 10:05 and escorted Richard back to her office. Her first impression of him centered on how incredibly young and harmless he looked. "Hardly the look of a killer," she thought as she reflected on Judge Hyde's stark description of him in the park yesterday.

"Have a seat," Maria told Rick as they arrived at her office (which was really just a cubicle). After he sat down, Maria got straight to it. "Tell me about the crime," she said.

Rick tearfully told her his version of what had happened on that tragic night. He told her that he had drunk two beers and taken two cold pills. He steadfastly maintained that he had never read the warnings on the cold medicine box (about drowsiness, especially when taken with alcohol). However, he still expressed great remorse for having driven after drinking any beer and especially after taking cold pills with the beer. He explained that though he was not honestly convinced that he had fallen asleep due to the beer and the pills, he did recognize the fact that this was possible. He certainly admitted that he had fallen asleep behind the wheel and had therefore wrongfully caused the death of the crash victims.

Maria found Rick to a very sympathetic figure. It was not often that she felt sorry for a "killer," but this time she did—a little bit anyway.

"Tell me about yourself," she suggested.

"What do you want to know?" Rick inquired.

"Tell me about your life in school, your friends, your family, and your dreams."

Rick spent the next 20 minutes telling Maria all about himself, his school, his friends, and his family. He told her about his love of math, his high grades, and his goal to become an economist someday—if that career would still be available to him as a convicted felon.

"What kind of sentence do you think you should get for this crime?" Maria finally asked.

Rick turned pale. "Do I have to give you a figure on that?" Rick asked.

"No."

"Then I'd rather not. Jail scares the whiz out of me."

"Why is that?" Maria inquired.

"I am not sure a regular guy like me has the particular set of skills needed to get by in such a tough place," Rick answered. "It is really going to suck to be me inside there."

Maria nodded with sympathy. She knew Rick's hunch that prison would be rough on a square like him was spot on. She would be recommending 36 months to the judge, the minimum mandatory sentence. Recommending the minimum allowed by law might be considered good news to some, but Maria sensed that this would not be the case with Rick. She decided to just say goodbye and leave it at that for now. "See you next week in court, Richard," was all she said in parting. "Thank you for coming in today on time."

After Rick left, Maria spent the next few minutes staring sadly down from the sixth floor window near her cubicle. Her eyes soon focused on the small park where she had eaten her lunch the day before. She watched as the squirrels looked for food. Before long, she noticed Rick walking on the sidewalk just outside of the front of the park toward his parents who were waiting outside their parked car. She shook her head in sympathy as she saw him get a hug from his mom. Then, suddenly, she saw Judge Hyde standing next to his parked car in his reserved parking stall a few yards from the park entrance. Judge Hyde was watching Rick as well; only the look on his face seemed to be one of resentment rather than one of sympathy. Just then, the judge glanced up to the courthouse sixth floor bank of windows from which Maria had been gazing. Startled, she lurched back out of sight, almost losing her balance. "Maybe my recommending 36 months would be kind of light," she considered. "After all, there was some real damage done to innocent people here." Then she thought of Rick in prison for three years, a sparrow being constantly harassed by vultures. "No, I think I will stick with the 36."

∽

## Key Terms Found in This Chapter

| | |
|---|---|
| Presentence investigation unit | Prior record score |
| Whole person | Mandatory sentencing guidelines |
| Sentencing guidelines | Non-mandatory sentencing guidelines |
| Statutory maximum penalty | PSI writer |
| Sentencing grid | Mandatory minimum sentence |
| Current offense gravity score | |

# Questions for Class Discussion

1. What county agency in the chapter housed the presentence investigation unit? Would you consider working in such a unit? Would you prefer it to being a regular probation and parole officer?

2. Why would it be unethical for Judge Hyde to lobby the presentence investigator about the Mahan case, given that he was the victim's biological father? Do you condemn Judge Hyde for doing this lobbying or feel sympathy for his actions?

3. What sort of information can presentence investigators get from police and other records for their reports, even before meeting with a defendant?

4. Why do judges want to know the "whole person" before sentencing someone? What sort of information is necessary to have in getting to know the "whole person"? Which of these pieces of information do you find the most important?

5. Who promulgates sentencing guidelines? Why do some states prefer to use them instead of just letting judges "do their thing"?

6. What is a sentencing grid? What two criteria does the plotter use in finding the correct place to land a defendant on the grid? Would it be better to wind up in the upper right corner of the grid or the lower left corner?

7. What argument could you make to a state legislature wanting to use a sentencing grid to have such grids be mere "nonmandatory" guides? What argument could you make to have such grids be binding and mandatory?

8. Do you like the idea of making some crimes come attached with mandatory minimum sentences? What are the pros and cons of such legislative oversight?

9. What place should remorse play in a presentence investigator's recommendation for a sentence?

10. Should a presentence investigator even worry about a defendant's prison survival skills if the person is going to have to serve some kind of long sentence anyway? Would your answer be any different in a minor case in which the investigator was seriously considering jail time versus probation as recommendation options?

11. If you were a judge in a nonmandatory guideline state, how much weight would you give sentencing recommendations made by presentence investigators?

# 41

## Sentencing

It was 9:10 a.m. on the 25th of the month. In 20 minutes, Judge Robert Price's court would be in session. First up this morning: the sentencing hearing on Rick's homicide by vehicle case. This hearing was the only nonroutine matter Judge Price would have to be working on this day. Everything else scheduled on his day's calendar was easy stuff. Still, he wished that it were a day scheduled with all easy stuff.

Judge Price was grateful for the information he had read late yesterday afternoon that was contained in Maria Hernandez's presentence investigation report. He wanted to know exactly what kind of a young man Rick was. After reading the report, he considered him to be a decent person who had done a bad thing on what turned out to be the worst day of his otherwise good life. He wanted to show the kid mercy but also believed that mercy should not decimate justice. There were two dead people, plus their surviving family members, who needed to be shown consideration as well.

There are **four classical goals of sentencing**: rehabilitation, deterrence, incapacitation, and retribution. Judges tend to gravitate more heavily to one or two of them than they do the others, and Judge Price was no exception.

Though popular with many judges and the public, Judge Price had little faith in rehabilitation. "People have to be habilitated before they can be rehabilitated," he liked to quip. He just did not see rehabilitation as being a very realistic goal of the criminal justice system. **Rehabilitation** (setting someone straight) assumes a **medical model of crime** in that it treats crimes as a sort of social disease that can be cured given the proper treatment. However, Judge Price believed that forcing someone into a program, be it plain incarceration or even a program inside a prison, had little hope of working. The prison's revolving door seemed to confirm that to him.

Price had even more cynical views regarding the goal of deterrence. Whether considering so-called **specific deterrence** (teaching an individual offender a lesson via sentencing so that he/she will not reoffend) or **general deterrence** (teaching society a group lesson by showing them what can happen to one of their own), Judge Price thought deterrence was largely a joke. "People obey the law because they believe it is wrong not to do so," he thought, "not because they are scared straight."

**Incapacitation** (segregating an offender from society so that he or she can no longer do harm — at least while incarcerated), was a goal Judge Price did believe in. He bristled when defense attorneys referred to incarceration as merely **warehousing** their clients who would come out no better a person than when they went in. "Yeah, but at least we get a break from them while they are put away," he would respond. Judge Price also knew that crime, especially serious crime, was primarily a "young man's game," and incarcerating dangerous people long enough often helped them to age out of crime.

**Retribution** was the goal that most attracted Judge Price. Some people like to call this concept "revenge," but he thought of it more as **just deserts**. He did not believe he could do much to deter people or to rehabilitate them, but he sure believed he could see to it that victimizers got what was coming to them. That said, Judge Price was not draconian in his sentencing by any means. He was known as being tough, but he was hardly the toughest judge in the courthouse when it came to stiff sentences. At most, he was third down on the list.

Rick could have drawn a much harsher sentencing judge than Judge Price.

Part of Judge Price's self-perceived duty was to see that justice for the victims was done. His philosophy was that Richard Mahan should be punished somehow not just for the one count of homicide that he was convicted of but also for both deaths that he had so obviously caused.

True, the jury had found Rick guilty of one count and not guilty of the other, but Judge Price found such a split verdict to be utterly irrational. "How on earth could the jury decide Mahan had somehow wrongfully caused the death of the passenger in the other vehicle but not the driver?" he thought. Price suspected that many on the jury must have engaged in some form of partial "jury nullification" in reaching their verdict.

**Jury nullification** is the power that all juries have to find someone not guilty even though the state has proven its case to their satisfaction beyond a reasonable doubt. Jury nullification can have a bright side (e.g., northern juries in the 1800s refusing to convict neighbors of violating the Fugitive Slave Act by playing a part in the Underground Railroad). Jury nullification also can have a sinister side (e.g., all-White, southern juries in the early 1900s refusing to convict obvious participants in lynch mobs). Some legal scholars consider jury nullification to be a right that juries have. Others (most) consider it merely to be a raw, naked power and therefore something to be endured but never legitimated. This latter view is the reason that most judges do not let defense lawyers tell juries of this power during their closing arguments. If juries wish to engage in jury nullification, they have to figure out their ability to do so all by themselves.

Judge Price thought that jury nullification was a disgrace. He could not stop a jury from engaging in it, but he could try to "clean up their mess" at sentencing if at least some of the charges stuck. Even so, he (being a rule-minded person) would never do anything that would itself be an act of lawlessness on his own part. The question that Judge Price was now struggling with in his chambers was, "Can I properly consider two dead bodies in my sentence even though the jury found the defendant only guilty of one count of vehicular homicide?"

Judge Price began to mull over the distinction between a "trial fact" and a "sentencing fact." Judges (not juries) sentence people, and so judges are permitted to determine so-called sentencing facts to help them design a proper sentence. For example, the facts outlined in Maria's presentence report to the judge were nearly all "sentencing facts." The jury did not have to determine Rick's "degree of remorsefulness" or whether or not he accepted "responsibility for the crimes." Neither did the judge have to leave it to the jury to determine Rick's educational level, family situation, or employment history. These are all clearly **sentencing facts** to be ultimately determined by the judge using a "preponderance" level of proof (i.e., more likely than not). **Trial facts**, on the other hand, are those facts that must be determined by a jury, not a judge. Furthermore, the jury must use the "beyond a reasonable doubt" standard in finding them and not just the mere "preponderance" level of proof, as is the case with judges finding their sentencing facts.

So was the fact that Rick killed two people instead of just one strictly a trial fact or rather a mere sentencing fact? Judge Price knew that the legal definition of a trial fact was a little hard to grasp. A trial fact is defined as any fact that, if found, would increase the defendant's length of sentence **beyond the statutory maximum** for the offense being punished. For example, if simple assault ordinarily carries a maximum sentence of 11 months in jail but simple assault motivated by racial hatred carries a maximum sentence of double that, the finding of race as the motivating factor for the assault would be a trial fact, not a sentencing fact. Similarly, if selling under 500 grams of cocaine calls for a maximum sentence of five years in prison, but selling over 500 grams calls for a maximum sentence of seven years, the amount of cocaine sold would be a trial fact rather than a sentencing fact. This is so, in both instances, because the fact in question would cause the defendant to receive a sentence that exceeded the normal statutory maximum for the crime originally contemplated and would therefore be a new crime entirely (since different crimes have different statutory maximums).

Judge Price knew the above was the law but was still not sure if he should sentence Rick for two deaths even though the jury found him responsible for just one. Despite the distinction between trial facts and sentencing facts as outlined above, the determination of trial facts versus sentencing facts in real life still can be very tricky. True, Judge Price sensed that he could maybe evade the letter of the law by giving Rick a stiff sentence for just one dead body without exceeding the statutory maximum for one homicide. This would especially be the case if he were to refrain from mentioning on the record any consideration of two (as opposed to just one) deaths. Yet, it bothered him that this might at least be evading the spirit of the law. In the end, Judge Price decided he would just sentence Mahan as though he had only caused the death of just one victim. Besides, he could properly give a very stiff sentence if he wanted to just for the one death.

Judge Price looked at the small clock on his desk. It was now 9:31. He figured he better get to the hearing.

"All rise," the bailiff called as the judge emerged from his chamber door into the courtroom. Judge Price walked pensively to his chair and motioned for everyone to sit down. He himself remained standing for a few seconds while silencing his cell phone and then took his seat as well.

"I believe we are here this morning for sentencing in the matter of Commonwealth v. Richard Mahan. Ms. Prosecutor, are you ready to proceed?"

"Yes, Your Honor," Kate replied.

"Defense counsel, are you ready to proceed?"

"Yes, Your Honor."

"Does either the Commonwealth or the defense have any corrections to be made to the facts outlined in the presentence report?" the judge inquired. Both attorneys told Judge Price that they were satisfied with the facts.

"Very well. Before I deliver the sentence of the court, I will ask both lawyers to argue any points they may have relevant to the sentencing decision. Ms. Page, you may go first."

Kate stood up and argued forcefully in favor of a sentence much longer than the mandatory minimum sentence of three years recommended by Maria in her presentence report. The prosecutor spoke of "justice" for the victims and their survivors repeatedly, knowing that Judge Price was a firm believer in said concept. She spoke of justice for society as a whole and of the scourge of DUI related deaths on our highways. She referred to the crash as "horrific" and said that "nobody should dignify this crash by using the term accident. It was a terrible crime; it was no accident." She asked the judge not to let the defendant's youth play too prominent a role in his punishment. "If he is old enough to drive, he is old enough to be held accountable for his driving," she suggested. She finally urged the court to give Richard a sentence "in the upper range of the penalty, something approaching the 10-year maximum for one count of this type of homicide." Then, Kate sat down. She looked at the trooper. He appeared pleased with her request for near maximum time.

It was now Jack's turn. He emphatically emphasized the fact that his client was young, in fact, only 17 years old. He spoke of Rick's stellar grades in school, his lack of a criminal record, and his freedom from addictions. He spoke of the "light drinking" that had taken place and the fact that the cold pills were "nonprescription." He suggested that even three years was far too long, and his client constituted a "poster boy" as to what can go wrong when legislatures force judges to mete out mandatory minimum sentences. He almost concluded by asking the judge not to warehouse his client for no good reason; he reconsidered this tactic at the last second and instead painted a concluding picture of young, defenseless Rick in a dark prison filled with violence. "Three years in a place like that for a conventional kid like Rick is more like nine years for a street-wise adult. Giving Rick three years will be about as much pain as giving him 'the upper end' of the sentencing range that the Ms. Page so harshly seems to think is fitting." With that, Jack sat down.

As he took his seat, Jack's young client leaned over and whispered in his ear. He asked Jack if he was crazy. "I can't do three years!" Rick pleaded in desperation.

"I know," Jack replied. "Today this judge is required by the state legislature to give you no less than three years. Let's hope for that for now, and we will try to get more relief later in our appeal."

"Are we going to appeal, Mr. Day?" Rick asked.

"Of course, for the 10th time, yes, we will appeal, Rick." Jack glanced up at the bench and saw Judge Price patiently waiting for them to finish their quiet discussion. He thought that the judge's look of patience might be a good sign. It was, in a sense. Judge Price had entered the courtroom tentatively planning to sentence Rick to seven years in prison. He thought that even just one dead body deserved a sentence of at least that long. Now, after having heard Jack's sentencing argument, his heart had softened a little.

Judge Price looked at Richard and instructed him to "please stand." Rick did so, with his knees now shaking vigorously. He looked bizarre, almost like an actor in a comedy. Yet, just like the earlier time he had stood shaking before the judge during the announcement of the verdicts, nobody in the room felt any impulse whatsoever to laugh.

Jack also rose to his feet to stand in customary solidarity with his client. The judge took a quick glance at the audience, then looking directly at Rick, announced his sentence. "After consideration of the arguments just heard, and after some careful thought before and during this hearing, it is the order of this court that Richard Mahan be sentenced as follows. On the misdemeanor conviction of reckless driving, you are sentenced to time served with credit given to time spent in jail prior to making bail. On the misdemeanor count of underage drinking, you are sentenced to time served. On the felony count of homicide by vehicle while driving under the influence of alcohol and/or drugs, I hereby sentence you to four years in the state penitentiary, with no credit for any pre-trial detention."

Judge Price paused briefly out of concern that Rick looked faint. "Please, be seated," he politely stated. Jack took Rick by the arm and helped lower him back down into his seat.

"Mr. Day, I understand that your client is not yet 18 years of age?"

"That is correct, Your Honor. He will turn 18 in six weeks."

"Very well, it is the order of the court that the defendant be housed in the county juvenile detention facility until his 18th birthday and then be transferred to the state prison once he reaches that age."

Jack stood back up and asked, "Your Honor, I ask that my client be allowed to remain free on bail pending final disposition of his appeal."

"Denied," the judge ruled. Judge Price always denied such requests since appeals took so long and were so infrequently successful.

"Then, Your Honor, I request that you allow my client to remain in the juvenile detention facility, not just for the six weeks until he turns 18, but until such time that his appeal is ultimately decided."

"Now that's not a bad idea," Judge Price thought to himself. He knew that the juvenile detention facility had a special wing for older delinquents who had reached 18 while living there but had not yet finished serving the full length of their juvenile "sentences" (juvenile correctional jurisdiction ends at age 21). Judge Price looked at Kate. "What is the Commonwealth's position on Mr. Day's request?" the judge inquired.

"The Commonwealth…" Ms. Page had to pause to think about this. After five seconds of silence, she finally objected. "Mr. Mahan did a real crime and needs to go to a real person's prison," she argued. However, Judge Price took her initial hesitation as a good indication that even she believed that Jack's idea was not without merit.

Judge Price shifted his attention now to the defense table. "I will grant the defense request. The defendant will serve his sentence in the county's secure juvenile detention facility until such time that the Superior Court of Pennsylvania determines his appeal of right. If his appeal is denied, he will at that point be immediately transferred to an adult prison to be determined by the State Department of Corrections."

Two sheriffs slowly approached the defense table from the side. One of them instructed Rick to place his hands behind him so that he could be handcuffed. Rick complied and was promptly led away through a side door. As he left the room, Rick looked at his parents. The look of concern in their eyes motivated him to act brave for their sakes. Acting brave helped him feel a little better also.

"What next?" Father Skelly asked Jack from his seat located a couple of rows behind Jack.

"We will appeal!" Jack said firmly.

"Do we have a shot?" asked Rick's father.

"Yes, I already have some clever ideas."

Kate was about to professionally tease Jack about having "clever ideas." Seeing the distress on the faces of the defendant's parents, she chose instead to keep her mouth shut — for now.

~

## Key Terms Found in This Chapter

Four classical goals of sentencing
Rehabilitation
Medical model of crime
Specific deterrence
General deterrence
Incapacitation
Warehousing

Retribution
Just Deserts
Jury nullification
Sentencing facts
Trial facts
Beyond the statutory maximum

## Questions for Class Discussion:

1. What are the four classical goals of sentencing? Would you, like some, add restitution as a modern fifth goal, or is restitution simply not an aspect of punishment?
2. Which of the four classical goals do you like best? Least?

3. How is the idea of rehabilitation linked to a medical model of crime? Do you have much faith in the criminal justice system being able to rehabilitate people?
4. What is the difference between specific and general deterrence? Does either work very well in our society? Can you give an example of general deterrence that seems to be working?
5. Why do some critics of incapacitation refer to it derisively as merely warehousing people? Do you agree that incapacitation is pointless?
6. Is retribution a moral goal of sentencing? Do you agree with an "eye for an eye, a tooth for a tooth"? Is retribution plain old-fashioned revenge, or is it more appropriate to label it "just deserts"?
7. Various scholars claim that the death penalty simply does not deter potential murderers. Why might this be the case? In your opinion, would a societal goal for retribution justify the death penalty in murder cases even if deterrence is futile?
8. What is jury nullification? Can you give a virtuous example of this concept? A wicked example?
9. In your opinion, is jury nullification a right that juries have or just a power? Should the ability to nullify the law be kept hidden from juries?
10. Who decides a trial fact? Who decides a sentencing fact? What is the level of proof required for each? Can you give an example of a trial fact and of a sentencing fact?
11. What test have appellate courts developed to distinguish a sentencing fact from a trial fact when it is not plainly obvious which type of fact is in play?
12. Jack made a passionate argument for mercy for his client during the sentencing hearing. If you were the defense attorney in another case, would you be able and willing to make a passionate argument in favor of mercy in a case involving a client you thought was purely evil?

# 42

# A Clever Idea

Jack spent the next week combing through the trial transcript trying to actually come up with his promised "clever ideas" for an appeal.
First, he meticulously combed through every line of the trial transcript,
zooming his attention on any point where the trial judge had ruled on
an objection. That is how lawyers usually **spot issues for appeal**. Lawyers
look in the trial transcript for where the trial judge may have messed up
in ruling incorrectly on some lawyer's objection during the trial. They
then pounce on that. Of course, nearly every trial judge makes some in-
correct rulings on objections during a trial (one judge admitted to Jack
once that he guessed on objections about a fourth of the time). That is
why appellate courts long ago came up with the so-called **harmless error
doctrine**. This rule requires a lawyer to prove not just that the judge had
mistakenly ruled on an objection during the trial, but that there was a
high risk that the mistake had altered the entire outcome of the trial.
Jack knew that unless a judge's mistake was very bad, the harmless error
doctrine would nearly always save the judge's day.

Jack's "issue spotting" examination of the trial transcript scored just a
few very weak issues he could argue, but that would obviously never survive the harmless error doctrine. He therefore was not in the mood even
to raise them unless he got very desperate. What about issues other than
those involving poor judicial rulings regarding objections during trial?
Off the top of his head, Jack could immediately come up with two such

appealable issues. One of these was that the "verdict was **against the clear weight** of the evidence." Here, Jack would be arguing that it was the jury rather than the judge who had committed error. To win on that one, he would have to convince an appellate court that no reasonable jury could possibly have convicted his client, given the facts that were established. "A sure loser of an issue if ever there was one," Jack reminded himself. Appellate courts hate acting as a **13th juror** by second guessing the triers of the facts. The standard used is not how the appellate judges would have voted if they had been on the jury. Rather, the appellate court would have to decide that the verdict, given the proof offered, was essentially asinine. Jack knew that the finding of vehicular homicide while DUI in Rick's trial was unfortunate but far from being outside the bounds of all reason.

The other issue that immediately popped into Jack's lawyer head was whether the sentence of four years for the vehicular homicide was so stiff as to be "grossly disproportionate" to the crime. If so, its excessive duration would be a form of cruel and unusual punishment. Jack would be suggesting that the judge acted unconstitutionally when he messed up the sentence. "Again, a loser issue," he thought. He knew very well that appellate courts leave sentences undisturbed even when they believe them to be disproportionate. **Gross disproportionality** is what gets appellate courts to vacate a sentence. Jack knew that no reviewing body was ever going to rule that giving someone four years for wrongfully causing someone's death was even disproportionate, let alone grossly disproportionate.

Jack also knew that the above two issues (verdict against the clear weight of the evidence and a grossly disproportionate sentence) were what desperate defense lawyers often made the centerpieces of their appeals. When appellate courts see these infamous, **two boilerplate issues** — and only these two issues — being raised, they often interpret this as a signal from the defense lawyer that "I've got nothing; it was clean trial. But my client is forcing me to appeal this to you, and I have to argue something."

Clients armed with their **appeal of right** (a first appeal that every convicted person has) can indeed force an attorney to appeal their conviction, unless the lawyer instead wants to go through the hideous process of filing an "Anders brief." In an **Anders brief**, a lawyer unable to find even one appealable issue must painstakingly go over every single ruling (on objections or otherwise) found in the trial transcript and explain why the judge had ruled correctly on every single one of them. Anders briefs are 10 times the work of coming up with some frivolous issues and simply arguing the least frivolous among them in a dramatically shorter traditional brief. In addition to constituting a mountain of work, Anders briefs really get the client angry. This is why so few lawyers file one. It is much easier to argue that the "verdict was against the weight of the evidence" or the sentence was "grossly disproportionate" and be done with it. These issues keep a naive client satisfied because they give the lawyers something to write about that sounds good. Every client seems to think that the verdict was against the weight of the evidence and his or her sentence was too harsh.

As suggested, the reason that every client can force an attorney to appeal is that every state, by statute, gives every criminal defendant convicted of a crime one "appeal of right." States also allow the possibility of appeals subsequent to the appeal of right, but these are all **discretionary appeals**. That means that the higher appellate court (e.g., a state supreme court) only has to hear such appeals if it finds the issue(s) raised to be highly interesting or of great public importance. Good luck with that.

Even though convicted clients get to decide whether to advance an initial "appeal of right"—with nothing to lose, they always choose "yes"—this does not mean that the client also gets to decide what issues to appeal. The latter is completely within the **domain of the lawyer**.

Jack was not about to stiff his client Rick by arguing the two hopeless boilerplate issues of insufficiency of the evidence or too stiff a sentence. Sure, he would throw them into his brief as many lawyers do (just in case his client might get lucky). However, he wanted something more: at least one issue with some real juice.

Jack decided that he could argue that the juvenile judge who had transferred (waived) Rick's case to adult court long ago had abused his discretion by doing so. Jack would suggest that the juvenile court judge was so hyper focused on the seriousness of the charges that he never engaged in the legally required, broader **detailed wavier inquiry** as to whether such a transfer to adult court was truly in the public interest. By state law, this detailed inquiry was to include certain specific factors. One very important factor was indeed the seriousness of the charges. However, the factors also included things such as the juvenile court judge contemplating the threat Rick would continue to pose to the safety of the public, Rick's degree of culpability, his prior record as a juvenile, and (most important) his amenability to treatment and rehabilitation as a ward of the juvenile correctional system. True, the juvenile judge at the time had repeatedly tried to get Rick's (then) public defender to bring up such matters during the transfer hearing. However, the defense lawyer had stupidly failed to do so adequately despite the constant prompts and invitations from the judge. Jack would vigorously argue that the fact that the defense attorney utterly had failed to guide the court into engaging in such a detailed inquiry would not excuse the judge from failing to have done so on his own volition, in other words, *sua sponte*.

State law was clear: juvenile judges contemplating waiver to adult court should exercise huge caution and be loath to transfer a child to the realm of the adults. The bottom line was that such discretionary transfers should constitute a clear, rare exception to the norm of retaining juvenile court jurisdiction.

Jack liked this potential issue very much, but he worried for an instant about whether or not he had waited too long to raise this issue. He wondered that perhaps he was required to have raised it immediately after the transfer decision had been made and before the jury trial in adult court had taken place. Luckily, no. In his state (as in many), the juvenile court judge's decision to grant transfer to adult court was **not immediately appealable**, meaning it had to wait until final disposition of the matter in adult court.

Jack thought he really might be onto something with his idea, but appellate tribunals, like lower court juries, can be rascals whose future decisions are never confidently predictable by anyone. Yet, Jack felt that he at least had something honestly decent to present to his client, Rick. There actually was some hope.

It was early afternoon when Jack arrived at the juvenile detention facility temporarily housing Rick. Rick would only be allowed to stay there until his appeal had been decided. If he lost, the state prison to which he would be transferred would be a lot worse. Yet, this secure juvenile correctional facility was no picnic either. Jack sensed some of his client's intense pain as he now looked deeply into the face of anguished, young Rick Mahan.

"How is my appeal going, Mr. Day?" Rick asked the very instant he sat down across from Jack at the table in the visitation room. A visibly anxious Rick had not even thought to say "hello" first.

"I think I might be on to something," Jack replied. He was trying to look very confident—even more than he really was. Clients fall apart when their lawyers do not seem confident.

"Really! What have you got?" Rick asked. "I heard from some of the guys in here that you should argue that the verdict was against the weight of the evidence."

"I will argue that, but I've got something much better than that," Rick countered. "I think the juvenile judge messed up in transferring your case to adult court. If I am right, and the appellate court agrees, your adult conviction will be overturned."

"Then I will go free?" Rick inquired with a mixture of excitement and hope.

"Well, not exactly," Jack explained. "Your case would be sent back to juvenile court to be processed there. We would start all over again there."

"I won't go free?" Rick said with some disappointment.

"Well, you might go free, or you might have to do some more time in this very place. It depends on what I can work out. The good news is that you will not have to go to adult prison. I might even have a chance at negotiating time served. I do not know. However, I have to win the appeal first."

"What happens if the appellate court rules that the verdict was against the weight of the evidence? Would I then go free?"

"Yes, yes, you would," Jack acknowledged. He was about to explain the near hopelessness of that result to young Rick but did not have the heart. Instead, he just left it at that.

"When will the court hear my appeal?" Rick was hoping Jack would give an answer indicating weeks but suspected it would be months.

"Oh, not for a few months, I am afraid, Rick," admitted his lawyer. "Appeals tend to take a while. There is a lot of hurry up and wait."

"When you say, 'a few months,' you mean like three?" Rick asked.

"More like five or six," Jack confessed. "First I have to file what is called 'post-trial motions' with the trial judge, Judge Price. I have three more weeks to file them. Then the trial judge will rule on them fast. He almost certainly will deny them. That is how the game is played. Once he denies them, I can file our appeal to the Superior Court in Philadelphia."

"What will you put down in your post-trial motions?" Rick wanted to know.

"I will list and argue before Judge Price the very same issues I want to eventually raise and argue on appeal. **Post-trial motions** give the trial judge a chance to make things right before pestering the higher court. Trial judges almost never want to admit that the trial was broken, though. Admitting that normally means that they messed up in a major way by ruling badly on some important objection made during trial. Our appeal is a little different, though, since we will be arguing that the juvenile court judge, not Judge Price, is the one that messed up. Still, I do not see Judge Price slamming his courthouse peer by ruling in our favor. Yet, we shall see."

"So, if we lose on our post-trial motions..." Rick was cut off by his attorney.

"If we lose on those, we then are given the green light to appeal those very same issues to the Superior Court of Pennsylvania. The Superior Court will not permit me to raise any new issues before them that I did not raise in my post-trial motions. Again, this is how the game is played."

Jack spent the rest of his visit with young Rick giving him some pointers on how to tolerate juvie hall better. "How many fights have you started so far?" he asked Rick. When Rick replied that he had yet to be the one to start a fight, Jack advised him to start one. "It does not matter so much whether you win or lose," he counseled the gentle youth. "To get the respect of the people here, you probably need to start a fight or two."

"Won't that get me into trouble with the staff?" Rick asked.

"Yes, but that is a good thing. Inmates like people who get in trouble with the hated staff."

"What am I supposed to start a fight about?" Rick waited for a response.

"Aren't there some creeps here who have constantly been giving you a hard time over and over again about nothing? Start with any one of them."

The time came for Jack to leave, but he promised to provide his client with a copy of his written post-trial motions soon. "I will have them done within the next four days," he advised his client.

"Wow, that fast?" Rick asked.

"Yeah, figuring out what issues to go with is the hard part. Once that is decided, the motions almost write themselves. I will put more polish into the appellate briefs, though. They are what will ultimately and probably count."

Jack shook Rick's hand, stood, and watched as a guard escorted Rick out of the room and back into the general population. Through an interior window, he watched with deep concern as a fellow resident began to mock Rick using various offensive jeering mannerisms. The creep laughed with delight. Jack watched approvingly as young Rick suddenly stopped, spun around, and slammed his fist into his tormentor's nose. A huge ruckus ensued. "My work is done here," Jack whispered to himself as he contentedly made his way toward an exit.

## Key Terms Found in This Chapter

| | |
|---|---|
| Spot issues for appeal | Anders brief |
| Harmless error doctrine | Discretionary appeals |
| Against the clear weight | Domain of the lawyer |
| Thirteenth juror | Detailed waiver inquiry |
| Gross disproportionality | Sua sponte |
| Two boilerplate issues | Not immediately appealable |
| Appeal of right | Post-trial motions |

## Questions for Class Discussion

1. How do lawyers use the trial transcript to spot issues for appeal? What are they looking for within the transcript?
2. Why is the harmless error doctrine necessary when it comes to errors made by judges during trials? Why do you suppose judges make frequent mistakes?
3. What does a lawyer have to establish in order to convince an appellate court that the verdict was against the clear weight of the evidence? Why is this so hard to do?
4. What do appellate judges mean when they say they do not want to sit as the "13th juror" in reviewing verdicts?

5. How out of bounds must sentences be before an appellate court will vacate them on the ground that they are excessively long? Why do you suppose it is not enough merely to demonstrate that the sentence was simply disproportionate to the crime?

6. What are the two infamous boilerplate issues that lawyers with nothing else like to raise on appeal? What signal does a lawyer send to appellate courts when they raise only these two issues? Why then do they even bother raising them?

7. What work is involved in writing an Anders brief? Why do lawyers hate writing them? How do clients react to them? What option can lawyers with nothing but hopeless issues pursue in lieu of writing the laborious Anders brief?

8. What is meant by an "appeal of right"? What do defendants (especially those with free lawyers) have to lose by insisting on this right? If you were convicted of a crime you knew you had done, would you exercise your right to appeal?

9. What does it mean that higher appeals are all "discretionary"? What sort of issues make it likely that a higher appellate court will want to hear your appeal?

10. What does it mean that "what issues will be raised are within the domain of the lawyer"? Why is this the case?

11. Jack came up with one decent issue to raise on appeal. What was it? What would happen to the case if the appellate court finds that Jack's idea is correct?

12. What does it mean for a judge to act *sua sponte*? Should judges probably act *sua sponte* more often than they seem to do?

13. What does it mean that an issue is "not immediately appealable"? When does it become "appealable"? Why do you suppose appellate courts consider most issues to be "not immediately appealable"?

14. What are post-trial motions? Why is this step necessary before taking your gripes to an appellate court? What is the relationship between issues raised in post-trial motions and those allowed on appeal?

# Unit 15
# Salvation

This unit completes the book. We see how an attorney goes about conducting and winning an appeal. Then we witness a new bargain being obtained, post-appeal. Ultimately, we see how a new life opens up for Jack.

# 43

## The Appeal

Jack promptly filed his post-trial motions with trial Judge Price who, as predicted, promptly denied all of them. Now it was time to appeal to higher authority.

Appealing to higher authority begins with an attorney filing a **notice of appeal**. This notice makes the higher court (in this case, the Pennsylvania Superior Court) aware of your client's existence and aware of their appeal. It also acts as a signal to the local clerk of court to send a copy of the trial transcript and other case records to the higher court. Not being new to this process, Jack was keenly aware that this notice of appeal had a **drop-dead date** of just 30 days from the denial of one's post-trial motions. Miss that deadline, and you forever miss the right to appeal. Jack met the deadline.

With the notice of appeal out of the way, Jack got down to the hard work of actually creating a **written brief** (a compilation of grievances and corresponding legal arguments) for the appellate court. By state law, his brief was due within 30 days of filing his notice of appeal. The prosecutor's **brief in response** would be due 30 days after receipt of the defense brief. He knew that most appeals are won even before the lawyers appear before the appellate tribunal for oral arguments (the next step). By then, most judges have already made up their minds by what they have read in the attorneys' briefs.

Generally speaking, appeals involve either "error correction" or "policy review." Policy review is the much more glitzy of the two. Think of cases such as *Roe v. Wade* (the famous abortion rights case) or *Miranda v. Arizona* (the case that gave us the famous Miranda warnings). In cases like those involving **policy review**, lawyers are asking appellate courts to create new constitutional law by interpreting the federal or a state constitution in such a way as to strike down a particular law or practice. Fun stuff and exciting stuff—the kind of thing one eventually hears discussed by law professors in law schools—but Jack did not care about that right now. He had the much more mundane task of simply saving Rick.

Jack was simply seeking error correction. He wanted to convince the Superior Court that Rick's process had been flawed due to human error. With **error correction**, an attorney is arguing that either a judge made a mistake (that was not harmless) by making a very bad ruling or a jury had made a mistake by returning a ridiculous verdict. Consequently, a defendant had been denied his or her fair day(s) in court.

In writing his brief, Jack would be producing something much more lengthier and detailed than the mere **memorandum of law** (a type of mini brief) that he had attached to his earlier post-trial motions to the trial judge. The Superior Court gave him an entire month to compose this brief and expected something more beefy than a memorandum. In this sense, briefs are usually nothing of the kind.

Jack began his so-called brief by first giving a **recitation of the facts** of the case. He told the reader about the crimes—who, what, when, where and how. While never lying, he made certain to sugarcoat the facts that favored his side. This sugarcoating had to be light, though. Too thick and it would backfire. Jack referred to the automobile crash as a "tragic accident" and to his client as a "boy" of 17 years of age. (Of course, in her response brief, Kate would refer to the crash as an act of "reckless abandon" and to Rick Mahan as "the young man" or simply as "Mahan.")

After a recitation of the facts, Jack's next task was to present each of the issues he wished to advance. The **issues** are those points of contention raised by the defense that it claims resulted in an unfair result of some kind. He had just three issues: abuse of discretion on the part of the juvenile court judge in transferring the matter to adult court, verdict in adult court against the clear weight of the evidence, and an ultimate sentence that was grossly disproportionate to the crime. Jack knew that he should start with his strongest issue first: abuse of juvenile court discretion in waving the matter to adult court.

In arguing this issue, Jack made use of all of the various **sources of legal authority** available to him. He cited **statutes** (e.g., the law passed by his state legislature that required juvenile judges to make a "detailed inquiry" into whether the transfer was really in the "public interest"). Jack cited **case law** (prior decisions of appellate courts that now serve as precedent to lower trial courts—there were a ton of those). Jack even cited a couple of **law review articles** (published articles written by law professors who explore topics in the law). Of course, Jack also directly cited various provisions of both the federal and state **constitutions** since he knew that constitutions trump every other type of legal authority.

Jack used all of these sources to argue his first issue vigorously: the juvenile judge absolutely abused his discretion in waiving this case to adult court. In the brief, Jack boldly asserted that the judge failed to make a detailed inquiry, focusing too intently on the seriousness of the charges (and perhaps the "advanced age" of the nearly grown-up defendant). According to Jack, the juvenile judge, Leonard Watson, failed to adequately consider such critical things as young Rick's amenability to rehabilitative treatment in the juvenile system, his total lack of any prior juvenile record, and the fact that he was unlikely to keep reoffending. Jack made sure to point out that rehabilitation was the main goal that juvenile courts are charged to focus upon, and that retribution was completely out of bounds in juvenile court. Finally, he admitted that the juvenile judge had tried several times to get the incompetent defense lawyer to address such things during the waiver hearing but failed. Jack portrayed these failed efforts on the part of the juvenile judge to motivate the defense lawyer to do his job as "proof" that the juvenile judge's conscience was pricking him. Yet, the exasperated judge had finally just "moved on!" He should never have just "moved on."

Jack went on to argue his other two issues. He first argued that the guilty verdict in adult court was against the clear weight of the evidence. The central point he made here was that there was a clear lack of causation in the case. True, Rick had consumed two beers and two cold pills. However, no reasonable jury (according to Jack) could have been convinced beyond a reasonable doubt that the crash had actually been caused by consumption of these products. Another theory almost as plausible existed to explain the crash: Rick had simply fallen asleep at the wheel due to natural causes, not intoxication.

Finally, Jack asked the court that if it was disinclined to do anything else, then it should at least reduce his client's sentence of incarceration from four years to just three (the mandatory minimum). He passionately argued that four years might be proper for an adult, but his client was still just a boy. He may have been transferred to adult court, but he really was still under 18. Three years was long enough for the mistake of someone of such a young age.

Jack concluded his brief by including a final required section clearly stating the **relief being sought**. He first asked the court to overturn the conviction entirely on the basis that the verdict was against the weight of the evidence. Jack knew that if the Superior Court was to do this, double jeopardy would kick in, and his client would be free. Next, he asked if that were not the outcome, then the juvenile judge should be found to have abused his discretion by ordering transfer to adult court. If the appellate court agreed, Jack asked that the case be **remanded** (sent back) to juvenile court for the matter to start from scratch there, where it belonged. Finally, if neither of these two remedies were granted, he asked that the court at least reduce his client's sentence from four years to just the minimum mandatory of three.

Jack's "brief" wound up totaling 20 pages in the end (four times longer than his earlier memorandum of law provided to the trial judge as part of his post-trial motions). He filed the brief electronically with the Superior Court (and mailed it a hard copy) and then sent copies (electronic and hard) to the district attorney's office and the local clerk of court.

Three and a half weeks later, Jack received his copy of the response brief filed by the district attorney's office. It was authored by Kate herself rather than by someone else in her office. (Some prosecutor offices expect the trial prosecutor to write this brief, while others have a full-time brief writer do it.) Since Kate herself had written the brief, Jack knew that she too would probably be the one from her office attending oral arguments.

Oral arguments wound up taking place nearly four months later. Young Rick spent all of this time waiting in juvenile lockup. He was already becoming a much harder and tougher version of his former self.

Jack knew that for survival purposes this was temporarily a good thing but not so great for the long-term life of his client.

When the day for **oral arguments** arrived, Jack and Kate rode the commuter train together from the leafy suburbs into ultra-urban, downtown Philadelphia. Arriving at the building housing the Superior Court, they took their seats in Courtroom 5 and waited for their turn. While waiting, they watched two attorneys scheduled for earlier arguments finishing their pitches. Nobody but lawyers and judges were in this room. This was a place solely for legal argumentation. No new evidence would be introduced, so there was no need for witnesses. There was no need for a jury. There was no need even for the defendant to be there. It was a room dedicated just for lawyers to stand at a podium and address a **tribunal** of three judges. (Nearly all oral arguments are heard by a subset of three judges, though some appeals are so momentous that the entire panel of 15 or so judges constituting the appellate court will sit on the case *en banc.*)

Jack and Kate nervously listened as one of the three judges announced that it was now time to hear from the attorneys on the case of *Commonwealth v. Richard Mahan.* Jack knew that it was his responsibility to go first. Defense lawyers always go first in appellate court. That is because only defense lawyers can appeal a verdict. Prosecutors cannot appeal a negative trial outcome even when they had been wronged due to process error. Double jeopardy sees to that.

Jack walked up to the podium and introduced himself to the judges. The judges smiled back.

"You have 15 minutes to present your argument," one of the judges told Jack. "There is a light on the top of your podium that will flash a few times when you have just two minutes left. It will start flashing again when your time is up. We are very strict about these time constraints. You may begin."

Jack did not want to waste his precious time arguing his two weaker issues. He got straight to arguing his contention that there had been an abuse of juvenile court discretion regarding the transfer of Rick to adult court. Rick had been talking for only 30 seconds when one of the judges interrupted him with a legal question.

"Uh oh," prosecutor Kate thought to herself as she watched. "Jack is actually getting some traction!" She knew that appellate judges only interrupt defense lawyers that soon if they think the lawyer's appeal has some real merit. Judges who sit quietly and politely listen while the lawyer who filed the appeal runs out the clock are not going to rule in that lawyer's favor.

Jack answered the first question directed at him by citing the Pennsylvania statue on "detailed inquiry." He then cited an earlier case from the Superior Court, fleshing out the legislative intent in that statute. Then he cited a case from the Pennsylvania Supreme Court that had a fact pattern that was vaguely similar to his own client's case. The cases seemed to be germane. Before Jack could even finish responding entirely to the first question, another of the judges asked him a second question. This was followed by a third, then a forth, then a fifth, then many more, in rapid succession.

Jack never was able to return to his prepared remarks before he saw the "two-minute warning" light begin to flash on his podium. He tried to start a summary but instead finished his time answering yet two more questions. Then the light flashed again. "Time's up," one of the judges observed. "Thank you, Mr. Day. We shall now be pleased to hear from Assistant District Attorney Page."

Kate walked toward the podium as Jack walked back. Jack winked at her subtly as they passed each other. "Cocky guy," she thought. Yet, she almost found his arrogance to be amusingly charming. "Jack has come a long way since his panic attacks in trial court," she silently considered.

Kate was not about to give up, not yet. She launched into an attack of Jack's interpretation of the statute and case law. She cited learned commentary on the statute that included some of the statute's legislative history. She cited precedent favorable to her side, case after case. She thought she was getting in some serious counterpunches until 10 minutes in she realized that the judges had thus far asked her just two questions. That was not good. As suggested earlier, oral argument is not meant to be a one-way lecture made by an attorney but rather a **Socratic dialog** of lively questions and answers between an attorney and the judges. When a dialog is not taking place, one is almost certainly losing. Very little back and forth was taking place now. When Kate got to the period of the two-minute warning, she finally got a couple of quite decent pro-prosecution questions in short order before time ran out. "Was it too little, too late?" she wondered. She would have to wait for the decision of the court to find out for sure.

Two more months passed. Jack was on cafeteria lunch duty at his high school when he felt his phone vibrating in his pocket. He sneaked a peek to see who would be bothering him at work. The call was coming from the district attorney's office. He eagerly pushed a button and whispered, "Hello?"

"Jack, is that you?" a voice on the other end called out. "This is Kate. Have you heard the news yet?"

"No!" Jack exclaimed. "What have you heard? Has the Superior Court issued their opinion?"

"Yes, we will both be getting an official letter soon. But my sources tell me that you won your appeal!"

"On what issue?" he asked. "On which particular issue?"

"You know on which issue," Kate deadpanned. "The Superior Court has held that the juvenile court judge abused his discretion by transferring your boy Mahan to adult court. The adult court conviction and related sentence have been vacated. The case is being remanded to juvenile court for adjudication from scratch there."

"Hot diggidy dang!" Jack shouted loudly into the phone. He started doing a hokey victory dance while continuing to shout, "Hot dang!" Four surprised students at a nearby table looked at Jack as if he were completely insane. He stopped dancing, looked straight at these students, and then nodded, winked, and whispered the words, "Hot dang!" The students looked at one another and smiled.

"Jack, we need to talk," Kate suggested in a calm voice.

"About what?" Jack asked.

"About where we might go from here."

## Key Terms Found in This Chapter

Notice of appeal

Drop-dead date

Written brief

Brief in response

Policy review

Error correction

Statutes

Case law

Law review articles

Constitutions

Relief being sought

Remanded

Memorandum of law
Recitation of the facts
Issues
Sources of legal authority

Oral arguments
Tribunal
En banc
Socratic dialogue

# Questions for Class Discussion

1. What are the purposes of the "notice of appeal"? What specific things does it accomplish or set in motion?
2. What is a drop-dead date? What happens to an appeal if it is not met? How would you react if you were a defendant whose lawyer missed the date?
3. What is the purpose of the written brief? What sorts of sections appear in it? How is it different from a memorandum of law?
4. Which side — prosecution or defense — typically files the "brief in response"? Why is this side virtually always the one who files a brief in response?
5. What is meant by "policy review"? Why is this such a glitzy thing?
6. What is meant by "error correction"? How do judges make errors during trials? What big error are juries often accused of making?
7. How should lawyers go about "sugarcoating" while drafting the "recitation of the facts"? How can this backfire if one is not careful? How did Jack sugarcoat the facts?
8. How many issues did Jack raise in his brief? Which did he argue first? Which two were more boilerplate? Was it worth including the boilerplate issues in this particular case?
9. What are the various sources of "legal authority" that attorneys cite in their appellate briefs? Which has the most punch?
10. What does "precedent" mean? Who must follow it?
11. What three types of "relief" did Jack specifically request in his brief? Why do you suppose appellate courts require that specific relief requests be spelled out?
12. Where are oral arguments made? How much time do attorneys have to make them? How many judges listen to them in most appeals? How many judges listen if the appeal is of great public importance?

13. What does it mean if judges are using up a lot of the lawyer's allotted time asking questions rather than just letting the attorney get through their prepared remarks? Why do you suppose this is so?
14. Who was Socrates? From what you can glean from this chapter, how did he probably like to engage in "dialogue" with his pupils?

# 44

## An Artful Deal

Rick was watching television with several other young detainees when a juvenile detention officer gently tapped him on the shoulder from behind. He turned expecting to see one of the many resident thugs wanting to bully him yet again. He was relieved to see that it was an adult employee instead.

"Mahan," the worker began, "Your attorney is here to see you. He told the folks up front he has some news about your appeal." Rick stared for a few seconds at the man in disbelief. "Follow me," the worker commanded. As the two walked from the day room, the other juveniles who had been within earshot exploded in excited speculations. "Good luck, Ricky boy!" one of them finally shouted.

Rick first saw his lawyer's face through the interior window separating the hallway from the visitation room. He hesitated for a few moments to study the face of his attorney through the window. Jack was sitting at a table looking very relaxed, even serene. That might mean good news, Rick decided.

"Mahan, are you coming?" the escort asked while holding open the door to the visitation room. Rick hurried through the door and shyly walked toward his attorney.

"Hello, Mr. Day," he uttered nervously. "Do you have news about my appeal?"

Jack smiled and rose to his feet. "I do indeed. Have a seat, Rick."

After the two sat down, Jack got straight to business. "I have good news, Rick," he said with a wink and a grin.

"I like good news," Rick replied. "What is it?"

"The Superior Court has granted our appeal by ruling that Juvenile Court Judge Leonard Watson messed up. They say he should never have transferred your case to adult court. Consequently, your adult court conviction has been vacated along with its nasty sentence."

"You mean it is all over? I get to go free? It's all finally over?"

"Well, the news is good but not quite that good. The appellate court has ordered your case be sent back to juvenile court for processing from scratch there."

"I guess that is good news," Rick agreed.

"It is good news!" Jack insisted. "First, people who are processed as juveniles can never be sent to an adult prison. Second, you no longer will have to go through life dealing with employers and others upset about public record convictions they can learn about. Juvenile court findings of delinquency result in **sealed records**—nobody outside of the juvenile court system will have access to them. Third, I spoke with the juvenile judge, and he has ordered that you be released pending your juvenile hearing. Fourth…"

"Wait!" Rick interjected. "They are letting me go home now?" This revelation made him intensely excited.

"Yes, I have already given the head office here a copy of the judge's signed order releasing you. When I leave, you are going with me. Your parents are waiting for you outside to give you a lift home. They would have come in, but it is after-hours. Only lawyers are permitted visits after hours."

"Yes!" Rick shouted. "I am so out of here!" Jack just laughed in response.

"Anyway, where was I?" Jack asked himself outloud.

"Fourth," Rick told him. "You were on your forth point."

"So, the fourth point is that the prosecutor and I came up with a deal that we approached the juvenile judge about. Unlike plea bargains in adult court, juvenile judges insist that they be involved in any negotiations. Anyway, the judge is on board if you and your parents agree to the terms. I must tell you, Rick, that I think the judge is being very reasonable in giving his blessing to these negotiated terms. My hunch is that he did not like being on some appellate court's radar. Juvenile judges are not used to having their decisions reviewed on appeal. This judge probably wants this case to go away now. So, there is a deal if you are open to it."

"I am listening, Mr. Day." Rick was indeed all ears.

"Well, the really good news is that if you accept the terms, you will not have to come back and do any more time locked up here in juvenile hall or elsewhere."

"I accept!" Rick said.

"Wait, there is more," Jack told him. "True, you will not have to do any more time locked up. However, you will spend the next two years on what they call **intensive probation**. This means that a juvenile probation officer will be hounding you night and day to make sure you stay out of trouble generally and that you stop drinking entirely — she or he will be doing almost daily breath machine tests to check up on you."

"I accept!"

"I am not quite done yet, Rick. There is more. You will also have to agree to attend at least six months of alcohol counseling, lose your driver's license for two years, and perform 500 hours of community service to be arranged and supervised by your probation officer."

"I accept!" Rick again confirmed unhesitatingly.

"Okay, your parents, as **interested adults**, will also have to agree to all of these conditions since you are still underage."

"They will," Rick said.

Jack wanted to make sure Rick understood exactly what he would be legally required to do to make the deal happen. "Rick, what you will have to do is to go into juvenile court and **admit the charges**, including the homicides. Admitting the charges is sort of like pleading guilty in adult court. Once you admit the charges, the juvenile judge will then enter an **adjudication of delinquency**. That means that the court is finding you responsible for doing harms that are serious enough to constitute crimes if you had been an adult. Of course, since a delinquent act is not actually a crime, there will be no public criminal record generated, and nobody will seek to punish you. That is how we got the deal. We were able to convince the judge that locking you up might be necessary for punishment, but it was not necessary for your rehabilitation."

Rick sensed that his attorney wanted him to say something. "Mr. Day,

I will have no problem admitting the charges in court. I am just grateful to get out of lockup and not to have to worry about having a criminal record."

"And you have no problem with being put on intensive probation and doing all those hours of community service?"

"Of course not. However, I refuse to give up my right to drive a car for two years."

"Are you kidding me?" Jack seemed perplexed.

"Yes, I am kidding you."

"So, then, are you now ready to get the hell out of here, Rick?" Jack nodded toward the exit door as he rose to his feet.

"You mean, right now, like right this very moment? They will just let me walk out?"

"Well, if you would rather spend one more night here to exchange goodbyes with all of your little friends, I am sure I can arrange that."

"No, no, no!" exclaimed Rick. "Let's go."

With that, Rick and Jack walked out into the night air. Rick felt on fire. Minutes earlier, he had been in months-long survival mode. Now, he felt as if he were entering a new, strange, wonderful world.

Rick's parents reacted to their son's sudden emergence by jumping out of their car and running over to embrace him. Everyone cried, except Jack. Jack could not stop smiling.

## Key Terms Found in This Chapter

Sealed records
Interested adults
Adjudication of delinquency

Intensive probation
Admit the charges

## Questions for Class Discussion

1.  How would you feel if you were Rick getting the "good news" about the results of the appeal from attorney Jack? What were some of the things in the news that would make you happy?

2. Intensive probation is just one step away from being incarcerated. However, what are some ways that it is a quite a big step away?

3. What are some things the juvenile probation office could come up with in terms of community service for Rick?

4. In what ways is "admitting the charges" similar to "pleading guilty" in adult court? In what ways is it different?

5. Why do you suppose that the juvenile court would require Rick's parents also to agree to the deal?

6. What is the similarity between a "delinquent act" and a "crime"? What are the differences?

7. What do you suppose it must be like to walk out of a lock-up into freedom for the first time in months? What things would you enjoy most?

# 45
## Liberty's New Champions

Five months had passed by since Rick had admitted the delinquent acts of homicide and related charges. During this time, he had graduated from high school and started working as a repairperson's helper at a local hospital. He appreciated being able to fib when asked on his employment application if he had ever been convicted of a criminal offense. He reported that he had not, knowing that his juvenile adjudication was sealed and would forever remain hidden from the outside world. Besides, technically, he never had been convicted of any crimes. Juvenile court is civil court, and nobody there ever leaves having been "convicted" of anything.

Rick would one day go on to become a doctor and wind up fixing people in the very hospital where he now fixed things. But what about his attorney, Jack?

Jack went back to his usual life of teaching math in his high school. Father Skelly, his principal, told him that if only Jack would convert to Catholicism, Skelly would see to it that he became the parochial school's next principal. Jack told Skelly that as a matter of conscience, he would have to remain a heathen even if it meant he could not advance to the front office. Upon hearing this, Skelly was not sure if he should be more worried about Jack's soul or about the fate of his beloved St. Francis High. He decided he was more worried about St. Francis. Jack's soul was too good for him to have to worry.

It was an ordinary late Monday afternoon when Jack looked out his empty classroom windows and saw an attractive woman in the distance looking into his car window out in the parking lot. "What is she up to?" Jack wondered. By the way she was dressed, she looked more like a businessperson than a car burglar. "Oh my gosh, it's Kate Page!" Jack suddenly realized. He hurriedly ran out to meet her.

"You know car burglary is a felony in this state," Jack shouted accusatorily as he approached his own car. Startled, Kate stopped looking in the window and spun around.

"Oh, Jack, it's you!" she exclaimed. "You shouldn't sneak up on someone like that."

"Are you thinking of buying my car?" Jack deadpanned. "It won't come cheap."

"No, no. I was just trying to see somehow if it was indeed your car or if you had already left for the day. There is something I would like to discuss with you if you have a few minutes." Jack could not imagine what Kate might want. "Maybe, she wants to ask me out on a date," he thoughtfully hoped.

"Let's talk in my car," Jack suggested as he unlocked the doors with his remote. The two of them climbed in. As they sat down in their seats, a male student walked past the front of the car, nodded at Kate, and then winked at Jack. Jack blushed but Kate kind of thought it was funny.

"How's life in the exciting district attorney's office these days?" Jack finally asked.

"I would not know," Kate said with a shrug. "I got fired right after Rick was put on intensive probation."

"You can't be serious!" Jack responded. "I never heard. Fired for what?"

"Apparently, some mystery judge in the courthouse got very upset about how I supposedly mishandled the Rick Mahan case, especially my losing the appeal."

"What judge?" Jack asked. "Was it Judge Price who presided over the trial in adult court?"

"I don't think so. I saw Price in the courthouse lobby an hour before my office fired me. He was very friendly and kind to me. Strangely sympathetic. I think he somehow knew what was about to befall me and felt bad."

"Then, what judge?" Jack inquired.

"I never did find out. The **first assistant** was the one who fired me.

She told me that I was a great attorney, but the DA himself told her that I had to go. She told me in confidence that it was necessary because one of the judges the DA apparently cares about insisted upon it. She would not tell me which judge or why the DA would even listen to such a judge in the first place. I am not even sure the first assistant knew herself who the particular judge was. She seemed very confused and embarrassed. Still, she fired me. It is not as if I had any civil service protection or anything. As an ADA, I was always just an **at-will employee** who could be dismissed for any reason and without warning."

"Maybe you should hire a lawyer," Jack suggested. Kate laughed, thinking he was joking. She tried to return the joke by suggesting that she could hire him. "No, really, hiring some lawyer to investigate this might not be a bad idea," Jack told her in all seriousness. "Something stinks here. Even at-will employment has some safeguards."

"Yeah, well, I've completely moved on," Kate stated with firm assurance. "However, I still would like to hire you as a lawyer." This time it was Jack who laughed at what he thought was a joke.

"No, I am serious," insisted Kate. "That is why I came to see you. I am starting a criminal defense practice in town and would like to recruit you as a partner. I already have a small office near the courthouse and am spreading the word around that I am accepting clients. In fact, I already got a client."

"Who?"

"A 26-year-old woman who shot her husband to death as he slept. She used his own gun to do it, the same gun he routinely would hold to her head and threaten her with."

"Sounds like a gem of a husband," Jack observed.

"Yeah, a real piece of work," Kate agreed. "My client suffered from two years of nonstop abuse at her husband's hands. He would wake her up each morning with a punch to her ribs. He made her eat dog food once or twice a week for dinner just for laughs. He made her prostitute herself for money. If she did need not meet his money quota, he would beat her silly. He told her if she ever went to the police or left him or told her widowed mother, he would kill her and her mother. Her mother is a successful oncologist at the University of Pennsylvania hospital in Philly. She is the one paying my legal fee, which is rather hefty."

"What is the prosecutor charging this tragic young woman with?"

"Murder. The DA's office says that killing someone, even a batterer, while he is asleep is not self-defense. The threat has to be imminent to justify lethal force. "

"What about battered wife syndrome as a defense?" Jack suggested. "Maybe she thought the threat was ongoing, never-ending."

"Our state no longer recognizes that defense. The legislature says it has been known sometimes to lead to vigilantism. I could still try a plain vanilla insanity defense though."

Jack spent the next 30 minutes advising Kate on how she should design her defense strategy. Kate literally took notes. Jack explained in detail how she could go about painting the dead husband in such a way that the jurors would wind up hating him enough to let the shooter off the hook. "Get them to be almost happy that she killed him; then give them the insanity defense so they have something on which to hang their hat."

"So, are you in?" Kate finally asked after listening to his long sermons. "Do you want to be my law partner?"

"Would I have to give up teaching?"

"Probably."

"I don't know," Jack stated after a long pause. "You see, I get panic attacks sometimes in court."

"Yeah, I know. I still want you as a partner. You are a fantastic negotiator, Jack, one of the best. Negotiating deals is 90% of the job. You also are great at writing appeals. Trials is where your anxieties might cause the most mischief, but we can do all of those while sitting at the table as **co-counsel**. We would always have one another's back in court."

"Okay, but won't we starve?" Jack countered. "I hear that starting up a law practice is usually an uphill financial battle for years. They always say that the **first rule of starting a practice** is don't do it."

"It almost always is a tough climb," Kate concurred. "The hard part will be attracting clients. However, I have this feeling that both you and I will be naturals at **rainmaking**. Remember, I already have this one fat case to get us kickstarted."

"How much is this fancy doctor paying you to represent her daughter?"

"Fifty thousand dollars, plus expenses. I told her that with all of my experience as a former full-time prosecutor, I was well worth it and would not consider less. Of course, if she were not so rich I most certainly would have demanded less."

"Fifty thousand dollars!" Jack whispered with astonishment. Jack paused while he thought about that for a while. "I'm in," he finally declared. "On one condition."

"What's that?" Kate asked.

"You be the one to tell Father Skelly that I am leaving St. Francis. He will get extremely upset. He is not the kind of guy you want to make upset."

"Do I get to have a panic attack, first?" Kate inquired. She was only half kidding.

∽

## Key Terms Found in This Chapter

First assistant
Co-counsel
Rainmaking

At-will employee
First rule of starting a practice

## Questions for Class Discussion

1. What duties do you imagine a first assistant district attorney to have? Why would an elected district attorney want/need such a person?
2. Do you agree that assistant district attorneys should be "at-will employees"? Are government workers normally "at-will"? How are assistant district attorneys different from teachers and most other people who work for the government?
3. What might be some reasons for a firing that would be illegal even when it is an "at-will" employee getting the ax?
4. If you were Kate, would you accept your firing without putting up a fight given the rumors that were circulating about?
5. What were some lawyerly tasks that Kate thought Jack would be quite good at despite issues with panic attacks? How did she propose to handle his anxieties during trials? Do you think that she could make that work?
6. What is the "first rule of starting a law practice"? Why is it usually a bad idea to start one from scratch?

7. What is rainmaking? Why is it so hard to do when one is just start-ing out? Why might Kate and Jack have an edge on rainmaking that most lawyers starting up a practice would not have?

8. Knowing what you know about Kate and Jack (the good and the bad), would you recommend their new law firm to a close relative charged with a serious crime?

9. Is Jack making a mistake to give up the noble profession of teach-ing in order to become a private criminal defense attorney? What do you suppose might be some of his motivations for making this switch?

10. As an old person on your deathbed, would you rather look back on a life of great teaching or a life of great criminal defense work?

# Index

General deterrence, 376
Getting out obsession, 54
Glacial pace, 161
Go along to get along, 170
Goals of sentencing, 375
Good a job or better, 51
Grand juries, 45
Grandstanding, 175
Gross disproportionality, 386
Group *voir dire, 204*
Hands-off supervision approach, 136
Harmless error doctrine, 385
Hate convicting people they love, 160
Horizontal representation, 42
Human desire for delay, 168
Humanized, 36
Hung jury, 346
Hypotheticals to assert guilt, 326
Impeach, 44, 282
In house counsel, 96
Incapable of safe driving, 119
Incapacitation, 376
Incarceration-related pre-trial harms, 68
Inconsistent verdict, 349
Incorrigible, 60
Indictment, 45
Indirect criminal contempt, 180
Individual *voir dire, 204*
Individual-level legal problems, 96
Ineffective assistance of counsel, 226, 320
Inflame the jury's passions, 326
Information, 45

Initial vote, 344
Inmate code, 62
Instruct the jury, 335
Intensive probation, 407
Interested adult, 32, 407
Issues, 396
Ivy League law school, 3
Joint problem-solving approach, 128
Judges of the facts, 335
Judges of the law, 335
Judge's veto, 128
Judicial economy, 326
Judicial regalia, 244
Jurors' tribal instincts, 282
Jury conviction rate, 158
Jury foreperson, 344
Jury instructions, 335
Jury leaders, 348
Jury nullification, 377
Jury selection, 203
Jury's first among equals, 197
Just deserts, 376
Just in time justice, 100
Justice delayed is justice denied, 165
Justice of the peace, 42, 177
Just-in-time resolution, 167
Juvenile correctional jurisdiction, 7
Juvenile court jurisdiction, 7
Juvenile intake workers, 24
Juvie Hall, 59
Key element of proof, 246
Kiddie court, 31
L.S.A.T., 11
Last remnant of aristocracy, 180